Analysis for
Financial Management

The McGraw-Hill/Irwin Series in Finance, Insurance, and Real Estate

Stephen A. Ross
Franco Modigliani Professor of Finance and Economics
Sloan School of Management
Massachusetts Institute of Technology
Consulting Editor

FINANCIAL MANAGEMENT

Adair
Excel Applications for Corporate Finance
First Edition

Benninga and Sarig
Corporate Finance: A Valuation Approach

Block and Hirt
Foundations of Financial Management
Eleventh Edition

Brealey, Myers, and Allen
Principles of Corporate Finance
Eighth Edition

Brealey, Myers, and Marcus
Fundamentals of Corporate Finance
Fifth Edition

Brooks
FinGame Online 4.0

Bruner
Case Studies in Finance: Managing for Corporate Value Creation
Fifth Edition

Chew
The New Corporate Finance: Where Theory Meets Practice
Third Edition

Chew and Gillan
Corporate Governance at the Crossroads: A Book of Readings
First Edition

DeMello
Cases in Finance
Second Edition

Grinblatt and Titman
Financial Markets and Corporate Strategy
Second Edition

Helfert
Techniques of Financial Analysis: A Guide to Value Creation
Eleventh Edition

Higgins
Analysis for Financial Management
Eighth Edition

Kester, Ruback, and Tufano
Case Problems in Finance
Twelfth Edition

Ross, Westerfield, and Jaffe
Corporate Finance
Seventh Edition

Ross, Westerfield, Jaffe, and Jordan
Corporate Finance: Core Principles and Applications
First Edition

Ross, Westerfield, and Jordan
Essentials of Corporate Finance
Fifth Edition

Ross, Westerfield, and Jordan
Fundamentals of Corporate Finance
Seventh Edition

Shefrin
Behavioral Corporate Finance: Decisions that Create Value
First Edition

Smith
The Modern Theory of Corporate Finance
Second Edition

White
Financial Analysis with an Electronic Calculator
Sixth Edition

INVESTMENTS

Bodie, Kane, and Marcus
Essentials of Investments
Sixth Edition

Bodie, Kane, and Marcus
Investments
Sixth Edition

Cohen, Zinbarg, and Zeikel
Investment Analysis and Portfolio Management
Fifth Edition

Corrado and Jordan
Fundamentals of Investments: Valuation and Management
Third Edition

Hirt and Block
Fundamentals of Investment Management
Eighth Edition

FINANCIAL INSTITUTIONS AND MARKETS

Cornett and Saunders
Fundamentals of Financial Institutions Management

Rose and Hudgins
Bank Management and Financial Services
Sixth Edition

Rose and Marquis
Money and Capital Markets: Financial Institutions and Instruments in a Global Marketplace
Ninth Edition

Santomero and Babbel
Financial Markets, Instruments, and Institutions
Second Edition

Saunders and Cornett
Financial Institutions Management: A Risk Management Approach
Fifth Edition

Saunders and Cornett
Financial Markets and Institutions: An Introduction to the Risk Management Approach
Third Edition

INTERNATIONAL FINANCE

Beim and Calomiris
Emerging Financial Markets

Eun and Resnick
International Financial Management
Fourth Edition

Analysis for Financial Management

Eighth Edition

ROBERT C. HIGGINS
Marguerite Reimers
Professor of Finance
The University of Washington

Boston   Burr Ridge, IL   Dubuque, IA   Madison, WI   New York   San Francisco   St. Louis
Bangkok   Bogotá   Caracas   Kuala Lumpur   Lisbon   London   Madrid   Mexico City
Milan   Montreal   New Delhi   Santiago   Seoul   Singapore   Sydney   Taipei   Toronto

ANALYSIS FOR FINANCIAL MANAGEMENT
Eighth Edition
International Edition 2007

10   09   08   07   06   05   04   03   02   01
20   09   08   07   06
CTF   ANL

Library of Congress Control Number: 2005053449

ISBN 007-125422-6 (without S&P card)

When ordering this title, use ISBN 007-125706-3

Printed in Singapore

www.mhhe.com

In memory of Alex Robichek
teacher, colleague, and friend.

Brief Contents

Contents

Preface

Like its predecessors, the eighth edition of *Analysis for Financial Management* is for nonfinancial executives and business students interested in the practice of financial management. It introduces standard techniques and recent advances in a practical, intuitive way. The book assumes no prior background beyond a rudimentary and perhaps rusty familiarity with financial statements—although a healthy curiosity about what makes business tick is also useful. Emphasis throughout is on the managerial implications of financial analysis.

Analysis for Financial Management should prove valuable to individuals interested in sharpening their managerial skills and to executive program participants. The book has also found a home in university classrooms as the sole text in Executive MBA and applied finance courses, as a companion text in case-oriented courses, and as a supplementary reading in more theoretical finance courses.

Analysis for Financial Management is my attempt to translate into another medium the enjoyment and stimulation I have received over the past three decades working with executives and college students. This experience has convinced me that financial techniques and concepts need not be abstract or obtuse; that recent advances in the field such as agency theory, market signaling, market efficiency, and capital asset pricing are important to practitioners; and that finance has much to say about the broader aspects of company management. I also believe that any activity in which so much money changes hands so quickly cannot fail to be interesting.

Part One looks at the management of existing resources, including the use of financial statements and ratio analysis to assess a company's financial health, its strengths, weaknesses, recent performance, and future prospects. Emphasis throughout is on the ties between a company's operating activities and its financial performance. A recurring theme is that a business must be viewed as an integrated whole and that effective financial management is possible only within the context of a company's broader operating characteristics and strategies.

The rest of the book deals with the acquisition and management of new resources. Part Two examines financial forecasting and planning with particular emphasis on managing growth and decline. Part Three considers the financing of company operations, including a review of the principal security types, the markets in which they trade, and the proper choice of security type by the issuing company. The latter requires a close look at financial leverage and its effects on the firm and its shareholders.

Part Four addresses the use of discounted cash flow techniques, such as the net present value and the internal rate of return, to evaluate investment opportunities. It also deals with the difficult task of incorporating risk into investment appraisal. The book concludes with an examination of business valuation and company restructuring within the context of the ongoing debate over the proper roles of shareholders, boards of directors, and incumbent managers in governing America's public corporations.

An extensive glossary of financial terms and suggested answers to odd-numbered, end-of-chapter problems follow the last chapter.

Changes in the Eighth Edition

Readers familiar with earlier editions of *Analysis for Financial Management* will note several changes and refinements in this edition, including

- Use of legendary motorcycle manufacturer Harley-Davidson, Inc., as the extended example throughout the book.

- A major streamlining of Chapter 8 to emphasize the effect of diversification on risk, estimating firm betas, and the use of multiple hurdle rates in investment appraisal.

- A major simplification of the appendix to Chapter 8 to focus on asset beta and Adjusted Present Value.

- Discussion of recent newsworthy companies including Dell's remarkable working capital practices, Google's Dutch auction initial public offering, and investor Carl Icahn's assault on Blockbuster's board.

- Addition of spreadsheet-based end-of-chapter problems available with suggested answers on the Web.

- Expanded coverage of accounting fundamentals, fair value accounting, international accounting standards, and cash budgeting.

- A de-emphasis of present value tables in favor of computers and calculators in present value calculations, plus coverage of equivalent annual costs or benefits, and differing compounding periods.

- More on the private equity form of organization, including its possible effectiveness in addressing incentive problems inherent in more traditional organizational structures.

As in earlier editions, you will continue to find annotated website references at the end of each chapter. Also available is an *Analysis for*

Financial Management website containing the following:

- Spreadsheet problems and suggested answers
- Supplementary end-of-chapter problems and suggested answers
- URLs of all websites mentioned in the book
- Complimentary software
- An annotated list of suggested cases to accompany the book
- PowerPoint versions of selected tables and figures.

The complimentary software consists of three easy-to-use Excel programs, which I often use to analyze financial statements, project financing needs, and evaluate investment opportunities. The URL for this cornucopia of treats is **www.mhhe.com/higgins8e.**

A word of caution: *Analysis for Financial Management* emphasizes the application and interpretation of analytic techniques in decision making. These techniques have proved useful for putting financial problems into perspective and for helping managers anticipate the consequences of their actions. But techniques can never substitute for thought. Even with the best technique, it is still necessary to define and prioritize issues, to modify analysis to fit specific circumstances, to strike the proper balance between quantitative analysis and more qualitative considerations, and to evaluate alternatives insightfully and creatively. Mastery of technique is only the necessary first step toward effective management.

I want to thank Eric Wehrly for continuing help on end-of-chapter problems. Eric will make a fine finance teacher in coming years. I am indebted to Andy Halula of Standard & Poor's for providing timely updates to Research Insight. The ability to access current Compustat data on compact disc was a great help in providing timely examples of current practice. I also owe a large thank you to the following people for their insightful reviews of the 7th edition and their constructive advice. They did an exceptional job, and any remaining short-comings are mine not theirs.

Roy Clemons
George Mason University

Salil Sarkar
University of Texas–Arlington

James Haltiner
College of William and Mary

Scott Hoover
Washington and Lee University

Jeffrey Allen
Southern Methodist University

Linda Bowen
University of North Carolina–Chapel Hill

Tom Nelson
University of Colorado–Boulder

Olaf Thorp
Babson College

Fred Yeager
Saint Louis University

Richard Proctor
Siena College

Peyton Foster Roden
University of North Texas

I appreciate the exceptional direction provided by Steve Patterson, Michelle Driscoll, Jim Labeots, Artemio Ortiz, and Debra Sylvester of McGraw-Hill/Irwin on the development, design, and editing of the book. Bill Alberts, David Beim, Dave Dubofsky, Bob Keeley, Jack McDonald, George Parker, Megan Partch, and Alan Shapiro have my continuing gratitude for their insightful help and support throughout the book's evolution. Thanks go as well to my daughter, Sara Higgins, for writing and editing the accompanying software. Finally, I want to express my appreciation to students and colleagues at the University of Washington, Stanford University, The Koblenz Graduate School of Management, The Gordon Institute of Business Science, The Swiss International Business School ZfU AG, Boeing, and Microsoft, among others, for stimulating my continuing interest in the practice and teaching of financial management.

I envy you learning this material for the first time. It's a stimulating intellectual adventure.

Robert C. (Rocky) Higgins
University of Washington
rhiggins@u.washington.edu

PART ONE

Assessing the Financial Health of the Firm

CHAPTER ONE

Interpreting Financial Statements

Financial statements are like fine perfume; to be sniffed but not swallowed.

Abraham Brilloff

Accounting is the scorecard of business. It translates a company's diverse activities into a set of objective numbers that provide information about the firm's performance, problems, and prospects. Finance involves the interpretation of these accounting numbers for assessing performance and planning future actions.

The skills of financial analysis are important to a wide range of people, including investors, creditors, and regulators. But nowhere are they more important than within the company. Regardless of functional specialty or company size, managers who possess these skills are able to diagnose their firm's ills, prescribe useful remedies, and anticipate the financial consequences of their actions. Like a ballplayer who cannot keep score, an operating manager who does not fully understand accounting and finance works under an unnecessary handicap.

This and the following chapter look at the use of accounting information to assess financial health. We begin with an overview of the accounting principles governing financial statements and a discussion of one of the most abused and confusing notions in finance: cash flow. Two recurring themes will be that defining and measuring profits is more challenging than one might expect, and that profitability alone does not guarantee success, or even survival. In Chapter 2, we look at measures of financial performance and ratio analysis.

The Cash Flow Cycle

Finance can seem arcane and complex to the uninitiated. However, a comparatively few basic principles should guide your thinking. One is that *a company's finances and operations are integrally connected*. A company's

FIGURE 1.1   **The Cash Flow–Production Cycle**

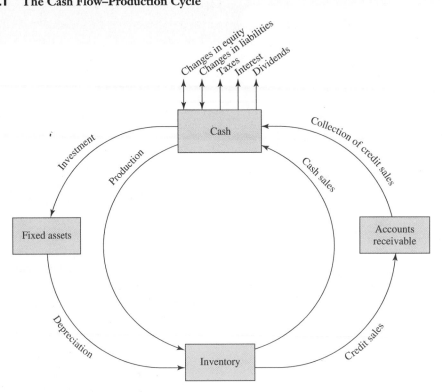

activities, method of operation, and competitive strategy all fundamentally shape the firm's financial structure. The reverse is also true: Decisions that appear to be primarily financial in nature can significantly affect company operations. For example, the way a company finances its assets can affect the nature of the investments it is able to undertake in future years.

The cash flow production cycle in Figure 1.1 illustrates the close interplay between company operations and finances. For simplicity, suppose the company shown is a new one that has raised money from owners and creditors, has purchased productive assets, and is now ready to begin operations. To do so, the company uses cash to purchase raw materials and hire workers; with these inputs, it makes the product and stores it temporarily in inventory. Thus, what began as cash is now physical inventory. When the company sells an item, the physical inventory changes back into cash. If the sale is for cash, this occurs immediately; otherwise, cash is not realized until some later time when the account receivable is collected. This simple movement of cash to inventory, to accounts receivable, and back to cash is the firm's *operating*, or *working capital*, *cycle*.

Another ongoing activity represented in Figure 1.1 is investment. Over a period of time, the company's fixed assets are consumed, or worn out, in the creation of products. It is as though every item passing through the business takes with it a small portion of the value of fixed assets. The accountant recognizes this process by continually reducing the accounting value of fixed assets and increasing the value of merchandise flowing into inventory by an amount known as *depreciation*. To maintain productive capacity and to finance additional growth, the company must invest part of its newly received cash in new fixed assets. The object of this whole exercise, of course, is to ensure that the cash returning from the working capital cycle and the investment cycle exceeds the amount that started the journey.

We could complicate Figure 1.1 further by including accounts payable and expanding on the use of debt and equity to generate cash, but the figure already demonstrates two basic principles. First, *financial statements are an important window on reality*. A company's operating policies, production techniques, and inventory and credit-control systems fundamentally determine the firm's financial profile. If, for example, a company requires payment on credit sales to be more prompt, its financial statements will reveal a reduced investment in accounts receivable and possibly a change in its revenues and profits. This linkage between a company's operations and its finances is our rationale for studying financial statements. We seek to understand company operations and predict the financial consequences of changing them.

The second principle illustrated in Figure 1.1 is that *profits do not equal cash flow*. Cash—and the timely conversion of cash into inventories, accounts receivable, and back into cash—is the lifeblood of any company. If this cash flow is severed or significantly interrupted, insolvency can occur. Yet the fact that a company is profitable is no assurance that its cash flow will be sufficient to maintain solvency. To illustrate, suppose a company loses control of its accounts receivable by allowing customers more and more time to pay, or suppose the company consistently makes more merchandise than it sells. Then, even though the company is selling merchandise at a profit in the eyes of an accountant, its sales may not be generating sufficient cash soon enough to replenish the cash outflows required for production and investment. When a company has insufficient cash to pay its maturing obligations, it is insolvent. As another example, suppose the company is managing its inventory and receivables carefully, but rapid sales growth is necessitating an ever-larger investment in these assets. Then, even though the company is profitable, it may have too little cash to meet its obligations. The company will literally be "growing broke." These brief examples illustrate why a manager must be concerned at least as much with cash flows as with profits.

To explore these themes in more detail and to sharpen your skills in using accounting information to assess performance, we need to review the basics of financial statements. If this is your first look at financial accounting, buckle up because we will be moving quickly. If the pace is too quick, take a look at one of the accounting texts recommended at the end of the chapter.

The Balance Sheet

The most important source of information for evaluating the financial health of a company is its financial statements, consisting principally of a balance sheet, an income statement, and a cash flow statement. Although these statements can appear complex at times, they all rest on a very simple foundation. To understand this foundation and to see the ties among the three statements, let us look briefly at each.

A *balance sheet* is a financial snapshot, taken at a point in time, of all the assets the company owns and all the claims against those assets. The basic relationship, and indeed the foundation for all of accounting, is

$$\text{Assets} = \text{Liabilities} + \text{Shareholders' equity}$$

It is as if a herd (flock? covey?) of accountants runs through the business on the appointed day, making a list of everything the company owns, and assigning each item a value. After tabulating the firm's assets, the accountants list all outstanding company liabilities, where a liability is simply an obligation to deliver something of value in the future—or more colloquially, some form of an "IOU." Having thus totaled up what the company *owns* and what it *owes*, the accountants call the difference between the two *shareholders' equity*. Shareholders' equity is the accountant's estimate of the value of the shareholders' investment in the firm just as the value of a homeowner's equity is the value of the home (the asset), less the mortgage outstanding against it (the liability). Shareholders' equity is also known variously as *owners' equity*, *stockholders' equity*, *net worth*, or simply *equity*.

It is important to realize that the basic accounting equation holds for individual transactions as well as for the firm as a whole. Thus when a retailer pays $1 million in wages, cash declines $1 million and shareholders' equity falls by the same amount. Similarly, when a company borrows $100,000, cash rises by this amount, as does a liability entitled something like *loans outstanding*. And when a company receives a $10,000 payment from a customer, one asset, cash, rises while another asset, accounts receivable, falls by this amount. In each instance the double-entry nature of accounting guarantees that the basic accounting equation holds for each transaction, and when summed across all transactions, for the company as a whole.

To see how the repeated application of this single formula underlies the creation of company financial statements, consider Worldwide Sports (WWS), a newly founded retailer of value-priced sporting goods. In January 2005, the founder invested $150,000 of his personal savings and borrowed an additional $100,000 from relatives to start the business. After buying furniture and display materials for $60,000 and merchandise for $80,000, WWS was ready to open its doors.

The following six transactions summarize WWS's activities over the course of its first year.

- Sell $900,000 worth of sports equipment, receiving $875,000 in cash with $25,000 still to be paid.

- Pay $190,000 in wages.

- Purchase $380,000 of merchandise at wholesale, with $20,000 still owing to suppliers, and $30,000 worth still in inventory at year-end.

- Spend $210,000 on other expenses, including utilities, rent, and taxes.

- Depreciate furniture and fixtures by $15,000.

- Pay $10,000 interest on loan from relatives.

Table 1.1 shows how an accountant would record these transactions. WWS's beginning balance, the first line in the table, shows cash of $250,000, a loan of $100,000, and equity of $150,000. But these numbers change quickly as the company buys fixtures and an initial inventory of merchandise. And they change further as each of the listed transactions occurs.

TABLE 1.1   Worldwide Sports Financial Transactions 2005 ($ thousands)

	Assets				=	Liabilities		+	Equity
	Cash	Accounts Receivable	Inventory	Fixed Assets		Accounts Payable	Loan from Relatives		Owners' Equity
Beginning balance 1/1/05	$ 250						$100		$ 150
Initial purchases	(140)		80	60					
Sales	875	25							900
Wages	(190)								(190)
Merchandise purchases	(360)		30			20			(350)
Other expenses	(210)								(210)
Depreciation				(15)					(15)
Interest payment	(10)								(10)
Ending balance 12/31/05	$ 215	$25	$110	$ 45		$20	$100		$ 275

Abstracting from the accounting details, there are two important things to note here. First, the basic accounting equation holds for each transaction. For every line in the table, assets equal liabilities plus owners' equity. Second, WWS's year-end balance sheet at the bottom of the table is just its beginning balance sheet plus the cumulative effect of the individual transactions. For example, ending cash on December 31, 2005, is beginning cash of $250,000 plus, or minus, the cash involved in each transaction. Incidentally, WWS's first year appears to have been an excellent one; owners' equity is up $125,000 over the course of the year.

If the balance sheet is a snapshot in time, the income statement and the cash flow statement are videos, highlighting changes in two especially important balance sheet accounts over time. Business owners are naturally interested in how company operations have affected the value of their investment. The income statement addresses this question by partitioning observed changes in owners' equity into revenues and expenses, where revenues are increases in owners' equity generated by sales, and expenses are reductions in owner's equity incurred to earn the revenue. The difference between revenues and expenses is earnings, or net income.

The focus of the cash flow statement is solvency, having enough cash in the bank to pay bills as they come due. The cash flow statement provides a detailed look at changes in the company's cash balance over time. As an organizing principle, the statement segregates changes in cash into three broad categories: cash provided, or consumed, by operating activities, by investing activities, and by financing activities. Figure 1.2 is a simple schematic diagram showing the close conceptual ties among the three principal financial statements.

See **harley-davidson.com** for more on the company, including financial statements.

To illustrate the techniques and concepts presented throughout this book, I will refer whenever possible to Harley-Davidson, Inc., legendary purveyors of motorcycles and attitude, primarily to middle-aged, married men. Headquartered in Milwaukee, Harley-Davidson is a New York Stock

FIGURE 1.2 **Ties among Financial Statements**

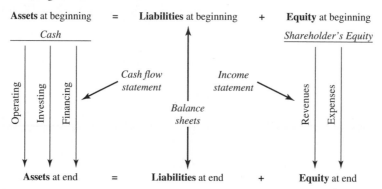

Exchange–traded company and a member of the Standard & Poors 500 index of leading American corporations. The company operates in two principal business segments: motorcycles and related products, and financial services, primarily wholesale and retail financing to Harley-Davidson dealers and customers. Tables 1.2 and 1.3 present Harley-Davidson's balance

TABLE 1.2   **Harley-Davidson, Inc., Balance Sheets ($ millions)***

	December 31		Change in Account
	2003	2004	
Assets			
Cash	$ 329.3	$ 275.2	$ (54.1)
Marketable securities	993.3	1,336.9	343.6
Accounts receivable, less reserve for possible losses	1,114.4	1,328.4	214.0
Inventories	207.7	226.9	19.2
Prepaid income taxes	51.2	60.5	9.3
Other current assets	33.2	38.3	5.1
Total current assets	2,729.1	3,266.2	
Property, plant, and equipment	2,191.2	2,193.4	2.2
Less accumulated depreciation and amortization	1,144.9	1,168.7	23.8
Net property, plant, and equipment	1,046.3	1,024.7	(21.6)
Finance receivables, net	735.9	905.2	169.3
Goodwill	53.7	59.5	5.8
Other assets	358.1	227.7	(130.4)
Total assets	$4,923.1	$ 5,483.3	
Liabilities and Shareholders' Equity			
Long-term debt due in one year	$ 324.3	$ 495.4	171.1
Accounts payable	223.9	244.2	20.3
Income taxes payable	54.8	53.5	(1.3)
Accrued expenses	197.2	197.1	(0.1)
Other current liabilities	155.6	182.4	26.8
Total current liabilities	955.8	1,172.6	
Long-term debt	670.0	800.0	130.0
Postretirement healthcare benefits	127.4	149.8	22.4
Deferred income taxes	125.8	51.4	(74.4)
Other long-term liabilities	86.3	90.8	4.5
Total liabilities	1,965.3	2,264.6	
Common stock	3.3	3.3	
Additional paid-in capital	419.5	533.1	
Retained earnings	3,121.2	3,832.5	
Less treasury stock	(586.2)	(1,150.4)	
Total shareholders' equity	2,957.8	3,218.5	260.7
Total liabilities and shareholders' equity	$4,923.1	$ 5,483.1	

*Totals may not add due to rounding.

TABLE 1.3 Harley Davidson, Inc., Income Statements ($ millions)

	December 31	
	2003	2004
Net sales	$4,903.7	$5,320.5
Cost of goods sold	2,855.7	2,995.5
Gross profit	2,048.0	2,325.0
Selling, general and engineering expenses	684.2	726.6
Depreciation	196.9	214.1
Total operating expenses	881.1	940.7
Operating income	1,166.9	1,384.3
Interest expense	21.5	22.7
Other nonoperating income	20.7	18.0
Total nonoperating expenses	0.8	4.7
Income before income taxes	1,166.1	1,379.6
Provision for income taxes	405.1	489.7
Net income	$ 761.0	$ 889.9

See www.nysscpa.org and select "Define a Term" for an exhaustive glossary of accounting terms.

sheets and income statements, respectively, for 2003 and 2004. If the precise meaning of every asset and liability category in Table 1.2 is not immediately apparent, be patient. We will discuss many of them in the following pages. In addition, all of the accounting terms used appear in the glossary at the end of the book.

Harley-Davidson's balance sheet equation for 2004 is

Assets   = Liabilities   + Shareholders' equity
$5,483.1 million = $2,264.6 million + $3,218.5 million

Current Assets and Liabilities

By convention, accountants list assets and liabilities on the balance sheet in order of decreasing liquidity, where liquidity refers to the speed with which an item can be converted to cash. Thus among assets cash, marketable securities, and accounts receivable appear at the top, while land, plant, and equipment are toward the bottom. Similarly on the liabilities side, short-term loans and accounts payable are toward the top, while shareholders' equity is at the bottom.

Accountants also arbitrarily define any asset or liability that is expected to turn into cash within one year as *current* and all others assets and liabilities as *long-term*. Inventory is a current asset because there is reason to believe it will be sold and will generate cash within one year. Accounts payable are short-term liabilities because they must be paid within one

---

A Word to the Unwary

Nothing puts a damper on a good financial discussion (if such exists) faster than the suggestion that if a company is short of cash, it can always spend some of its shareholders' equity. Equity is on the liabilities side of the balance sheet, not the asset side. It represents owners' claims against existing assets. In other words, that money has already been spent.

---

year. Note that even though Harley-Davidson is primarily a manufacturer, approximately 60 percent of its assets are current. We will say more about this in the next chapter.

Note too that the company has two entries for accounts receivable, one a short-term asset and the other a long-term asset. The short-term asset represents payments due to the company's finance subsidiary, Harley-Davidson Financial Services, within the coming year. The long-term asset, labeled "Finance receivables, net," records payments due beyond the coming year.

Shareholders' Equity

A common source of confusion is the large number of accounts appearing in the shareholders' equity portion of the balance sheet. Harley-Davidson has four, beginning with common stock and ending with treasury stock (see Table 1.2). Unless forced to do otherwise, my advice is to forget these distinctions. They keep accountants and attorneys employed, but seldom make much practical difference. As a first cut, just add up everything that is not an IOU and call it shareholders' equity.

Income Statement

Looking at Harley-Davidson's operating performance in 2004, the basic income statement relation appearing in Table 1.3 is

Revenues	−	Expenses				=	Net income
Net sales	−	Cost of goods sold	− Operating expenses	− Nonoperating expenses	− Taxes	=	Net income
$5,320.5	−	$2,995.5	− $940.7	− $4.7	− $489.7	=	$889.9

Net income records the extent to which net sales generated during the accounting period exceeded expenses incurred in producing the sales. For variety, net income is also commonly referred to as *earnings* or *profits*, frequently with the word *net* stuck in front of them; net sales are often called *revenues* or *net revenues*; and cost of goods sold is labeled *cost of sales*. I have never found a meaningful distinction between these terms. Why so many words to say the same thing? My personal belief is that accountants are so rule-bound in their calculations of the various amounts that their creativity runs a bit amok when it comes to naming them.

Income statements are commonly divided into operating and nonoperating segments. As the names imply, the operating segment reports the results of the company's major, ongoing activities, while the nonoperating segment summarizes all ancillary activities. In 2004, Harley-Davidson reported operating income of $1,384.3 million and nonoperating expenses of $4.7 million, consisting of $22.7 million in interest expense and $18 million in income, primarily interest income on the company's large investment in marketable securities appearing on the balance sheet.

Measuring Earnings

This is not the place for a detailed discussion of accounting. But because earnings, or lack of same, are a critical indicator of financial health, several technical details of earnings measurement deserve mention.

Accrual Accounting

The measurement of accounting earnings involves two steps: (1) identifying revenues for the period and (2) matching the corresponding costs to revenues. Looking at the first step, it is important to recognize that revenue is not the same as cash received. According to the *accrual principle* (a cruel principle?) of accounting, revenue is recognized as soon as "the effort required to generate the sale is substantially complete and there is a reasonable certainty that payment will be received." The accountant sees the timing of the actual cash receipts as a mere technicality. For credit sales, the accrual principle means that revenue is recognized at the time of sale, not when the customer pays. This can result in a significant time lag between the generation of revenue and the receipt of cash. Looking at Harley-Davidson, we see that revenue in 2004 was $5,320.5 million but accounts receivable increased $383.3 million over the year ($214 million increase in short-term accounts receivable plus $169.3 increase in long-term finance receivables). We conclude that cash received from sales during 2004 was only $4,937.2 million ($5,320.5 million − $383.3 million). The other $383.3 million still awaits collection.

Depreciation

Fixed assets and their associated depreciation present the accountant with a particularly challenging problem in matching. Suppose that in 2006, a company constructs for $50 million a new facility that has an expected productive life of 10 years. If the accountant assigns the entire cost of the facility to expenses in 2006, some weird results follow. Income in 2006 will appear depressed due to the $50 million expense, while income in the following nine years will look that much better as the new facility contributes to revenue but not to expenses. Thus, charging the full cost of a long-term asset to one year clearly distorts reported income.

The preferred approach is to spread the cost of the facility over its expected useful life in the form of depreciation. Because the only cash outlay associated with the facility occurs in 2006, the annual depreciation listed as a cost on the company's income statement is not a cash outflow. It is a *noncash charge* used to match the 2006 expenditure with resulting revenue. Said differently, depreciation is the allocation of past expenditures to future time periods to match revenues and expenses. A glance at Harley-Davidson's income statement reveals that in 2004, the company included a $214.1 million noncash charge for depreciation and amortization among their operating expenses. In a few pages, we will see that during the same year, the company spent $213.6 million acquiring new property, plant, and equipment.

To determine the amount of depreciation to take on a particular asset, three estimates are required: the asset's useful life, its salvage value, and the method of allocation to be employed. These estimates should be based on economic and engineering information, experience, and any other objective data about the asset's likely performance. Broadly speaking, there are two methods of allocating an asset's cost over its useful life. Under the *straight-line* method, the accountant depreciates the asset by a uniform amount each year. If an asset costs $50 million, has an expected useful life of 10 years, and has an estimated salvage value of $10 million, straight-line depreciation will be $4 million per year ([$50 million − $10 million]/10).

The second method of cost allocation is really a family of methods known as *accelerated depreciation*. Each technique charges more depreciation in the early years of the asset's life and correspondingly less in later years. Accelerated depreciation does not enable a company to take more depreciation in total; rather, it alters the timing of the recognition. While the specifics of the various accelerated techniques need not detain us here, you should recognize that the life expectancy, the salvage value, and the allocation method a company uses can fundamentally affect reported earnings. In general, if a company is conservative and depreciates its assets rapidly, it will tend to understate current earnings, and vice versa.

Taxes

A second noteworthy feature of depreciation accounting involves taxes. Most U.S. companies, except very small ones, keep at least two sets of financial records: one for managing the company and reporting to shareholders and another for determining the firm's tax bill. The objective of the first set is, or should be, to accurately portray the company's financial performance. The objective of the second set is much simpler: to minimize taxes. Forget objectivity and minimize taxes. These differing objectives mean the accounting principles used to construct the two sets of books differ substantially. Depreciation accounting is a case in point. Regardless of the method used to report to shareholders, company tax books will minimize current taxes by employing the most rapid method of depreciation over the shortest useful life the tax authorities allow.

This dual reporting means that actual cash payments to tax authorities usually differ from the provision for income taxes appearing on a company's income statement, sometimes trailing the provision and other times exceeding it. To illustrate, Harley-Davidson's $489.7 million provision for income taxes appearing on its 2004 income statement is the tax payable according to the accounting techniques used to construct the company's published statements. But because Harley-Davidson has used different accounting techniques over the years when reporting to the tax authorities, taxes actually paid in 2004 were considerably greater than this amount. To confirm this fact, note that Harley-Davidson has one tax account on the asset side of its balance sheet, called "prepaid income taxes," and two more tax accounts on the liabilities side called "income taxes payable" and "deferred income taxes." The asset account reflects prepayment of taxes not yet due, while the liability accounts reflect tax obligations not yet paid. The net change in these balance sheet accounts during 2004 indicates that Harley-Davidson's tax liability fell $85 million over the year, so that taxes paid must have been $85 million higher than the provision for taxes appearing on the income statement. Harley-Davidson's aggressive deferral of tax obligations in past years resulted in a 2004 tax payment in excess of the tax obligation appearing on its income statement. Here is a detailed accounting.

Provision for income taxes	$489.7
+ Increase in prepaid income taxes	9.3
+ Reduction in income taxes payable	1.3
+ Reduction in deferred income taxes	74.4
Taxes paid	$574.7

At the end of 2004, Harley-Davidson's net tax liability appearing on its balance sheet was $44.4 million ($53.5 income taxes payable + $51.4 deferred income taxes − $60.5 prepaid income taxes). This sum represents money Harley-Davidson must pay tax authorities in future years, but in the meantime can be used to finance the business. Tax deferral techniques create the equivalent of interest-free loans from the government. In Japan

Defining Earnings

Creditors and investors look to company earnings for help in answering two fundamental questions: How did the company do last period, and how might it do in the future? To answer the first question it is important to use a broad-based measure of income that includes everything affecting the company's performance over the accounting period. However, to answer the second we want a narrower income measure that abstracts from all unusual, nonrecurring events to focus strictly on the company's steady state, or ongoing, performance.

The accounting profession and the Securities and Exchange Commission obligingly provide two such official measures, known as net income and operating income, and require companies to report them on their financial statements.

Net income, or net profit, is the proverbial "bottom line," defined as total revenue less total expenses.

Operating income is profit realized from day-to-day operations excluding taxes, interest income and expense, and what are known as extraordinary items. An extraordinary item is one that is both unusual in nature and infrequent in occurrence.

For a variety of sometimes-legitimate reasons, corporate executives and business analysts have increasingly argued that these official income measures are inadequate or inappropriate for their purposes and have encouraged a whole new cottage industry devoted to creating and promoting new, improved earnings measures. Here are some of the more popular ones:

Pro forma earnings, also known as operating earnings, core earnings, or ongoing earnings, are total revenues less total expenses, omitting any and all expenses the company believes might cloud investor perceptions of the true earning power of the business. If this sounds vague, it is. Each company has license to decide what expenses are to be ignored, and to change its mind from year to year. In the first three quarters of 2001, the 100 largest firms traded on the Nasdaq stock exchange reported pro forma earnings of $20 billion. For the same period, they reported losses under Generally Accepted Accounting Principles of $82 billion.[a] Happily executives' enthusiasm for pro forma earnings has waned since the bursting of the dot-com bubble.

EBIT (pronounced E-bit) is earnings before interest and taxes, a useful and widely used measure of a business's income before it is divided among creditors, owners, and the taxman.

EBITDA (pronounced E-bit-da) is earnings before interest, taxes, depreciation, and amortization. EBITDA has its uses in some industries, such as broadcasting, where depreciation charges may routinely overstate true economic depreciation. However, as Warren Buffett notes, treating EBITDA as equivalent to earnings is tantamount to saying that a business is the commercial equivalent of the pyramids—forever state-of-the-art, never needing to be replaced, improved, or refurbished. In Buffett's view, EBITDA is a number favored by investment bankers when they cannot justify a deal based on EBIT.

EIATBS (pronounced E-at-b-s) is earnings ignoring all the bad stuff, which is the earnings concept too many executives and analysts appear to prefer.

[a] "A Survey of International Finance," *Economist,* May 18, 2002, p. 20.

and other countries that do not allow the use of separate accounting techniques for tax and reporting purposes, these complications never arise.

Research and Marketing

Now that you understand how accountants use depreciation to spread the cost of long-lived assets over their useful lives to better match revenues and costs, you may think you also understand how they treat research and marketing expenses. Because R&D and marketing outlays promise benefits over a number of future periods, it is only logical that an accountant would show these expenditures as assets when they are incurred and then spread the costs over the assets' expected useful lives in the form of a noncash charge such as depreciation. Impeccable logic, but this isn't what accountants do, at least not in the United States. Because the magnitude and duration of the prospective payoffs from research and development (R&D) and marketing expenditures are difficult to estimate, accountants typically duck the problem by forcing companies to record the entire expenditure as an operating cost in the year incurred. Thus, although a company's research outlays in a given year may have produced technical breakthroughs that will benefit the firm for decades to come, all of the costs must be shown on the income statement in the year incurred. The requirement that companies expense all research and marketing expenditures when incurred commonly understates the profitability of high-tech and high-marketing companies and complicates comparison of American companies with those in other nations that treat such expenditures more liberally.

Sources and Uses Statements

Two very basic but valuable things to know about a company are where it gets its cash and how it spends the cash. At first blush, it might appear that the income statement will answer these questions because it records flows of resources over time. But further reflection will convince you that the income statement is deficient in two respects: It includes accruals that are not cash flows, and it lists only cash flows associated with the sale of goods or services during the accounting period. A host of other cash receipts and disbursements do not appear on the income statement. Thus, Harley-Davidson increased its investment in inventories by almost $20 million in 2004 (Table 1.2) with little or no trace of this buildup on its income statement. Harley-Davidson also increased long-term debt by $171.1 million with little or no effect on its income statement.

To gain a more accurate picture of where a company got its money and how it spent it, we need to look more closely at the balance sheet or, more precisely, two balance sheets. Use the following two-step procedure. First, place two balance sheets for different dates side by side, and note all of the changes in accounts that occurred over the period. The changes for Harley-Davidson in 2004 appear in the rightmost column of Table 1.2. Second, segregate the changes into those that generated cash and those that consumed cash. The result is a *sources and uses statement*.

Here are the guidelines for distinguishing between a source and a use of cash:

- *A company generates cash in two ways: by reducing an asset or by increasing a liability.* The sale of used equipment, the liquidation of inventories, and the reduction of accounts receivable are all reductions in asset accounts and are all sources of cash to the company. On the liabilities side of the balance sheet, an increase in a bank loan and the sale of common stock are increases in liabilities, which again generate cash.

- *A company also uses cash in two ways: to increase an asset account or to reduce a liability account.* Adding to inventories or accounts receivable and building a new plant all increase assets and all use cash. Conversely, the repayment of a bank loan, the reduction of accounts payable, and an operating loss all reduce liabilities and all use cash.

Because it is difficult to spend money you don't have, total uses of cash over an accounting period must equal total sources.

Table 1.4 presents a 2004 sources and uses statement for Harley-Davidson. It reveals that the company got most of its cash from lenders in

TABLE 1.4 Harley-Davidson, Inc., Sources and Uses Statement, 2004 ($ millions)*

Sources	
Reduction in cash	$ 54.1
Reduction in net property, plant, and equipment	21.6
Reduction in other assets	130.4
Increase in long-term debt due in one year	171.1
Increase in notes payable	20.3
Increase in other current liabilities	26.8
Increase in long-term debt	130.0
Increase in postretirement healthcare benefits	22.4
Increase in other long-term liabilities	4.5
Increase in shareholders' equity	260.7
Total sources	**$841.9**
Uses	
Increase in marketable securities	$343.6
Increase in accounts receivable	214.0
Increase in inventories	19.2
Increase in prepaid income taxes	9.3
Increase in other current assets	5.1
Increase in finance receivables, net	169.3
Increase in goodwill	5.8
Reduction in income taxes payable	1.3
Reduction in accrued expenses	0.1
Reduction in deferred income taxes	74.4
Total uses	**$842.1**

*Totals do not add due to rounding.

How Can a Reduction in Cash Be a Source of Cash?

One potential source of confusion in Table 1.4 is that the decline in cash in 2004 appears as a source of cash. How can a reduction of cash be a source of cash? Simple. It is the same as when you withdraw money from your checking account: You reduce your bank balance but have more cash on hand to spend. Conversely, a deposit in your bank account increases your balance but reduces spendable cash in your pocket.

the form of increases in long-term debt. A second important source of cash, as evidenced by the increase in shareholders' equity, was the retention of profits earned throughout the year. The company, in turn, used cash to increase its investment in marketable securities and to add to accounts receivable and finance company receivables. The sharp increase in marketable securities to over $1.3 billion hints that the company may be generating more cash than it can profitably use in the business. We will revisit this topic in more detail in later chapters.

The Two-Finger Approach

I personally do not spend a lot of time constructing sources and uses statements. It might be instructive to go through the exercise once or twice just to convince yourself that sources really do equal uses. But once beyond this point, I recommend using a "two-finger approach." Put the two balance sheets side by side, and quickly run any two fingers down the columns in search of big changes. This should enable you to quickly observe that the great majority of Harley-Davidson's cash came from lenders and increased shareholders' equity while additions to marketable security and various receivables accounts were the principal uses to which the cash was put. In 30 seconds or less, you have the essence of a sources and uses analysis and are free to move on to more stimulating activities. The other changes are largely window dressing of more interest to accountants than to managers.

The Cash Flow Statement

Identifying a company's principal sources and uses of cash is a useful skill in its own right. It is also an excellent starting point for considering the cash flow statement, the third major component of financial statements along with the income statement and the balance sheet.

In essence, a cash flow statement just expands and rearranges the sources and uses statement, placing each source or use into one of three broad categories. The categories and their values for Harley-Davidson in 2004 are as follows:

Category	Source (or Use) of Cash ($ millions)
1. Cash flows from operating activities	$969.7
2. Cash flows from investing activities	($707.7)
3. Cash flows from financing activities	($316.1)

Double-entry bookkeeping guarantees that the sum of the cash flows in these three categories equals the change in cash balances over the accounting period.

Table 1.5 presents a complete cash flow statement for Harley-Davidson in 2004. The first category, "cash flows from operating activities," can be

TABLE 1.5   **Harley-Davidson, Inc., Cash Flow Statement, 2004 ($ millions)***

Cash Flows from Operating Activities	
Net income	$ 889.8
Adjustments to reconcile net income to net cash provided by operating activities:	
Depreciation	214.1
Deferred income taxes	(42.0)
Changes in assets and liabilities	
Increase in accounts receivables	(212.4)
Increase in inventories	(19.2)
Increase in accounts payables	39.6
Other asset and liabilities, net change	(45.3)
Tax benefit from the exercise of stock options	51.5
Other	93.6
Net cash provided by operating activities	969.7
Cash Flows from Investing Activities	
Capital expenditures	(213.6)
Investment in securitized receivables, net	(146.3)
Net purchases of marketable securities	(349.0)
Other, net	1.2
Net cash used by investing activities	(707.7)
Cash Flows from Financing Activities	
Net increase in long-term borrowings	305.0
Dividends paid	(119.2)
Repurchase of common stock	(564.1)
Issuance of common stock under employee stock option plans	62.2
Net cash provided by financing activities	(316.1)
Net increase (decrease) in cash	(54.1)
Cash at beginning of year	329.3
Cash at end of year	$ 275.2

*Totals do not add due to rounding.

thought of as a rearrangement of Harley-Davidson's financial statements to eliminate the effects of accrual accounting on net income. First, we add all noncash charges, such as depreciation and amortization, back to net income, recognizing that these charges did not entail any cash outflow. Then we add the changes in current assets and liabilities to net income, acknowledging, for instance, that some sales did not increase cash because customers had not yet paid, while some expenses did not reduce cash because the company had not yet paid. Changes in other current assets and liabilities, such as inventories, appear here because the accountant, following the matching principle, ignored these cash flows when calculating net income. Interestingly, the cash generated by Harley-Davidson's operations was a full $80 million more than the firm's income. A principal reason for the difference is that the income statement includes a $214.1 million noncash charge for depreciation.

In many textbook examples, the cash flow statement is a simple rearrangement of the sources and uses statement. In real companies the situation is invariably more complicated. Harley-Davidson illustrates two such complications. The first involves an addition to cash flow from operating activities entitled "tax benefit from the exercise of stock options." It arises as follows. In most instances when employees exercise stock options, the employee owes tax on the difference between the value of the stock on the exercise date and the exercise price specified in the option. The tax consequences for the company are just the opposite. It is able to claim a tax-deductible expense for precisely the same amount—even though the company incurs no cash cost when it first issues the option or when the employee later exercises it. In 2004 such noncash expenses reduced Harley-Davidson's tax bill by $51.5 million. The same figure, of course, lies hidden somewhere among the various tax accounts on the sources and uses statement, but management has chosen to highlight the number in the cash flow statement.

To put this tax benefit in perspective, it is interesting to note that in 2000 Cisco Systems, the leading builder of Internet networking gear, reported record net income of $2.7 billion, and a tax benefit from the exercise of employee stock options of $3.1 billion. Stock options are complex and controversial, and this is certainly not the place for a detailed discussion of the topic. At the same time I can't resist noting that the enthusiasm for stock options evinced by many high-tech executives is easier to understand after learning that options can help companies report record profits and greatly reduced taxes in the same year.

A second complication appearing on Harley-Davidson's cash flow statement is a $146.3 million cash outflow from investing activities labeled "investment in securitized receivables, net." When Harley-Davidson's finance subsidiary loans money to a customer to buy a Harley cycle, the customer signs a legal document promising to repay the loan. The finance subsidiary can retain this document as a "finance receivable," or it can sell the document to someone else for immediate cash. To facilitate sale, it is common practice to *securitize* the receivable. This involves bundling a number of receivables together into a diversified portfolio and selling investors new securities representing ownership interests in the portfolio. To further enhance the appeal of the portfolio, the finance company commonly retains an ownership interest. This is the origin of Harley-Davidson's $146.3 million investment in securitized receivables. During 2004, the company originated and securitized almost $2 billion in receivables, while retaining a $146.3 million interest in the portfolios. The word "net" stuck on the end of this entry tells us the amount is net of a reserve to cover expected bad debt losses. I have no idea why this figure differs from the $169.3 million increase in "finance receivables, net" appearing on the sources and uses statement.

Some analysts maintain that net cash provided by operating activities, appearing on the cash flow statement, is a more reliable indicator of firm performance than net income. They argue that because net income depends on a myriad of estimates, allocations, and approximations, devious managers can easily manipulate it. Numbers appearing on a company's cash flow statement, on the other hand, record the actual movement of cash, and are thus more objective measures of performance.

There is certainly some merit to this view, but also two problems. First, low or even negative net cash provided by operating activities does not necessarily indicate poor performance. Rapidly growing businesses in particular must customarily invest in current assets, such as accounts receivable and inventories, to support increasing sales. And although such investments reduce net cash provided by operating activities, they do not in any way suggest poor performance. Second, cash flow statements turn out to be less objective, and thus less immune to manipulation than might be supposed. Harley-Davidson's treatment of finance receivables is a case in point. If Harley-Davidson sold motorcycles on simple open account, the increase in accounts receivable accompanying each sale would reduce net cash provided by operating activities. But because the company loans money to customers to enable them to make immediate payment, and because it chooses to classify these loans as investments rather than increases in accounts receivable, net cash provided by operating activities is undiminished by the credit extension. So although the customer owes Harley-Davidson money in either case, net cash provided by operating activities appears lower in the first case than in the second. Because the criteria for apportioning cash flows among operating, investing, and financing activities are ambiguous, subjective judgment must be used in the preparation of cash flow statements.

What Is Cash Flow?

So many conflicting definitions of *cash flow* exist today that the term has almost lost meaning. At one level, cash flow is very simple. It is the movement of money into or out of a cash account over a period of time. The problem arises when we try to be more specific. Here are four common types of cash flow you are apt to encounter.

$$\text{Net cash flow} = \text{Net income} + \text{Noncash items}$$

Often known in investment circles as cash earnings, net cash flow is intended to measure the cash a business generates, as distinct from the earnings—a laudable objective. Applying the formula to Harley-Davidson's 2004 figures (Table 1.5), net cash flow was $1,155.4 million, equal to net income plus depreciation, and tax benefit from exercise of stock options.

A problem with net cash flow as a measure of cash generation is that it implicitly assumes a business's current assets and liabilities are either unrelated to operations or do not change over time. In Harley-Davidson's case, the cash flow statement reveals that changes in a number of current assets and liabilities consumed $237.6 million in cash. A more inclusive measure of cash generation is therefore cash flow from operating activities as it appears on the cash flow statement.

$$\text{Cash flow from operating activities} = \text{Net cash flow} \\ \pm \text{ Changes in current assets and liabilities}$$

A third, even more inclusive measure of cash flow, popular among finance specialists is

$$\text{Free cash flow} = \frac{\text{Total cash available for distribution to owners and creditors}}{\text{after funding all worthwhile investment activities}}$$

Free cash flow extends cash flow from operating activities by recognizing that some of the cash a business generates must be plowed back into the business, in the form of capital expenditures, to support growth. Abstracting from a few technical details, free cash flow is essentially cash flow from operating activities less capital expenditures. As we will see in Chapter 9, free cash flow is a fundamental determinant of the value of a business. Indeed, one can argue that the principal means by which a company creates value for its owners is to increase free cash flow.

Yet another widely used cash flow is

$$\text{Discounted cash flow} = \frac{\text{A sum of money today having the same value}}{\text{as a future stream of cash receipts and disbursements}}$$

Discounted cash flow refers to a family of techniques for analyzing investment opportunities that take into account the time value of money. A standard approach to valuing investments and businesses uses discounted cash flow techniques to calculate the present value of projected free cash flows. This is the focus of the last three chapters of this book.

My advice when tossing cash flow terms about is to either use the phrase broadly to refer to a general movement of cash or to define your terms carefully.

Much of the information contained in a cash flow statement can be gleaned from careful study of a company's income statement and balance sheet. Nonetheless, the statement has three principal virtues. First, accounting neophytes and those who do not trust accrual accounting have at least some hope of understanding it. Second, the statement provides more accurate information about certain activities, such as taxes and securitization, than one can infer from income statements and balance sheets alone. Third, it casts a welcome light on the issue of firm solvency by highlighting the extent to which operations are generating or consuming cash.

Financial Statements and the Value Problem

To this point, we have reviewed the basics of financial statements and grappled with the distinction between earnings and cash flow. This is a valuable start, but if we are to use financial statements to make informed business decisions, we must go further. We must understand the extent to which accounting numbers reflect economic reality. When the accountant tells us that Harley-Davidson's total assets were worth $5,483.3 million on December 31, 2004, is this literally true, or is the number just an artificial accounting construct? To gain perspective on this issue, and in anticipation of later discussions, I want to conclude by examining a recurring problem in the use of accounting information for financial decision making.

Market Value versus Book Value

Part of what I will call the *value problem* involves the distinction between the market value and the book value of shareholders' equity. Harley-Davidson's 2004 balance sheet states that the value of shareholders' equity is $3,218.5 million. This is known as the *book value* of Harley-Davidson's equity. However, Harley-Davidson is not worth $3,218.5 million to its shareholders or to anyone else, for that matter. There are two reasons. One is that financial statements are *transactions based*. If a company purchased an asset for $1 million in 1950, this transaction provides an objective measure of the asset's value, which the accountant uses to value the asset on the company's balance sheet. Unfortunately, it is a 1950 value that may or may not have much relevance today. To further confound things, the accountant attempts to reflect the gradual deterioration of an asset over time by periodically subtracting depreciation from its balance sheet value. This practice makes sense as far as it goes, but depreciation is the only change in value an American accountant customarily recognizes. The $1 million asset purchased in 1950 may be technologically obsolete and therefore virtually worthless today; or, due to inflation, it may be worth much more than its original purchase price. This is especially true of land, which can be worth several times its original cost.

It is tempting to argue that accountants should forget the original costs of long-term assets and provide more meaningful current values. The problem is that objectively determinable current values of many assets do not exist. Faced with a choice between relevant but subjective current values and irrelevant but objective historical costs, accountants opt for irrelevant historical costs. Accountants prefer to be precisely wrong rather than vaguely right. This means it is the user's responsibility to make any adjustments to historical-cost asset values she deems appropriate.

Check **www.cfo.com**, search for "fair value" for more on fair value accounting.

Prodded by regulators and investors, the Financial Accounting Standards Board, accounting's principal rule-making fraternity, increasingly stresses what is known as *fair value* accounting, according to which certain assets and liabilities must appear on company financial statements at their market values instead of their historical costs. Such "marking to market" applies to selected assets and liabilities that trade actively on financial markets, including many common stocks and bonds. Proponents of fair value accounting acknowledge it will never be possible to eliminate historical cost accounting entirely, but maintain that market values should be used whenever possible. Skeptics respond that mixing historical costs and market values in the same financial statement will only heighten confusion, and that periodically revaluing company accounts to reflect changing market values introduces unwanted subjectivity, distorts reported earnings, and greatly increases earnings volatility. They point out that under fair value accounting changes in owners' equity no longer mirror the results of company operations but also include potentially large and volatile gains and losses from changes in the market values of certain assets and liabilities. The gradual movement toward fair value accounting was greeted with howls of protest, especially from financial institutions concerned that the move would increase apparent earnings volatility and, more menacingly, might reveal that some enterprises are worth less than historical-cost financial statements suggest. To these firms the appearance of benign stability is apparently more appealing than the hint of an ugly reality.

To understand the second, more fundamental reason Harley-Davidson is not worth $3,218.5 million, recall that equity investors buy shares for the future income they hope to receive, not for the value of the firm's assets. Indeed, if all goes according to plan, most of the firm's existing assets will be consumed in generating future income. The problem with the accountant's measure of shareholders' equity is that it bears little relation to future income. There are two reasons for this. First, because the accountant's numbers are backward looking and cost based, they often provide few clues about the future income a company's assets might generate. Second, companies typically have a great many assets and liabilities that do not appear on their balance sheets but affect future income nonetheless. Examples include patents and trademarks, loyal customers, proven mailing lists, superior technology, and, of course, better management. It is said that in

TABLE 1.6 The Book Value of Equity Is a Poor Surrogate for the Market Value of Equity, December 31, 2004

Company	Value of Equity ($ millions)		Ratio, Market Value to Book Value
	Book	Market	
Aetna Inc.	$ 9,081	$ 22,186	2.4
Affymetric Inc.	249	2,576	10.3
Coca-Cola Co.	15,935	101,224	6.4
Dana Corp.	2,435	2,069	0.8
First Advantage Corp.	290	143	0.5
General Motors Corp.	27,726	22,639	0.8
Google Inc.	2,929	52,925	18.1
Harley-Davidson Inc.	3,219	17,880	5.6
Hewlett-Packard Co.	37,726	59,011	1.6
Home Depot Inc.	24,158	85,445	3.5
IBM	29,747	146,708	4.9
Intel Corp.	38,579	145,774	3.8
Kraft Foods	29,911	17,141	0.6
Winn-Dixie Stores Inc.	364	143	0.4
Yahoo! Inc.	7,101	43,849	6.2

many companies, the most valuable assets go home to their spouses in the evening. Examples of unrecorded liabilities include pending lawsuits, inferior management, and obsolete production processes. The accountant's inability to measure assets and liabilities such as these means that book value is customarily a highly inaccurate measure of the value perceived by shareholders.

It is a simple matter to calculate the market value of shareholders' equity when a company's shares are publicly traded: Simply multiply the number of common shares outstanding by the market price per share. On December 31, 2004, Harley-Davidson's common shares closed on the New York Stock Exchange at $60.75 per share. With 294.32 million shares outstanding, this yields a value of $17,879.9 million, or more than 5.5 times the book value ($17,879.9/$3,218.5 million). This $17,879.9 million is the market value of Harley-Davidson's equity.

Table 1.6 presents the market and book values of equity for 15 representative companies. It demonstrates clearly that book value is a poor proxy for market value.

Goodwill

There is one instance in which intangible assets, such as brand names and patents, find their way onto company balance sheets. It occurs when one company buys another at a price above book value. Suppose an acquiring firm pays $100 million for a target firm and the target's assets have a book value of only $40 million and an estimated replacement value of only $60 million. To record the transaction, the accountant will allocate $60 million of the acquisition price to the value of the assets acquired and assign the remaining $40 million to a new asset commonly known as "goodwill."[1] The acquiring company paid a handsome premium over the fair value of the target's recorded assets because it places a high value on its unrecorded, or intangible, assets. But not until the acquisition creates a piece of paper with $100 million written on it is the accountant willing to acknowledge this value.

Economic Income versus Accounting Income

A second dimension of the value problem is rooted in the accountant's distinction between *realized* and *unrealized* income. To anyone who has not studied too much accounting, income is what you could spend during the period and be as well off at the end as you were at the start. If Mary Siegler's assets, net of liabilities, are worth $100,000 at the start of the year and rise to $120,000 by the end, and if she receives and spends $70,000 in wages during the year, most of us would say her income was $90,000 ($70,000 in wages + $20,000 increase in net assets).

But not the accountant. Unless Mary's investments were in marketable securities with readily observable prices, he would say Mary's income was only $70,000. The $20,000 increase in the market value of assets would not qualify as income because the gain was not *realized* by the sale of the assets. Because the value of the assets could fluctuate in either direction before the assets are sold, the gain is only *on paper*, and accountants generally do not recognize paper gains or losses. They consider *realization* the objective evidence necessary to record the gain, despite the fact that Mary is probably just as pleased with the unrealized gain in assets as with another $20,000 in wages.

It is easy to criticize accountants' conservatism when measuring income. Certainly the amount Mary could spend, ignoring inflation, and be as well off as at the start of the year is the commonsense $90,000, not the accountant's $70,000. Moreover, if Mary sold her assets for $120,000 and immediately repurchased them for the same price, the $20,000 gain would

---

[1] For years, accounting authorities required companies to write this goodwill off as a noncash expense against income over a number years. Now goodwill need not be written off unless there is objective evidence its market value has declined.

become realized and, in the accountant's eyes, become part of income. That income could depend on a sham transaction such as this is enough to raise suspicions about the accountant's definition.

However, we should note two points in the accountant's defense. First, if Mary holds her assets for several years before selling them, the gain or loss the accountant recognized on the sale date will just equal the sum of the annual gains and losses we nonaccountants would recognize. So it's really not total income that is at issue here but simply the timing of its recognition. Second, it is extremely difficult to measure the periodic change in the value of many assets unless they are actively traded. Thus, even if an accountant wanted to include "paper" gains and losses in income, she would often have great difficulty doing so. In the corporate setting, this means the accountant frequently must be content to measure realized rather than economic income.

Imputed Costs

A similar but subtler problem exists on the cost side of the income statement. It involves the cost of equity capital. Harley-Davidson's accountants acknowledge that in 2004 the company had use of $3,218.5 million of shareholders' money, measured at book value. They would further acknowledge that Harley-Davidson could not have operated without this money and that this money is not free. Just as creditors earn interest on loans, equity investors expect a return on their investments. Yet if you look again at Harley-Davidson income statement (Table 1.3), you will find no mention of the cost of this equity; interest expense appears, but a comparable cost for equity does not.

While acknowledging that equity capital has a cost, the accountant does not record it on the income statement because the cost must be imputed, that is, estimated. Because there is no piece of paper stating the amount of money Harley-Davidson is obligated to pay owners, the accountant refuses to recognize any cost of equity capital. Once again, the accountant would rather be reliably wrong than make a potentially inaccurate estimate. The result has been serious confusion in the minds of less knowledgeable observers and continuing "image" problems for corporations.

Following is the bottom portion of Harley-Davidson's 2004 income statement as prepared by its accountant and as an economist might prepare it. Observe that while the accountant shows earnings of $889.9 million, the economist records a profit of only $568.0 million. These numbers differ because the economist includes a $321.9 million charge as a cost of equity capital, while the accountant pretends equity is free.

(We will consider ways to estimate a company's cost of equity capital in Chapter 8. Here I have assumed a 10 percent annual equity cost and applied it to the book value of Harley-Davidson's equity [$321.9 million = 10% × $3,218.5 million].)

	Accountant	Economist
Operating income	$1,384.3	$1,384.3
Interest expense	22.7	22.7
Other nonoperating income	18.0	18.0
Cost of equity		**321.9**
Income before taxes	1,379.6	1,057.7
Provision for taxes	489.7	489.7
Accounting earnings	$ 889.9	
Economic earnings		$ 568.0

The distinction between accounting earnings and economic earnings might be only a curiosity if everyone understood that positive accounting earnings are not necessarily a sign of superior or even commendable performance. But when many labor unions and politicians view accounting profits as evidence that a company can afford higher wages, higher taxes, or more onerous regulation, and when most managements view such profits as justification for distributing handsome performance bonuses, the distinction can be an important one. Keep in mind, therefore, that the right of equity investors to expect a competitive return on their investments is every bit as legitimate as a creditor's right to interest and an employee's right to wages. All voluntarily contribute scarce resources, and all are justified in expecting compensation. Remember too that a company is not shooting par unless its economic profits are zero or greater. By this criterion, Harley-Davidson had a fine but not fantastic year in 2004. On closer inspection, you will find that many companies reporting apparently large earnings are really performing like weekend duffers when the cost of equity is included.

We will look at the difference between accounting and economic profits again in more detail in Chapter 8 under the rubric of economic value added, or EVA. In recent years, EVA has become a popular yardstick for assessing company and managerial performance.

In sum, those of us interested in financial analysis eventually develop a love-hate relationship with accountants. The value problem means that financial statements typically yield distorted information about company earnings and market value. This limits their applicability for many important managerial decisions. Yet financial statements frequently provide the best information available, and if we bear their limitations in mind, they can be a useful starting point for analysis. In the next chapter, we consider the use of accounting data for evaluating financial performance.

SUMMARY

1. This chapter reviewed the accounting principles governing financial statements and the use of accounting information in financial decision making.
2. Two recurring themes throughout the chapter were that defining and measuring profits is a challenging task and that profitability alone does not guarantee success, or even survival.
3. A company's finances and its business operations are integrally related. We study a company's financial statements because they are a window on the firm's operations.
4. Earnings are not cash flow. The wise manager watches both.
5. A balance sheet is a snapshot of a company's assets and liabilities at a point in time. An income statement records sales, related expenses, and earnings over a period of time.
6. Income statements and balance sheets rely on the accrual principle. As a result, revenues and expenses are not synonymous with cash inflow and outflows.
7. A cash flow statement eliminates the effects of accrual accounting to present the firm's cash receipts and disbursements over the accounting period.
8. A sources and uses statement can be thought of as a "poor man's" cash flow statement. Two steps are necessary to create one: calculate changes in balance sheet accounts over the accounting period, and segregate them into sources and uses.
9. Because financial statements are largely transactions based, they must be used with caution in financial decision making. In particular, accounting asset values commonly differ from economic values because accounting values are tied to historical costs. Moreover, accounting income customarily differs from economic income because accountants are hesitant to recognize unrealized gains and losses and because they often ignore imputed costs.

ADDITIONAL RESOURCES

Anthony, Robert N. and Leslie P. Breitner. *Essentials of Accounting*.
8th ed. Englewood Cliffs, NJ: Prentice Hall, 2002. 110 pages.
> The lead author is a distinguished emeritus Harvard professor. A
> great way to review or pick up the basics of accounting on your own.
> Available in paperback, about $54.

Downes, John; and Jordan Elliot Goodman. *Dictionary of Finance and
Investment Terms*. 6th ed. New York: Barron's Educational Services, Inc.,
2002. 736 pages.
> More than 4,000 terms clearly defined. Available in paperback,
> about $12.

Horngren, Charles T.; Gary L. Sundem; and John A. Elliott. *Introduction
to Financial Accounting*. 8th ed. Englewood Cliffs, NJ: Prentice Hall,
2002. 648 pages.
> The high-octane stuff—best-selling college text. Everything you ever
> wanted to know about the topic and then some. $108.

Tracy, John A. *How to Read a Financial Report: Wringing Vital Signs Out of
the Numbers*. 6th ed. New York: John Wiley & Sons, 2004. 203 pages.
> A lively, accessible look at practical aspects of financial statement
> analysis. Available in paperback, about $15.

Welton, Ralph E.; and George T. Friedlob. *Keys to Reading an Annual
Report*. 3rd ed. New York: Barron's Educational Services, Inc., 2001.
193 pages.
> A no-nonsense, practical guide to understanding financial reports.
> About $8.

WEBSITES

philanthropy.ml.com/ipo/resources/financial.html
From this site you can download a free copy of Merrill Lynch's classic
"How to Read a Financial Report" as a PDF file.

www.duke.edu/~charvey/Classes/wpg/glossary.htm
Duke Professor Campbell Harvey's glossary of finance with more than
8,000 terms defined and more than 18,000 hyperlinks.

www.edgarscan.pwcglobal.com
Edgar, a Securities and Exchange Commission site, contains virtually all
filings of public companies in the United States. It is a treasure trove
of financial information, including annual and quarterly reports. The
referenced site offers a slick way to access Edgar, including direct
downloading into a spreadsheet and hyperlinked access to specific

portions of SEC filings. "Benchmarking Assistant" performs graphical financial benchmarking against peer companies. I use it often.

PROBLEMS

Answers to odd-numbered problems appear at the end of the book. For additional problems with answers, see **www.mhhe.com/higgins8e**.

1. a. Is a company better or worse off when the market value of its liabilities falls $10 million? Why?
   b. If you owned a company, would you prefer the market value of its assets to rise $10 million or the market value of its liabilities to fall $10 million? Why?

2. What does it mean when cash flow from operations on a company's cash flow statement is negative? Is this bad news? Is it dangerous?

3. Why do you suppose financial statements are constructed on an accrual basis rather than a cash basis when cash accounting is so much easier to understand?

4. Explain briefly how each of the following transactions would affect a company's balance sheet. (Remember, assets must equal liabilities plus owners' equity before and after the transaction.)
   a. Purchase of a new $40 million building, financed 25 percent with cash and 75 percent with a bank loan.
   b. Purchase of a new building for $40 million cash.
   c. A $10,000 payment to trade creditors.
   d. Sale of $100,000 of merchandise for cash.
   e. Sale of $100,000 of merchandise for credit.

5. The book value of Nott's Nursery's total assets is $400,000. Suppose Golden Gardens Inc. acquires Nott's Nursery's assets for $1 million and finances the purchase by selling $600,000 in new stock, $300,000 in new debt, and reducing cash by $100,000. Describe how the acquisition affects Golden Gardens Inc.'s balance sheet.

6. Table 3.1 in Chapter 3 presents financial statements over the period 2002–2005 for R&E Supplies, Inc.
   a. Construct a sources and uses statement for the company over this period (one statement for all three years).
   b. What insights, if any, does the sources and uses statement give you about the financial position of R&E Supplies?

7. You are responsible for labor relations in your company. During heated labor negotiations, the General Secretary of your largest union exclaims, "Look, this company has $10 billion in assets, $5 billion in

equity, and made a profit last year of $200 million—due largely, I might add, to the effort of union employees. So don't tell me you can't afford our wage demands." How would you reply?

8. You manage a real estate investment company. One year ago the company purchased 10 parcels of land distributed throughout the community for $1 million each. A recent appraisal of the properties indicates that five of the parcels are now worth $800,000 each, while the other five are worth $1.6 million each.

   Ignoring any income received from the properties and any taxes paid over the year, calculate the investment company's accounting earnings and its economic earnings in each of the following cases:

   a. The company sells all of the properties at their appraised values today.
   b. The company sells none of the properties.
   c. The company sells the properties that have fallen in value and keeps the others.
   d. The company sells the properties that have risen in value and keeps the others.
   e. After returning from a property management seminar, an employee recommends the company adopt an end-of-year policy of always selling properties that have risen in value since purchase, and always retaining properties that have fallen in value. The employee explains that with this policy the company will never show a loss on its real estate investment activities. Do you agree with the employee? Why, or why not?

9. Please ignore taxes for this problem. During 2004, Beckey Construction earned net income of $250,000. The firm neither bought nor sold any capital assets. The book value of its assets declined by the year's depreciation charge, which was $200,000. The firm's operating cash flow for the year was $450,000. The market value of its assets increased by $300,000. What was Beckey Construction's economic income for the year? Why is this figure different from its accounting income?

10. Martha currently performs for a ballet company that pays her a salary of $30,000 a year. She is considering quitting this job and opening her own dance company. She estimates the annual revenues from the company will be $95,000 and that total annual expenses for operating the company, ignoring any payments to Martha, will be $75,000. Martha's accountant friend advises her to start her own company because it will be a profitable enterprise. Do you agree with the accountant? Why or why not?

11. Selected information about Sam 'n' Ella's Chicken Delight, a chain of hot new restaurants, follows.

	($ in millions)	
	2005	2006
Net sales	$104	$156
Cost of goods sold	60	82
Depreciation	20	24
Net income	10	16
Finished goods inventory	12	10
Accounts receivable	20	30
Accounts payable	12	18
Net fixed assets	$160	$168

a. During 2006 how much cash did Sam 'n' Ella's collect from sales?

b. During 2006 what was the cost of goods produced by the company?

c. Assuming the company neither sold nor salvaged any assets during the year, what were the company's capital expenditures during 2006?

12. Below are summary cash flow statements for three roughly equal-size companies

	($ millions)		
	A	B	C
Net cash flows from operations	$ (300)	$(300)	$ 300
Net cash used in investing activities	(900)	(30)	(90)
Net cash from financing activities	1,200	210	(240)
Cash balance at beginning of year	150	150	150

a. Calculate each company's cash balance at the end of the year.

b. Explain what might cause company C's net cash from financing activities to be negative.

c. Looking at companies A and B, which company would you prefer to own? Why?

d. Is company C's cash flow statement cause for any concern on the part of C's management or shareholders? Why or why not?

13. Epic Record's equity has a market value of $5 million with 500,000 shares outstanding. The book value of its equity is $1,750,000.

a. What is Epic's stock price per share? What is its book value per share?

b. If the company repurchases 20 percent of its shares in the stock market, how will this affect the book value of equity if all else remains the same?

c. If there are no taxes or transaction costs, and investors do not change their perceptions of the firm, what should the market value of the firm be after the repurchase?

14. Use Standard & Poor's Market Insight website (**www.mhhe.com/ edumarketinsight**) for this problem. Yahoo Inc. reported a $92.8 million loss in 2001.

    a. Does this necessarily mean the company's operating activities consumed cash in 2001? Explain.

    b. Looking at the company's 2001 Annual Statement of Cash Flows, did operating activities consume cash or generate cash? How much?

    c. What was Yahoo's single largest *operating* source of cash in 2001? Explain how this could be a source of cash.

15. Use Standard & Poor's Market Insight website (**www.mhhe.com/ edumarketinsight**) for this problem.

    a. What was the ratio of the market value of equity to the book value of equity for eBay, Inc. at year-end 2003? (From the "Excel Analytics" tools on the left of the screen, consult "Valuation Data, Profitability.")

    b. What growth rate in sales did eBay achieve in 2002 and 2003? (From the Excel Analytics tools, consult Annual Income Statements and select the % Change tab on the spreadsheet.)

    c. Might eBay's high market-to-book ratio be due to its growth rate? Explain.

16. An Excel spreadsheet containing the Whistler Corporation's financial statements is available for download at **www.mhhe.com/higgins8e**. (Select Student Edition > Choose a Chapter > Excel Spreadsheets.) Use the statements to create a sources and uses statement and a cash flow statement for the company in 2005. If you are new to Excel, see **www.extension.iastate.edu/Pages/Excel/homepage.html** for a free, interactive tutorial.

CHAPTER TWO

Evaluating Financial Performance

You can't manage what you can't measure.

William Hewlett

The cockpit of a 747 jet looks like a three-dimensional video game. It is a sizable room crammed with meters, switches, lights, and dials requiring the full attention of three highly trained pilots. When compared to the cockpit of a single-engine Cessna, it is tempting to conclude that the two planes are different species rather than distant cousins. But at a more fundamental level, the similarities outnumber the differences. Despite the 747's complex technology, the 747 pilot controls the plane in the same way the Cessna pilot does: with a stick, a throttle, and flaps. And to change the altitude of the plane, each pilot makes simultaneous adjustments to the same few levers available for controlling the plane.

Much the same is true of companies. Once you strip away the facade of apparent complexity, the levers with which managers affect their companies' financial performance are comparatively few and are similar from one company to another. The executive's job is to control these levers to ensure a safe and efficient flight. And like the pilot, the executive must remember that the levers are interrelated; one cannot change the business equivalent of the flaps without also adjusting the stick and the throttle.

The Levers of Financial Performance

In this chapter, we analyze financial statements for the purpose of evaluating performance and understanding the levers of management control. We begin by studying the ties between a company's operating decisions, such as how many units to make this month and how to price them, and its financial performance. These operating decisions are the levers by which management controls financial performance. Then we broaden the discussion to consider the uses and limitations of ratio analysis as a tool for evaluating performance. To keep things practical, we will again use the financial statements for Harley-Davidson, Inc., presented in Tables 1.2, 1.3, and 1.5 of the last chapter, to illustrate the techniques. The chapter concludes with an evaluation of Harley-Davidson's financial performance relative to its competition. (See Additional Resources at the end of the chapter for information about HISTORY, complimentary software for calculating company ratios. Also at the end of the chapter, Table 2.5 presents summary definitions of the principal ratios appearing throughout the chapter.)

Return on Equity

By far the most popular yardstick of financial performance among investors and senior managers is the *return on equity (ROE)*, defined as

$$\text{Return on equity} = \frac{\text{Net income}}{\text{Shareholders' equity}}$$

Harley-Davidson's ROE for 2004 was

$$\text{ROE} = \frac{\$889.9}{\$3,218.5} = 27.6\%$$

It is not an exaggeration to say that the careers of many senior executives rise and fall with their firms' ROEs. ROE is accorded such importance because it is a measure of the *efficiency* with which a company employs owners' capital. It is a measure of earnings per dollar of invested equity capital or, equivalently, of the percentage return to owners on their investment. In short, it measures bang per buck.

Later in this chapter, we will consider some significant problems with ROE as a measure of financial performance. For now, let us accept it provisionally as at least widely used and see what we can learn.

The Three Determinants of ROE

To learn more about what management can do to increase ROE, let us rewrite ROE in terms of its three principal components:

$$\text{ROE} = \frac{\text{Net income}}{\text{Sales}} \times \frac{\text{Sales}}{\text{Assets}} \times \frac{\text{Assets}}{\text{Shareholders' equity}}$$

Denoting the last three ratios as the profit margin, asset turnover, and financial leverage, respectively, the expression can be written as

$$\frac{\text{Return on}}{\text{equity}} = \frac{\text{Profit}}{\text{margin}} \times \frac{\text{Asset}}{\text{turnover}} \times \frac{\text{Financial}}{\text{leverage}}$$

This says that management has only three levers for controlling ROE: (1) the earnings squeezed out of each dollar of sales, or the *profit margin*;

(2) the sales generated from each dollar of assets employed, or the *asset turnover;* and (3) the amount of equity used to finance the assets, or the *financial leverage.*[1] With few exceptions, whatever management does to increase these ratios increases ROE.

Note too the close correspondence between the levers of performance and company financial statements. Thus, the profit margin summarizes a company's income statement performance by showing profit per dollar of sales. The asset turnover ratio summarizes the company's management of the asset side of its balance sheet by showing the resources required to support sales. And the financial leverage ratio summarizes management of the liabilities side of the balance sheet by showing the amount of shareholders' equity used to finance the assets. This is reassuring evidence that despite their simplicity, the three levers do capture the major elements of a company's financial performance.

We find that Harley-Davidson's 2004 ROE was generated as follows:

$$\frac{\$889.9}{\$3,218.5} = \frac{\$889.9}{\$5,320.5} \times \frac{\$5,320.5}{\$5,483.3} \times \frac{\$5,483.3}{\$3,218.5}$$

$$27.6\% = 16.7\% \times 1.0 \times 1.7$$

Table 2.1 presents ROE and its three principal components for 10 highly diverse businesses. It shows quite clearly that there are many paths to heaven: The companies' ROEs are very similar, but the combinations of profit margin, asset turnover, and financial leverage producing this end result vary widely. Thus, ROE ranges from a high of 33.6 percent for Merck & Co., a major drug firm, to a low of 11.6 percent for Internet auction house eBay, Inc., while the range for the profit margin, to take one example, is from a low of 3.5 percent for Whole Foods Market to a high of 24.8 percent for Merck. ROE differs by about 3 to 1 high to low, but the profit margin varies by a factor of more than 7 to 1. Comparable ranges for asset turnover and financial leverage are 42 to 1 and 9 to 1, respectively.

Why are ROEs similar across firms while profit margins, asset turnovers, and financial leverages differ dramatically? The answer, in a word, is competition. Attainment of an unusually high ROE by one company acts as a magnet to attract rivals anxious to emulate the superior performance. As rivals enter the market, the heightened competition drives the

---

[1] At first glance the ratio of assets to shareholders' equity may not look like a measure of financial leverage, but consider the following:

$$\frac{\text{Assets}}{\text{Equity}} = \frac{\text{Liabilities} + \text{Equity}}{\text{Equity}} = \frac{\text{Liabilities}}{\text{Equity}} + 1$$

And the liabilities-to-equity ratio clearly measures financial leverage.

TABLE 2.1 ROEs and Levers of Performance for 10 Diverse Companies, 2004*

	Return on Equity (ROE) (%)	=	Profit Margin (P) (%)	×	Asset Turnover (A) (times)	×	Financial Leverage (T) (times)
Bank of America	14.2	=	21.6	×	0.06	×	11.17
ChevronTexaco	29.5	=	9.3	×	1.53	×	2.06
eBay	11.6	=	23.8	×	0.41	×	1.19
Florida Power and Light	11.8	=	8.4	×	0.37	×	3.76
Genentech	11.6	=	17.0	×	0.49	×	1.39
Harley-Davidson	27.6	=	16.7	×	0.97	×	1.70
Merck	33.6	=	24.8	×	0.55	×	2.46
Netflix	13.8	=	4.3	×	2.01	×	1.61
Norfolk Southern	11.6	=	12.6	×	0.30	×	3.10
Whole Foods Market	13.9	=	3.5	×	2.54	×	1.54

*Totals do not add due to rounding.

successful company's ROE back toward the average. Conversely, unusually low ROEs repel potential new competitors and drive existing companies out of business so that over time, survivors' ROEs rise toward the average.

To understand how managerial decisions and a company's competitive environment combine to affect ROE, we will examine each lever of performance in more detail. In anticipation of the discussion of ratio analysis to follow, we will also consider related commonly used financial ratios. See Additional Resources at the end of the chapter for published sources of business ratios.

The Profit Margin

The profit margin measures the fraction of each dollar of sales that trickles down through the income statement to profits. This ratio is particularly important to operating managers because it reflects the company's pricing strategy and its ability to control operating costs. As Table 2.1 indicates, profit margins differ greatly among industries depending on the nature of the product sold and the company's competitive strategy.

Note too that profit margin and asset turnover tend to vary inversely. Companies with high profit margins tend to have low asset turns, and vice versa. This is no accident. Companies that add significant value to a product, such as Florida Power and Light and Genentech, can demand high profit margins. However, because adding value to a product usually requires lots of assets, these same firms tend to have lower asset turns. At the other extreme, grocery stores, such as Whole Foods Market, bring the product in the store on forklift trucks, sell for cash, and make the customer carry out his own purchases. Because they add little value to the product, they have very low profit margins and correspondingly high asset turns. It should be apparent, therefore, that a high profit margin is not necessarily better or worse than a low one—it all depends on the combined effect of the profit margin and the asset turnover.

Return on Assets

To look at the combined effect of margins and turns, we can calculate the *return on assets (ROA)*:

$$\text{ROA} = \frac{\text{Profit}}{\text{margin}} \times \frac{\text{Asset}}{\text{turnover}} = \frac{\text{Net income}}{\text{Assets}}$$

Harley-Davidson's ROA in 2004 was

$$\text{Return on assets} = \frac{\$889.9}{\$5,483.3} = 16.2\%$$

This means Harley-Davidson earned an average of 16.2 cents on each dollar tied up in the business.

ROA is a basic measure of the efficiency with which a company allocates and manages its resources. It differs from ROE in that it measures profit as a percentage of the money provided by owners *and* creditors as opposed to only the money provided by owners.

Some companies, such as Merck and Norfolk Southern, a railroad, produce their ROAs by combining a high profit margin with a low asset turn; others, such as Whole Food Market, adopt the reverse strategy. A high profit margin *and* a high asset turn is ideal, but can be expected to attract considerable competition. Conversely, a low profit margin combined with a low asset turn will attract only bankruptcy lawyers.

Gross Margin

When analyzing profitability, it is often interesting to distinguish between variable costs and fixed costs. Variable costs change as sales vary, while fixed costs remain constant. Companies with a high proportion of fixed costs are more vulnerable to sales declines than other firms, because they cannot reduce fixed costs as sales fall. This means falling sales will produce major profit declines in high-fixed-cost businesses.

Unfortunately, the accountant does not differentiate between fixed and variable costs when constructing an income statement. However, it is usually safe to assume that most expenses in cost of goods sold are variable, while most of the other operating costs are fixed. The gross margin enables us to distinguish, insofar as possible, between fixed and variable costs. It is defined as

$$\text{Gross margin} = \frac{\text{Gross profit}}{\text{Sales}} = \frac{\$2,325.0}{\$5,320.5} = 43.7\%$$

where gross profit equals net sales less cost of sales. Approximately 43.7 percent of Harley-Davidson's sales dollar is a *contribution to fixed cost and profits;* 43.7 cents of every sales dollar is available to pay for fixed costs and to add to profits.

One common use of the gross margin is to estimate a company's break-even sales volume. Harley-Davidson's income statement tells us that total operating expenses in 2004 were $940.7 million. If we assume these expenses are fixed and if 43.7 cents of each Harley-Davidson sales dollar is available to pay for fixed costs and add to profits, the company's zero-profit sales volume must be $940.7/0.437, or $2,152.6 million.[2] Assuming operating expenses and the gross margin are independent of sales, Harley-Davidson loses money when sales are below $2,152.6 million and makes money when sales are above this figure.

Asset Turnover

Some newcomers to finance believe assets are a good thing: the more the better. The reality is just the opposite: Unless a company is about to go out of business, its value is in the income stream it generates, and its assets are simply a necessary means to this end. Indeed, the ideal company would be one that produced income without any assets; then no investment would be required, and returns would be infinite. Short of this fantasy, our ROE equation tells us that, other things constant, financial performance improves as asset turnover rises. This is the second lever of management performance.

The asset turnover ratio measures the sales generated per dollar of assets. Harley-Davidson's asset turnover of 1.0 means that Harley-Davidson generated $1.00 of sales for each dollar invested in assets. This ratio measures asset intensity, with a low asset turnover signifying an asset-intensive business and a high turnover the reverse.

The nature of a company's products and its competitive strategy strongly influence asset turnover. A steel mill will never have the asset turnover of a grocery store. But this is not the end of the story, because management diligence and creativity in controlling assets are also vital determinants of a company's asset turnover. When product technology is similar among competitors, control of assets is often the margin between success and failure.

---

[2] Income = Sales − Variable costs − Fixed costs = Sales × Gross margin − Fixed costs. Setting income to zero and solving for sales, Sales = Fixed costs/Gross margin.

Dell Computer is a case in point. Between 1991 and 2004 the company relentlessly drove its asset turnover up from 1.6 to 2.1 times, a figure that compares with a turnover of only 1.0 for Apple Computer. Partially as a result, Dell's ROE in 2004 was a robust 46.9 percent, while Apple's was 5.4 percent. To put Dell's performance in perspective, Dell's 2004 ROE would have been only 35.5 percent had it not improved its asset turnover so aggressively.[3]

Control of current assets is especially critical. You might think the distinction between current and fixed assets based solely on whether the asset will revert to cash within one year is artificial. But more is involved than this. Current assets, especially accounts receivable and inventory, have several unique properties. One is that if something goes wrong—if sales decline unexpectedly, customers delay payment, or a critical part fails to arrive—a company's investment in current assets can balloon very rapidly. When even manufacturing companies routinely invest one-half or more of their money in current assets, it is easy to appreciate that even modest alterations in the management of these assets can significantly affect company finances.

A second distinction is that unlike fixed assets, current assets can become a source of cash during business downturns. As sales decline, a company's investment in accounts receivable and inventory should fall as well, thereby freeing cash for other uses. (Remember, a reduction in an asset account is a source of cash.) The fact that in a well-run company current assets move in an accordionlike fashion with sales is appealing to creditors. They know that during the upswing of a business cycle rising current assets will require loans, while during a downswing falling current assets will provide the cash to repay the loans. In bankers' jargon, such a loan is said to be *self-liquidating* in the sense that the use to which the money is put creates the source of repayment.

It is often useful to analyze the turnover of each type of asset on a company's balance sheet individually. This gives rise to what are known as *control ratios*. Although the form in which each ratio is expressed may vary, every control ratio is simply an asset turnover for a particular type of asset. In each instance, the firm's investment in the asset is compared to net sales or a closely related figure.

Why compare assets to sales? The fact that a company's investment in, say, accounts receivable has risen over time could be due to two forces:

---

[3] In 2004, Dell's profit margin was 6.2 percent, and its asset-to-equity ratio was 3.58 times. Combining these numbers with Dell's 1991 asset turnover ratio of 1.6 yields an ROE of 35.5 percent (35.5% = 6.2% × 1.6 × 3.58). Dell's fiscal year-end is January 31. The dates referred to are for the prior calendar year.

(1) Perhaps sales have risen and simply dragged receivables along, or (2) management may have slackened its collection efforts. Relating receivables to sales in a control ratio corrects for changes in sales, enabling the analyst to concentrate on the more important effects of changing management control. Thus, the control ratio distinguishes between sales-induced changes in investment and other, perhaps more sinister causes. Following are some standard control ratios and their values for Harley-Davidson in 2004.

Inventory Turnover

Inventory turnover is expressed as

$$\text{Inventory turnover} = \frac{\text{Cost of goods sold}}{\text{Ending inventory}} = \frac{\$2,995.5}{\$226.9} = 13.2 \text{ times}$$

An inventory turn of 13.2 times means that items in Harley-Davidson's inventory turn over 13.2 times per year on average; said differently, the typical item sits in inventory about 28 days before being sold (365 days/ 13.2 times = 27.7 days).

Several alternative definitions of the inventory turnover ratio exist, including sales divided by ending inventory and cost of goods sold divided by average inventory. Cost of goods sold is a more appropriate numerator than sales because sales include a profit markup that is absent from inventory. But beyond this, I see little to choose from among the various definitions.

The Collection Period

The *collection period* highlights a company's management of accounts receivable. For Harley-Davidson

$$\text{Collection period} = \frac{\text{Accounts receivable}}{\text{Credit sales per day}} = \frac{\$1,328.4}{\$5,320.5/365} = 91.1 \text{ days}$$

Credit sales appear here rather than net sales because only credit sales generate accounts receivable. As a company outsider, however, I do not know what portion of Harley-Davidson's net sales, if any, are for cash, so I assume they are all on credit. Credit sales per day is defined as credit sales for the accounting period divided by the number of days in the accounting period, which for annual statements is obviously 365 days.

Two interpretations of Harley-Davidson's collection period are possible. We can say that Harley-Davidson has an average of 91.1 days' worth of credit sales tied up in accounts receivable, or we can say that the average time lag between sale and receipt of cash from the sale is 91.1 days.

If we like, we can define a simpler asset turnover ratio for accounts receivable as just credit sales/accounts receivable. However, the collection

Beware of Seasonal Companies

Interpreting many ratios of companies with *seasonal sales* can be tricky. For example, suppose a company's sales peak sharply at Christmas, resulting in high year-end accounts receivable. A naive collection period calculated by relating year-end accounts receivable to average daily sales for the whole year will produce an apparently very high collection period because the denominator is insensitive to the seasonal sales peak. To avoid being misled, a better way to calculate the collection period for a seasonal company is to use credit sales per day based only on the prior 60 to 90 days' sales. This matches the accounts receivable to the credit sales actually generating the receivables.

period format is more informative, because it allows us to compare a company's collection period with its terms of sale. Thus, if a company sells on 90-day terms, a collection period of 65 days is excellent, but if the terms of sale were 30 days, our interpretation would be quite different.

Interpretation of Harley-Davidson's collection period is complicated by the fact that in addition to short-term receivables, the company also carries long-term accounts receivables generated by its finance company. A more inclusive measure of the company's trade credit extended combines short- and long-term receivables in a single calculation as follows

$$\text{Collection period for total receivables} = \frac{\$1,328.4 + \$905.2}{\$5,320.5/365}$$

$$= 153.2 \text{ days}$$

Days' Sales in Cash

Harley-Davidson's days' sales in cash is

$$\frac{\text{Days' sales}}{\text{in cash}} = \frac{\text{Cash and securities}}{\text{Sales per day}} = \frac{\$275.2 + \$1,336.9}{\$5,320.5/365} = 110.6 \text{ days}$$

Harley-Davidson has 110.6 days' worth of sales in cash and securities. It is difficult to generalize about whether or not this amount is appropriate for Harley-Davidson. Companies require modest amounts of cash to facilitate transactions and are sometimes required to carry substantially larger amounts as compensating balances for bank loans. In addition, cash and marketable securities can be an important source of liquidity for a firm in an emergency. So the question of how much cash and securities a company should carry is often closely related to the broader question of how important liquidity is to the company and how best to provide it. Nonetheless, 110.6 days' sales in cash and securities appears quite ample. For comparison, the median figure for 500 large nonfinancial companies in 2004 was 47.3 days.

So how did Dell improve its asset turnover so sharply? By aggressively managing its working capital. Between 1991 and 2004, Dell's inventory turnover rose an amazing 18-fold from 4.7 times to 86.8 times—or every 4.2 days—the collection period fell from 68 days to 33, and the payables period rose from 60 days to 82. During this period, Dell systematically reduced inventory, accelerated collections, and delayed payments. Much of this improvement can be attributed to the company's increasing emphasis on Web-based sales, and its revolutionary build-to-order manufacturing strategy. But whatever the cause, the collective effect of these improvements was to free up $15.1 billion in cash that Dell put to use financing growth, while simultaneously repurchasing shares and maintaining conservative debt levels.[4]

Payables Period

The *payables period* is a control ratio for a liability. It is simply the collection period applied to accounts payable. For Harley-Davidson

$$\frac{\text{Payables}}{\text{period}} = \frac{\text{Accounts payable}}{\text{Credit purchases per day}} = \frac{\$244.2}{\$2995.5/365} = 29.8 \text{ days}$$

The proper definition of the payables period uses credit purchases, because they are what generate accounts payable. However, an outsider seldom knows credit purchases, so it is frequently necessary to settle for the closest approximation: cost of goods sold. This is what I have done above for Harley-Davidson; $2,995.5 million is Harley-Davidson's cost of goods sold, not its credit purchases. Cost of goods sold can differ from credit purchases for two reasons. First, the company may be adding to or depleting inventory, that is, purchasing at a different rate than it is selling. Second, all manufacturers add labor to material in the production process, thereby making cost of goods sold larger than purchases. Because of these differences, it is tricky to compare a manufacturing company's payables period, based on cost of goods sold, to its purchase terms. For Harley-Davidson, it is almost certain that cost of goods sold overstates credit purchases per day and that Harley-Davidson's suppliers are waiting a good bit longer than 29.8 days on average to receive payment.

Fixed-Asset Turnover

Companies or industries requiring large investments in long-lived assets to produce their goods are said to be capital intensive. Because a preponderance of their costs are fixed, capital-intensive businesses, such as auto manufacturers and airlines, are especially sensitive to the state of the economy, prospering in good times as sales rise relative to costs and suffering in bad

---

[4] Had Dell's 1991 figures for inventory turnover, collection period, and payables period prevailed in 2004, the company's investment in working capital would have been $15.1 billion higher.

Microsoft's Levers of Performance

Software giant Microsoft's 2004 levers of performance make instructive reading. As shown below, the company combined an attractive profit margin and conservative financial leverage with an abysmally low asset turnover of only 0.40 times to generate a modest ROE of 10.9 percent. This is poor performance for a company selling at 26 times the last 12-month's earnings and thought by many to be a monopolist.

How can a software giant generate an asset turnover more like that of a steel mill or a public utility? A look at Microsoft's balance sheet explains the mystery. At fiscal year-end in June 2004, fully $60.6 billion, or almost two-thirds of Microsoft's assets, were in cash and marketable securities. It's as if the company had merged with a mid-sized commercial bank. And Microsoft is not alone. It is now common practice for leading technology companies to build huge war chests, which they argue are necessary to finance continued growth and to facilitate possible acquisitions—like maybe Panama or South Dakota. Others, including Ralph Nader, see a more sinister purpose: to keep the money out of the hands of shareholders and to avoid taxes. Little wonder then that Microsoft recently relented and paid a record $32 billion special dividend.

To focus on Microsoft's operating performance as opposed to its ability to invest excess cash, we can strip cash and marketable securities out of the analysis. To do this, imagine the company returned 90 percent of its cash and securities to shareholders as a giant dividend. (In fact, it only distributed about half its cash and securities.) This would cut assets and shareholders' equity by about $55 billion, and assuming a modest 2 percent after-tax return on cash and securities, would knock $1.1 billion from net income. The resulting revised levers of performance appear below. Asset turnover is now a more plausible, but still low, 0.99 times, and ROE is up to a robust 35.7 percent. These numbers more accurately reflect the economics of Microsoft's business.

	Return on Equity	=	Profit Margin	×	Asset Turnover	×	Financial Leverage
As reported	10.9%	=	22.2%	×	0.40	×	1.24
Revised	35.7%	=	19.2%	×	0.99	×	1.89

Totals do not add due to rounding.

as the reverse occurs. Capital intensity, also referred to as operating leverage, is of particular concern to creditors because it magnifies the basic business risks faced by a firm.

Fixed-asset turnover is a measure of capital intensity, with a low turnover implying high intensity. The ratio in 2004 for Harley-Davidson was

$$\text{Fixed-asset turnover} = \frac{\text{Sales}}{\text{Net property, plant, and equipment}} = \frac{\$5,320.5}{\$1,024.7}$$

$$= 5.2 \text{ times}$$

where $1,024.7 million is the book value of Harley-Davidson's net property, plant, and equipment.

Financial Leverage

The third lever by which management affects ROE is financial leverage. A company increases its financial leverage when it raises the proportion of debt relative to equity used to finance the business. Unlike the profit margin and the asset turnover ratio, where more is generally preferred to less, financial leverage is not something management necessarily wants to maximize, even when doing so increases ROE. Instead, the challenge of financial leverage is to strike a prudent balance between the benefits and costs of debt financing. Later we will devote all of Chapter 6 to this important financial decision. For now it is sufficient to recognize that more leverage is not necessarily preferred to less and that while companies have considerable latitude in their choice of how much financial leverage to employ, there are economic and institutional constraints on their discretion.

As Table 2.1 suggests, the nature of a company's business and its assets influence the financial leverage it can employ. In general, businesses with highly predictable and stable operating cash flows, such as Florida Power and Light, can safely undertake more financial leverage than firms facing a high degree of market uncertainty, such as Netflix and Genentech. In addition, businesses such as commercial banks, which have diversified portfolios of readily salable, liquid assets, can also safely use more financial leverage than the typical business.

Another pattern evident in Table 2.1 is that ROA and financial leverage tend to be inversely related. Companies with low ROAs generally employ more debt financing, and vice versa. This is consistent with the previous paragraph. Safe, stable, liquid investments tend to generate low returns but substantial borrowing capacity. Commercial banks are extreme examples of this pattern. Bank of America combines what by manufacturing standards would be a horrible 1.3 percent ROA with an astronomical leverage ratio of 11.17 to generate a representative ROE of 14.2 percent. The key to this pairing is the safe, liquid nature of the bank's assets. (Past loans to Third World dictators and Texas energy companies are, of course, another story—one the bank would just as soon forget.)

The following ratios measure financial leverage, or debt capacity, and the related concept of liquidity.

Balance Sheet Ratios

The most common measures of financial leverage compare the book value of a company's liabilities to the book value of its assets or equity. This gives rise to the *debt-to-assets ratio* and the *debt-to-equity ratio*, defined as

$$\text{Debt-to-assets ratio} = \frac{\text{Total liabilities}}{\text{Total assets}} = \frac{\$2,264.6}{\$5,483.3} = 41.3\%$$

$$\text{Debt-to-equity ratio} = \frac{\text{Total liabilities}}{\text{Shareholders' equity}} = \frac{\$2,264.6}{\$3,218.5} = 70.4\%$$

The first ratio says that money to pay for 41.3 percent of Harley-Davidson's assets, in book value terms, comes from creditors of one type or another. The second ratio says the same thing in a slightly different way: Creditors supply Harley-Davidson with $70.4 cents for every dollar supplied by shareholders. As footnote 1 demonstrated earlier, the lever of performance introduced earlier, the assets-to-equity ratio, is simply the debt-to-equity ratio plus 1.

Coverage Ratios

A number of variations on these balance sheet measures of financial leverage exist. Conceptually, however, there is no reason to prefer one over another, for they all focus on balance sheet values, and hence all suffer from the same weakness. The financial burden a company faces by using debt financing ultimately depends not on the size of its liabilities relative to assets or to equity but on its ability to meet the annual cash payments the debt requires. A simple example will illustrate the distinction. Suppose two companies, A and B, have the same debt-to-assets ratio, but A is very profitable and B is losing money. Chances are that B will have difficulty meeting its annual interest and principal obligations, while A will not. The obvious conclusion is that balance sheet ratios are of primary interest only in liquidation, when the proceeds of asset sales are to be distributed among creditors and owners. In all other instances, we should be more interested in comparing the annual burden the debt imposes to the cash flow available for debt service.

This gives rise to what are known as *coverage ratios*, the most common of which are *times interest earned* and *times burden covered*. Letting EBIT represent *earnings before interest and taxes*, these ratios are defined as:

$$\text{Times interest earned} = \frac{\text{EBIT}}{\text{Interest expense}} = \frac{\$1,402.3}{\$22.7} = 61.8 \text{ times}$$

$$\text{Times burden covered} = \frac{\text{EBIT}}{\text{Interest} + \left(\dfrac{\text{Principal repayment}}{1 - \text{Tax rate}}\right)}$$

$$= \frac{\$1,402.3}{\$22.7 + \$495.4/(1 - \$489.7/\$1,379.6)}$$

$$= 1.8 \text{ times}$$

Both ratios compare income available for debt service in the numerator to some measure of annual financial obligation. For both ratios, the income available is EBIT.[5] This is the earnings the company generates that can be used to make interest payments. EBIT is before taxes because interest payments are before-tax expenditures, and we want to compare like quantities. Harley-Davidson's times-interest-earned ratio of 61.8 means the company earned its interest obligation 61.8 times over in 2004; EBIT was 61.8 times as large as interest.

Though dentists may correctly claim that if you ignore your teeth they'll eventually go away, the same cannot be said for principal repayments. If a company fails to make a principal repayment when due, the outcome is the same as if it had failed to make an interest payment. In both cases, the company is in default and creditors can force it into bankruptcy. The times-burden-covered ratio reflects this reality by expanding the definition of annual financial obligations to include debt principal repayments as well as interest. When including principal repayment as part of a company's financial burden, we must remember to express the figure on a before-tax basis comparable to interest and EBIT. Unlike interest payments, principal repayments are not a tax-deductible expense. This means that if a company is in, say, the 50 percent tax bracket, it must earn $2 before taxes to have $1 after taxes to pay creditors. The other dollar goes to the tax collector. For other tax brackets, the before-tax burden of a principal repayment is found by dividing the repayment by 1 minus the company's tax rate. Adjusting the principal repayment in this manner to its before-tax equivalent is known in the trade as *grossing up* the principal—about as gross as finance ever gets.

An often-asked question is: Which of these coverage ratios is more meaningful? The answer is that both are important. If a company could always roll over its maturing obligations by taking out new loans as it repaid old ones, the *net* burden of the debt would be merely the interest expense, and times interest earned would be the more important ratio. The problem is that the replacement of maturing debt with new debt is not an automatic feature of capital markets. In some instances, when capital markets are unsettled or a company's fortunes decline, creditors may refuse to renew maturing obligations. Then the burden of the debt suddenly becomes interest plus principal payments, and the times-burden-covered ratio assumes paramount importance. This happened to Burmah Oil, a large British company, some years ago when it took out a large, short-term loan to finance an acquisition, thinking it could roll over the maturing short-term debt into more permanent financing. However, before Burmah could pull off the refinancing, a bank failure in Germany made

---

[5] I calculated EBIT here as income before income taxes + interest expense ($1,379.6 + $22.7 = $1,402.3).

creditors suddenly very skittish, and no one was willing to lend Burmah the money. A major crisis was averted only when the British government stepped into the breach. In sum, it is fair to conclude that the times-burden-covered ratio is too conservative assuming the company will pay its existing loans down to zero, but the times-interest-earned ratio is too liberal assuming the company will roll over all of its obligations as they mature.

Another common question is: How much coverage is enough? I cannot answer this question precisely, but several generalizations are possible. If a company has ready access to cash in the form of unused borrowing capacity, sizable cash balances, or readily salable assets, it can operate safely with lower coverage ratios than competitors without such reserves. The ready access to cash gives the company a means of payment it can use whenever operating earnings are insufficient to cover financial obligations. A second generalization is that coverage should increase with the *business risk* the firm faces. For example, National Semiconductor operates in a dynamic environment characterized by rapid technological change and high rates of product obsolescence. In view of this high business risk, the company would be ill advised to take on the added financial risk that accompanies low coverage ratios. Said another way, a food processor that has very stable, predictable cash flows can operate safely with much lower coverage ratios than a company such as National Semiconductor, which has trouble forecasting more than three or four years into the future.

Market Value Leverage Ratios

A third family of leverage ratios relates a company's liabilities to the *market value of its equity* or the *market value of its assets*. For Harley-Davidson in 2004,

$$\frac{\text{Market value of debt}}{\text{Market value of equity}} = \frac{\text{Market value of debt}}{\text{Number of shares of stock} \times \text{Price per share}}$$

$$= \frac{\$2,264.6}{\$17,879.9} = 12.7\%$$

$$\frac{\text{Market value of debt}}{\text{Market value of assets}} = \frac{\text{Market value of debt}}{\text{Market value of debt} + \text{equity}}$$

$$= \frac{\$2,264.6}{\$2,264.6 + \$17,879.9} = 11.2\%$$

Careful readers will note that I have assumed the market value of debt equals the book value of debt in both of these ratios. Strictly speaking, this is seldom true, but in most instances the difference between the two quantities is small. Also, accurately estimating the market value of debt often turns out to be a tedious, time-consuming chore that is best avoided—unless, of course, you are being paid by the hour.

Market value ratios are clearly superior to book value ratios simply because book values are historical, often irrelevant numbers, while market values indicate the true worth of creditors' and owners' stakes in the business. Recalling that market values are based on investors' expectations about future cash flows, market value leverage ratios can be thought of as coverage ratios extended over many future periods. Instead of comparing income to financial burden in a single year as coverage ratios do, market value ratios compare today's value of expected future income to today's value of future financial burdens.

Market value ratios are especially helpful when assessing the financial leverage of rapidly growing, start-up businesses. Even when such companies have terrible or nonexistent coverage ratios, lenders may still extend them liberal credit if they believe future cash flows will be sufficient to service the debt. McCaw Communications offers an extreme example of this. At year-end 1990, McCaw had over $5 billion in debt; a debt-to-equity ratio, in book terms, of 330 percent; and annualized interest expenses of *more than 60 percent of net revenues*. Moreover, despite explosive growth, McCaw had never made a meaningful operating profit in its principal cellular telephone business. Why then did otherwise intelligent creditors loan McCaw $5 billion? Because creditors and equity investors believed it was only a matter of time before the company would begin to generate huge cash flows. This optimism was handsomely rewarded in late 1993 when AT&T paid $12.6 billion to acquire McCaw. Including the $5 billion in debt assumed by AT&T, the acquisition ranked as the second largest in corporate history at the time.

Another example is Amazon.com. In 1998 the company recorded its largest-ever loss of $124 million, had never earned a profit, and had only $139 million left in shareholders' equity. But not to worry: Lenders were still pleased to extend the company $350 million in long-term debt. Apparently creditors are willing to overlook a number of messy details when a borrower's sales are growing 300 percent a year and the market value of its equity tops $17 billion—especially when the debt is convertible into equity. After all, in market value terms, Amazon's debt-to-equity ratio was only 3 percent.

Economists like market value leverage ratios because they are accurate indicators of company indebtedness at a point in time. But you should be aware that market value ratios are not without problems. One is that they ignore rollover risks. When creditors take the attitude that debt must be repaid with cash, not promises of future cash, modest market value leverage ratios can be of hollow comfort. Also, despite these ratios' conceptual appeal, few companies use them to set financing policy or to monitor debt levels. This may be due in part to the fact that volatile stock prices can make market value ratios appear somewhat arbitrary and beyond management's control.

Liquidity Ratios

As noted, one determinant of a company's debt capacity is the liquidity of its assets. An asset is liquid if it can be readily converted to cash, while a liability is liquid if it must be repaid in the near future. As the Burmah Oil debacle illustrates, it is risky to finance illiquid assets such as fixed plant and equipment with liquid, short-term liabilities, because the liabilities will come due before the assets generate enough cash to pay them. Such "maturity mismatching" forces borrowers to roll over, or refinance, maturing liabilities to avoid insolvency.

Two common ratios intended to measure the liquidity of a company's assets relative to its liabilities are the *current ratio* and the *acid test*. For Harley-Davidson,

$$\text{Current ratio} = \frac{\text{Current assets}}{\text{Current liabilities}}$$

$$= \frac{\$3,266.2}{\$1,172.6} = 2.8 \text{ times}$$

$$\text{Acid test} = \frac{\text{Current assets} - \text{Inventory}}{\text{Current liabilities}}$$

$$= \frac{\$3,266.2 - \$226.9}{\$1,172.6} = 2.6 \text{ times}$$

The current ratio compares the assets that will turn into cash within the year to the liabilities that must be paid within the year. A company with a low current ratio lacks liquidity in the sense that it cannot reduce its current assets for cash to meet maturing obligations. It must rely instead on operating income and outside financing.

The acid-test ratio, sometimes called the *quick ratio*, is a more conservative liquidity measure. It is identical to the current ratio except that the numerator is reduced by the value of inventory. Inventory is subtracted because it is frequently illiquid. Under distress conditions, a company or its creditors may realize little cash from the sale of inventory. In liquidation sales, sellers typically receive 40 percent or less of the book value of inventory.

You should recognize that these ratios are rather crude measures of liquidity, for at least two reasons. First, rolling over some obligations, such as accounts payable, involves virtually no insolvency risk provided the company is at least marginally profitable. Second, unless a company intends to go out of business, most of the cash generated by liquidating current assets cannot be used to reduce liabilities because it must be plowed back into the business to support continued operations.

Is ROE a Reliable Financial Yardstick?

To this point, we have assumed management wants to increase the company's ROE, and we have studied three important levers of performance by which they can accomplish this: the profit margin, asset turnover, and financial leverage. We concluded that whether a company is IBM or the corner drugstore, careful management of these levers can positively affect ROE. We also saw that determining and maintaining appropriate values of the levers is a challenging managerial task that requires an understanding of the company's business, the way the company competes, and the interdependencies among the levers themselves. Now it is time to ask how reliable ROE is as a measure of financial performance. If company A has a higher ROE than company B, is it necessarily a better company? If company C increases its ROE, is this unequivocal evidence of improved performance?

ROE suffers from three critical deficiencies as a measure of financial performance, which I will refer to as the *timing* problem, the *risk* problem, and the *value* problem. Seen in proper perspective, these problems mean ROE is seldom an unambiguous measure of performance. ROE remains a useful and important indicator, but it must be interpreted in light of its limitations, and no one should automatically assume a higher ROE is always better than a lower one.

The Timing Problem

It is a cliché to say that successful managers must be forward looking and have a long-term perspective. Yet ROE is precisely the opposite: backward looking and focused on a single year. So it is little wonder that ROE can at times be a skewed measure of performance. When, for example, a company incurs heavy startup costs to introduce a hot new product, ROE will initially fall. However, rather than indicating worsening financial performance, the fall simply reflects the myopic, one-period nature of the yardstick. Because ROE necessarily includes only one year's earnings, it fails to capture the full impact of multiperiod decisions.

The Risk Problem

Business decisions commonly involve the classic "eat well–sleep well" dilemma. If you want to eat well, you had best be prepared to take risks in search of higher returns. If you want to sleep well, you will likely have to forgo high returns in search of safety. Seldom will you realize both high returns and safety. (And when you do, please give me a call.)

The problem with ROE is that it says nothing about what risks a company has taken to generate it. Here is a simple example. Take-a-Risk, Inc., earns an ROA of 6 percent from wildcat oil exploration in Cambodia, which it combines with an assets-to-equity ratio of 5.0 to produce an ROE of 30 percent (6% × 5.0). Never-Dare, Ltd., meanwhile, has an ROA of 10 percent on its investment in government securities, which it finances with equal portions of debt and equity, yielding an ROE of 20 percent (10% × 2.0). Which company is the better performer? My answer is Never-Dare. Take-a-Risk's ROE is high, but its high business risk and extreme financial leverage make it a very uncertain enterprise. I would prefer the more modest but eminently safer ROE of Never-Dare.[6] Security analysts would make the same point by saying that Take-a-Risk's ROE might be higher but that the number is much lower quality than Never-Dare's ROE, meaning that it is much riskier. In sum, because ROE looks only at return while ignoring risk, it can be an inaccurate yardstick of financial performance.

Return on Invested Capital

To circumvent the distorting effects of leverage on ROE and ROA, I recommend calculating *return on invested capital (ROIC)*, also known as *return on net assets (RONA)*:

$$\text{ROIC} = \frac{\text{EBIT}(1 - \text{Tax rate})}{\text{Interest-bearing debt} + \text{Equity}}$$

Harley-Davidson's 2004 ROIC was

$$\frac{\$1,402.3(1 - \$489.7/\$1,379.6)}{\$495.4 + \$800.0 + \$3,218.5} = 20.0\%$$

The numerator of this ratio is the earnings after tax the company would report if it were all equity financed, and the denominator is the sum of all sources of cash to the company on which a return must be earned. Thus, while accounts payable are a source of cash to the company, they are excluded because they carry no explicit cost. In essence, ROIC is the rate of return earned on the total capital invested in the business without regard for whether it is called debt or equity.

---

[6] Even if I preferred eating well to sleeping well, I would still choose Never-Dare and finance my purchase with a little personal borrowing to lever my return on investment. See the appendix to Chapter 6 for more on the substitution of personal borrowing for company borrowing.

To see the virtue of ROIC, consider the following example. Companies A and B are identical in all respects except that A is highly levered and B is all equity financed. Because the two companies are identical except for capital structure, we would like a return measure that reflects this fundamental similarity. The following table shows that ROE and ROA fail this test. Reflecting the company's extensive use of financial leverage, A's ROE is 18 percent, while B's zero-leverage position generates a lower but better-quality ROE of 7.2 percent. ROA is biased in the other direction, punishing company A for its extensive use of debt and leaving B unaffected. Only ROIC is independent of the different financing schemes the two companies employ, showing a 7.2 percent return for both firms. ROIC thus reflects the company's fundamental earning power before it is confounded by differences in financing strategies.

	Company	
	A	**B**
Debt @ 10% interest	$ 900	$ 0
Equity	100	1,000
Total assets	$1,000	$1,000
EBIT	$120	$120
– Interest expense	90	0
Earnings before tax	30	120
– Tax @ 40%	12	48
Earnings after tax	$ 18	$ 72
ROE	18.0%	7.2%
ROA	1.8%	7.2%
ROIC	7.2%	7.2%

The Value Problem

ROE measures the return on shareholders' investment; however, the investment figure used is the *book value* of shareholders' equity, not the *market value*. This distinction is important. Harley-Davidson's ROE in 2004 was 27.6 percent, and indeed this is the return you could have earned had you been able to buy the company's equity for its book value of $3,218.5 million. But that would have been impossible, for, as noted in the previous chapter, the market value of Harley-Davidson's equity was $17,879.9 million. At this price, your annual return would have been only 5.0 percent, not 27.6 percent ($889.9/$17,879.9 = 5.0%). The market value of equity is more significant to shareholders because it measures the current, realizable worth of the shares, while book value is only history.

So even when ROE measures management's financial performance, it may not be synonymous with a high return on investment to shareholders. Thus, it is not enough for investors to find companies capable of generating high ROEs; these companies must be unknown to others, because once they are known, the possibility of high returns to investors will melt away in higher stock prices.

The Earnings Yield and the P/E Ratio

It might appear that we can circumvent the value problem by simply replacing the book value of equity with its market value in the ROE. But the resulting *earnings yield* has problems of its own. For Harley-Davidson,

$$\text{Earnings yield} = \frac{\text{Net income}}{\text{Market value of shareholders' equity}}$$

$$= \frac{\text{Earnings per share}}{\text{Price per share}} = \frac{\$3.02}{\$60.75} = 5.0\%$$

Is earnings yield a useful measure of financial performance? No! The problem is that a company's stock price is very sensitive to investor expectations about the future. A share of stock entitles its owner to a portion of *future* earnings as well as present earnings. Naturally, the higher an investor's expectations of future earnings, the more she will pay for the stock. This means that a bright future, a high stock price, and a *low* earnings yield go together. Clearly, a high earnings yield is not an indicator of superior performance; in fact, it is more the reverse. Said another way, the earnings yield suffers from a severe timing problem of its own that invalidates it as a performance measure.

Turning the earnings yield on its head produces the *price-to-earnings ratio*, or *P/E ratio*. Harley-Davidson's 2004 P/E ratio is

$$\frac{\text{Price per share}}{\text{Earnings per share}} = \frac{\$60.75}{\$3.02} = 20.1 \text{ times}$$

The P/E ratio adds little to our discussion of performance measures, but its wide use among investors deserves comment. The P/E ratio is the price of one dollar of current earnings and is a means of normalizing stock prices for different earnings levels across companies. At year end 2004, investors were paying $20.10 per dollar of Harley-Davidson's earnings. A company's P/E ratio depends principally on two things: its future earnings prospects and the risk associated with those earnings. Stock price, and hence the P/E ratio, rises with improved earnings prospects and falls with increasing risk. A sometimes confusing pattern occurs when a company's earnings are weak but investors believe the weakness is temporary. Then prices remain buoyant in the face of depressed earnings, and the P/E ratio *rises*. In general, the P/E ratio says little about a company's current financial performance, but it does indicate what investors believe about future prospects.

ROE or Market Price?

For years academicians and practitioners have been at odds over the proper measure of financial performance. Academicians criticize ROE for the reasons just cited and argue that the correct measure of financial performance is the firm's stock price. Moreover, they contend that management's goal should be to maximize stock price. Their logic is persuasive: Stock price represents the value of the owners' investment in the firm, and if managers want to further the interests of owners, they should take actions that increase value to owners. Indeed, the notion of "value creation" has become a central theme in the writings of many academicians and consultants.

Practitioners acknowledge the logic of this reasoning but question its applicability. One problem is the difficulty of specifying precisely how operating decisions affect stock price. If we are not certain what impact a change in, say, the business strategy of a division will have on the company's stock price, the goal of increasing price cannot guide decision making. A second problem is that managers typically know more about their company than do outside investors, or at least think they do. Why, then, should managers consider the assessments of less informed investors when making business decisions? A third practical problem with stock price as a performance measure is that it depends on a whole array of factors outside the company's control. One can never be certain whether an increase in stock price reflects improving company performance or an improving external economic environment. For these reasons, many practitioners remain skeptical of stock market–based indicators of performance, even while academicians and consultants continue to work on translating value creation into a practical financial objective. One popular effort along these lines is *economic value added (EVA)*, popularized by the consulting firm Stern Stewart Management Services. We will look more closely at EVA in Chapter 8.

Ratio Analysis

In our discussion of the levers of financial performance, we defined a number of financial ratios. It is now time to consider the systematic use of these ratios to analyze financial performance. Ratio analysis is widely used by managers, creditors, regulators, and investors. At root it is an elementary process involving little more than comparing a number of

Can ROE Substitute for Share Price?

Figures 2.1 and 2.2 suggest that the gulf between academicians and practitioners over the proper measure of financial performance may be narrower than supposed. The graphs plot the market value of equity divided by the book value of equity against ROE for two representative groups of companies. The ROE figure is a weighted-average ROE over the most recent three years. The solid line in each figure is a regression line indicating the general relation between the two variables. The noticeable positive relationship visible in both graphs suggests that high-ROE companies tend to have high stock prices relative to book value, and vice versa. Hence, working to increase ROE appears to be generally consistent with working to increase stock price.

The proximity of the company dots to the fitted regression line is also interesting. It shows the importance of factors other than ROE in determining a company's market-to-book ratio. As we should expect, these other factors play a significant role in determining the market value of a company's shares.

For interest, I have indicated the positions of several companies on the graphs. Note in Figure 2.1 that Harley-Davidson is virtually on the regression line, indicating that based purely on historical ROEs, Harley-Davidson's stock is fairly priced compared with those of other recreational products companies.

In Figure 2.2, Altria Group, formerly known as Philip Morris, takes the prize with an ROE of almost 40 percent, although Schlumberger, an oil and gas field services company, and Procter & Gamble win market-to-book honors at 6.8 times. General Motors, on the other hand, appears to be the Rodney Dangerfield of the stock market. Despite a respectable ROE of 13.5 percent, it "can't get no respect" among investors who assign it a very modest market-to-book ratio of 0.6. It's almost as if investors do not expect GM to keep up its past performance.

To summarize, these graphs offer tantalizing evidence that despite its weaknesses, ROE may serve as at least a crude proxy for share price in measuring financial performance.

FIGURE 2.1 **Market Value to Book Value of Equity versus Return on Equity for 30 Recreational Products Companies**

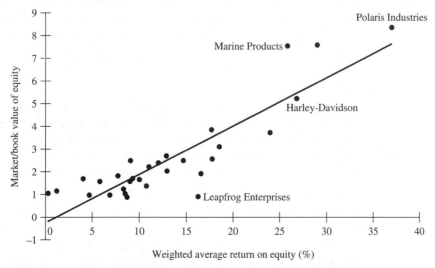

The regression equation is MV/BV = −0.24 + 0.21ROE, where MV/BV is the market value of equity relative to the book value of equity in the first quarter of 2005 and ROE is a weighted-average of return on equity in 2004 and the prior two years. Companies with negative ROEs were eliminated. Adjusted R^2 = 0.78.

FIGURE 2.2 Market Value to Book Value of Equity versus Return on Equity for 82 Large Corporations

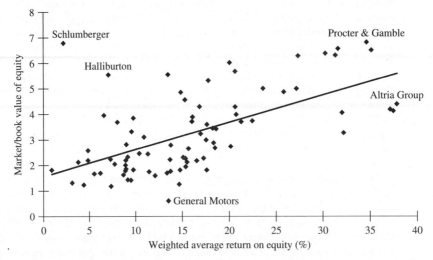

Companies are members of the Standard and Poor's 100 Index of the largest U.S. corporations. Those with negative values and outliers with ROEs above 40 percent were eliminated. The regression equation is MV/BV = 1.56 + 0.11ROE, where MV/BV is the market value of equity relative to book value at the end of the first quarter of 2005 and ROE is a weighted average return on equity for 2004 and the prior two years. Adjusted R^2 = 0.35.

company ratios to one or more performance benchmarks. Used with care and imagination, the technique can reveal much about a company. But there are a few things to bear in mind about ratios. First, a ratio is simply one number divided by another, so it is unreasonable to expect the mechanical calculation of one or even several ratios to automatically yield important insights into anything as complex as a modern corporation. It is best to think of ratios as clues in a detective story. One or even several ratios might be misleading, but when combined with other knowledge of a company's management and economic circumstances, ratio analysis can tell a revealing story.

A second point to bear in mind is that a ratio has no single correct value. Like Goldilocks and the three bears, the observation that the value of a particular ratio is too high, too low, or just right depends on the perspective of the analyst and on the company's competitive strategy. The current ratio, previously defined as the ratio of current assets to current liabilities, is a case in point. From the perspective of a short-term creditor, a high current ratio is a positive sign suggesting ample liquidity and a high likelihood of repayment. Yet an owner of the company might look on the same current ratio as a negative sign suggesting that the company's assets are being deployed too conservatively. Moreover, from an operating perspective, a high current ratio could be a sign of conservative management or the natural result of a competitive strategy that emphasizes liberal credit terms and sizable inventories. In this case, the important question is not whether the current ratio is too high but whether the chosen strategy is best for the company.

Using Ratios Effectively

If ratios have no universally correct values, how do you interpret them? How do you decide whether a company is healthy or sick? There are three approaches, each involving a different performance benchmark: Compare the ratios to rules of thumb, compare them to industry averages, or look for changes in the ratios over time. Comparing a company's ratios to rules of thumb has the virtue of simplicity but has little else to recommend it. The appropriate ratio values for a company depend too much on the analyst's perspective and on the company's specific circumstances for rules of thumb to be very helpful. The most positive thing one can say about them is that over the years, companies conforming to these rules of thumb apparently go bankrupt somewhat less frequently than those that do not.

Comparing a company's ratios to industry ratios provides a useful feel for how the company measures up to its competitors, provided you bear in mind that company-specific differences can result in entirely justifiable deviations from industry norms. Also, there is no guarantee that the industry as a whole knows what it is doing. The knowledge that one railroad was much like its competitors was cold comfort in the depression of the 1930s, when virtually all railroads got into financial difficulties.

The most useful way to evaluate ratios involves trend analysis: Calculate ratios for a company over several years, and note how they change over time. Trend analysis avoids the need for cross-company and cross-industry comparisons, enabling the analyst to draw firmer conclusions about the company's financial health and its variation over time.

Moreover, the levers of performance suggest one logical approach to trend analysis: Instead of calculating ratios at random, hoping to stumble across one that might be meaningful, take advantage of the structure implicit in the levers. As Figure 2.3 illustrates, the levers of performance organize ratios into three tiers. At the top, ROE looks at the performance of the enterprise as a whole; in the middle, the levers of performance indicate how three important segments of the business contributed to ROE; and on the bottom, many of the other ratios discussed reveal how the management of individual income statement and balance sheet accounts contributed to the observed levers. To take advantage of this structure, begin at the top by noting the trend in ROE over time. Then narrow your focus and ask what changes in the three levers account for the observed ROE pattern. Finally, get out your microscope and study individual accounts for explanations of the observed changes in the levers. To illustrate, if

FIGURE 2.3 The Levers of Performance Suggest One Road Map for Ratio Analysis

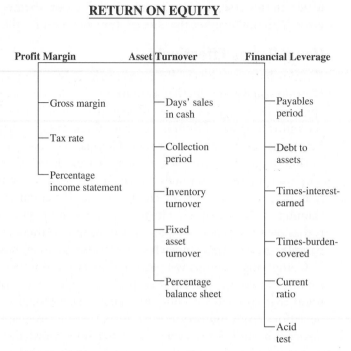

RETURN ON EQUITY

Profit Margin   Asset Turnover   Financial Leverage

Profit Margin	Asset Turnover	Financial Leverage
Gross margin	Days' sales in cash	Payables period
Tax rate	Collection period	Debt to assets
Percentage income statement	Inventory turnover	Times-interest-earned
	Fixed asset turnover	Times-burden-covered
	Percentage balance sheet	Current ratio
		Acid test

ROE has plunged while the profit margin and financial leverage have remained constant, examine the control of individual asset accounts in search of the culprit or culprits.

Ratio Analysis of Harley-Davidson, Inc.

As a practical demonstration of ratio analysis, let us see what the technique can tell us about Harley-Davidson. Table 2.2 presents previously discussed ratios for Harley-Davidson over the years 2000 to 2004 and median industry figures for 2004. (For summary definitions of the ratios, see Table 2.5 at end of chapter.) The comparison industry consists of five representative competitors noted at the bottom of the table. As an example of similar, readily available industry data, Table 2.4 at the end of the chapter presents selected ratios from Dun & Bradstreet Information Services for representative industries, including median, upper-quartile, and lower-quartile values for the represented ratios.[7]

---

[7] For any ratio, if we array all of the values for the companies in the industry from the highest to the lowest, the figure falling in the middle of the series is the *median,* the ratio halfway between the highest value and the median is the *upper quartile,* and the ratio halfway between the lowest value and the median is the *lower quartile.* Data are from *Industry Norms and Key Business Ratios: Library Edition 2003–04,* Dun & Bradstreet Credit Services, 2004.

TABLE 2.2 Ratio Analysis of Harley-Davidson, Inc., 2000–2004, and Industry Medians, 2004

	2000	2001	2002	2003	2004	Industry Median*
Profitability ratios:						
Return on equity (%)	**24.7**	**24.9**	**26.0**	**25.7**	**27.6**	**27.2**
Return on assets (%)	14.3	14.0	15.0	15.5	16.2	13.2
Return on invested capital (%)	18.7	19.0	19.6	19.6	20.0	26.7
Profit margin (%)	**11.4**	**12.3**	**13.5**	**15.5**	**16.7**	**5.9**
Gross margin (%)	39.4	40.7	39.8	41.8	43.7	26.0
Price-to-earnings ratio (X)	34.5	37.6	24.1	18.8	20.1	18.6
Turnover-control ratios:						
Asset turnover (X)	**1.3**	**1.1**	**1.1**	**1.0**	**1.0**	**2.3**
Fixed-asset turnover (X)	4.0	4.0	4.2	4.7	5.2	9.3
Inventory turnover (X)	9.6	11.6	11.9	13.7	13.2	7.2
Collection period (days)	75.4	79.8	81.8	82.9	91.1	15.1
Days' sales in cash (days)	50.3	65.4	67.5	98.4	110.6	34.9
Payables period (days)	33.6	33.8	32.0	28.6	29.8	27.3
Leverage and liquidity ratios:						
Assets to equity (X)	**1.7**	**1.8**	**1.7**	**1.7**	**1.7**	**2.0**
Debt to assets (%)	42.3	43.7	42.2	39.9	41.3	48.8
Debt to equity (%)	73.3	77.6	72.9	66.4	70.4	95.4
Times interest earned (X)	18.0	27.8	50.3	55.2	61.8	85.1
Times burden covered (X)	3.2	1.9	1.5	2.3	1.8	85.1
Debt to assets (market value, %)	7.9	7.6	10.4	12.1	11.2	12.9
Debt to equity (market value, %)	8.6	8.3	11.6	13.7	12.7	14.8
Current ratio (X)	2.6	2.3	2.1	2.9	2.8	2.6
Acid test (X)	2.2	2.1	1.9	2.6	2.6	1.3

*Sample consists of five representative competitors in the "leisure travel" industry: Arctic Cat, Brunswick, Polaris Industries, Marine Products, and Winnebago Industries. (March 2004, data for Arctic Cat.)

Beginning with Harley-Davidson's return on equity, we see a modest, steady growth from 24.7 percent in 2000 to 27.6 percent in 2004. The most recent figure is only slightly above the peer group median of 27.2 percent, but well above the 14.6 percent ROE chalked up by a broad spectrum of American companies in that year.[8] Harley-Davidson's return on invested capital shows a similarly improving trend, rising to 20 percent in 2004. This compares favorably with a figure of only 10.2 percent for a broad spectrum on companies, but is noticeably below the peer

[8] The median return on equity in 2004 for companies listed in the Standard & Poor's 500 Index, generally the largest 500 companies in the United States, was 14.6 percent. The comparable figure for return on invested capital was 10.2 percent.

group median of 26.7 percent. I am inclined to attribute this relative shortfall to the fact that Harley-Davidson has a finance subsidiary, while peer group firms do not. I expect the finance subsidiary to generate lower but safer returns than the company's manufacturing activities. Indeed if I strip the finance subsidiary out of Harley-Davidson's numbers, I find a revised ROIC of 24.3 percent—much closer to the peer group median.[9] I find Harley-Davidson's steady improvement in ROE and ROIC in the past five years to be especially impressive in light of the fact that the lower-margin finance company was growing rapidly throughout the period.

Looking next at the company's levers of performance, Harley-Davidson's profit margin reflects the power of its legendary brand. The company is consistently able to translate visions of halcyon days astride a Dyna Glide or a Softail into premium product prices. Harley-Davidson's profit margin in 2004 is a robust 16.7 percent, up about 50 percent since 2000, and almost three times that of its peers. To put this increased margin in perspective, had Harley-Davidson's profit margin remained at its 2000 level of 11.4 percent, ROE in 2004 would have been down some 30 percent below actual ($11.4\% \times 1.0 \times 1.7 = 19.4\%$). Harley-Davidson's asset turnover makes much less attractive reading, having fallen steadily over the period to a level less than half that of its peers. I will say more about this ratio shortly. Looking last at financial leverage, we see a conservatively financed business in a conservative industry. The assets-to-equity ratio has been very stable at 1.7 times, somewhat below the peer group median of 2.0. Harley-Davidson's ROE is thus a somewhat better quality number than that of peers.

Digging a little deeper into these broad trends, the sharp improvement in Harley-Davidson's profit margin is due primarily to an increasing gross margin, which is up over four percentage points since 2000. This improvement suggests some combination of more aggressive pricing and better cost control in manufacturing. Given the declining growth rate in sales over the past several years, I am inclined to attribute most of the improved margin to aggressive pricing. Harley-Davidson's low asset turnover ratio relative to peers has three causes: (1) lower fixed-asset turnover, (2) a much higher collection period, and (3) a much higher days' sales in cash ratio. The lower fixed-asset turnover is

---

[9] Harley-Davidson's annual report identifies all company debt as finance company borrowings and it reveals that operating income from financial services in 2004 was $188.6 million. I calculated the revised ROIC by reducing EBIT $188.6 million and eliminating debt from the denominator of the ratio.

worrisome. It might harmlessly reflect more capital-intensive production processes or more in-house production than peer firms, but it might also signal poor asset utilization by Harley-Davidson. While comforted by the steady recent improvement in fixed-asset turns, I would still like to know more about this disparity. The second cause, a sharply higher collection period, is almost certainly because Harley-Davidson provides customer financing, whereas peer firms do not. I note too that the finance subsidiary is responsible for an added drag on asset turnover in the form of $905.5 million in long-term finance receivables, net. I will say more about the third cause, a large and growing cash hoard, in a few paragraphs. Harley-Davidson's asset turnover ratio is not only low relative to peers but continues to fall. This decline masks two opposing trends: improving fixed asset and inventory turns, offset by a sharply rising collection period and days' sales in cash. I am especially impressed by the rising inventory turnover, which is now approaching double that of peers. I also am somewhat comforted by the fact that improving fixed asset turns and inventory turns both suggest increasing manufacturing efficiency.

Harley-Davidson's leverage and liquidity ratios show growing conservatism. Liquidity, as evidenced by the current and acid-test ratios, is above peers and generally rising. The company's balance sheet leverage ratios offer somewhat mixed signals, with the book value numbers suggesting considerable stability, while the market value ratios signal rising debt levels. The source of these contradictory signals is Harley-Davidson's stock price, which has failed to rise in concert with the book value of equity or assets. The lagging stock price causes the company's debt to rise relative to market values even as it remains constant relative to book values. To sort through these mixed signals, we can look at the times interest earned ratio, my nominee for the most informative indicator of financial leverage. Harley-Davidson's interest coverage improved steadily and dramatically from 18 times in 2000 to 61.8 times in 2004, despite the fact that growing finance company debt works against this trend. As we will see in Chapter 6, this is very substantial coverage—although still below the peer group median. Evidently, debt financing is not especially popular in this industry. Finally, I am not concerned about Harley-Davidson's low times-burden-covered ratio. The company can easily refinance this debt as it comes due, and I know that finance companies customarily use lots of short-term financing tied to customer loans.

Table 2.3 presents what are known as *common-size financial statements* for Harley-Davidson for 2000 to 2004, as well as industry averages for 2004. A common-size balance sheet simply presents each asset and liability as a

TABLE 2.3 Harley-Davidson, Inc., Common-Size Financial Statements, 2000–2004, and Industry Averages, 2004

	2000	2001	2002	2003	2004	Industry Average*
Assets						
Cash	17.2%	14.1%	7.3%	6.7%	5.0%	25.6%
Marketable securities	–	6.3	13.3	20.2	24.4	
Accounts receivable, net	25.8	24.9	25.0	22.6	24.2	9.0
Inventories	7.9	5.8	5.7	4.2	4.1	23.6
Other current assets	2.4	2.4	2.3	1.7	1.8	6.4
Total current assets	53.3	53.4	53.5	55.4	59.6	64.6
Property, plant, and equipment	58.5	54.7	52.0	44.5	40.0	48.6
Less accumulated depreciation	27.5	26.1	25.2	23.3	21.3	27.1
Net property, plant, and equipment	31.0	28.6	26.7	21.3	18.7	21.5
Finance receivables, net	9.6	12.2	15.3	15.0	16.5	2.1
Goodwill	2.2	1.6	1.3	1.1	1.1	5.7
Other assets	4.0	4.2	3.2	7.3	4.2	6.2
Total assets	100.0%	100.0%	100.0%	100.0%	100.0%	100.0%
Liabilities and Shareholders' Equity						
Long-term debt due in one year	3.7%	7.0%	9.9%	6.6%	9.0%	0.0%
Accounts payable	7.0	6.2	5.9	4.6	4.5	11.1
Income taxes payable	2.1	2.1	1.8	1.1	1.0	1.0
Accrued expenses	4.6	4.5	4.9	4.0	3.6	17.4
Other current liabilities	3.0	3.1	3.2	3.2	3.3	0.6
Total current liabilities	20.4	23.0	25.6	19.4	21.4	30.2
Long-term debt	14.6	12.2	9.8	13.6	14.6	3.8
Deferred taxes	0.6	0.6	0.8	2.6	0.9	2.4
Other long-term liabilities	6.7	8.0	5.9	4.3	4.4	7.5
Total liabilities	42.3	43.7	42.2	39.9	41.3	43.8
Total shareholders' equity	57.7	56.3	57.8	60.1	58.7	56.2
Total liabilities and shareholders' equity	100.0%	100.0%	100.0%	100.0%	100.0%	100.0%
Income Statements						
Net sales	100.0%	100.0%	100.0%	100.0%	100.0%	100.0%
Cost of goods sold	60.6	59.3	60.2	58.2	56.3	75.8
Gross profit	39.4	40.7	39.8	41.8	43.7	24.2
Selling, general and engineering expenses	17.2	17.0	14.9	14.0	13.7	12.3
Depreciation	4.4	4.3	4.1	4.0	4.0	2.5
Total operating expenses	21.6	21.3	19.0	18.0	17.7	14.9
Operating income	17.9	19.4	20.9	23.8	26.0	9.4
Interest expense	1.0	0.7	0.4	0.4	0.4	0.2
Other nonoperating income	1.1	0.3	0.1	0.4	0.3	0.4
Income before income taxes	18.0	19.0	20.6	23.8	25.9	9.5
Provision for income taxes	6.6	6.7	7.1	8.3	9.2	3.4
Net income	11.4%	12.4%	13.5%	15.5%	16.7%	6.2%

*Sample consists of five representative competitors in the "leisure travel" industry: Arctic Cat, Brunswick, Polaris Industries, Marine Products, and Winnebago Industries. (March 2004, data for Arctic Cat.)
Totals may not add due to rounding.

percentage of total assets. A common-size income statement is analogous except that all items are scaled in proportion to net sales instead of to total assets. The purpose of scaling financial statements in this fashion is to concentrate on underlying trends by abstracting from changes in the dollar figures caused by growth or decline. In addition, common-size statements are useful for removing simple scale effects when comparing different-size companies.

Looking first at Harley-Davidson's balance sheet, observe that the biggest changes on the asset side are increasing cash and securities, which rise from 17.2 percent of assets to 29.4, and declining net property, plant, and equipment, which fall from 31.0 percent to 18.7. Relative to peers, Harley-Davidson has invested much more in accounts receivable and finance receivables, and much less in inventories. Note too that about 60 percent of Harley-Davidson's assets are short-term. This percentage again highlights the importance of working-capital management to most businesses. When a large proportion of a company's investment is in assets as volatile as inventory and accounts receivable, that investment bears close watching.

On the liabilities side of Harley-Davidson's balance sheet, we again see a stable liabilities-to-assets ratio about equal to that of peers, but we also see a greater amount of interest-bearing debt. I attribute Harley-Davidson's greater reliance on interest-bearing debt to the funding needs of the company's finance subsidiary.

Harley-Davidson's common-size income statements again evidence high and growing operating margins, due in part, I am sure, to an improving economy over the period. One general observation: Although small percentage changes on an income statement may appear inconsequential—especially when it's not your performance bonus on the line—they seldom are. For example, the steady decline in Harley-Davidson's selling, general, and engineering expenses may not seem like a big deal compared with sales. After all, how important can 3.5 percentage points be? The answer is very important when compared with income. Because Harley-Davidson's income before taxes was 25.9 percent of sales in 2004, the decline in selling, general, and engineering expenses boosted company profits by almost 14 percent (3.5/25.9 = 13.5%). This effect is even more pronounced for companies with less lofty operating margins. The median ratio of income before taxes to sales among 500 large American firms in 2004 was only 11.8 percent, meaning that every one-percentage-point reduction in cost relative to sales boosts profits by almost 8.5 percent (1/11.8 = 8.5%).

Some beginners are inclined to think of all operating expenses as fixed and to fault management for allowing them to rise with sales. Where are the economies of scale they ask? The answer is that scale economies are usually not so simple. If they were, very large companies such as Sears and Rite Aid would quickly dominate smaller competitors and eventually monopolize markets. In fact, while some activities exhibit economies of scale, others are subject to diseconomies of scale, meaning the company becomes less efficient with size. Moreover, many activities exhibit scale economies over only a limited range of activity and then require a large investment to increase capacity. So on balance, I see no reason to criticize Harley-Davidson for its management of operating expenses.

To summarize our review of Harley-Davidson, ratio analysis reveals a highly profitable, conservatively financed company on the cusp of change. For the seven years between 1995 and 2002, Harley-Davidson's sales grew at an average annual rate of 18.0 percent. However, despite an improving economy and record low interest rates, growth fell to 14.0 percent in 2003 and declined further to 8.5 percent in 2004. Looking at Table 2.2, investor concern about slackening growth is readily apparent in the sharp decline in the company's price-to-earnings ratio, which fell from 37.6 times in 2001 to only 20.1 times in 2004. Concern heightened further just last week when management announced cuts in planned production to better match sales, causing the stock price to plummet 17 percent in a single day.

The financial effect of high profitability and stalling sales is the rapid build up of excess cash. Growth requires continuing investment in receivables, inventories, and fixed plant to support added sales, and when this growth diminishes, cash that would otherwise go to financing these investments begins to accumulate. Harley-Davidson clearly illustrates this dynamic. The firm's cash flow statement tells us that since 2003, when sales growth first began to slow, Harley-Davidson has added $78 million to dividends and repurchased $668 million of company stock; yet despite these outflows, cash and marketable securities have still more than doubled to over $1.6 billion. Harley-Davidson is clearly generating much more cash than it knows what to do with. Newly designated Chief Executive Officer Jim Ziemer's principal financial challenge as he takes office will be to find a productive use for this cash by either rekindling internal growth, expanding into new markets, or returning the cash to shareholders in an orderly manner. Spending excess cash might sound like fun, but Mr. Ziemer knows better. He realizes that failure to make productive use of this cash flow will further depress Harley-Davidson's stock price, antagonize his board of directors, and potentially invite a hostile takeover attempt. We will say much more about how best to address Mr. Ziemer's challenge in coming chapters.

TABLE 2.4 Selected Ratios for Representative Industries, 2003 (upper-quartile, median, and lower-quartile values)

Lines of Business and Number of Firms Reporting	Current Ratio (times)	Total Liabilities to Net Worth (%)	Collection Period (days)	Net Sales to Inventory (times)	Total Assets to Net Sales (%)	Profit Margin (%)	Return on Assets (%)	Return on Equity (%)
Agriculture, forestry, and fishing								
Beef cattle, feedlot (16)	2.2	97.3	17.9	6.0	50.0	8.9	11.1	25.3
	1.4	**156.9**	**34.0**	**4.8**	**62.4**	**4.0**	**4.6**	**13.3**
	1.2	217.0	46.6	2.8	112.9	1.9	3.5	9.1
Lawn and graden services (304)	2.9	46.1	23.2	109.8	25.0	6.3	17.7	41.2
	1.6	**110.2**	**41.3**	**42.2**	**33.8**	**2.5**	**5.6**	**14.9**
	1.1	220.4	61.7	12.4	49.1	0.2	0.5	2.4
Manufacturing								
Mens and boys shirts (19)	3.1	49.6	34.0	7.7	41.3	5.6	10.1	53.0
	2.0	**157.5**	**44.9**	**4.1**	**57.1**	**3.6**	**6.2**	**11.2**
	1.5	266.2	67.6	2.6	72.3	1.4	3.8	7.7
Motors and generators (49)	3.5	31.0	35.8	9.0	43.5	8.5	11.2	21.7
	2.2	**83.9**	**47.3**	**6.9**	**64.8**	**1.0**	**3.0**	**6.1**
	1.4	175.3	62.1	4.1	110.9	(2.4)	(3.2)	(2.4)
Semiconductors and related devices (208)	5.8	16.4	37.6	12.3	69.1	7.4	6.9	10.8
	3.3	**39.6**	**49.6**	**8.0**	**139.6**	**(5.1)**	**(2.8)**	**(2.0)**
	2.0	100.9	63.9	4.8	237.5	(42.5)	(25.0)	(36.6)
Process control instruments (98)	5.4	17.4	41.3	12.0	41.2	5.8	9.3	18.3
	3.1	**45.5**	**54.0**	**7.0**	**61.4**	**1.5**	**3.0**	**4.9**
	1.9	120.3	66.4	4.3	76.7	(1.6)	(2.0)	(0.7)
Wholesale trade								
Sporting and recreational goods (191)	3.8	36.9	18.6	11.3	24.9	3.6	9.7	21.8
	2.1	**101.8**	**28.1**	**7.3**	**33.4**	**1.4**	**4.0**	**7.1**
	1.4	241.9	42.7	4.8	43.6	0.2	0.6	2.1
Women's and children's clothing (168)	3.2	46.8	13.1	14.9	22.7	6.1	19.3	49.6
	2.0	**114.0**	**29.8**	**8.7**	**31.8**	**2.4**	**8.0**	**19.6**
	1.3	296.0	53.7	5.3	51.7	0.6	1.3	4.9

Source: *Industry Norms & Key Business Ratios, 2003–2004*, Desktop Edition, Dun & Bradstreet, a company of The Dun & Bradstreet Corporation. Reprinted with permission.

TABLE 2.4 Selected Ratios for Representative Industries, 2003 (upper-quartile, median, and lower-quartile values) (*Continued*)

Lines of Business and Number of Firms Reporting	Current Ratio (times)	Total Liabilities to Net Worth (%)	Collection Period (days)	Net Sales to Inventory (times)	Total Assets to Net Sales (%)	Profit Margin (%)	Return on Assets (%)	Return on Equity (%)
Retail trade								
Department stores (133)	5.2	24.6	2.6	6.5	35.8	3.9	7.1	14.2
	2.7	**66.5**	**8.4**	**4.6**	**47.6**	**1.5**	**3.3**	**6.4**
	1.8	124.2	21.2	2.8	69.2	0.1	—	0.2
Grocery stores (406)	2.9	43.1	0.7	28.9	14.3	2.2	9.2	21.2
	1.6	**92.0**	**2.9**	**19.1**	**20.2**	**0.8**	**4.1**	**8.4**
	1.1	256.1	6.6	13.5	30.8	0.2	0.8	2.1
Jewelry stores (297)	5.2	24.7	3.9	3.5	47.7	4.2	7.0	12.6
	2.9	**68.1**	**15.2**	**2.5**	**63.8**	**1.3**	**1.8**	**4.6**
	2.0	153.6	35.8	1.6	93.1	(0.3)	(0.5)	(0.7)
Services								
Beauty shops (26)	2.0	55.6	1.5	114.5	22.1	16.2	31.5	150.7
	1.2	**152.6**	**25.4**	**58.9**	**32.8**	**5.3**	**13.5**	**39.7**
	0.6	334.4	149.3	27.6	58.9	2.9	6.3	20.0
Dental laboratories (13)	2.3	68.0	36.7	81.5	25.1	4.2	8.4	26.4
	1.4	**198.6**	**38.3**	**59.8**	**29.4**	**1.9**	**5.6**	**10.7**
	1.2	370.0	43.8	43.5	57.8	0.5	1.9	4.8
College and universities (123)	2.9	22.2	12.8	110.6	160.3	12.2	5.0	8.8
	1.9	**46.7**	**21.2**	**54.6**	**228.6**	**4.5**	**2.3**	**4.2**
	1.2	83.6	49.3	42.1	316.4	(3.8)	(1.4)	(1.7)

TABLE 2.5   **Definitions of Principal Ratios Appearing in Chapter**

Profitability Ratios

Return on equity	= **Net income/Shareholders' equity**
Return on assets	= Net income/Assets
Return on invested capital	= $\dfrac{\text{Earnings before interest and taxes} \times (1 - \text{Tax rate})}{\text{Interest-bearing debt} + \text{Shareholders' equity}}$
Profit margin	= **Net income/Sales**
Gross margin	= Gross profit/Sales
Price to earnings	= Price per share/Earnings per share

Turnover-Control Ratios

Asset turnover	= **Sales/Assets**
Fixed-asset turnover	= Sales/Net property, plant, and equipment
Inventory turnover	= Cost of goods sold/Ending inventory
Collection period	= Accounts receivable/Credit sales per day (If credit sales unavailable, use sales)
Days' sales in cash	= Cash and securities/Sales per day
Payables period	= Accounts payable/Credit purchases per day (If purchases unavailable, use cost of goods sold)

Leverage and Liquidity Ratios

Assets to equity	= **Assets/Shareholders' equity**
Debt to assets	= Total liabilities/Assets (Interest-bearing debt is often substituted for total liabilities)
Debt to equity	= Total liabilities/Shareholders' equity
Times interest earned	= Earnings before interest and taxes/Interest expense
Times burden covered	= $\dfrac{\text{Earnings before interest and taxes}}{\text{Interest exp.} + \text{Prin. pay.}/(1 - \text{Tax rate})}$
Debt to assets (market value)	= $\dfrac{\text{Total liabilities}}{\text{No. equity shares} \times \text{Price/share} + \text{Total liabilities}}$
Debt to equity (market value)	= $\dfrac{\text{Total liabilities}}{\text{No. equity shares} \times \text{Price/share}}$
Current ratio	= Current assets/Current liabilities
Acid test	= $\dfrac{\text{Current assets} - \text{Inventory}}{\text{Current liabilities}}$

APPENDIX

International Differences in Financial Structure

Those French have a different word for everything.

Steve Martin

To this point, we have spoken almost entirely of American practices and norms. It is natural to ask how universal these customs are and to wonder how financial structure varies from one country to another. This appendix attempts to answer these questions and to review the more popular explanations for the differences observed. Definitive answers will not be possible in these few pages, but we will survey the most comprehensive data available and briefly summarize the best of emerging research.

Comparisons among Foreign Companies Trading on U.S. Markets

Table 2A.1 presents standard ratios for foreign companies whose shares trade in U.S. markets. The companies are grouped by country of incorporation, and the reported ratios are median 2004 values. For comparison, I have also included analogous ratios for companies listed in the S&P 100 Index, Standard & Poor's index of the largest 100 U.S. industrial firms. The four countries and two regions represented are hardly exhaustive, but the selected countries and regions are economically important and offer geographic and economic diversity.

Looking first at the profitability ratios, we see that Germany and Japan are laggards, with returns on invested capital little more than half those of others. A little historical research indicates that the Japanese number is not an anomaly. Indeed, the ROE for the Japanese sample has not been in double figures since 1984, long before the Asian crisis and the Japanese bubble economy of the late 1980s. Such returns are consistent with the reputed emphasis of Japanese firms on growth in market share to the detriment of short-run profits, except that the short run has lasted longer than expected and the Japanese economy continues to suffer.

A second noteworthy pattern in the data is the low asset turns and higher profit margins among the Asian and Latin American samples. Rather than indicating any differences in performance, I think this pattern reflects the reality that these samples are composed largely of capital-intensive firms from such industries as mining, power, and transportation.

TABLE 2A.1 Ratio Analysis of Companies in Various Countries and Regions, 2004, Median Values

	UK	Germany	Japan	Asia	Latin America	U.S. S&P
Number of companies	59	16	35	36	65	82
Profitability ratios						
Return on equity (%)	13.6	11.3	6.0	12.7	10.1	16.1
Return on assets (%)	5.7	3.5	2.8	5.0	4.4	6.0
Return on invested capital (%)	11.6	6.7	5.1	9.3	9.0	11.0
Profit margin (%)	5.3	3.4	2.9	11.3	6.2	7.6
Gross margin (%)	32.1	35.2	33.5	44.4	44.3	39.4
Price to earnings (X)	16.8	16.3	14.6	12.1	11.5	20.6
Turnover-control ratios						
Asset turnover (X)	0.8	0.9	0.9	0.5	0.6	0.8
Fixed-asset turnover (X)	3.7	3.0	3.9	0.9	1.4	3.5
Inventory turnover (X)	6.3	5.6	6.0	10.9	7.2	5.9
Collection period (days)	58.7	77.3	69.9	47.2	65.8	48.5
Days' sales in cash (days)	31.3	44.4	66.4	53.1	48.8	40.6
Payables period (days)	47.3	53.3	76.3	56.2	61.2	47.2
Leverage and liquidity ratios						
Assets to equity (%)	2.4	2.6	2.9	1.9	2.4	2.7
Debt to assets (%)	63.7	64.1	65.2	50.1	59.6	64.4
Debt to equity (%)	142.0	163.6	187.5	89.9	136.8	170.8
Times interest earned (X)	4.7	5.0	21.7	6.2	3.0	6.5
Times burden covered (X)	2.1	0.7	1.0	1.6	1.0	2.3
Debt to assets (market value, %)	35.8	50.8	50.2	40.3	51.7	33.3
Debt to equity (market value, %)	55.8	103.5	101.2	67.4	107.1	49.9
Current ratio (X)	1.3	1.5	1.4	1.0	1.2	1.4
Acid test (X)	1.0	1.2	1.1	0.9	1.0	1.1

Sample consists of companies incorporated in indicated geographic regions whose stock trades on U.S. markets, most as American Depository Receipts (ADRs). Financial firms and utilities are excluded. The Asia sample excludes Japan. Companies in the S&P sample are members of the Standard & Poor's index of the 100 largest U.S. industrial firms. Smaller companies with sales less than $300 million are omitted.

Looking at the turnover-control ratios, observe that Japanese firms have lengthy collection periods and payables periods. This is usually attributed to the importance of banks in financing Japanese business and a unique form of corporate organization known as *keiretsu*. A *keiretsu* is a form of mutual aid society composed of a number of companies, usually including a "main bank," that purchase sizable ownership interests in one another as a way to cement business relations and to repel possible takeover threats from outsiders. A principal way to finance *keiretsu* has been for the main bank to lend generously to the major *keiretsu* members—companies such as Toyota, Sony, and so on—which then pass some of the money downstream to other *keiretsu* members in the form of liberal trade credit. Hence the larger accounts receivable and accounts payable balances.

FIGURE 2A.1   **Average Interest Coverage Ratio, 1996**

Source: World Bank staff calculations based on the Financial Times Information's Extel database.

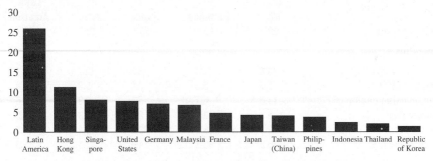

Note: Ratio of operating cash flows (operating income before interest, taxes, and depreciation) to interest payable on loans.

Although the *keiretsu* form of organization is rapidly unwinding, vestiges still remain.

Finally, looking at the leverage and liquidity ratios, it is difficult to argue that there are any significant differences in the level of indebtedness employed by sample firms. Asian and Latin American firms have somewhat lower balance sheet debt ratios, but their coverage ratios are representative of other samples. Japanese firms have the distinction of showing the highest debt-to-equity ratio and the highest interest coverage ratio, all made possible by near-zero interest rates in Japan. German, Japanese, and Latin American firms report low burden-covered ratios, suggesting a large proportion of their debt is short-term.

Public Companies

Turning to a different data source, Figure 2A.1 shows the average interest coverage ratio for companies in 12 countries and Latin America in 1996. The figure is from a study by Michael Pomerleano, a World Bank economist.[1] Rather than confining himself to companies trading in U.S. markets, Pomerleano's sample includes companies trading in any public market, local as well as foreign. This greatly expands the number of firms in his sample, but also increases the likelihood that differences in accounting and reporting practices will distort his results. The obvious conclusion from the figure is that Latin American companies are quite modestly indebted, while companies in developed economies such as the United States, Germany, France, and Japan are moderately indebted. At the other

---

[1] Michael Pomerleano, "Corporate Finance Lessons from the East Asian Crisis," *Public Policy for the Private Sector,* Note No. 155, The World Bank Group, October 1998, p. 3.

extreme, companies in several Asian economies, such as Korea, Thailand, and Indonesia, are up to their eyeballs in debt. Pomerleano argues convincingly that debt levels such as these were an important contributing factor to the financial crisis that struck Asia in 1997.

When interpreting this figure and the earlier table it is important to bear in mind that publicly traded firms are not necessarily representative of the economy as a whole. This is especially true in developing economies where publicly traded firms represent a small and often elite portion of the total economy. Note too that the similarity of debt levels among companies trading in U.S. markets evident in Table 2A.1 most likely reflects the requirements of U.S. investors rather than any inherent similarities among home country practices. It is entirely possible that the elite firms trading in U.S. markets will have similar capital structures, while other, purely domestic firms carry much different debt loads.

Why, in Figure 2A.1, are Korean, Thai, and Indonesian companies so heavily indebted, while Latin American companies are not? It is always dangerous to generalize about diverse countries scattered across the globe, but here is my take on the situation. Begin by noting two common characteristics among developing economies, whether in East Asia or Latin America. First, wealthy families and the state control a high percentage of public firms. For example, Stijn Claessens and colleagues report that in 1996 the top 10 families in Korea, Thailand, and Indonesia controlled between 37 and 58 percent of the *total* value of listed equities in these countries.[2] Second, public financial markets in emerging economies are generally small and unstable. As a result most company financing comes from one of three sources: controlling family members, state-owned or (often) influenced banks, or the state itself.

A principal reason Korean, Thai, and Indonesian companies are heavily indebted is that the state in these countries has often used the banking system to implement economic development strategies. This involves directing or encouraging banks to lend generously to targeted companies and, when necessary, cajoling banks to bail out troubled targets without excessive regard to creditworthiness. In return, the governments have not been above pumping public money into the banking system to keep favored companies and the banking system itself afloat.

Conversely, Latin American companies evidence modest debt financing because governments in the region have historically been less committed to top-down economic development programs and have been less inclined to view their banking systems as vehicles for allocating resources

---

[2] Stijn Claessens, Simeon Djankov, and Larry H.P. Lang, "The Separation of Ownership and Control in East Asian Corporations," *Journal of Financial Economics,* October–November 2000, pp. 81–112.

among companies. As a result, bank lending in Latin America more accurately reflects the creditworthiness of borrowers and the absence of implicit government loan guarantees. The low debt levels are also undoubtedly a product of the high and volatile inflation characteristic of the region. Because erratic inflation greatly increases the risks borne by fixed-rate investors, few lenders are willing to make long-run commitments in such an environment.

The Move Toward International Accounting Standards

A problem inherent in any cross-country comparison of accounting numbers is that accountants in different countries do not always keep score by the same rules. Companies in German-speaking countries, for example, have a long tradition of secrecy. Indeed, it was not many years ago that *Fortune* magazine remarked of Roche, the giant Swiss pharmaceutical company, "The only number in Hoffman-LaRoche's annual report you can believe is the year on the front."

See **www.accaglobal.com/ifrs/** for a comprehensive, if somewhat opaque, source of information on international financial accounting standards.

Happily times are changing, and what optimists might call international accounting standards are beginning to emerge. The European Union (EU) has taken the lead in this initiative as part of its much broader effort to hammer out a common, integrated marketplace among member countries. After some 30 years of study, debate, and political wrangling, the accounting initiative became a reality on January 1, 2005, when all 7,000 publicly traded companies in Europe dumped their national accounting rules in favor of the newly designated International Financial Accounting Standards (IFAS). At the same time, some 80 other countries spread over six continents have also adopted IFAS, either directly or by aligning national rules to the new international standards.

Even Japan is changing. In 1996, after some 15 years of economic malaise and in response to the increasing internationalization of its economy, Japan initiated a series of economic reforms since known as the "financial big bang." One important reform was to rewrite Japanese accounting rules to make them more consistent with those of the European Union and the United States. Being Japan, it should come as no surprise to learn that the country's accounting big bang has proven to be more of a sustained whimper, with changes occurring only gradually between 1999 and 2006. Nonetheless, the changes are fundamental, including the following:

- Consolidated financial statements are now the primary focus of attention. Before they were often treated as supplementary to parent company statements and buried in footnotes.

- Managers must now expense research and development costs as incurred. Before they had the choice of expensing the costs or capitalizing them to be written off, like depreciation, over time.

- Clearer rules on the use of fair value accounting to value shares owned in other companies make it much more difficult for firms to manipulate reported earnings.

Some observers believe these changes will help Japanese companies attract foreign investment as firms become more transparent to international investors. Others further argue that the changes are already affecting firm behavior, encouraging a greater emphasis on profitability over market share and instilling greater financial discipline in company investment choices.[3] With any luck, future editions of this book might even report that ROEs for Japanese firms have climbed into double-digits.

United States accounting authorities have traditionally viewed American accounting rules as the gold standard to which other countries could only hope to aspire. And their approach to international accounting standards has been to invite the rest of the world to adopt ours. But accounting scandals at Enron and WorldCom, and the ensuing demise of the accounting firm Arthur Andersen, have made Americans a bit more humble about their accounting rules and a bit more willing to compromise.

Historically, a major barrier to greater transatlantic cooperation on accounting standards has been differing philosophical perspectives on the role such standards should play. The European philosophy has been to articulate broad accounting principles and to charge accountants and executives to prepare company accounts consistent with the spirit of those principles. Concerned that principles alone leave too much room for manipulation, the American approach has been to lay down voluminous, detailed rules defining how each transaction is to be recorded and demanding strict conformance to the letter of those rules.

Ironically, this rules-based philosophy seems to have backfired in recent years. Rather than limiting accounting manipulation, the American "bright-line" approach appears on occasion to have encouraged it. It has done so by shifting executives' focus from preparing fair and accurate statements to figuring out how best to beat the rules. The ability to argue "we didn't break any rules, so we must be innocent" appears to have given some executives a rationale for shirking their professional responsibilities in pursuit of better looking numbers. One response to this breakdown in U.S. accounting standards was passage of the Sarbanes-Oxley Act of 2002.

[3] Mitsuru Mizuno, "The Impact of New Accounting Standards on Japanese Companies," *Pacific Economic Review,* 9:4 (2004), pp. 357–369.

Among numerous changes to corporate governance and reporting practices, Sarbanes-Oxley requires chief executive officers and chief financial officers to personally attest to the appropriateness, fairness, and accuracy of their company's financial reports. A second response on the part of some U.S. accountants and regulators has been to express renewed interest in the European, broad-brush approach, and to open the door at least a bit to the possibility of increased international cooperation.

In sum, our cursory review of accounting practices internationally indicates that differences in national standards are rapidly diminishing and that further integration is likely. This trend is driven by several forces, including the growing globalization of business and finance, EU attempts to create a single marketplace among member countries, Japan's efforts to revive their stagnating economy, and U.S. reactions to recent accounting scandals. This is not to say the era of a single, world standard is neigh, but rather that differences among various national standards are rapidly declining in number and severity. A distinct side benefit of this trend is that the challenge inherent in making cross-border comparisons of accounting numbers is falling rapidly and should continue doing so in future years.

SUMMARY

1. Although a major corporation and the corner drugstore may seem vastly different, the levers by which managers in both firms affect performance are similar and few in number. This chapter studied the ties between these levers and the firm's financial performance.

2. Return on equity is the most popular single yardstick of financial performance, although it does suffer from timing, risk, and value problems.

3. The primary components of return on equity are the profit margin, the asset turnover ratio, and financial leverage. The profit margin summarizes income statement performance. The asset turnover ratio focuses on the asset side of the balance sheet and indicates how efficiently management has used the firm's assets. Financial leverage looks at the liabilities side of the balance sheet and how the company has financed its assets.

4. Turnover control ratios indicate the efficiency with which the company uses a specific type of asset, such as accounts receivable or inventory. Such information is especially important for managing potentially volatile current assets and liabilities.

5. More financial leverage is not always better than less. Financial leverage can be measured by using balance sheet ratios or coverage ratios.

Coverage ratios compare the annual burden of the debt to the operating cash flow available to service the debt. Coverage ratios are usually superior for measuring long-term indebtedness.

6. Companies display widely differing profit margins, asset turnovers, and financial leverage, depending on the production technologies and strategies employed. The product of these three ratios is return on equity. Competition ensures that there is less variation in return-on-equity ratios than in its constituents.

7. Return on equity and return on assets reflect the combined effect of the earning power of a company's assets and the way those assets are financed. Return on invested capital is insensitive to company financing and thus is a better measure of earning power.

8. Ratio analysis is the systematic examination of a number of company ratios in search of insights into the firm's operations and its financial vitality.

9. Two productive ratio analysis techniques are to compare a company's ratios with those of competitors, and to observe changes in the company's ratios over time. Used creatively, ratios are useful tools but can be misleading if applied mechanically.

ADDITIONAL RESOURCES

Fridson, Martin S.; and Fernando Alvarez. *Financial Statement Analysis: A Practitioner's Guide*. 3rd ed. John Wiley and Sons, 2002. 424 pages.
> A Merrill Lynch executive and an academic combine to write a thorough practical overview of the topic. $74.

Palepu, Krishna G.; Paul M. Healy; and Victor L. Bernard. *Business Analysis and Valuation: Using Financial Statements*. 2nd ed. Cincinnati: South-Western College Publishing, 2003. 352 pages.
> Part finance, part accounting. An innovative look at the use of accounting information to address selected financial questions, especially business valuation. Available in paperback. $100.

Jablonsky, Stephen F.; and Noah P. Barsky. *The Manager's Guide to Financial Statement Analysis*, 2nd ed. New York: John Wiley & Sons, Inc., 2001. 304 pages.
> A practical introduction to financial statement analysis. $34.97.

Jiambalvo, James. *Managerial Accounting*. 2nd ed. New York: John Wiley & Sons, Inc., 2003. 544 pages.
> A straightforward and concise introduction to the use of managerial accounting in planning, budgeting, management control, and decision making. $100.

SOFTWARE

Designed to accompany this text, HISTORY produces a financial analysis of up to five years of user-supplied, historical financial data about a company. Results appear in four convenient tables of one page each. Balance sheet and income statement entries can be customized to a limited degree to reflect the reporting practices of individual companies. For a complimentary copy, visit **www.mhhe.com/higgins8e.**

WEBSITES

www.annualreportservice.com
As the name suggests, this site offers links to thousands of annual reports.

www.bigcharts.com
Provides an extensive array of company information, including profiles, stock prices, and financial statements, and great historical stock price graphs for most U.S. public companies.

www.moneycentral.msn.com/investor/invsub/results/compare.asp
Select a company and this CNBC site provides a variety of financial ratios and a comparison of company ratios to industry and S&P 500 figures.

SOURCES FOR BUSINESS RATIOS

Check your library for the following:

Troy, Leo. *Almanac of Business and Industrial Ratios 2005*. Aspen Law and Business, 2004. 768 pages.
   Based on IRS tax filings. Especially good on ratios for small companies.
Compact Disclosure. *Annual Report Information for U.S. Companies*.
   Extensive balance sheet and income statement information, including standard ratios, for virtually all publicly traded U.S. companies. Available on compact disk.
Dun & Bradstreet Business Credit Services. *Industry Norms and Key Business Ratios*. New York: published annually.
   Percentage balance sheets and 14 ratios for more than 1 million U.S. corporations, partnerships, and proprietorships, both public and private, representing 800 lines of business as defined by SIC codes. Median-, upper-, and lower-quartile values.
Annual Statement Studies 2004–2005: Financial Ratio Benchmarks. Risk Management Association. Philadelphia: published annually.

Common-size financial statements and widely used ratios in many business lines. Ratios broken out into six size ranges by sales and by assets. Also contains comparative historical data. One limitation is that only companies with assets of $250 million or less are included. Excellent bibliography entitled "Sources of Composite Financial Data."
Standard & Poor's. *Analysts Handbook*. New York: published annually, with monthly supplements.

Income statement, balance sheet, and share price data by industry for all companies in S&P 500 stock averages.

PROBLEMS

Answers to odd-numbered problems are at end of book. For additional problems with answers, see **www.mhhe.com/higgins8e.**

1. Following are selected ratios for Houston Exploration Corp. (an oil and gas exploration company) and Dean Foods Co. (a dairy products firm) for the year 2000. Which set of ratios belongs to Houston. Why do you think so?

	Company A	Company B
Asset turnover ratio	2.15	0.40
Profit margin	0.04	0.47

2. a. Which company would you expect to have the higher debt-to-equity ratio, a financial institution or a high-technology company? Why?
   b. Which company would you expect to have a higher profit margin, an appliance manufacturer or a wholesale grocer? Why?
   c. Which company would you expect to have a higher price-to-earnings ratio, Mantis Tractors or Glue-gull Internet Inc.? Why?
   d. Which company would you expect to have a higher current ratio, a jewelry store or a retail bookstore? Why?

3. True or false?
   a. A company's return on equity will always equal or exceed its return on assets.
   b. A company's assets-to-equity ratio always equals one plus its liabilities-to-equity ratio.
   c. A company's collection period should always be less than its payables period.
   d. A company's current ratio must always be larger than its acid-test ratio.

e. Economic earnings are more volatile than accounting earnings.

f. Ignoring taxes and transactions costs, unrealized paper gains are less valuable than realized cash earnings.

4. Your firm is considering the acquisition of a very promising Internet company. One executive argues against the move, pointing out that because the Internet company is presently losing money, the acquisition will cause your firm's return on equity to fall.

a. Is the executive correct in predicting that ROE will fall?

b. How important should changes in ROE be in this decision?

5. Financial data for HomeDepot.com Inc. follows: ($ in thousands)

	Year 1	Year 2
Sales	$193,730	$320,115
Cost of goods sold	159,937	261,801
Net income	122,642	−299,460
Cash flow from operations	−40,971	−15,810
Balance Sheet		
Cash	247,403	179,609
Marketable securities	230,644	32,695
Accounts receivable	15,520	26,129
Inventories	3,886	48,220
Total current assets	497,453	286,653
Accounts payable	19,204	19,066
Accrued liabilities	39,627	89,820
Total current liabilities	$ 58,831	$108,886

a. Calculate the current and quick ratio at the end of each year. How has the company's short-term liquidity changed over this period?

b. Assuming a 365-day year for all calculations, compute the following:

(1) The collection period each year based on sales.

(2) The inventory turnover, and the payables period each year based on cost of goods sold.

c. What is your interpretation of the company's performance?

6. Top management measures your division's performance by calculating the division's return on investment (ROI), defined as division-operating income per period divided by division assets. Your division has done quite well lately; its ROI is 30 percent. You believe the division should invest in a new production process, but a colleague disagrees, pointing out that because the new investment's first-year ROI is only 25 percent, it will hurt performance. How would you respond?

7. Answer the questions below based on the following information. Taxes are 35 percent and all dollars are in millions.

	Company X	Company Z
Earnings before interest and taxes	$400	$ 420
Debt (at 10% interest)	200	1,200
Equity	800	300

    a. Calculate each company's ROE, ROA, and ROIC.

    b. Why is company Z's ROE so much higher than X's? Does this mean Z is a better company? Why or why not?

    c. Why is company X's ROA higher than Z's? What does this tell you about the two companies?

    d. How do the two companies' ROICs compare? What does this suggest about the two companies?

8. Table 3.1 in Chapter 3 presents financial statements over the period 2002 through 2005 for R&E Supplies, Inc.

    a. Use these statements to calculate as many of the ratios in Table 2.2 as you can.

    b. What insights do these ratios provide about R&E's financial performance? What problems, if any, does the company appear to have?

9. Terravision Inc.'s sales last year totaled $75 million, and 80 percent of its sales are on credit. Terravision's collection period is 60 days. What was Terravision's year-end accounts receivable balance?

10. In 2004, Natural Selection, a nationwide computer dating service, had $200 million of assets and $80 million of liabilities. Earnings before interest and taxes were $50 million, interest expense was $12 million, the tax rate was 40 percent, principal repayment requirements were $10 million, and annual dividends were 25 cents per share on 10 million shares outstanding.

    a. Calculate:

        (1) Natural Selection's liabilities-to-equity ratio

        (2) Times interest earned ratio

        (3) Times burden covered

    b. What percentage decline in earnings before interest and taxes could Natural Selection have sustained before failing to cover

        (1) Principal repayment requirements

        (2) Common dividend payments?

11. Given the following information, complete the balance sheet shown below.

Collection period	50 days
Days sales in cash	15 days
Current ratio	2.4
Inventory turnover	6 times
Liabilities to assets	80%
Payables period	28 days

(All sales are on credit. All calculations assume a 365-day year. Payables period is based on cost of goods sold.)

Assets

Current:	
Cash	$ 500,000
Accounts receivable	
Inventory	1,000,000
Total current assets	
Net fixed assets	_____
Total assets	5,000,000

Liabilities and shareholders' equity

Current liabilities:	
Accounts payable	
Short-term debt	_____
Total current liabilities	
Long-term debt	
Shareholders' equity	_____
Total liabilities and equity	

12. You will need to use the Standard & Poor's Market Insight website (**www.mhhe.com/edumarketinsight**) for this problem. Observe the sales-to-net property, plant, and equipment ratio for fiscal 2003 for each of the following companies: AMR Corp., Oracle Corp., Alcan Inc., and Yahoo Inc. (From among the Excel Analytics programs on the left of your screen, consult the Annual Ratio Report.)

    a. What does the ratio tell you about these companies?

    b. How can you explain the wide differences you observe in the ratio?

13. An Excel spreadsheet containing Costco Wholesale Corporation's financial statements for 2001–2003 is available for download at **www.mhhe.com/higgins8e**. (Select Student Edition > Choose a Chapter > Excel Spreadsheets.) Use the spreadsheet to calculate as many of

the company's Profitability, Turnover-Control, and Leverage and Liquidity ratios as you can for 2001 through 2003 (see Table 2.5).

eXcel

14. Use Gap, Inc.'s, financial statements available on the Web at **www.mhhe.com/higgins8e** to answer the questions below. (Select Student Edition > Choose a Chapter > Excel Spreadsheets.) Use the company's Operating Profit as an approximation of its EBIT, and you may assume a 40 percent tax rate for your calculations.

a. For the fiscal years ending in January of 2003 and 2004, calculate
    (1) Gap's total liabilities-to-equity ratio;
    (2) Times interest earned ratio; and
    (3) Times burden covered.

b. What percentage decline in earnings before interest and taxes could Gap have sustained in fiscal years 2003 and 2004 before failing to cover
    (1) Principal repayment requirements,
    (2) Common dividend payments?

c. Prepare common-size financial statements for Gap, Inc., for 2002–2004.

PART TWO

Planning Future
Financial Performance

CHAPTER THREE

Financial Forecasting

Planning is the substitution of error for chaos.

Anonymous

To this point we have looked at the past, evaluating existing financial statements and assessing past performance. It is now time to look to the future. We begin in this chapter with an examination of the principal techniques of financial forecasting and a brief overview of planning and budgeting as practiced by large, modern corporations. In the following chapter, we look at planning problems unique to the management of company growth. Throughout this chapter our emphasis will be on the techniques of forecasting and planning; so as a counterweight, it will be important that you bear in mind that proper technique is only a part of effective planning. At least as critical is the development of creative market strategies and operating policies that underlie the financial plans.

Pro Forma Statements

Finance is central to a company's planning activities for at least two reasons. First, much of the language of forecasting and planning is financial. Plans are stated in terms of financial statements, and many of the measures used to evaluate plans are financial. Second, and more important, the financial executive is responsible for a critical resource: money. Because virtually every corporate action has financial implications, a vital part of any plan is determining whether the plan is attainable given the company's limited resources.

Companies typically prepare a wide array of plans and budgets. Some, such as production plans and staff budgets, focus on a particular aspect of the firm, while others, such as pro forma statements, are much broader in scope. Here we will begin with the broader techniques and talk briefly about more specialized procedures later when we address planning in large corporations.

Pro forma financial statements are the most widely used vehicles for financial forecasting. A pro forma statement is simply a prediction of what the company's financial statements will look like at the end of the forecast period. These predictions may be the culmination of intensive, detailed operating plans and budgets or nothing more than rough, back-of-the-envelope projections. Either way, the pro forma format displays the information in a logical, internally consistent manner.

A major purpose of pro forma forecasts is to estimate a company's future need for external funding, a critical first step in financial planning. The process is a simple one. If the forecast says a company's assets will rise next year to $100, but liabilities and owners' equity will total only $80, the obvious conclusion is that $20 in external funding will be required. The forecast is silent about what form this new financing should take—whether trade credit, bank borrowing, new equity, or whatever—but one way or another a fresh $20 is necessary. Conversely, if the forecast says assets will fall below projected liabilities and owners' equity, the obvious implication is that the company will generate more cash than necessary to run the business. And management faces the pleasant task of deciding how best to deploy the excess. In equation form,

$$\frac{\text{External}}{\text{funding required}} = \frac{\text{Total}}{\text{assets}} - \left(\text{Liabilities} + \frac{\text{Owners'}}{\text{equity}} \right)$$

Practitioners often refer to external funding required as the "plug" because it is the amount that must be plugged into the balance sheet to make it balance.

Percent-of-Sales Forecasting

As Victor Borge first noted, "Forecasting is always difficult, especially with regard to the future." One straightforward yet effective way to simplify the challenge is to tie many of the income statement and balance sheet figures to future sales. The rationale for this *percent-of-sales* approach is the tendency, noted in Chapter 2, for all variable costs and most current assets and current liabilities to vary directly with sales. Obviously, this will not be true for all of the entries in a company's financial statements, and certainly some independent forecasts of individual items, such as plant and equipment, will be required. Nonetheless, the percent-of-sales method does provide simple, logical estimates of many important variables.

The first step in a percent-of-sales forecast should be an examination of historical data to determine which financial statement items have varied in proportion to sales in the past. This will enable the forecaster to decide which items can safely be estimated as a percentage of sales and which must be forecast using other information. The second step is to forecast sales. Because so many other items will be linked mechanically to the sales forecast, it is critical to estimate sales as accurately as possible. Also, once the pro forma statements are completed, it is a good idea to test the sensitivity of the results to reasonable variations in the sales forecast. The final step in the percent-of-sales forecast is to estimate individual financial statement items by extrapolating the historical patterns to the newly estimated sales. For instance, if inventories have historically been about 20 percent of sales and next year's sales are forecast to be $10 million, we would expect inventories to be $2 million. It's that simple.

To illustrate the use of the percent-of-sales method, consider the problem faced by Suburban National Bank. R&E Supplies, Inc., a modest-size wholesaler of plumbing and electrical supplies, has been a customer of the bank for a number of years. The company has maintained average deposits of approximately $30,000 and has had a $50,000 short-term, renewable loan for five years. The company has prospered, and the loan has been renewed annually with only cursory analysis.

In late 2005, the president of R&E Supplies visited the bank and requested an increase in the short-term loan for 2006 to $500,000. The president explained that despite the company's growth, accounts payable had increased steadily and cash balances had declined. A number of suppliers had recently threatened to put the company on COD for future purchases unless they received payments more promptly. When asked why he was requesting $500,000, the president replied that this amount seemed "about right" and would enable him to pay off his most insistent creditors and rebuild his cash balances.

Knowing that the bank's credit committee would never approve a loan request of this magnitude without careful financial projections, the lending officer suggested that he and the president prepare pro forma financial statements for 2006. He explained that these statements would provide a more accurate indication of R&E's credit needs.

The first step in preparing the pro forma projections was to examine the company's financial statements for the years 2002 through 2005, shown in Table 3.1, in search of stable patterns. The results of this ratio analysis appear in Table 3.2. The president's concern about declining liquidity and increasing trade payables is well founded; cash and securities have fallen from 22 days sales to 7 days sales, while accounts payable have risen from a payables period of 39 days to 66 days.[1] Another worrisome trend is the increase in cost of goods sold and general, selling, and administrative expenses in proportion to sales. Earnings clearly are not keeping pace with sales.

---

[1] See Table 2.5 in Chapter 2 for definitions of ratios used in this chapter.

TABLE 3.1 Financial Statements for R&E Supplies, Inc., December 31, 2002–2005 ($ thousands)

Income Statements				
	2002	2003	2004	2005*
Net sales	$11,190	$13,764	$16,104	$20,613
Cost of goods sold	9,400	11,699	13,688	17,727
Gross profit	1,790	2,065	2,416	2,886
Expenses:				
General, selling, and administrative expenses	1,019	1,239	1,610	2,267
Net interest expense	100	103	110	90
Earnings before tax	671	723	696	529
Tax	302	325	313	238
Earnings after tax	$ 369	$ 398	$ 383	$ 291
Balance Sheets				
Assets				
Current assets:				
Cash and securities	$ 671	$ 551	$ 644	$ 412
Accounts receivable	1,343	1,789	2,094	2,886
Inventories	1,119	1,376	1,932	2,267
Prepaid expenses	14	12	15	18
Total current assets	3,147	3,728	4,685	5,583
Net fixed assets	128	124	295	287
Total assets	$ 3,275	$ 3,852	$ 4,980	$ 5,870
Liabilities and Owners' Equity				
Current liabilities:				
Bank loan	$ 50	$ 50	$ 50	$ 50
Accounts payable	1,007	1,443	2,426	3,212
Current portion long-term debt	60	50	50	100
Accrued wages	5	7	10	18
Total current liabilities	1,122	1,550	2,536	3,380
Long-term debt	960	910	860	760
Common stock	150	150	150	150
Retained earnings	1,043	1,242	1,434	1,580
Total liabilities and owners' equity	$ 3,275	$ 3,852	$ 4,980	$ 5,870

*Estimate.

The last column in Table 3.2 contains the projections agreed to by R&E's president and the lending officer. In line with recent experience, sales are predicted to increase 25 percent over 2005. General, selling, and administrative expenses will continue to rise as a result of an unfavorable labor settlement. After comparing R&E's cash balances to historical levels and to those of competitors, the president believes cash and securities

TABLE 3.2 Selected Historical Financial Ratios for R&E Supplies, Inc., 2002–2005

	History				Forecast
	2002	2003	2004	2005E	2006F
Annual growth rate in sales	—	23%	17%	28%	25%
	Ratios Tied to Sales				
Cost of goods sold (% of sales)	84	85	85	86	86
General, selling, and administrative expenses (% of sales)	9	9	10	11	12
Cash and securities (days sales in cash)	22	15	15	7	18
Accounts receivable (collection period)	44	47	47	51	51
Inventories (inventory turnover)	8	9	7	8	9
Accounts payable (payables period)	39	45	65	66	59
	Other Ratios in Percent				
Tax/earnings before tax*	45	45	45	45	45
Dividends/earnings after tax	50	50	50	50	50

E = Estimate
F = Forecast
*Including state and local taxes.

should rise to at least 18 days' sales. Because cash and securities are generally low return assets, this figure represents the minimum amount the president believes is necessary to operate the business efficiently. This reasoning is reinforced by the fact that any cash or securities balances above this minimum will just add to the loan amount and thus cost the company more money. Since much of R&E's cash balances will sit in his bank, the lending officer readily agrees to the projected increase in cash. The president also thinks accounts payable should decline to no more than a payables period of 59 days. The tax rate and the dividends-to-earnings, or payout, ratio are expected to stay constant.

The resulting pro forma financial statements appear in Table 3.3. Looking first at the income statement, the implication of the preceding assumptions is that earnings after tax will decline to $234,000, down 20 percent from the prior year. The only entry on this statement requiring further comment is net interest expense. Net interest expense will clearly depend on the size of the loan the company requires. However, because we do not know this yet, net interest expense has initially been assumed to equal last year's value, with the understanding that this assumption may have to be modified later.

Estimating the External Funding Required

To most operating executives, a company's income statement is more interesting than its balance sheet because the income statement measures

TABLE 3.3   Pro Forma Financial Statements for R&E Supplies, Inc., December 31, 2006 ($ thousands)

Income Statement		
	2006	**Comments**
Net sales	$25,766	25% increase
Cost of goods sold	22,159	86% of sales
Gross profit	3,607	
Expenses:		
General, selling, and administrative expenses	3,092	12% sales
Net interest expense	90	Initially constant
Earnings before tax	425	
Tax	191	45% tax rate
Earnings after tax	$ 234	

Balance Sheet		
Assets		
Current assets:		
Cash and securities	$ 1,271	18 days sales
Accounts receivable	3,600	51 day collection period
Inventories	2,462	9 times turnover
Prepaid expenses	20	Rough estimate
Total current assets	7,353	
Net fixed assets	280	See text discussion
Total assets	$ 7,633	
Liabilities and Owners' Equity		
Current liabilities:		
Bank loan	$ 0	
Accounts payable	3,582	59 day payables period
Current portion of long-term debt	100	See text discussion
Accrued wages	22	Rough estimate
Total current liabilities	3,704	
Long-term debt	660	
Common stock	150	
Retained earnings	1,697	See text discussion
Total liabilities and owners' equity	$ 6,211	
External funding required	**$ 1,422**	

profitability. The reverse is true for the financial executive. When the object of the exercise is to estimate future financing requirements, the income statement is interesting only insofar as it affects the balance sheet. To the financial executive, the balance sheet is key.

The first entry on R&E's pro forma balance sheet (Table 3.3) requiring comment is prepaid expenses. Prepaid expenses, like accrued wages below, is a small item that increases erratically with sales. Since the amounts are small and the forecast does not require a high degree of precision, rough estimates will suffice.

When asked about new fixed assets, the president indicated that a $43,000 capital budget had already been approved for 2003. Further, depreciation for the year would be $50,000, so net fixed assets would decline $7,000 to $280,000 ($280,000 = $287,000 + $43,000 − $50,000).

Note that the bank loan is initially set to zero. We will calculate the external funding required momentarily and will then be in a position to consider a possible bank loan. Continuing down the balance sheet, "current portion of long-term debt" is simply the principal repayment due in 2007. It is a contractual commitment specified in the loan agreement. As this required payment becomes a current liability, the accountant shifts it from long-term debt to current-portion long-term debt.

The last entry needing explanation is retained earnings. Since the company does not plan to sell new equity in 2006, common stock remains constant. Retained earnings are determined as follows:

$$\frac{\text{Retained}}{\text{earnings '06}} = \frac{\text{Retained}}{\text{earnings '05}} + \frac{\text{Earnings}}{\text{after tax '06}} - \text{Dividends '06}$$

$$\$1,697,000 = \$1,580,000 + \$234,000 - \$117,000$$

In words, when a business earns a profit larger than its dividend, the excess adds to retained earnings. The retained earnings account is the principal bridge between a company's income statement and its balance sheet; so as profits rise, retained earnings grow and loan needs decline.[2]

The last step in constructing R&E's pro formas is to estimate the amount of external funding required. Using the expression defined earlier,

$$\frac{\text{External}}{\text{funding required}} = \frac{\text{Total}}{\text{assets}} - \left(\text{Liabilities} + \frac{\text{Owners'}}{\text{equity}} \right)$$

$$= \$7,633,000 - \$6,211,000$$

$$= \$1,422,000$$

According to our first-pass forecast, R&E Supplies needs not $500,000 but more than *$1.4 million* to achieve the president's objectives.

Mindful of the cautionary tale of the grateful borrower who rises to shake the hand of his banker and exclaims, "I don't know how I'll ever

---

[2] Sometimes companies will complicate this equation by charging certain items, such as gains or losses on foreign currency translation, directly to retained earnings. But this is not a problem here.

repay you," the lending officer for Suburban National Bank is apt to be of two minds about this result. On the one hand, R&E has a projected 2006 accounts receivable balance equal to $3.6 million, which would probably provide excellent security for a $1.4 million loan. On the other hand, R&E's cavalier attitude toward financial planning and the president's obvious lack of knowledge about where his company is headed are definite negatives. But before getting too involved in the implications of the forecast, we need to recall that our projection does not yet include the higher interest expense on the new, larger loan.

Interest Expense

One thing that bothers attentive novices about pro forma forecasting is the circularity involving interest expense and indebtedness. As noted earlier, interest expense cannot be estimated accurately until the amount of external funding required has been determined. Yet because the external funding depends in part on the amount of interest expense, it would appear one cannot be accurately estimated without the other.

There are two common ways around this dilemma. The more responsible approach is to use a computer spreadsheet to solve for the interest expense and external funding simultaneously. We will look at this approach in more detail below. The other, more cavalier approach is to ignore problem with the expectation that the first-pass estimate will be close enough. Given the likely errors in predicting sales and other variables, the additional error caused by a failure to determine interest expense accurately is usually not all that critical.

To illustrate, R&E Supplies' first-pass pro formas assumed a net interest expense of $90,000, whereas the balance sheet indicates total interest-bearing debt of almost $2.2 million. At a 10 percent interest rate, this implies an interest expense of about $220,000, or $130,000 more than our first-pass estimate. But think what happens as we trace the impact of a $130,000 addition to interest expense through the income statement. First, the $130,000 expense is before taxes. At a 45 percent tax rate, the decline in earnings after tax will be only $71,500. Second, because R&E Supplies distributes half of its earnings as dividends, a $71,500 decline in earnings after tax will result in only a $35,750 decline in the addition to retained earnings. So after all the dust settles, our estimate of the addition to retained earnings and, by implication, the external funding required will be about $35,750 low. But when the need for new external financing is already over $1.4 million, what's another $35,750 among friends? Granted, increased interest expense has a noticeable percentage effect on earnings, but by the time the increase filters through taxes and dividend payments, the effect on the external funding needed is modest. The moral to the story is that quick-and-dirty financial forecasts really can be quite useful. Unless you are naturally inclined toward green eyeshades or have the luxury of charging by the hour, you will find that handmade forecasts are just fine for many purposes.

Seasonality

A more serious potential problem with pro forma statements—and, indeed, with all of the forecasting techniques mentioned in this chapter—is that the results are applicable only on the forecast date. The pro formas in Table 3.3 present an estimate of R&E Supplies' external financing requirements on December 31, 2006. They say nothing about the company's need for financing on any other date before or after December 31. If a company has seasonal financing requirements, knowledge of year-end loan needs may be of little use in financial planning, since the year end may bear no relation whatever to the date of the company's peak financing need. To avoid this problem, you should make monthly or quarterly forecasts rather than annual ones. Or, if you know the date of peak financing need, you can simply make this date the forecast horizon.

Pro Forma Statements and Financial Planning

To this point, R&E's pro forma statements simply display the financial implications of the company's operating plans. This is the forecasting half of the exercise. It is time now for R&E to do some serious financial planning. Using the techniques described in earlier chapters, management must analyze the forecast carefully to decide if it is acceptable or whether it must be changed to avoid identified problems. In particular, R&E management must decide whether the estimated external funding requirement is too large. If the answer is yes, either because R&E does not want to borrow $1.4 million or because the bank is unwilling to grant such a large loan, management must change its plans to conform to the financial realities. This is where operating plans and financial plans merge (or, too often, collide) to create a coherent strategy. Fortunately, the pro forma forecast provides an excellent template for such iterative planning.

To illustrate the process, suppose that Suburban National Bank, concerned about R&E management's obvious lack of financial acumen, will not lend the company more than $1 million. Ignoring the possibility of trying another bank, or selling new equity, R&E's challenge is to modify its operating plans to shave $400,000 off the projected external funding requirement. There are many ways to meet this challenge, each involving subtle trade-offs among growth, profitability, and funding needs. And while we are not in a position to evaluate these trade-offs, as R&E management would be, we can illustrate the mechanics. Suppose that after much debate management decides to test the following revised operating plan:

- Tighten up collection of accounts receivable so that the collection period falls from 51 days to 47.

- Settle for a more modest improvement in trade payables so that the payables period rises from 59 days to 60.

Finally because a tougher collection policy will drive away some customers and higher trade payables will sacrifice some prompt payment discounts, let us presume that management believes the revised plan will reduce sales growth from 25 percent to 20 percent and increase general, selling, and administrative expenses from 12 percent to 12.5 percent.

To test this revised operating plan we need only make the indicated changes in assumptions and roll out a revised pro forma forecast. Table 3.4 presents the results of this exercise. The good news is that external funding required is now below the $1 million target; the bad news is that this improvement is not free. Earnings after tax in the revised forecast trail the original projection in Table 3.3 by 34 percent [($234 − 155)/$234].

Is R&E Supplies' revised operating plan optimal? Is it superior to all other possible plans? We cannot say; these are fundamental questions of business strategy that can never be answered with complete assurance. We can say, however, that pro forma forecasts contribute mightily to the planning process by providing a vehicle for evaluating alternative plans, by quantifying the anticipated costs and benefits of each, and by indicating which plans are financially feasible.

Computer-Based Forecasting

Readily available spreadsheets have made it possible for anyone with a modicum of computer skill to spin out elegant (and occasionally useful) pro forma forecasts and sophisticated risk analysis. To demonstrate how easy computer-based forecasting is Table 3.5 (page 99) presents an abbreviated one-year forecast for R&E Supplies as it might appear on a computer screen. (If you are a computer novice, I suggest skipping this section or developing a basic understanding of spreadsheet programs before continuing.) The first area on the simulated screen is an *assumptions box*, containing all of the information and assumptions required to construct the forecast. (It is a good idea to leave some room here initially so that if you are unable to think of all the necessary information immediately, you can add it later.) Gathering all of the necessary input information in an

TABLE 3.4   Revised Pro Forma Financial Statements for R&E Supplies, Inc., December 31, 2006 ($ thousands, changes in bold)

Income Statement		
	2006	**Comments**
Net sales	**$24,736**	**20% increase**
Cost of goods sold	21,273	86% of sales
Gross profit	3,463	
Expenses:		
General, selling, and administrative expenses	**3,092**	**12.5% sales**
Net interest expense	90	Initially constant
Earnings before tax	281	
Tax	126	45% tax rate
Earnings after tax	$ 155	
Balance Sheet		
Assets		
Current assets:		
Cash and securities	$ 1,220	18 days sales
Accounts receivable	**3,185**	**47 day collection period**
Inventories	2,364	9 times turnover
Prepaid expenses	20	Rough estimate
Total current assets	6,789	
Net fixed assets	280	See text discussion
Total assets	$ 7,069	
Liabilities and Owners' Equity		
Current liabilities:		
Bank loan	$ 0	
Accounts payable	**3,497**	**60 day payables period**
Current portion of long-term debt	100	See text discussion
Accrued wages	22	Rough estimate
Total current liabilities	3,619	
Long-term debt	660	
Common stock	150	
Retained earnings	1,657	See text discussion
Total liabilities and owners' equity	$ 6,086	
External funding required	$ 982	

assumptions box can be a real timesaver later if you want to change assumptions. The 2006 data in the assumptions box correspond closely to the data used earlier in our original handmade forecast for R&E Supplies.

The forecast begins immediately below the assumptions box. The first column, labeled "Equations 2006," is included for explanatory purposes

Why Are Lenders So Conservative?

Some would answer, "Too much Republican in-breeding," but there is another possibility: low returns. Simply put, if expected loan returns are low, lenders cannot accept high risks.

Let us look at the income statement of a representative bank lending operation with say, 100, $1 million loans, each paying 10 percent interest:

($ thousands)	
Interest income (10% × 100 × $1 million)	$10,000
Interest expense	7,000
Gross income	3,000
Operating expenses	1,000
Income before tax	2,000
Tax at 40% rate	800
Income after tax	$ 1,200

The $7 million interest expense represents a 7 percent return the bank must promise depositors and investors to raise the $100 million lent. (In bank jargon, these loans offer a 3 percent lending margin, or spread.) Operating expenses include costs of the downtown office towers, the art collection, wages, and so on.

These numbers imply a minuscule return on assets of 1.2 percent ($1.2 million/100 × $1 million). We know from the levers of performance that to generate any kind of reasonable return on equity, banks must pile on the financial leverage. Indeed, to generate a 12 percent ROE, our bank needs a 10-to-1 assets-to-equity ratio or, equivalently, $9 in liabilities for every $1 in equity.

Worse yet, our profit figures are too optimistic because they ignore the reality that not all loans are repaid. Banks typically are able to recover only about 40 percent of the principal value of defaulted loans, implying a loss of $600,000 on a $1 million default. Ignoring tax losses on defaulted loans, this means that if only two of the bank's 100 loans go bad annually, the bank's $1.2 million in expected profits will evaporate. Stated differently, a loan officer must be almost certain that each loan will be repaid just to break even. (Alternatively, the officer must be almost certain of being promoted out of lending before the loans start to go bad.) So why are lenders conservative? Because the aggressive ones have long since gone bankrupt.

and would not appear on a conventional forecast. Entering the equations shown causes the computer to calculate the quantities appearing in the second column, labeled "Forecast 2006." The third column, labeled "Forecast 2007," is presently blank.

Two steps are required to get from the assumptions to the completed forecast. First, it is necessary to enter a series of equations tying the inputs to the forecasted outputs. These are the equations appearing in the first column. Here is how to read them. The first equation for net sales is = B3 + B3 * C4. This instructs the computer to get the number in cell B3 and add to it that number times the number in cell C4, in other words,

TABLE 3.5 Forecasting with a Computer Spreadsheet: Pro Forma Financial Forecast for R&E Supplies, Inc., December 31, 2006 ($ thousands)

	A	B	C	D
1				
2	Year	2005 Actual	2006	2007
3	Net sales	$20,613		
4	Growth rate in net sales		25.0%	
5	Cost of goods sold/net sales		86.0%	
6	Gen., sell., and admin. expenses/net sales		12.0%	
7	Long-term debt	$ 760	$660	
8	Current portion long-term debt	$ 100	$100	
9	Interest rate		10.0%	
10	Tax rate		45.0%	
11	Dividend/earnings after tax		50.0%	
12	Current assets/net sales		29.0%	
13	Net fixed assets		$280	
14	Current liabilities/net sales		14.5%	
15	Owners' equity	$1,730		
16	**INCOME STATEMENT**			
17		Equations	Forecast	Forecast
18	Year	2006	2006	2007
19	Net sales	=B3 + B3*C4	$25,766	
20	Cost of goods sold	=C5*C19	22,159	
21	Gross profit	=C19 − C20	3,607	
22	Gen., sell., and admin. exp.	=C6*C19	3,092	
23	Interest expense	=C9*(C7 + C8 + C40)	231	
24	Earnings before tax	=C21 − C22 − C23	285	
25	Tax	=C10*C24	128	
26	Earnings after tax	=C24 − C25	156	
27	Dividends paid	=C11*C26	78	
28	Additions to retained earnings	=C26 − C27	78	
29				
30	**BALANCE SHEET**			
31	Current assets	=C12*C19	7,472	
32	Net fixed assets	=C13	280	
33	Total assets	=C31 + C32	7,752	
34				
35	Current liabilities	=C14*C19	3,736	
36	Long-term debt	=C7	660	
37	Equity	=B15 + C28	1,808	
38	Total liabilities and shareholders'	=C35 + C36 + C37	6,204	
39	equity			
40	**EXTERNAL FUNDING REQUIRED**	=C33 − C38	**$ 1,548**	

$20,613 + \$20,613 \times 25\%$. The second equation instructs the computer to multiply forecasted net sales by the forecasted cost of goods sold percentage. The third says to calculate gross profit by subtracting cost of goods sold from net sales.

There are only three tricky equations. Interest expense, row 23, is the interest rate times end-of-period long-term debt, including the current portion, plus the forecasted external funding required. As discussed earlier, the tricky part here is the interdependency between interest expense and external funding required. (I will talk more about this in step 2.) The other two equations are simple by comparison. The equity equation, row 37, is end-of-period equity plus additions to retained earnings; the external funding required equation, row 40, is total assets minus total liabilities and shareholders' equity.

The second required step is to incorporate the interdependence between interest expense and external funding required. Without some adjustment, the computer will likely signal "circular reference" and then stall when you enter the equation for interest expense. To avoid this, you need to shift to what spreadsheeters call *manual calculation*. With Excel software, you need to do the following. Select "Tools" from the menu, followed by "Options." Select the "Calculation" tab, then choose "Manual" calculation and click the "iteration" toggle. Finally, set the maximum number of iterations to something above, say, 5, and press OK. With the program no longer in automatic calculation mode, you will now need to tell the computer when to calculate. Do this by pressing the F9 key. Your forecast should now be complete.

Now the fun begins. To modify a forecast assumption, just change the appropriate entry in the assumptions box, press F9, and *voilà:* The computer instantly makes all the necessary changes and shows the revised forecast. To extend the forecast one more year, just complete the entries in the assumptions box, highlight the 2006 forecast, and copy or fill one column to the right. Then make some obvious changes in the equations for net sales and equity, press the F9 key, and the computer does the rest. (See Additional Resources at the end of the chapter for information about PROFORMA, complimentary software for constructing pro forma forecasts.)

Coping with Uncertainty

Sensitivity Analysis

Several techniques exist to help executives grapple with the uncertainty inherent in all realistic financial projections. The simplest is *sensitivity analysis*, known colloquially as "what if" questions: What if R&E's sales grow by

15 percent instead of 25 percent? What if cost of goods sold is 84 percent of sales instead of 86 percent? It involves systematically changing one of the assumptions on which the pro forma statements are based and observing how the forecast responds. The exercise is useful in at least two ways. First, it provides information about the range of possible outcomes. For example, sensitivity analysis on R&E Supplies' original forecast might reveal that depending on the future sales volume attained, the company's need for external financing could vary between $1.4 million and $2 million. This would tell management that it had better have enough flexibility in its financing plans to add an extra $600,000 in external funding as the future unfolds. Second, sensitivity analysis encourages management by exception. It enables managers to determine which assumptions most strongly affect the forecast and which are secondary. This allows them to concentrate their data-gathering and forecasting efforts on the most critical assumptions. Subsequently, during implementation of the financial plan, the same information enables management to focus on those factors most critical to the plan's success.

Scenario Analysis

Sensitivity analysis has its uses, but it is important to realize that forecasts seldom err on one assumption at a time. That is, whatever events throw one assumption in a financial forecast off the mark will likely affect other assumptions as well. For example, suppose we want to estimate R&E Supplies' external financing needs assuming sales fall 15 percent below expectations. Sensitivity analysis would have us simply cut forecasted sales growth by 15 percent and recalculate the external financing required. However, this approach implicitly assumes the shortfall in sales will not affect any of the other estimates underlying the forecast. If the proper assumptions are that inventories will initially rise when sales drop below expectations and the profit margin will decline as the company slashes prices to maintain volume, failure to include these complementary effects will cause an underestimate of the need for outside financing.

Instead of manipulating one assumption at a time, *scenario analysis* broadens the perspective to look at how a number of assumptions might change in response to a particular economic event. The first step in a scenario analysis is to identify a few carefully chosen events, or scenarios, that might plausibly befall the company. Common scenarios include loss of a major customer, successful introduction of a major new product, or entry of an important new competitor. Then, for each scenario identified, the second step is to carefully rethink the variables in the original forecast to either reaffirm the original assumption or substitute a new, more accurate one. The last step in the analysis is to generate a separate forecast for each scenario. The result is a limited number of detailed projections describing the range of contingencies the business faces.

Simulation

Simulation is a computer-assisted extension of sensitivity analysis. To perform a simulation, begin by assigning a probability distribution to each uncertain element in the forecast. The distribution describes the possible values the variable could conceivably take on and states the probability of each value occurring. Next, ask a computer to pick at random a value for each uncertain variable consistent with the assigned probability distribution and generate a set of pro forma statements based on the selected values. This creates one trial. Performing the last step many times produces a large number of trials. The output from a simulation is a table or, more often, a graph summarizing the results of many trials.

As an example, Figure 3.1 displays the results of a simulation of R&E's external funding needs using Crystal Ball, a popular simulation program. Our original forecast assumed a 25 percent sales growth in 2006, but this, of course, is only a guess. The figure shows a frequency chart of R&E's external funds required as the estimated sales growth varies in a range of about 10 to 40 percent. To generate the chart, I selected a bell-shaped, normal distribution for the sales growth estimate from the gallery of distributions provided by Crystal Ball and shown at the bottom of the figure. Then, using the spreadsheet model in Table 3.5, I asked Crystal Ball to display the results of 500 trials as a frequency chart. In less than a minute, I had the result shown. I could have allowed virtually all of the assumptions in the spreadsheet to vary, and to vary in correlation with one another, but this is enough to provide a taste of how easy simulations have become.

The principal advantage of simulation relative to sensitivity analysis and scenario analysis is that it allows all of the uncertain input variables to change at once. The principal disadvantage, in my experience, is that the results are often hard to interpret. One reason is that few executives are used to thinking about future events in terms of probabilities. The frequency chart in Figure 3.1 indicates there is a 2.00 percent chance that R&E's external funding needs will exceed $1.844 million. Is a 2.00 percent chance so remote that R&E can safely raise less than $1.844 million, or might the prudent course be to raise even more just in case? How big a chance should the company be willing to take that it will be unable to meet its external funding requirement: 10 percent, 2 percent, or is .02 percent the right number? The answer isn't obvious. A second difficulty with simulation in practice recalls President Eisenhower's dictum "It's not the plans but the planning that matters." With simulation much of the

FIGURE 3.1   Simulating R&E Supplies' Need for External Funding: Frequency Chart and Distribution Gallery for Sales Growth

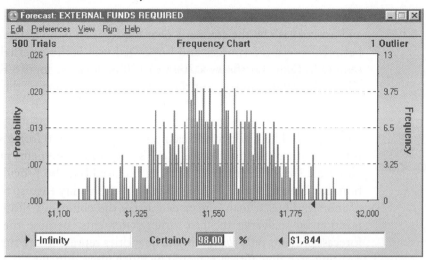

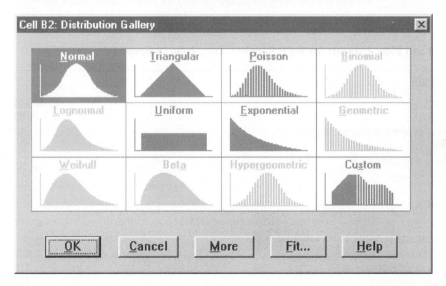

"planning" goes on inside the computer, and managers too often see only the results. Consequently, they may not gain the depth of insight into the company and its future prospects that they would if they used simpler techniques.

The complete Crystal Ball program is available on a one-week trial basis at **www.crystalball.com.** For practice using the program to build a simulation model, see problem 12 at the end of this chapter.

Cash Flow Forecasts

A cash flow forecast is simply a listing of all anticipated sources of cash to and uses of cash by the company over the forecast period. The difference between forecasted sources and forecasted uses is the external financing required. Table 3.6 shows a 2006 cash flow forecast for R&E Supplies. The assumptions underlying the forecast are the same as those used to construct R&E's initial pro forma statements in Table 3.3.

Cash flow forecasts are straightforward, easily understood, and commonly used. Their principal weakness compared to pro forma statements is that they are less informative. R&E's pro forma statements not only indicate the size of the external funding required but also provide information that is useful for evaluating the company's ability to raise this amount of money. Thus, a loan officer can assess the company's future financial position by analyzing the pro forma statements. Because the cash flow forecast presents only *changes* in the quantities represented, a similar analysis using cash flow forecasts would be much more difficult.

TABLE 3.6 **Cash Flow Forecast for R&E Supplies, Inc., 2006 ($ thousands)**

Sources of Cash	
Net income	$ 234
Depreciation	50
Decreases in assets or increases in liabilities:	
Increase in accounts payable	370
Increase in accrued wages	4
Total sources of cash	$ 658
Uses of Cash	
Dividends	$ 117
Increases in assets or decreases in liabilities:	
Increase in cash and securities	859
Increase in accounts receivable	714
Increase in inventories	195
Increase in prepaid expenses	2
Investment in fixed assets	43
Decrease in long-term debt	100
Decrease in short-term debt	50
Total uses of cash	$2,080

Determination of external funding required:
    Total sources + External funding required = Total uses
        $658,000 + External funding required = $2,080,000
External funding required = $1,422,000

Cash Budgets

A *cash budget* is what you and I are apt to prepare when we are worried about our personal finances. We make a list of all expected cash inflows and outflows over coming months, and earnestly hope the former exceeds the latter. When the news is bad, and outflows exceed inflows, we know that reduced savings or a new loan is in our future. Similarly, a corporate cash budget is a simple listing of projected cash receipts and disbursements over a forecast period for the purpose of anticipating future cash shortages or surpluses. Many firms use a nested set of financial forecasts, relying on pro forma projections to plan operations and estimate external funding needs, and cash budgets, prepared on a weekly or even daily basis, to manage short-term cash.

The only conceptual challenge to preparing a cash budget for a company lies in the fact that company accounts are based on accrual accounting, while cash budgets use strictly cash accounting. This makes it necessary to translate company projections regarding sales and purchases into their cash equivalents. For credit sales, this means adjusting for the time lag between a sale and receipt of cash from the sale. Analogously, for credit purchases, it means adjusting for the lag between the purchase of an item and payment of the resulting account payable.

To see the mechanics, Table 3.7 presents Jill Clair Fashions' monthly cash budget for the third quarter of 2006. Jill Clair is a modest-sized manufacturer and distributor of women's apparel. Sales are quite seasonal, reaching a peak in midsummer, and the company treasurer is concerned about maintaining adequate cash balances during this critical period. For simplicity, the table presents a monthly cash budget. In practice, a treasurer working with volatile sales and limited cash would likely want weekly and perhaps daily budgets as well.

The top part of the budget, labeled "Determination of Cash Collections and Payments," makes the necessary conversion between accrual and cash accounting. The company's stated credit terms are 2%/10 net 30 days, meaning customers receive a 2 percent discount when they pay within 10 days, but otherwise the bill is due in full in 30 days. Based on past experience, the treasurer anticipates that 30 percent of customers will pay in the month of purchase and claim the discount, 60 percent will pay in the following month, and 10 percent will pay two months after purchase. Looking at July's numbers, we see that projected sales are $300,000 but collections are only $223,000. Approximately $88,000 of this total comes from collections of sales made in July. This figure equals 30 percent of 98 percent of July's sales. (Ninety-eight percent reflects the two percent discount for prompt payment.) Approximately $120,000 of July collections comes from

TABLE 3.7 **Cash Budget for Jill Clair Fashions, 3rd Quarter, 2006 ($ thousands)**

	Actual		Projected		
	May	**June**	**July**	**Aug.**	**Sept.**
I. Determination of Cash Collections and Payments					
Projected sales	$150	$200	$300	$400	$250
Collection of sales					
During month of sale			88	118	74
(0.3) (.98) (month's sales)					
During 1st month after sale			120	180	240
0.6 (prior month's sales)					
During 2nd month after sale			15	20	30
0.1 (sales two months ago)					
Total collections			$223	$318	$344
Purchases 0.6 (next month's projected sales)		$180	$240	$150	
Payments (prior month's purchases)			$180	$240	$150
II. Cash Receipts and Disbursements					
Total collections (from above)			$223	$318	$344
Sale of used equipment				79	
Total cash receipts			$223	$397	$344
Payments (from above)			180	240	150
Wages and salaries			84	82	70
Interest payments			8	8	8
Rent			10	10	10
Taxes					12
Principal payment on loan					40
Other disbursements			1	27	14
Total cash disbursements			$283	$367	$304
Net cash receipts (disbursements)			$(60)	$ 30	$ 40
III. Determination of Cash Surplus or Deficit					
Beginning cash			220	160	190
Net cash receipts (disbursements)			(60)	30	40
Ending cash			160	190	230
Minimum desired cash			200	200	200
Cash surplus (deficit)			$ (40)	$ (10)	$ 30

sales booked in June, reflecting the expectation that 60 percent of June buyers will pay the following month. Finally, $15,000 of July collections originates from sales made two months ago and equals 10 percent of May sales.

Jill Clair purchases raw materials equal to 60 percent of next month's projected sales. So with August projected sales of $400,000, July purchases are

$240,000. However, because the company pays its accounts payable 30 days after purchase, cash payments equal June purchases, or only $180,000.

The second section in Table 3.7, labeled "Cash Receipts and Disbursements," records all anticipated cash inflows and outflows for each month. Also appearing is the monthly difference between these quantities, labeled "Net cash receipts (disbursements)." Observe that Jill Clair anticipates receiving cash from two sources: collections from credit sales, as estimated in the top part of the table, and an additional $79,000 from the sale of used equipment. Other possible sources of cash not contemplated here include such things as proceeds from a new bank loan, interest income, and cash from the exercise of employee stock options. In the lower part of this section, cash disbursements record all anticipated cash payments for each month, including payments for credit purchases as estimated above, wages and salaries, interest payments, rent, taxes, a loan principal payment, and other miscellaneous disbursements. In each category the treasurer has recorded the anticipated cash cost in the month paid. Note that depreciation does not appear among the disbursements because as a noncash charge it has no place in a cash budget.

The bottom portion of Jill Clair's cash budget shows the effect of the company's anticipated cash inflows and outflows on its need for external funding. The logic is quite simple. One month's ending cash balance becomes the next month's beginning balance, and throughout each month cash rises or falls according to that month's net cash receipts or disbursements. For example, August's beginning cash balance of $160,000 is July's ending balance, and during August net cash receipts of $30,000 boost cash to an ending figure to $190,000. Comparing each month's ending cash balance with the minimum desired level of cash as specified by the treasurer yields a monthly estimate of the company's cash surplus or deficit. A deficit measures the amount of money the company must raise on the forecast date to cover anticipated disbursements, and leave ending cash at the desired minimum. A forecasted surplus, on the other hand, means the company can cover anticipated disbursements and still have cash in excess of the desired minimum. Stated differently, the cash surplus or deficit figures in a cash budget are equal in all respects to the figures for external funding required appearing on a pro forma projection or a cash flow forecast. They all measure the company's future need for external financing or its projected surplus cash.

Jill Clair's cash budget suggests that the treasurer needs to borrow $40,000 in July, but should be able to reduce the loan to $10,000 the following month, and will be able to repay the loan in full by the end of September. In fact, it appears the company will have $30,000 in excess cash by then, which can be used to pay down other debt, purchase marketable securities, or invest elsewhere in the business.

The Techniques Compared

Although the formats differ, it should be a relief to learn that all of the forecasting techniques considered in this chapter produce the same results. As long as the assumptions are the same and no arithmetic or accounting mistakes are made, all of the techniques will produce the same estimate of external funding required. Moreover, if your accounting skills are up to the task, it is possible to reconcile one format with another. Problems 6, 7, and 8 at the end of the chapter allow you to demonstrate this fact for yourself.

A second reassuring fact is that regardless of which forecasting technique is used, the resulting estimate of new financing needs is not biased by inflation. Consequently, there is no need to resort to elaborate inflation adjustments when making financial forecasts in an inflationary environment. This is not to say that the need for new financing is independent of the inflation rate; indeed, as will become apparent in the next chapter, the financing needs of most companies rise with inflation. Rather, it means that direct application of the previously described forecasting techniques will correctly indicate the need for external financing even in the presence of inflation.

Mechanically, then, the three forecasting techniques are equivalent, and the choice of which one to use can depend on the purpose of the forecast. For most planning purposes and for credit analysis, I recommend pro forma statements because they present the information in a form suitable for additional financial analysis. For short-term forecasting and the management of cash, the cash budget is appropriate. A cash flow forecast lies somewhere between the other two. It presents a broader picture of company operations than a cash budget does and is easier to construct and more accessible to accounting novices than pro formas are, but it is also less informative than pro formas.

Planning in Large Companies

In a well-run company, financial forecasts are only the tip of the planning iceberg. Executives throughout the organization devote substantial time and effort to developing strategic and operating plans that eventually become the basis for the company's financial plans. This formalized planning process is especially important in large, multidivision corporations because it is frequently a key means of coordination, communication, and motivation within the organization.

In a large company, effective planning usually involves three formal stages that recur on an annual cycle. In broad perspective, these stages

A Problem with Depreciation

XYZ Corporation is forecasting its financing needs for next year. The original forecast shows an external financing need of $10 million. On reviewing the forecast, the production manager, having just returned from an accounting seminar, recommends increasing depreciation next year—for reporting purposes only, not for tax purposes—by $1 million. She explains, rather condescendingly, that this will reduce net fixed assets by $1 million and, because a reduction of an asset is a source of cash, this will reduce the external funding required by a like amount. Explain why the production manager is incorrect.

Answer: Increasing depreciation will reduce net fixed assets. However, it will also reduce provision for taxes and earnings after tax by the same amount. Since both are liability accounts and reduction of a liability is a use of cash, the whole exercise is a wash with respect to determination of external financing requirements. This is consistent with cash budgeting, which ignores depreciation entirely. Here is a numerical example:

	Original Depreciation	Increase in Depreciation	Change in Liability Account
Operating income	$10,000	$10,000	
Depreciation	4,000	5,000	
Earnings before tax	6,000	5,000	
Provision for tax @ 40%	2,400	2,000	−400
Earnings after tax	3,600	3,000	
Dividends	1,000	1,000	
Additions to retained earnings	$ 2,600	$ 2,000	−$600
Total change in liabilities			−$1,000

can be viewed as a progressive narrowing of the strategic choices under consideration. In the first stage, headquarters executives and division managers hammer out a corporate strategy. This involves a broad-ranging analysis of the market threats and opportunities the company faces, an assessment of the company's own strengths and weaknesses, and a determination of the performance goals to be sought by each of the company's business units. At this initial stage, the process is creative and largely qualitative. The role of financial forecasts is limited to outlining in general terms the resource constraints the company faces and testing the financial feasibility of alternative strategies.

In the second stage, division managers and department personnel translate the qualitative, market-oriented goals established in stage 1 into a set of internal division activities deemed necessary to achieve the agreed-on goals. For example, if a stage 1 goal is to increase product X's market share by at least 2 percent in the next 18 months, the stage 2 plans define what division management must do to achieve this objective. At this point, top management will likely have indicated in general terms the resources to be allocated to each division, although no specific spending plans will have been authorized. So division management will find it necessary to prepare at least rough financial forecasts to ensure that its plans are generally consistent with senior management's resource commitments.

In the third stage of the planning process, department personnel develop a set of quantitative plans and budgets based on the activities defined in stage 2. This essentially involves putting a price tag on the agreed-on division activities. The price tag appears in two forms: operating budgets and capital budgets. Although each company has its own definition of which expenditures are to appear on which budget, capital budgets customarily include expenditures on costly, long-lived assets, whereas operating budgets include recurring expenditures such as materials, salaries, and so on.

The integration of these detailed divisional budgets at headquarters produces the corporation's financial forecast. If management has been realistic about available resources throughout the planning process, the forecast will contain few surprises. If not, headquarters executives may discover that in the aggregate, the spending plans of the divisions exceed available resources and some revisions in division budgets will be necessary.

As company plans evolve from broad strategies to concrete marching orders, the forecasting techniques described in this chapter take on increasing importance, first as a means of articulating the financial implications of a chosen strategy, and then as a vehicle for testing alternative strategies. In proper perspective, then, financial forecasting is a family of techniques for translating creative ideas and strategies into concrete action plans, and while proper technique cannot guarantee success, the lack of same certainly heightens the odds of failure.

SUMMARY

1. This chapter presented the principal techniques of financial forecasting and planning.
2. Pro forma statements are the best all-around means of financial forecasting. They are a projection of the company's income statement and balance sheet at the end of the forecast period.
3. Percent-of-sales forecasting is a simple and useful technique in which many income statement and many balance sheet entries are assumed to change in proportion to sales.
4. Most operating managers are concerned chiefly with the income statement. When the goal is forecasting the need for outside financing, the balance sheet is the principal source of concern.

5. Financial forecasting involves the extrapolation of past trends and agreed-on changes into the future. Financial planning occurs when management evaluates the forecasts and considers possible modifications.

6. Computers are valuable allies in financial planning. They gracefully solve the interdependency problem between interest expense and external funding needs, and they greatly facilitate use of sensitivity analysis, scenario analysis, and simulation to "stress test" the plans.

7. A cash budget is a less general way to forecast than pro forma statements. It consists of a list of anticipated cash receipts and disbursements and their net effect on the firm's cash balances. When done correctly and using the same assumptions, cash budgets and pro forma statements generate the same estimated need for outside financing.

8. Planning in most large companies involves three continuing cycles: (*a*) a strategic planning cycle in which senior management is most active, (*b*) an operational cycle in which divisional managers translate qualitative strategic goals into concrete plans, and (*c*) a budgeting cycle that essentially puts a price tag on the operational plans. Financial forecasting and planning are increasingly important in each succeeding stage of the process.

ADDITIONAL RESOURCES

Benninga, Simon. *Financial Modeling*. 2nd ed. Cambridge, MA:
The MIT Press, 2000. 622 pages.
  Covers a number of financial models, including pro forma forecasting and simulation techniques, as well as more advanced models such as portfolio analysis, options, duration, and immunization. Microsoft Excel is used throughout. $70.00.
Mayes, Timothy R., and Todd M. Shank. *Financial Analysis with Microsoft Excel*. 3rd ed. South-Western College Publishing, 2003, 432 pages.
  An introductory-level look at the use of Microsoft Excel for financial analysis. Nowhere near as sophisticated or ambitious as the Benninga book. $50.00.

SOFTWARE

Written to accompany this text, PROFORMA converts user-supplied information and assumptions about a company into pro forma financial forecasts for as many as five years into the future. It also performs a ratio analysis and a sustainable growth analysis of the results. Additional "what if" analysis is easy to perform. For a complimentary copy, visit **www.mhhe.com/higgins8e.**

Visit us at www.mhhe.com/higgins8e

WEBSITES

www.crystalball.com
Visit this site to download a full-featured, one-week trial copy of Crystal Ball, a powerful addition to Excel for simulation analysis.

www.extension.iastate.edu/Pages/Excel/homepage.html
An interactive Excel tutorial for beginners prepared by a group of university computer experts.

www.exinfm.com/free_spreadsheets.html
Links to 69, and counting, free, Excel computer programs for use in analyzing a wide variety of financial issues. Gathered by a financial consultant.

PROBLEMS

Answers to odd-numbered problems are at end of book. For additional problems with answers, see **www.mhhe.com/higgins8e.**

1. Suppose you constructed a pro forma balance sheet for a company and the estimate for external financing required was negative. How would you interpret this result?

2. Harlin Fencing Company's sales, all on credit, for the past three months were:

August	September	October
$60,000	$90,000	$45,000

   a. Estimate Harlin's cash receipts in October if the company's collection period is 30 days.

   b. Estimate Harlin's cash receipts in October if the company's collection period is 45 days.

3. Suppose you constructed a pro forma balance sheet and a cash budget for a company for the same time period and the external financing required from the pro forma forecast exceeded the cash deficit estimated on the cash budget. How would you interpret this result?

4. Table 3.5 presents a computer spreadsheet for estimating R&E Supplies' external financing required for 2006. The text mentions that with modifications to the equations for equity and net sales, the forecast can easily be extended through 2007. Write the modified equations for equity and net sales.

5. Using a computer spreadsheet, the information presented below, and the modified equations determined in question 4 above, extend the forecast for R&E Supplies contained in Table 3.5 through 2007. Is R&E's external financing required in 2007 higher or lower than in 2006?

R&E Supplies Assumptions for 2007 ($ thousands)			
Growth rate in net sales	30.0%	Tax rate	45.0%
Cost of good sold/net sales	86.0%	Dividend/earnings after tax	50.0%
General, selling, and administrative expenses/net sales	11.0%	Current assets/net sales	29.0%
		Net fixed assets	$270
Long-term debt	$560	Current liabilities/net sales	14.4%
Current portion long-term debt	$100		
Interest rate	10.0%		

6. This and the following two problems demonstrate that pro forma forecasts, cash budgets, and cash flow forecasts all yield the same estimated need for external financing—provided you don't make any mistakes. For problems 6, 7, and 8, you may ignore the effect of added borrowing on interest expense.

   The treasurer of Pepperton, Inc., a wholesale distributor of household appliances, wants to estimate his company's cash balances for the first three months of 2006. Using the information below, construct a monthly cash budget for Pepperton for January through March 2006. Does it appear from your results that the treasurer should be concerned about investing excess cash or looking for a bank loan?

Pepperton Selected Information	
Sales (20 percent for cash, the rest on 30-day credit terms):	
2005 Actual	
October	$360,000
November	420,000
December	1,200,000
2006 Projected	
January	$600,000
February	240,000
March	240,000
Purchases (all on 60-day terms):	
2005 Actual	
October	$510,000
November	540,000
December	1,200,000

(Continued)

Pepperton Selected Information
Sales (20 percent for cash, the rest on 30-day credit terms):

2006 Projected

January	$300,000
February	120,000
March	120,000
Wages payable monthly	$180,000
Principal payment on debt due in March	210,000
Interest due in March	90,000
Dividend payable in March	300,000
Taxes payable in February	180,000
Addition to accumulated depreciation in March	30,000
Cash balance on January 1, 2006	$300,000
Minimum desired cash balance	150,000

7. Continuing problem 6, Pepperton's annual income statement and balance sheet for December 31, 2005 appear below. Additional information about the company's accounting methods and the treasurer's expectations for the first quarter of 2006 appear in the footnotes.

a. Use this information and the information in problem 6 to construct a pro forma income statement for the first quarter of 2006 and a pro forma balance sheet for March 31, 2006. What is your estimated external financing need for March 31?

b. Does the March 31, 2006, estimated external financing equal your cash surplus (deficit) for this date from your cash budget in problem 6? Should it?

c. Do your pro forma forecasts tell you more than your cash budget does about Pepperton's financial prospects?

d. What do your pro forma income statement and balance sheet tell you about Pepperton's need for external financing on February 28, 2006?

Pepperton Annual Income Statement
December 31, 2005 ($ thousands)

Net sales	$6,000
Cost of goods sold[1]	3,900
Gross profits	2,100
Selling and administrative expenses[2]	1,620
Interest expense	90
Depreciation[3]	90
Net profit before tax	300
Tax (33%)	99
Net profit after tax	$ 201

(Continued)

Balance Sheet
December 31, 2005 ($ thousands)

Assets	
Cash	$ 300
Accounts receivable	960
Inventory	1,800
Total current assets	3,060
Gross fixed assets	900
Accumulated depreciation	150
Net fixed assets	750
Total assets	$3,810
Liabilities	
Bank loan	$ 0
Accounts payable	1,740
Miscellaneous accruals[4]	60
Current portion long-term debt[5]	210
Taxes payable	300
Total current liabilities	2,310
Long-term debt	990
Shareholders' equity	510
Total liabilities and equity	$3,810

[1]Cost of goods sold consists entirely of items purchased in first quarter.
[2]Selling and administrative expenses consist entirely of wages.
[3]Depreciation is at the rate of $30,000 per quarter.
[4]Miscellaneous accruals are not expected to change in the first quarter.
[5]$210 due March 2006. No payments for remainder of year.

8. Based on your answer to question 7, construct a first-quarter 2006 cash flow forecast for Pepperton.

9. Toys-4-Kids manufactures plastic toys. Sales and production are highly seasonal. Below is a quarterly pro forma forecast indicating external financing needs for 2006. Assumptions are in parentheses.

   a. How do you interpret the negative numbers for income taxes in the first two quarters?

   b. Why are cash balances in the first two quarters greater than the minimum required $200,000? How were these numbers determined?

   c. How was "external financing required" appearing at the bottom of the forecast determined?

   d. Do you think Toys-4-Kids will be able to borrow the external financing required as indicated by the forecast?

Toys-4-Kids
2006 Quarterly Pro Forma Forecast
($ 000 thousands)

	Qtr 1	Qtr 2	Qtr 3	Qtr 4
Net sales	$ 300	$ 375	$3,200	$5,000
Cost of sales (70% of sales)	210	263	2,240	3,500
Gross profit	90	113	960	1,500
Operating expenses	560	560	560	560
Profit before tax	(470)	(448)	400	940
Income taxes	(188)	(179)	160	376
Profit after tax	$ (282)	$ (269)	$ 240	$ 564
Cash (minimum balance = $200,000)	$1,235	$ 927	$ 200	$ 200
Accounts receivable (75% of quarterly sales)	225	281	2,400	3,750
Inventory (12/31/05 balance = $500,000)	500	500	500	500
Current assets	1,960	1,990	3,120	4,450
Net plant and equipment	1,000	1,000	1,000	1,000
Total assets	$2,960	$2,708	$4,100	$5,450
Accounts payable (10% of quarterly sales)	30	38	320	500
Accrued taxes (payments quarterly in arrears)	(188)	(179)	160	376
Current liabilities	(158)	(142)	480	876
Long-term debt	400	400	400	400
Equity (12/31/05 balance = $3,000,000)	2,718	2,450	2,690	3,254
Total liabilities and equity	$2,960	$2,708	$3,570	$4,530
External financing required	$ 0	$ 0	$ 530	$ 920

10. Continuing with Toys-4-Kids introduced in the preceding problem, the company's production manager has argued for years that it is inefficient to produce on a seasonal basis. She believes the company should switch to level production throughout the year, building up finished goods inventory in the first two quarters to meet the peak selling needs in the last two. She believes the company can reduce its cost of goods sold from 70 to 65 percent with level production.

a. Prepare a revised pro forma forecast assuming level production. In your forecast assume that quarterly accounts payable under level production equal 10 percent of *average* quarterly sales for the year. To estimate quarterly inventory use the following two formulas.

$$\text{Inventory}_{eoq} = \text{Inventory}_{boq} + \text{Quarterly production} - \text{Quarterly cost of sales}$$

Quarterly production = Annual cost of sales/4

where eoq and boq refer to end of quarter and beginning of quarter, respectively. Please ignore the effect of increased external financing required on interest expense.

b. What is the effect of the switch from seasonal to level production on annual profits?

c. What effect does the switch have on the company's ending inventory? On the company's need for external financing?

d. Do you think the company will be able to borrow the amount of money required by level production? What obsolescence risks does the company incur by building up inventory in anticipation of future sales? Might this be a concern to lenders?

STANDARD
&POOR'S

11. You will need to use the Standard & Poor's Market Insight website (**www.mhhe.com/edumarketinsight**) for this problem. Market Insight presents a spreadsheet entitled "Forecasted Values." (Excel Analytics, Valuation Data, Forecasted Values.)

a. How are these forecasts generated? Are they more than simple extrapolation of past trends?

b. How useful might these forecasts be for projecting a company's future financing needs?

12. This problem asks you to construct a simple simulation model. If you do not own simulation software, you can download to your computer a free, full-strength version of Crystal Ball for a one-week trial. Point your browser to **www.crystalball.com** and select download.

a. Problem 5 above asked you to extend the forecast for R&E Supplies contained in Table 3.5 through 2007. Using the same spreadsheet, simulate R&E Supplies' external funding requirements in 2007 under the following assumptions.

(1) Represent the growth rate in net sales as a triangular distribution with a mean of 30 percent and a range 25 percent to 35 percent.

(2) Represent the interest rate as a uniform distribution varying from 9 percent to 11 percent.

(3) Represent the tax rate as a lognormal distribution with a mean of 45 percent and a standard deviation of 2 percent.

b. If the treasurer wants to be 95 percent certain of raising enough money in 2007, how much should he raise? (Grab the triangle below the frequency chart on the right and move it to the left until 95.00 appears in the "Certainty" window.)

eXcel

13. This problem asks you to prepare one- and five-year financial forecasts for Jasmine Apparel Company. An Excel spreadsheet containing the company's 2005 financial statements and management's projections is available for download at **www.mhhe.com/higgins8e**. (Select Student Edition > Choose a Chapter > Excel Spreadsheets.) Use this information to answer the questions posed in the spreadsheet.

14. The financial statements and additional information for Suunto Equipment Corp. appear at **www.mhhe.com/higgins8e.** (Select Student Edition > Choose a Chapter > Excel Spreadsheets.) The company's fiscal year end is September 30. Suunto's management wants to estimate the company's cash balances for the last three months of calendar year 2005, which are the first three months of fiscal year 2006. The questions accompanying the spreadsheet ask you to prepare a monthly cash budget, pro forma financial statements, and a cash flow forecast for this period.

CHAPTER FOUR

Managing Growth

Alas, the road to success is always under repair.

Anonymous

Growth and its management present special problems in financial planning, in part because many executives see growth as something to be maximized. They reason simply that as growth increases, the firm's market share and profits should rise as well. From a financial perspective, however, growth is not always a blessing. Rapid growth can put considerable strain on a company's resources, and unless management is aware of this effect and takes active steps to control it, rapid growth can lead to bankruptcy. Companies can literally grow broke. It is a sad truth that rapid growth has driven almost as many companies into bankruptcy as slow growth has. It is doubly sad to realize that those companies that grew too fast met the market test by providing a product people wanted and failed only because they lacked the financial acumen to manage their growth properly.

At the other end of the spectrum, companies growing too slowly have a different but no less pressing set of financial concerns. As will become apparent, if these companies fail to appreciate the financial implications of slow growth, they will come under increasing pressure from restive shareholders, irate board members, and potential raiders. In either case, the financial management of growth is a topic worthy of close inspection.

We begin our look at the financial dimensions of growth by defining a company's *sustainable growth rate*. This is the maximum rate at which company sales can increase without depleting financial resources. Then we look at the options open to management when a company's target growth rate exceeds its sustainable growth rate and, conversely, when growth falls below sustainable levels. An important conclusion will be that growth is not necessarily something to be maximized. In many companies, it may be necessary to limit growth to conserve financial strength. In others, the money used to finance unprofitable growth might better be returned to owners. The need to limit growth is a hard lesson for operating managers used to thinking that more is better; it is a critical one, however, because operating executives bear major responsibility for managing growth.

Sustainable Growth

We can think of successful companies as passing through a predictable life cycle. The cycle begins with a startup phase in which the company loses money while developing products and establishing a foothold in the market. This is followed by a rapid growth phase in which the company is profitable but is growing so rapidly that it needs regular infusions of outside financing. The third phase is maturity, characterized by a decline in growth and a switch from absorbing outside financing to generating more cash than the firm can profitably reinvest. The last phase is decline, during which the company is perhaps marginally profitable, generates more cash than it can reinvest internally, and suffers declining sales. Mature and declining companies frequently devote considerable time and money to seeking investment opportunities in new products or firms that are still in their growth phase.

We begin our discussion by looking at the growth phase, when financing needs are most pressing. Later we will consider the growth problems of mature and declining firms. Central to our discussion is the notion of sustainable growth. Intuitively, sustainable growth is merely a formalization of the old adage "It takes money to make money." Increased sales require more assets of all types, which must be paid for. Retained profits and the accompanying new borrowing generate some cash, but only limited amounts. Unless the company is prepared to sell common stock or borrow excessive amounts, this limit puts a ceiling on the growth it can achieve without straining its resources. This is the firm's sustainable growth rate.

The Sustainable Growth Equation

Let's begin by writing a simple equation to express the dependence of growth on financial resources. For this purpose, assume

- The company has a target capital structure and a target dividend policy it wishes to maintain.

- Management is unable or unwilling to sell new equity.

We will say more about these assumptions soon. For now it is enough to realize that although they may not be appropriate for all firms, the assumptions describe a great many.

Figure 4.1 shows the rapidly growing company's plight. It represents the firm's balance sheet as two rectangles, one for assets and the other for liabilities and owners' equity. The two long, unshaded rectangles represent the balance sheet at the beginning of the year. The rectangles are, of course, the same height because assets must equal liabilities plus owners'

FIGURE 4.1   New Sales Require New Assets, Which Must Be Financed

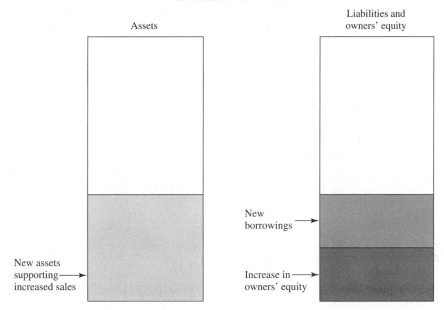

equity. Now, if the company wants to increase sales during the coming year, it must also increase assets such as inventory, accounts receivable, and productive capacity. The shaded area on the assets side of the figure represents the value of new assets necessary to support the increased sales. Because the company will not be selling equity by assumption, the cash required to pay for this increase in assets must come from retained profits and increased liabilities.

We want to know what limits the rate at which the company in Figure 4.1 can increase sales. Assuming, in effect, that all parts of a business expand in strict proportion like a balloon, what limits the rate of this expansion? To find out, start in the lower-right corner of the figure with owners' equity. As equity grows, the firm can borrow more money without altering the capital structure; together, the growth of liabilities and the growth of equity determine the rate at which assets expand. This, in turn, limits the growth rate in sales. So after all the dust settles, what limits the growth rate in sales is the rate at which owners' equity expands. A company's sustainable growth rate therefore is nothing more than its growth rate in equity.

Letting g^* represent the sustainable growth rate,

$$g^* = \frac{\text{Change in equity}}{\text{Equity}_{\text{bop}}}$$

where bop denotes beginning-of-period equity. Because the firm will not be selling any new shares by assumption, the only source of new equity will be from retained profits, so we can rewrite this expression as

$$g^* = \frac{R \times \text{Earnings}}{\text{Equity}_{\text{bop}}}$$

where R is the firm's "retention rate." R is the fraction of earnings retained in the business, or 1 minus the dividend payout ratio. If a company's target dividend policy is to distribute 10 percent of earnings as dividends, its retention ratio is 90 percent.

The ratio "Earnings/Equity" in this expression should look familiar; it is the firm's return on equity, or ROE. Thus

$$g^* = R \times \text{ROE}_{\text{bop}}$$

Finally, recalling the levers of performance discussed in Chapter 2, we can rewrite this expression yet again as

$$g^* = PRA\hat{T}$$

where P, A, and $\hat{T}$ are our old friends from Chapter 2, the levers of performance. Recall that P is the profit margin, A is the asset turnover ratio, and $\hat{T}$ is the assets-to-equity ratio. The assets-to-equity ratio wears a hat here as a reminder that it is assets divided by *beginning-of-period* equity instead of end-of-period equity as defined in Chapter 2.

This is the sustainable growth equation.[1] Let's see what it tells us. Given the assumptions just noted, the equation says that a company's sustainable growth rate in sales, g^*, equals the product of four ratios, P, R, A, and $\hat{T}$. Two of these ratios, P and A, summarize the operating performance of the business, while the other two describe the firm's principal financial policies. Thus, the retention rate, R, captures management's attitudes toward the distribution of dividends, and the assets-to-equity ratio, $\hat{T}$, reflects its policies regarding financial leverage.

An important implication of the sustainable growth equation is that g^* *is the only growth rate in sales that is consistent with stable values of the four ratios.* If a company increases sales at any rate other than g^*, one or more of the ratios *must* change. This means that when a company grows at a rate in excess of its sustainable growth rate, it had better improve operations (represented by an increase in the profit margin or the asset turnover ratio) or prepare to alter its financial policies (represented by increasing its retention rate or its financial leverage).

---

[1] I shall refrain from admonishing you to avoid "$\text{pra}\hat{t}$" falls.

Too Much Growth

This is the crux of the sustainable growth problem for rapidly expanding firms: Because increasing operating efficiency is not always possible and altering financial policies is not always wise, we see that it is entirely possible for a company to grow too fast for its own good. This is particularly true for smaller companies, which may do inadequate financial planning. Such companies see sales growth as something to be maximized and think too little of the financial consequences. They do not realize that rapid growth has them on a treadmill; the faster they grow, the more cash they need, even when they are profitable. They can meet this need for a time by increasing leverage, but eventually they will reach their debt capacity, lenders will refuse additional credit requests, and the companies will find themselves without the cash to pay their bills. All of this can be prevented if managers understand that growth above the company's sustainable rate creates financial problems that must be anticipated and solved.

Balanced Growth

Here is another way to think about sustainable growth. Recalling that a company's return on assets, ROA, can be expressed as the product of its profit margin times its asset turnover, we can rewrite the sustainable growth equation as[2]

$$g^* = R\hat{T} \times \text{ROA}$$

Here R and $\hat{T}$ reflect the company's financial policies, while ROA summarizes its operating performance. So if a company's retention ratio is 25 percent and its assets-to-equity ratio is 1.6, its sustainable growth equation becomes simply

$$g^* = 0.4 \times \text{ROA}$$

This equation says that given stable financial policies, sustainable growth varies linearly with return on assets. Figure 4.2 graphs this relationship with sales growth on the vertical axis, ROA on the horizontal axis, and the sustainable growth equation as the upward-sloping, solid, diagonal line. The line bears the label "Balanced growth" because the company can self-finance only the sales growth–ROA combinations lying on this line. All growth-return combinations lying off this line generate either cash deficits or cash surpluses. Thus, rapidly growing, marginally profitable

[2] Strictly speaking, this equation should be expressed in terms of return on invested capital, not return on assets, but the gain in precision is too modest to justify the added mathematical complexity. See Gordon Donaldson, *Managing Corporate Wealth* (New York: Praeger, 1984), Chapter 4, for a more rigorous exposition.

FIGURE 4.2 **A Graphical Representation of Sustainable Growth**

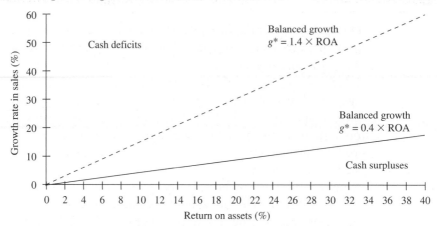

companies will plot in the upper-left portion of the graph, implying cash deficits, while slowly expanding, highly profitable companies will plot in the lower-right portion, implying cash surpluses. I should emphasize that the phrase "self-finance" does not imply constant debt but rather a constant debt-to-equity ratio. Debt can increase but only in proportion to equity.

When a company experiences unbalanced growth of either the surplus or the deficit variety, it can move toward the balanced growth line in any of three ways: It can change its growth rate, alter its return on assets, or modify its financial policies. To illustrate the last option, suppose the company with the balanced growth line depicted in Figure 4.2 is in the deficit region of the graph and wants to reduce the deficit. One strategy would be to increase its retention ratio to, say, 50 percent and its assets-to-equity ratio to, say, 2.8 to 1, thereby changing its sustainable growth equation to

$$g^* = 1.4 \times \text{ROA}$$

In Figure 4.2, this is equivalent to rotating the balanced growth line upward to the left, as shown by the dotted line. Now any level of profitability will support a higher growth rate than before.

In this perspective, the sustainable growth rate is the nexus of all growth-return combinations yielding balanced growth, and the sustainable growth problem is that of managing the surpluses or deficits caused by unbalanced growth. We will return to strategies for managing growth after looking at a numerical example.

Biosite, Inc.'s Sustainable Growth Rate

To illustrate the growth management challenges a rapidly growing business faces, let's look at Biosite, Inc., a developer, manufacturer, and marketer of

TABLE 4.1 **A Sustainable Growth Analysis of Biosite, Inc., 2000–2004***

	2000	2001	2002	2003	2004
Required ratios:					
Profit margin, P (%)	11.2	10.3	12.7	14.3	16.9
Retention ratio, R (%)	100.0	100.0	100.0	100.0	100.0
Asset turnover, A (times)	0.66	0.64	0.80	0.89	0.86
Financial leverage, $\hat{T}$ (times)	1.46	1.41	1.44	1.80	1.85
Biosite's sustainable growth rate, g^* (%)	10.8	9.3	14.6	22.9	26.9
Biosite's actual growth rate in sales, g (%)	25.8	19.4	60.3	64.8	41.3

	What If?		
	Asset Turnover 0.96 Times	**Financial Leverage 1.95 Times**	**Both Occur**
Biosite's sustainable growth rate in 2004 (%)	30.0	28.3	31.6

*Totals may not add due to rounding.

medical diagnostic products in San Diego, California. If you wanted to test for parasites, drug abuse, or congestive heart failure, you would be wise to contact Biosite. Table 4.1 presents the company's actual and sustainable growth rates in sales from 2000 through 2004. For each year, I calculated Biosite's sustainable growth rate by plugging the four required ratios for the relevant year into the sustainable growth equation. I calculated the four required ratios from the company's financial statements, which are not shown. Observe that Biosite's actual growth rate exceeded its sustainable rate in every year by a considerable margin.

How did Biosite cope with actual growth above sustainable levels? A look at the four required ratios reveals that the company increased every ratio except R, which was already equal to 1.0. Comparing 2004 with 2000, Biosite's profit margin, asset turnover, and financial leverage rose, 51 percent, 30 percent, and 27 percent, respectively. Had Biosite not improved its operating performance, as reflected in its profit margin and asset turnover, the financial leverage required to generate the company's 2004 sustainable growth rate would have been almost twice as high as observed.[3]

Figure 4.3 says the same thing graphically. It shows Biosite's balanced growth lines in 2000 and 2004, and the growth-return combinations the

[3] Assume Biosite's profit margin and asset turnover had remained at 2000 levels of 11.2 percent and 0.66 times, respectively, and let Y equal the financial leverage ratio required to generate the company's 2004 sustainable growth rate.

$$26.9\% = 11.2\% \times 100.0\% \times 0.66 \times Y$$

Solving for Y, $Y = 3.64$.

FIGURE 4.3 Biosite, Inc.'s Sustainable Growth Challenges, 2000–2004

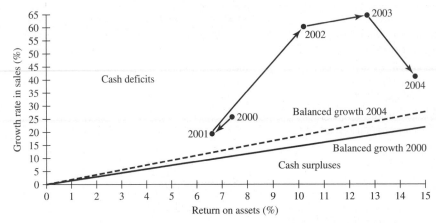

company achieved each year. Despite a significant increase in the slope of the company's balanced growth line, Biosite remained in the cash deficit portion of the graph throughout the period. The ongoing gap between the yearly growth-return combinations and the balanced growth lines confirms that despite the lower growth rate in 2004, Biosite's growth remains unbalanced, and thus a continuing challenge to management.

"What If" Questions

When management faces sustainable growth problems, the sustainable growth equation can be useful in searching for solutions. This is done through a series of "what if" questions as shown in the bottom portion of Table 4.1. We see, for example, that in coming years Biosite can raise its sustainable growth rate to 30.0 percent by speeding up its asset turnover from 0.86 to 0.96 times. Alternatively, it can boost its sustainable growth rate to 28.3 percent by raising its financial leverage to 1.95 times. Doing both simultaneously would raise sustainable growth to 31.6 percent.

What to Do When Actual Growth Exceeds Sustainable Growth

We have now developed the sustainable growth equation and illustrated its use for rapidly growing companies. The next question is: What should management do when actual growth exceeds sustainable growth? The first step is to determine how long the situation will continue. If the company's growth rate is likely to decline in the near future as the firm reaches maturity, the problem is only a transitory one that can probably be solved by further borrowing. In the future, when the actual growth rate falls below the sustainable rate, the company will switch from being

---

Dell Grows Up

Even well-known, successful companies such as $50 billion Dell, Inc., have experienced life-threatening growing pains. The company's young founder, Michael Dell, now admits that in 1993 Dell's growth spurt had come at the expense of a sound financial position. He says the company's cash reserves were down to $20 million at one point. "We could have used that up in a day or two. For a company our size, that was ridiculous. I realized we had to change the priorities."

Had Dell's priorities remained "growth, growth, growth," it might not be around today. Michael Dell founded Dell Computer before he was 20 years old. After several years of prodigious growth and with his company at the financial precipice, he lacked the expertise to manage the growth. Fortunately, he had the sense to hire more seasoned managers who could calm security analysts and steer Dell in a more conservative direction. Those managers urged Dell to focus on earnings and liquidity rather than sales growth. Slowing growth in 1994 cost the company market share, but it also helped convert a loss a year earlier into a $106.6 million profit. The company also instituted formal planning and budgeting processes. Today Dell is one of the world's largest computer manufacturers, with a healthy balance sheet, solid growth, and rapidly growing cash balances.

---

an absorber of cash to being a generator of cash and can repay the loans. For longer-term sustainable growth problems, some combination of the following strategies will be necessary.

- Sell new equity
- Increase financial leverage
- Reduce the dividend payout
- Prune away marginal activities
- Outsource some or all of production
- Increase prices
- Merge with a "cash cow"

Let's consider each of these strategies in more detail.

Sell New Equity

If a company is willing and able to raise new equity capital by selling shares, its sustainable growth problems vanish. The increased equity, plus whatever added borrowing it makes possible, become sources of cash with which to finance further growth.

The problem with this strategy is that it is unavailable to many companies and unattractive to others. In most countries throughout the world, equity markets are poorly developed or nonexistent. To sell equity in these countries, companies must go through the laborious and expensive task of seeking out investors one by one to buy the new shares. This is a difficult undertaking because without active stock market trading of the shares,

TABLE 4.2 **Sources of Capital to U.S. Nonfinancial Corporations, 1985–2004**

Source: Federal Reserve System, *Flow of Funds Accounts of the United States.* Available at http://www.federalreserve.gov/releases/z1/current/data.htm

Internal		
Retained profits	10.6%	
Depreciation	51.9	
Subtotal	62.4%	
External		
Increased liabilities	45.4%	
New equity issues	−7.9	
Subtotal	37.6%	
Total		100.0%

new investors will be minority owners of illiquid securities. Consequently, those investors interested in buying the new shares will be limited largely to family and friends of existing owners.

Even in countries with well-developed stock markets, such as the United States and Britain, many companies find it very difficult to raise new equity. This is particularly true of smaller concerns that, unless they have a glamorous product, find it difficult to secure the services of an investment banker to help them sell the shares. Without such help, the firms might just as well be in a country without developed markets, for a lack of trading in the stock will again restrict potential buyers largely to family and friends.

Finally, even many companies that are able to raise new equity prefer not to do so. This is evidenced in Table 4.2, which shows the sources of capital to U.S. nonfinancial corporations from 1985 through 2004. Observe that internal sources, depreciation and increases in retained earnings, were by far the most important sources of corporate capital, accounting for over 60 percent of the total. At the other extreme, *new equity has been not a source of capital at all but a use*, meaning American corporations on average retired more stock than they issued over this period.

We will return to the puzzling question of why companies do not issue more new equity at the end of the chapter. For now let us provisionally accept that many companies cannot or will not sell new stock, and consider other strategies for managing unsustainably rapid growth.

Increase Leverage

If selling new equity is not a solution to a company's sustainable growth problems, two other financial remedies are possible. One is to cut the dividend payout ratio, and the other is to increase financial leverage. A cut in the payout ratio raises sustainable growth by increasing the proportion of earnings retained in the business, while increasing the leverage ratio raises the amount of debt the company can add for each dollar of retained profits.

I like to think of increasing leverage as the "default" option, in two senses of the word. From a computer programming perspective, an increase in leverage will be what occurs by default when management does not plan ahead. Over time the company will find there is too little cash to pay creditors in a timely fashion, and accounts payable will rise by default. Increasing leverage is also the default option in the financial sense that creditors will eventually balk at rising debt levels and force the company into default—step one on the path to bankruptcy.

We will have considerably more to say about financial leverage in the next two chapters. It should be apparent already, however, that there is an upper limit to a company's use of debt financing. And part of the growth management challenge is to identify an appropriate degree of financial leverage for a company and to ensure this ceiling is not broached.

Reduce the Payout Ratio

Just as there is an upper limit to leverage, there is a lower limit of zero to a company's dividend payout ratio. Indeed, most companies are already at this limit, for in 1999 fewer than one company in four paid any dividends at all.[4] In general, owners' interest in dividend payments varies inversely with their perceptions of the company's investment opportunities. If owners believe the retained profits can be put to productive use earning attractive rates of return, they will happily forgo current dividends in favor of higher future ones. (There have been few complaints among eBay's shareholders about the lack of dividends.) On the other hand, if company investment opportunities do not promise attractive returns, a dividend cut will anger shareholders, prompting a decline in stock price. An additional concern for closely held companies is the effect of dividend changes on owners' income and on their tax obligations.

Profitable Pruning

Beyond modifications in financial policy, a company can make several operating adjustments to manage rapid growth. One is called "profitable pruning." During much of the 1960s and early 1970s, some financial

---

[4] Eugene F. Fama and Kenneth R. French, "Disappearing Dividends: Changing Firm Characteristics or Lower Propensity to Pay?" *Journal of Financial Economics,* April 2001, pp. 2–43.

experts emphasized the merits of product diversification. The idea was that companies could reduce risk by combining the income streams of businesses in different product markets. The thought was that as long as these income streams were not affected in exactly the same way by economic events, the variability inherent in each stream would "average out" when combined with others. We now recognize two problems with this conglomerate diversification strategy. First, although it may reduce the risks seen by management, it does nothing for the shareholders. If shareholders want diversification, they can get it on their own by just purchasing shares of different independent companies. Second, because companies have limited resources, they cannot be important competitors in a large number of product markets at the same time. Instead, they are apt to be followers in many markets, unable to compete effectively with the dominant firms.

Profitable pruning is the opposite of conglomerate merger. This strategy recognizes that when a company spreads its resources across too many products, it may be unable to compete effectively in any. Better to sell off marginal operations and plow the money back into remaining businesses.

Profitable pruning reduces sustainable growth problems in two ways: It generates cash directly through the sale of marginal businesses, and it reduces actual sales growth by eliminating some of the sources of the growth. Many businesses have successfully employed this strategy in recent years, including Cooper Industries, a large Texas company. Beginning in the 1970s, Cooper sold several of its operations, not because they were unprofitable but because Cooper believed it lacked the resources to become a dominant factor in the markets involved.

Profitable pruning is also possible for a single-product company. Here the idea is to prune out slow-paying customers or slow-turning inventory. This lessens sustainable growth problems in three ways: It frees up cash, which can be used to support new growth; it increases asset turnover; and it reduces sales. Sales decline because tightening credit terms and reducing inventory selection drive away some customers.

Outsourcing

Outsourcing involves the decision of whether to perform an activity in-house or purchase it from an outside vendor. A company can increase its sustainable growth rate by outsourcing more and doing less in-house. When a company outsources, it releases assets that would otherwise be tied up in performing the activity, and it increases its asset turnover. Both results diminish growth problems. An extreme example of this strategy is a franchisor who sources out virtually all of the company's capital-intensive activities to franchisees and, as a result, has very little investment.

The key to effective outsourcing is to determine where the company's unique abilities—or, as consultants would put it, "core competencies"—lie. If certain activities can be performed by others without jeopardizing the firm's core competencies, these activities are candidates for outsourcing.

Pricing

An obvious inverse relationship exists between price and volume. When sales growth is too high relative to a company's financing capabilities, it may be necessary to raise prices to reduce growth. If higher prices increase the profit margin, the price increase will also raise the sustainable growth rate.

In effect, the recommendation here is to make growth itself a decision variable. If rapid growth is a problem, attack the problem directly by cutting growth. And while closing early on alternate Wednesdays or turning away every 10th customer might get the job done, the most effective way to cut growth is usually to raise prices.

Is Merger the Answer?

When all else fails, it may be necessary to look for a partner with deep pockets. Two types of companies are capable of supplying the needed cash. One is a mature company, known in the trade as a "cash cow," looking for profitable investments for its excess cash flow. The other is a conservatively financed company that would bring liquidity and borrowing capacity to the marriage. Acquiring another company or being acquired is a drastic solution to growth problems, but it is better to make the move when a company is still financially strong than to wait until excessive growth forces the issue.

Too Little Growth

Slow-growth companies—those whose sustainable growth rate exceeds actual growth—have growth management problems too, but of a different kind. Rather than struggling continually for fresh cash to stoke the fires of growth, slow-growth companies face the dilemma of what to do with profits in excess of company needs. This might appear to be a trivial or even enviable problem, but to an increasing number of enterprises it is a very real and occasionally frightening one.

To get a closer look at the difficulties insufficient growth creates, let's look again at Harley-Davidson, Inc. Table 4.3 presents a five-year, sustainable growth analysis of Harley-Davidson. (Harley-Davidson's financial statements for 2003 and 2004 appear in Tables 1.2 and 1.3 in Chapter 1; other relevant ratios are given in Table 2.2 in Chapter 2.)

TABLE 4.3   A Sustainable Growth Analysis of Harley-Davidson, Inc., 2000–2004*

	2000	2001	2002	2003	2004
Required ratios:					
Profit margin, P (%)	11.4	12.3	13.5	15.5	16.7
Retention ratio, R (%)	91.3	91.9	92.8	92.2	86.6
Asset turnover, A (times)	1.25	1.14	1.11	1.00	0.97
Financial leverage, $\hat{T}$ (times)	2.10	2.22	2.20	2.20	1.85
Harley-Davidson's sustainable growth rate, g^* (%)	27.3	28.6	30.6	31.4	26.0
Harley-Davidson's actual growth rate, g (%)	17.8	16.4	21.4	14.0	8.5

*Totals may not add due to rounding.

FIGURE 4.4   Harley-Davidson, Inc.'s Sustainable Growth Challenges, 2000–2004

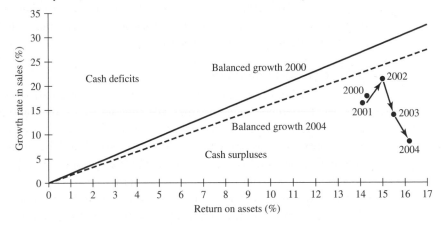

In each of the past five years Harley-Davidson's sustainable growth rate in sales exceeded its actual growth rate by a large amount. What did management do with all the excess cash? They returned a lot of it to owners in the form of dividends and share repurchases, and they invested heavily in their finance subsidiary receivables. But this was not nearly enough, for the largest single use of funds in the last five years was to increase cash and marketable securities. Looking forward, Harley-Davidson faces two related problems: to rekindle sales growth or, failing that, to find a more productive home for its money than marketable securities. This might involve introducing new products or acquiring other companies, but it might also involve increasing dividends and repurchasing even more shares.

Figure 4.4 says the same thing graphically. Reductions in Harley-Davidson's asset turnover and financial leverage lowered the company's balanced growth line. Nonetheless, high and growing profit margins pushed the company consistently into the cash surplus region of the graph, with the spread between balanced and actual growth rising sharply in the past two years. If present trends continue, the company will keep on generating much more cash than it needs to run the existing business efficiently.

What to Do When Sustainable Growth Exceeds Actual Growth

The first step in addressing problems of inadequate growth is to decide whether the situation is temporary or longer term. If temporary, management can simply continue accumulating resources in anticipation of future growth.

When the difficulty is longer term, the issue becomes whether the lack of growth is industrywide—the natural result of a maturing market—or unique to the company. If the latter, the reasons for inadequate growth and possible sources of new growth are to be found within the firm. In this event, management must look carefully at its own performance to identify and remove the internal constraints on company growth, a potentially painful process involving organizational changes as well as increased developmental expenses. The nerve-wracking aspect of such soul searching is that the strategies initiated to enhance growth must bear fruit within a few years or management will be forced to seek other, often more drastic solutions.

When a company is unable to generate sufficient growth from within, it has three options: ignore the problem, return the money to shareholders, or buy growth. Let us briefly consider each alternative.

Ignore the Problem

This response takes one of two forms: Management can continue investing in its core businesses despite the lack of attractive returns, or it can simply sit on an ever-larger pile of idle resources as Harley-Davidson has been doing. The difficulty with either response is that, like dogs to a fire hydrant, underutilized resources attract unwelcome attention. Poorly utilized resources depress a company's stock price and make the firm a feasible and attractive target for a raider. If a raider has done her sums correctly, she can redeploy the target firm's resources more productively and earn a substantial profit in the process. And among the first resources to be redeployed in such a raid is usually incumbent managers, who find themselves suddenly reading help-wanted ads. Even if a hostile raid does not occur, boards of directors and institutional shareholders are increasingly likely to give the boot to underperforming managements.

Another way to characterize the relationship between investment and growth is to distinguish between good growth and its evil twin, bad growth. Good growth occurs when the company invests in activities offering returns in excess of cost, including the cost of capital employed. Good growth benefits owners and is rewarded by a higher stock price and reduced threat of takeover. Bad growth involves investing in activities with returns at or below cost. Because ill-advised activities are always readily available, a bad growth strategy is easy to execute. If all else fails, the company can always overpay to purchase the sales and assets of another business. Such a strategy disposes of excess cash and makes the firm larger, but these cosmetic results only mask the fact that a bad growth strategy wastes valuable resources—and stock markets are increasingly adept at distinguishing between good and bad growth, and punishing the latter. The moral to the story, then, is that it is not enough for slow-growth companies to grow more rapidly; they must do so in a way that benefits shareholders. All other forms of growth are a snare and a delusion. (We will say more about value-creating investment activities in Chapters 7 and 8.)

Return the Money to Shareholders

The most direct solution to the problem of idle resources is to simply return the money to owners by increasing dividends or repurchasing shares. However, while this solution is becoming more common, it is still not the strategy of choice among many executives. The chief reason is that many executives appear to have a bias in favor of growth, even when the growth creates little or no value for shareholders. At the personal level, many managers resist paying large dividends because the practice hints of failure. Shareholders entrust managers with the task of profitably investing their capital, and for management to return the money suggests an inability to perform a basic managerial function. A cruder way to say the same thing is that dividends reduce the size of management's empire, an act counter to basic human nature.

Gordon Donaldson and others also document a bias toward growth at the organizational level.[5] In a carefully researched review and synthesis of the decision-making behavior of senior executives in a dozen large companies, Donaldson noted that executives commonly opt for growth, even uneconomic growth, out of concern for the long-run viability of their organizations. As senior managers see it, size offers some protection against the vagaries of the marketplace. Moreover, growth contributes significantly to company morale by creating stimulating career opportunities

[5] Donaldson, *Managing Corporate Wealth.*

for employees throughout the organization, and when growth slackens, the enterprise risks losing its best people.

Buy Growth

The third way to eliminate slow-growth problems is to buy growth. Motivated by pride in their ability as managers, concern for retaining key employees, and fear of raiders, managers often respond to excess cash flow by attempting to diversify into other businesses. Management systematically searches for worthwhile growth opportunities in other, more vibrant industries. And because time is a factor, this usually involves acquiring existing businesses rather than starting new ones from scratch.

The proper design and implementation of a corporate acquisition program is a challenging task that need not detain us here. Two points, however, are worth noting. First, in many important respects, the growth management problems of mature or declining companies are just the mirror image of those faced by rapidly growing firms. In particular, slow-growth businesses are generally seeking productive uses for their excess cash, while rapidly growing ones are in search of additional cash to finance their unsustainably rapid growth. It is natural, therefore, that high- and low-growth companies frequently solve their respective growth management problems by merging so that the excess cash generated by one organization can finance the rapid growth of the other. Second, after a flurry of optimism in the 1960s and early 1970s, accumulating evidence increasingly suggests that, from the shareholders' perspective, buying growth is distinctly inferior to returning the money to owners. More often than not, the superior growth prospects of potential acquisitions are fully reflected in the target's stock price, so that after paying a substantial premium to acquire another firm, the buyer is left with a mediocre investment or worse. The conflict between managers and owners in this regard is a topic of Chapter 9.

Sustainable Growth and Inflation

Growth comes from two sources: increasing volume and rising prices. Unfortunately, the amount of money a company must invest to support a dollar of inflationary growth is about the same as the investment required to support a dollar of real growth. Imagine a company that has no real growth—it makes and sells the same number of items every year—but is experiencing 10 percent inflationary growth. Then, even though it has the same number of units in inventory, each unit will cost more dollars to build, so the total investment in inventory will be higher. The same is true of accounts receivable: The same volume of customers will purchase the same number of units, but because each unit has a higher selling price, the total investment in accounts receivable will rise.

A company's investment in fixed assets behaves similarly under infla-tion, but with a delay. When the inflation rate increases, there is no im-mediate need for more fixed assets. The existing fixed assets can produce the same number of units. But as existing assets wear out and are replaced at higher prices, the company's investment in fixed assets rises.

This inflationary increase in assets must be financed just as if it were real growth. It is fair to say, then, that inflation worsens a rapidly expand-ing company's growth management problems. How much worse depends primarily on the extent to which management and creditors understand the impact of inflation on company financial statements.

Inflation does at least two things to company financial statements. First, as just noted, it increases the amount of external financing required. Second, in the absence of new equity financing, it increases the company's debt-to-equity ratio *when measured on its historical-cost financial statements*. This combination can spell trouble. If management or creditors require that the company's historical-cost debt-to-equity ratio stay constant over time, inflation will lower the company's real sustainable growth rate. If the sustainable growth rate is 15 percent without inflation, the real sustainable growth rate will fall to about 5 percent when the inflation rate is 10 per-cent. Intuitively, under inflation, cash that would otherwise support real growth must be used to finance inflationary growth.

If managers and creditors understand the effects of inflation, this in-verse relation between inflation and the sustainable growth rate need not exist. True, the amount of external financing required does rise with the inflation rate, but because the real value of liabilities declines as companies become able to repay their loans with depreciated dollars, the *net* increase in external financing may be little affected by inflation.

In sum, with historical-cost financial statements, inflationary growth appears to substitute for real growth on almost a one-for-one basis; each percentage point increase in inflation appears to reduce the real sustain-able growth rate by the same amount. More accurate, inflation-adjusted financial statements show, however, that inflation turns out to have rela-tively little effect on sustainable growth. Let us hope that executives can convince their bankers of this fact. I have not been able to do so.

Sustainable Growth and Pro Forma Forecasts

It is important to keep the material presented here in perspective. I find that comparison of a company's actual and sustainable growth rates reveals a great deal about the principal financial concerns confronting senior man-agement. When actual growth exceeds sustainable growth, management's focus will be on getting the cash to fund expansion; conversely, when actual growth falls below sustainable growth, the financial agenda will swing 180 degrees to one of productively spending the excess cash flow. The sustainable growth equation also describes the way many top executives view their jobs: Avoid external equity financing and work to balance operating strategies, growth targets, and financial policies so that the disparity between actual and sustainable growth is manageable. Finally, for nonfinancial types, the sustainable growth equation is a useful way to highlight the tie between a company's growth rate and its financial resources.

The sustainable growth equation, however, is essentially just a simplification of pro forma statements. If you really want to study a company's growth management problems in detail, therefore, I recommend that you take the time to construct pro forma financial statements. The sustainable growth equation may be great for looking at the forest but is considerably less helpful when studying individual trees.

New Equity Financing

Earlier in the chapter I noted that a fundamental assumption of sustainable growth analysis is that the company cannot or will not issue new equity. Consistent with this assumption I also noted in Table 4.2 that over the past 20 years new equity has been a use of cash to American companies, not a source, meaning that businesses have retired more stock than they have issued. It is time now to explore this phenomenon in more detail with particular emphasis on explaining why companies are so reticent to sell new stock.

Figure 4.5 shows the value of new equity issues, net of repurchases and retirements, on a year-by-year basis for the United States from 1965 through 2003. Net new equity issues grew erratically to about $28 billion in 1983, then plunged dramatically, and have been essentially negative ever since. In 1998, net new equity issues reached an all-time low of *minus* $267 billion; in other words, stock repurchases and retirements by American companies exceeded new issues by this amount. Companies reduce common stock outstanding in two ways: by repurchasing their own stock or acquiring the stock of another firm for cash or debt. Figure 4.5 attests to the huge wave of share repurchases and acquisitions on the part of U.S. companies in the past 15 years.

For comparison, the figure also includes the U.S. dollar value of net new equity issues by nonfinancial companies in Japan and the United Kingdom beginning in 1981. These figures show quite clearly that the dramatic reduction in equity outstanding among American companies

FIGURE 4.5 **Net New Equity Issues, 1965–2004**

Sources: Federal Reserve System, *Flow of Funds Accounts of the United States,* **www.federalreserve.gov/releases/z1/current/data.htm.** Bank of Japan, *Flow of Funds, Non-financial Corporations,* **www.boj.or.jp/.** U.K. Office of National Statistics, *Financial Account: Non-financial Corporations,* **www.statistics.gov.uk/.**

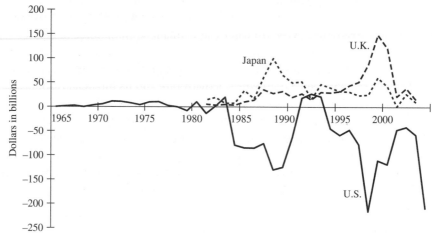

Note: $169.4 billion of equity issued by Vodafone to acquire Mannesmann in 2000 are omitted from U.K. figures because German equity falls by an equal amount.

has not occurred elsewhere. The best available evidence suggests that the tremendous reduction in equity outstanding in the United States was triggered initially by the hostile takeover battles that swept through the economy in the last half of the 1980s and was less prevalent or nonexistent elsewhere. In addition, share repurchase in many countries is illegal or just recently legalized. In more recent years, the reduction in U.S. equity appears attributable to the growing popularity of share repurchase as a way to distribute cash to shareholders and to manage reported earnings per share. If stock analysts are projecting a 15 percent growth in earnings-per-share but management believes they can only increase earnings 10 percent, one way to meet the analysts' target is to repurchase five percent of the shares outstanding.

These data suggesting that new equity capital is not a source of financing to American business are consistent with evidence showing that in an average year, only about 5 percent of publicly traded companies in the United States sell additional common stock. This means that a typical publicly traded company raises new equity capital in public markets only once every 20 years.[6]

Like the statistician who drowned crossing a stream because he heard it was only five feet deep on average, we need to remember that the equity

[6] U.S. Securities and Exchange Commission, *Report of the Advisory Committee on the Capital Formation and Regulatory Process,* July 24, 1996, Figure 4.

FIGURE 4.6 Gross Public Equity Issues and Initial Public Offerings, 1970–2003

Sources: *Federal Reserve Bulletin*, Table 1.46, "New Security Issues U.S. Corporations," various issues for gross public equity issues; Securities Data Corporation as cited in Jay R. Ritter, "Some Factoids About the 2004 IPO Market," **http://bear.cba.ufl.edu/ritter.**

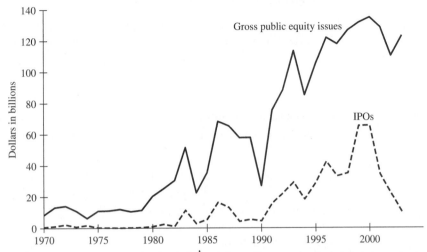

Note: New equity is publicly issued stock including preferred stock. IPOs exclude overallotment options but include the international tranche, if any.

figures presented are the net result of new issues and retirements. Figure 4.6 shows the gross proceeds from new common stock sales for U.S. companies from 1970 to 2003. The 34-year average was $59.8 billion, and the high in 2000 was $134.9 billion. To put these numbers in perspective, gross proceeds from new stock sales equaled 9 percent of total sources of capital to corporations over the period. The comparable figure as a percent of external sources was 22 percent.

Figure 4.6 also shows the money raised from initial public offerings of common stock (IPOs) from 1970 through 2003. Observe that the aggregate amount of money raised is comparatively modest, amounting to about one-quarter of gross new equity proceeds over the period. In 2000, the peak year for IPOs, total money raised equaled only 5 percent of total corporate external sources of capital.

These graphs are a testament to the dynamism of the American economy in which many firms are retiring equity at the same time others are selling new shares. On balance, the appropriate conclusion is that while the stock market is not an important source of capital to corporate America in the aggregate, it is critical to some companies. Companies making extensive use of the new equity market tend to be what brokers call "story paper," potentially high-growth enterprises with a particular product or concept that brokers can hype to receptive investors (the words high-tech and biotech come most readily to mind).

Why Don't U.S. Corporations Issue More Equity?

Here are several reasons. We will consider others in Chapter 6 when we review financing decisions in more detail.

- In recent years, companies in the aggregate simply did not need new equity. Retained profits and new borrowing were sufficient.

- Equity is expensive to issue. Issues costs commonly run in the neighborhood of 5 to 10 percent of the amount raised, and the percentage on small issues is even higher. These figures are at least twice as high as the issue costs for a comparable-size debt issue. (On the other hand, the equity can be outstanding forever, so its effective annualized cost is less onerous.)

- Many managers, especially U.S. managers, have a fixation with earnings per share (EPS). They translate a complicated world into the simple notion that whatever increases EPS must be good and whatever reduces EPS must be bad. In this view, a new equity issue is bad because, at least initially, the number of shares outstanding rises but earnings do not. EPS is said to be *diluted*. Later, as the company makes productive use of the money raised, earnings should increase but in the meantime EPS suffers. Moreover, as we will see in Chapter 6, EPS is almost always higher when debt financing is used in favor of equity.

- Then there is the "market doesn't appreciate us" syndrome. When a company's stock is selling for $10 a share, management tends to think the price will be a little higher in the future as soon as the current strategy begins to bear fruit. When the price rises to $15, management begins to believe this is just the beginning and the price will be even higher in the near future. Managers' inherent enthusiasm for their company's prospects produces a feeling that the firm's shares are undervalued at whatever price they currently command, and this view creates a bias toward forever postponing new equity issues. A recent survey of 371 chief financial officers of U.S. corporations by John Graham and Campbell Harvey at Duke University illustrates this syndrome. Despite the fact that the Dow Jones Industrial Averages were approaching a new record high of 10,000 at the time of the survey, fewer than one-third of respondents thought the stock market correctly valued their stock; only 3 percent believed their stock was overvalued, and fully 69 percent felt it was undervalued.[7]

---

[7] John R. Graham and Campbell R. Harvey, "The Theory and Practice of Corporate Finance: Evidence from the Field," *Journal of Financial Economics,* May–June 2001, pp. 187–243.

- Finally, many managers perceive the stock market to be an unreliable funding source. In addition to uncertainty about the price a company can get for new shares, managers also face the possibility that during some future periods the stock market will not be receptive to new equity issues on any reasonable terms. In finance jargon, the "window" is said to be shut at these times. Naturally, executives are reluctant to develop a growth strategy that depends on such an unreliable source of capital. Rather, the philosophy is to formulate growth plans that can be financed from retained profits and accompanying borrowing and relegate new equity finance to a minor backup role. More on this topic in later chapters.

SUMMARY

1. This chapter highlighted the financial management of growth and decline.

2. More growth is not always a blessing. Without careful financial planning, companies can literally grow broke.

3. A company's sustainable growth rate is the maximum rate at which it can grow without depleting financial resources. Sustainable growth does not assume constant debt. It assumes debt will increase in proportion to the growth in equity.

4. Sustainable growth equals the product of four ratios: the profit margin, the retention ratio, the asset turnover ratio, and financial leverage, defined here as assets divided by beginning-of-period equity. Alternatively, sustainable growth equals the firm's retention ratio times return on beginning-of-period equity. If a company's sales expand at any rate other than the sustainable growth rate, one or some combination of its four constituent ratios must change.

5. If a company's actual growth rate temporarily differs from its sustainable growth rate, change in company debt can probably accommodate the imbalance.

6. When the actual growth rate exceeds the sustainable for an extended period, management must formulate a financial strategy from among the following options: sell new equity, permanently increase financial leverage, reduce dividends, liquidate marginal operations, outsource activities, cut growth by increasing prices, or find a merger partner with deep pockets.

7. When actual growth is less than the sustainable growth rate, management's principal financial challenge is finding productive uses for the

excess cash flow. Options are to increase dividends, repurchase common shares, reduce liabilities, increase assets, or buy growth—that is, acquire other companies for their growth potential.

8. If managers and creditors base decisions on historical-cost financial statements, inflation reduces the company's sustainable growth rate. If they are more perceptive, inflation will have comparatively little effect on sustainable growth.

9. For a variety of reasons, some of which are yet to be discussed, most businesses are reluctant to sell new equity. Indeed, since 1984, the market value of shares extinguished through repurchase and acquisition for cash by American corporations has far exceeded the value of shares issued.

ADDITIONAL RESOURCES

Higgins, Robert C. "Sustainable Growth under Inflation." *Financial Management*, August 1981, pp. 36–40.

A look at the dependence of a company's sustainable growth rate on the inflation rate. The paper concludes that inflation will reduce sustainable growth only if an "inflation illusion" exists.

WEBSITES

www.research.stlouisfed.org/fred2/
Lots of good data on interest rates, employment, and so on. A treasure trove of current and historical economic data.

www.pages.stern.nyu.edu/~adamodar/
NYU professor Aswath Damodaran's home page, this site contains an exhaustive but no-nonsense selection of financial data sets and spreadsheets, as well as quite a bit of academic and instructional material. Data sets include bond ratings; spreads and interest coverage ratios by firm; historical returns on stocks, bonds, and bills; and return on equity and levers of performance by industry.

PROBLEMS

Answers to odd-numbered problems are at the end of the book. For additional problems with answers, see **www.mhhe.com/higgins8e.**

1. True or false? Why?
   a. A company's sustainable growth rate is the highest growth rate in sales it can attain without issuing new stock.

b. The stock market is a ready source of new capital when a company is incurring heavy losses.

c. Share repurchases usually increase earnings per share.

d. Companies often buy back their stock because managers believe the shares are undervalued.

e. Only rapidly growing firms have growth management problems.

f. Increasing growth increases stock price.

2. Table 3.1 in the last chapter presents R&E Supplies' financial statements for the period 2002 through 2005, and Table 3.5 presents a pro forma financial forecast for 2006. Use the information in these tables to answer the following questions.

a. Calculate R&E Supplies' sustainable growth rate in each year from 2003 through 2006.

b. Comparing the company's sustainable growth rate with its actual and projected growth rates in sales over these years, what growth management problems does R&E Supplies appear to face in this period?

c. How did the company cope with these problems? Do you see any difficulties with the way it addressed its growth problems over this period? If so, what are they?

d. What advice would you offer management regarding managing future growth?

3. PCA International, Inc., is one of the largest color portrait photography chains in North America. The company photographs, develops, and sells portrait packages through studios operated in Kmart stores. Following are selected financial data for the company for the period 1991–1995.

	1991	1992	1993	1994	1995
Profit margin (%)	4.8	5.5	3.3	3.0	5.3
Retention ratio (%)	78.4	65.7	53.9	47.8	71.9
Asset turnover ($\times$)	4.3	3.1	2.7	2.4	2.4
Financial leverage ($\times$)	5.6	4.2	2.0	2.0	1.8
Growth rate in sales (%)	6.9	8.0	(6.2)	(2.9)	(0.1)

a. Calculate PCA's sustainable growth rate in each year.

b. Comparing the company's sustainable growth rate with its actual growth rate in sales, what growth problems did PCA face over this period?

c. How did the company cope with these problems?

d. In March 1995, PCA announced a $7.5 million stock buy back, about equal in size to earnings that year. From a growth management perspective, was this a wise move?

4. Robert Half International, Inc. (RHI), headquartered in Menlo Park, California, is the world's first and largest provider of temporary and permanent personnel in accounting, finance, and information technology with 330 offices worldwide. The following are selected financial data for the company for the period 2000–2004.

	2000	2001	2002	2003	2004
Profit margin (%)	6.89	4.94	0.11	0.32	5.25
Retention ratio (%)	100.0	100.0	100.0	100.0	78.27
Asset turnover ($\times$)	2.78	2.47	2.03	2.00	2.23
Financial leverage ($\times$)	1.69	1.38	1.16	1.32	1.52
Growth rate in sales (%)	22.89	−10.05	−28.76	3.55	26.19

a. Calculate Robert Half's sustainable growth rate in each year.

b. Comparing the company's sustainable growth rate with its actual growth rate in sales, what growth problems did the company face over this period?

c. Considering economic conditions over the period, what was a likely cause of these problems?

d. Robert Half paid its first dividends in 2004. As an analyst, assess the company's decision to pay dividends.

5. Union Fidelity Company (UFC) has the following ratios for the years 1999 through 2003:

	1999	2000	2001	2002	2003
Profit margin (%)	38.5	37.9	37.3	38.5	38.7
Retention ratio (%)	100.0	100.0	100.0	100.0	100.0
Asset turnover ($\times$)	0.2	0.2	0.3	0.3	0.3
Financial leverage ($\times$)	1.3	1.4	1.4	1.5	1.8
Growth rate in sales (%)	53.2	36.4	46.5	49.3	40.6

a. Calculate UFC's sustainable growth rate for each year.

b. Does UFC have a growth problem?

c. How did UFC cope with its sustainable growth problems?

d. Calculate UFC's sustainable growth rate in 2003 assuming the asset turnover increases to 0.4 and the financial leverage decreases to 1.6 times.

**STANDARD
&POOR'S**

6. You will need to use the Standard & Poor's Market Insight website (**www.mhhe.com/edumarketinsight**) for this problem.

   a. For fiscal year 2004, what is the largest single asset on Boeing Company's balance sheet, on Oracle Corp's. balance sheet?

   b. Calculate the ratio of cash and equivalents to total assets for Boeing and Oracle for fiscal year 2004.

   c. In general terms, how does Oracle's huge investment in cash affect its return on equity and its sustainable growth rate?

   d. As an Oracle shareholder, would you endorse Oracle's investment in cash? As an Oracle senior executive, how would you defend the policy?

*e**X**cel*

7. Chapter 3, Problem 13, asks you to construct a five-year financial projection for Jasmine Apparel beginning in 2006. Based on your forecast, or the suggested answer at **www.mhhe.com/higgins8e** (Select Student Edition > Choose a Chapter > Excel Spreadsheets) calculate Jasmine Apparel's sustainable and actual growth rates in these years. What do these numbers suggest to you?

*e**X**cel*

8. An Excel spreadsheet containing selected financial information for Eight Ball Sporting Goods is available at **www.mhhe.com/higgins8e.** (Select Student Edition > Choose a Chapter > Excel Spreadsheets.) Using this information, answer the questions appearing in the spreadsheet regarding Eight Ball's growth management challenges.

PART THREE

Financing Operations

CHAPTER FIVE

Financial Instruments and Markets

Don't tell mom I'm an investment banker. She still thinks I play piano in a brothel.

Anonymous

A major part of a financial executive's job is to raise money to finance current operations and future growth. In this capacity, the financial manager acts much as a marketing executive. He or she has a product—claims on the company's future cash flow—that must be packaged and sold to yield the highest price to the company. The financial manager's customers are creditors and investors who put money into the business in anticipation of future cash flows. In return these customers receive a piece of paper such as a stock certificate, a bond, or a loan agreement, that describes the nature of their claim on the firm's future cash flow. When the paper can be bought and sold in financial markets, it is customarily called a *financial security*.

In packaging the product, the financial executive must select or design a financial security that meets the needs of the company and is attractive to potential creditors and investors. To do this effectively requires knowledge of financial instruments, the markets in which they trade, and the merits of each instrument to the issuing company. In this chapter, we consider the first two topics, financial instruments and markets. In the next chapter, we look at a company's choice of the proper financing instrument.

Although corporate financing decisions are usually the responsibility of top executives and their finance staffs, there are several reasons managers at all levels need to understand the logic on which these decisions rest. First, we all make similar financing decisions in our personal lives whenever we borrow money to buy a home, a car, or return to school. Second, as investors we are often consumers of the financial securities that companies issue, and it is always wise to be an informed consumer. Third, and most important for present purposes, sound financing decisions are central to effective financial management. This is witnessed by the fact that financial leverage is one of the levers of performance by which managers seek to generate competitive returns, and it is a principal determinant of a company's sustainable growth rate. So failure to appreciate the logic driving an enterprise's financing decisions robs managers of a complete understanding of their company and its challenges.

Before beginning, a few words about what this chapter is not. "Financial markets" is the name given to a dynamic, heterogeneous distribution system through which cash-surplus entities provide money to cash-deficit entities. Businesses are by no means the only, or even the most prominent players in these markets. Other active participants include national, state, and local governments and agencies, pension funds, endowments, individuals, commercial banks, insurance companies, and the list goes on and on. This chapter is not a balanced overview of financial markets; rather it is a targeted look at the financing instruments most used by nonfinancial corporations and the means by which they are sold. A further restriction is that we will not consider short-term instruments. When speaking of financial markets it is common to distinguish between *money markets*, in which securities having a maturity of less than one year trade, and *capital markets*, in which longer-term instruments are bought and sold. Because nonfinancial businesses rely much more on capital markets for financing, we will say little about money markets, even though they are the larger and more liquid of the two. (For a balanced, comprehensive look at financial markets and instruments, see one of the books recommended at the end of this chapter.)

Financial Instruments

Fortunately, lawyers and regulators have not yet taken all of the fun and creativity out of raising money. When selecting a financial instrument for sale in securities markets, a company is *not* significantly constrained by law or regulation. The company is largely free to select or design any instrument, provided only that the instrument appeals to investors and meets the needs of the company. Securities markets in the United States are regulated by the Securities and Exchange Commission (SEC) and, to a lesser extent, by state authorities. SEC regulation can create red tape and delay, but the SEC does not pass judgment on the investment merits of a security. It requires only that investors have access to all information relevant to valuing the security and have adequate opportunity to evaluate it before purchase. This freedom has given rise to such unusual securities as Foote Minerals' $2.20 cumulative, if earned, convertible preferred stock and Sunshine Mining's silver-indexed bonds. My favorite is a 6 percent bond issued by Hungary in 1983 that, in addition to paying interest, included a firm promise of telephone service within three years. The usual wait for a phone at the time was said to run up to 20 years. A close second is a bond proposed by a group of Russian vodka distillers. Known as *Lial*, or "Liter" bonds, they were to pay annual interest of 20 percent in hard currency or 25 percent in vodka. According to one of the promoters, "Vodka has been currency for 1,000 years. We have just made the relationship formal."

But do not let the variety of securities obscure the underlying logic. When designing a financial instrument, the financial executive works with three variables: investors' claims on future cash flow, their right to participate in company decisions, and their claims on company assets in liquidation. We will now describe the more popular security types in terms of these three variables. In reading the descriptions, bear in mind that the characteristics of a specific financial instrument are determined by the terms of the contract between issuer and buyer, not by law or regulation. So the descriptions that follow should be thought of as indicating general security types rather than exact definitions of specific instruments.

Bonds

Economists like to distinguish between physical assets and financial assets. A physical asset, such as a home, a business, or a painting, is one whose value depends on its physical properties. A financial asset is a piece of paper or, more formally, a security representing a legal claim to future cash payouts. The entity agreeing to make the payouts is the issuer, and the recipient is the investor. It is often useful to draw a further distinction among financial assets depending on whether the claim to future payments is fixed as to dollar amount and timing or residual, meaning the investor receives any cash remaining after all prior fixed claims have been paid. Debt instruments offer fixed claims, while equity, or common stock, offers residual claims. Human ingenuity being what it is, you should not be surprised to learn that some securities, such as convertible preferred stock, are neither fish nor fowl, offering neither purely fixed nor purely residual claims.

A bond, like any other form of indebtedness, is a *fixed-income* security. The holder receives a specified annual interest income and a specified amount at maturity—no more and no less (unless the company goes bankrupt). The difference between a bond and other forms of indebtedness such as trade credit, bank loans, and private placements is that bonds are sold to the public in small increments, usually $1,000 per bond. After issue, the bonds can be traded by investors on organized security exchanges.

I noted in the last chapter that internal financing, in the form of retained profits and depreciation, has historically provided about 60 percent of the money used by American business. Looking at external financing, aggregate data indicate that over the past two decades corporate bonds have been the largest source, accounting for about 34 percent of the total. Loans and advances of various kinds from banks and others have contributed another 15 percent. Before dismissing bank loans as of only secondary importance, it is important to bear in mind that although they are not a major source of financing in the aggregate, they are important to smaller firms. For example, in 2004 the ratio of bank loans to total liabilities among billion dollar–plus manufacturing firms was only 7 percent, while the comparable number for small manufacturers having assets of $25 million or less was 37 percent.[1]

Three variables characterize a bond: its *par value*, its *coupon rate*, and its *maturity date*. For example, a bond might have a $1,000 par value, a 9 percent coupon rate, and a maturity date of December 31, 2015. The par value is the amount of money the holder will receive on the bond's maturity date. By custom, the par value of bonds issued in the United States is usually $1,000. The coupon rate is the percentage of par value the issuer promises to pay the investor annually as interest income. Our bond will pay $90 per year in interest (9% × $1,000), usually in two semiannual payments of $45 each. On the maturity date, the company will pay the bondholder $1,000 per bond and will cease further interest payments.

On the issue date, companies usually try to set the coupon rate on the new bond equal to the prevailing interest rate on other bonds of similar maturity and quality. This ensures that the bond's initial market price will about equal its par value. After issue, the market price of a bond can differ substantially from its par value as market interest rates and credit risk perceptions change. As we will see in Chapter 7, when interest rates rise, bond prices fall, and vice versa.

Most forms of long-term indebtedness require periodic repayment of principal. This principal repayment is known as a *sinking fund*. Readers who have studied too much accounting will know that technically a sinking fund is a sum of money the company sets aside to meet a future obligation, and this is the way bonds used to work, but no more. Today a bond sinking fund is a direct payment to creditors that reduces principal. Depending on the indenture agreement, there are several ways a firm can meet its sinking-fund obligation. It can repurchase a certain number of bonds in

[1] U.S. Federal Reserve, "Flow of Funds Accounts of the United States," Table B.102 Balance Sheet of Nonfarm, Nonfinancial Corporate Business, 2004. **www.federalreserve.gov/releases/z1/**. U.S. Census Bureau, "Quarterly Financial Report for Manufacturing, Mining, and Trade Corporations," Tables 1.1 and 56.1. Fourth Quarter, 2004. **www.census.gov/prod/www/abs/qfr-mm.html**.

securities markets, or it can retire a certain number of bonds by paying the holders par value. When a company has a choice, it will naturally repurchase bonds if the market price of the bonds is below par value, which occurs whenever interest rates rise after the bond is issued.

I have just described a fixed-interest-rate bond. An alternative more common to loans than bonds is floating-rate debt in which the interest rate is tied to a short-term interest rate such as the 90-day U.S. Treasury bill rate. If a floating-rate instrument promises to pay, say, one percentage point over the 90-day bill rate, the interest to be paid on each payment date will be calculated anew by adding one percentage point to the then prevailing 90-day bill rate. Because the interest paid on a floating-rate instrument varies in harmony with changing interest rates over time, the instrument's market value always approximates its principal value.

Call Provisions

Some corporate bonds contain a clause giving the issuing company the option to retire the bonds prior to maturity. Frequently the call price for early retirement will be at a modest premium above par; or the bond may have a *delayed call*, meaning the issuer may not call the bond until it has been outstanding for a specified period, usually 5 or 10 years.

Companies want call options on bonds for two obvious reasons. One is that if interest rates fall, the company can pay off its existing bonds and issue new ones at a lower interest cost. The other is that the call option gives a company flexibility. If changing market conditions or changing company strategy requires it, the call option enables management to rearrange its capital structure.

At first glance, it may appear that a call option works entirely to the company's advantage. If interest rates fall, the company calls the bonds and refinances at a lower rate. But if rates rise, investors have no similar option. They must either accept the low interest income or sell their bonds at a loss. From the company's perspective, it looks like "heads I win, tails you lose," but investors are not so naive. As a general rule, the more attractive the call provisions to the issuer, the higher the coupon rate on the bond.

Covenants

Under normal circumstances, no creditors, including bondholders, have a direct voice in company decisions. Bondholders and other long-term creditors exercise control through *protective covenants* specified in the indenture agreement. Typical covenants include a lower limit on the company's current ratio, an upper limit on its debt-to-equity ratio, and perhaps a requirement that the company not acquire or sell major assets without prior creditor approval. Creditors have no say in company operations as long as the firm is current in its interest and sinking-fund payments and no covenants have been violated. If the company falls behind in its payments or violates a covenant, it is in *default*, and creditors gain considerable power. At the extreme, creditors can force the company into bankruptcy and possible liquidation. In liquidation, the courts supervise the sale of company assets and distribution of the proceeds to the various claimants.

Rights in Liquidation

The distribution of liquidation proceeds in bankruptcy is determined by what is known as the *rights of absolute priority*. First in line are, naturally, the government for past-due taxes. Among investors, the first to be repaid are *senior* creditors, then *general* creditors, and finally *subordinated* creditors. Preferred stockholders and common shareholders bring up the rear. Because each class of claimant is paid off in full before the next class receives anything, equity shareholders frequently get nothing in liquidation.

Secured Creditors

A *secured credit* is a form of senior credit in which the loan is collateralized by a specific company asset or group of assets. In liquidation, proceeds from the sale of this asset go only to the secured creditor. If the cash generated from the sale exceeds the debt to the secured creditor, the excess cash goes into the pot for distribution to general creditors. If the cash is insufficient, the lender becomes a general creditor for the remaining liability. Mortgages are a common example of a secured credit in which the asset securing the loan is land or buildings.

Bonds as an Investment

For many years, investors thought bonds to be very safe investments. After all, interest income is specified and the chances of bankruptcy are remote. However, this reasoning ignored the pernicious effects of inflation on fixed-income securities. For although the *nominal* return on fixed-interest-rate bonds is specified, the value of the resulting interest and principal payments to the investor is much less when inflation is high. This implies that investors need to concern themselves with the *real*, or inflation-adjusted, return on an asset, not the nominal return. And according to this yardstick, even default-free bonds can be quite risky in periods of high and volatile inflation.

Table 5.1 presents the nominal rate of return investors earned on selected securities over the period 1900 to 2004. Looking at long-term corporate bonds, you can see that had an investor purchased a representative portfolio of corporate bonds in 1899 and held them through 2004 (while reinvesting all interest income and principal payments in similar

TABLE 5.1 Rate of Return on Selected U.S. Securities, 1900–2004

Source: Elroy Dimson, Paul Marsh, and Mike Staunton. *Global Investment Returns Yearbook 2005*. (London, UK: ABN-AMRO, February 2005). p. 177. Return on long-term corporate bonds estimated by author.

Security	Return*
Common stocks	11.7%
Long-term corporate bonds	5.8
Long-term government bonds	5.3
Short-term government bills	4.0
Consumer price index	3.1

*Arithmetic mean annual returns ignoring taxes and assuming reinvestment of all interest and dividend income.

bonds), the annual return would have been 5.8 percent over the entire 104-year period. By comparison, the annual return on an investment in long-term U.S. government bonds would have been 5.3 percent over the same period. We can attribute the 0.5 percent difference to a "risk premium." This is the added return investors in corporate bonds earn over government bonds as compensation for the risk that the corporations will default on their liabilities or call their bonds prior to maturity.

The bottom entry in Table 5.1 contains the annual percentage change in the consumer price index over the period. Subtracting the annual inflation rate from 1900 through 2004 of 3.1 percent from these nominal returns yields real, or inflation-adjusted, returns of 2.7 percent for corporates and 2.2 percent for governments.[2] Long-term bonds did little more than keep pace with inflation over this period.

Bond Ratings

Several companies analyze the investment qualities of many publicly traded bonds and publish their findings in the form of bond ratings. A bond rating is a letter grade, such as AA, assigned to an issue that reflects the analyst's appraisal of the bond's default risk. Analysts determine these ratings using many of the techniques discussed in earlier chapters, including analysis of the company's balance sheet debt ratios and its coverage ratios relative to competitors. Table 5.2 contains selected debt-rating definitions of Standard & Poor's, a major rating firm. Table 6.4 in the next chapter shows the differences in key performance ratios by rating category.

---

[2] These numbers are approximate. The exact equation is $i_r = (1 + i_n)/(1 + p) - 1$, where i_r = real return, i_n = nominal return, and p = inflation rate. Applying this equation, the real returns on corporate and government bonds are 2.6 percent and 2.1 percent, respectively.

TABLE 5.2 **Selected Standard & Poor's Debt-Rating Definitions**

Source: Standard and Poor's Definitions, **www.standardpoor.com**

A Standard & Poor's issue credit rating is a current opinion of the creditworthiness of an obligor with respect to a specific financial obligation, a specific class of financial obligations, or a specific financial program. . . . It takes into consideration the creditworthiness of guarantors, insurers, or other forms of credit enhancement on the obligation and takes into account the currency in which the obligation is denominated. The issue credit rating is not a recommendation to purchase, sell, or hold a financial obligation, inasmuch as it does not comment as to market price or suitability for a particular investor. . .

Issue credit ratings are based, in varying degrees, on the following considerations:

(1) Likelihood of payment, capacity, and willingness of the obligor to meet its financial commitment on an obligation in accordance with the terms of the obligation.
(2) Nature of and provisions of the obligation.
(3) Protection afforded by, and relative position of, the obligation in the event of bankruptcy, reorganization, or other arrangement under the laws of bankruptcy and other laws affecting creditors' rights. . .

AAA An obligation rated 'AAA' has the highest rating assigned by Standard & Poor's. The obligor's capacity to meet its financial commitment on the obligation is extremely strong.

•
•

BBB An obligation rated 'BBB' exhibits adequate protection parameters. However, adverse economic conditions or changing circumstances are more likely to lead to a weakened capacity of the obligor to meet its financial commitment on the obligation.

•
•

CCC An obligation rated 'CCC' is currently vulnerable to nonpayment, and is dependent upon favorable business, financial, and economic conditions for the obligor to meet its financial commitment on the obligation. In the event of adverse business, financial, or economic conditions, the obligor is not likely to have the capacity to meet its financial commitment on the obligation.

•
•

D An obligation rated 'D' is in payment default. The 'D' rating category is used when payments on an obligation are not made on the date due even if the applicable grace period has not expired, unless Standard & Poor's believes that such payments will be made during such grace period. The 'D' rating also will be used upon the filing of a bankruptcy petition or the taking of a similar action if payments on an obligation are jeopardized.

Plus (+) or minus (−): The ratings from 'AA' to 'CCC' may be modified by the addition of a plus (+) or minus (−) sign to show relative standing within the major rating categories.

Junk Bonds

A company's bond rating is important because it affects the interest rate the company must offer. Moreover, many institutional investors are prohibited from investing in bonds that are rated less than "investment" grade, usually defined as BBB− and above. As a result, there have been periods in the past when companies with lower-rated bonds had great difficulty raising debt in public markets. Below-investment-grade bonds are known variously as *speculative*, *high-yield*, or simply *junk* bonds.

Until the emergence of a vibrant market for speculative-grade bonds in the 1980s, public debt markets were largely the preserve of huge, blue-chip corporations. Excluded from public bond markets, smaller, less

---

When Investing Internationally, What You See Isn't Always What You Get

A 10 percent interest rate on a dollar-denominated bond is not comparable to a 6 percent rate on a yen bond or a 14 percent rate on a British sterling bond. To see why, let's calculate the rate of return on $1,000 invested today in a one-year, British sterling bond yielding 14 percent interest. Suppose today's exchange rate is 1£ = $1.50 and the rate in one year is 1£ = $1.35.

$1,000 will buy £666.67 today ($1,000/1.50 = £666.67), and in one year interest and principal on the sterling bond will total £760 (£666.67 [1 + 0.14] = £760). Converting this amount back into dollars yields $1,026 in one year (£760 × 1.35 = $1,026). So the investment's rate of return, measured in dollars, is only 2.6 percent ([$1,026 − $1,000]/$1,000 = 2.6%).

Why is the dollar return so low? Because investing in a foreign asset is really two investments: purchase of a foreign-currency asset and speculation on future changes in the dollar value of the foreign currency. Here the foreign asset yields a healthy 14 percent, but sterling depreciates 10 percent against the dollar ([$1.50 − $1.35]/$1.50); so the combined return is roughly the difference between the two. The exact relationship is

$$(1 + \text{Return}) = (1 + \text{Interest rate})(1 + \text{Change in exchange rate})$$
$$(1 + \text{Return}) = (1 + 14\%)(1 - 10\%)$$
$$\text{Return} = 2.6\%$$

Incidentally, we know that sterling depreciated relative to the dollar over the year because a pound costs less at the end of the year than at the start.

---

prominent companies in need of debt financing were forced to rely on bank and insurance company loans. Although bond markets are still closed to most smaller businesses, the junk bond market has been a boon to many mid-size and emerging companies, which now find public debt an attractive alternative to traditional bank financing. The market has also been an important financing source to corporate raiders and private equity investors for use in highly levered transactions.

Common Stock

Common stock is a *residual income* security. The stockholder has a claim on any income remaining after the payment of all obligations, including interest on debt. If the company prospers, stockholders are the chief beneficiaries; if it falters, they are the chief losers. The amount of money a stockholder receives annually depends on the dividends the company chooses to pay, and the board of directors, which makes this decision quarterly, is under no obligation to pay any dividend at all.

Shareholder Control

At least in theory, stockholders exercise control over company affairs through their ability to elect the board of directors. In the United States, the wide distribution of share ownership and the laws governing election of the board have frequently combined to greatly reduce this authority, although the winds of change are blowing. In some companies, ownership of as little as 10 percent of the stock has been sufficient to control the entire board. In many others, there is no dominant shareholder group, and management has been able to control the board even if it owns little or none of the company's shares.

This does not imply that managers in such companies are free to ignore shareholder interests entirely, for they face at least two potential constraints on their actions. One is created by their need to compete in product markets. If management does not make a product or provide a service efficiently and sell it at a competitive price, the company will lose market share to more aggressive rivals and will eventually be driven from the industry. The actions managers take to compete effectively in product markets are consistent with shareholder interests.

Securities markets provide a second check on management discretion. If a company wants to raise debt or equity capital in future years, it must maintain its profitability to attract money from investors. Moreover, if managers ignore shareholder interests, stock price will suffer, and the firm may become the target of a hostile takeover. Even when not facing a takeover, a growing number of company boards, often prodded by large institutional shareholders, have become more diligent in monitoring management performance and replacing poor performers. Such corporate stalwarts as Hewlett-Packard, Campbell Soup, Aetna, and Mattel, to name but a few, have experienced such palace revolts in recent years. We will have more to say about corporate takeovers and the evolving role of the board of directors in Chapter 9.

German and Japanese owners exercise much more direct control over company managements than do their U.S. or English counterparts. In Germany, the legal ability of banks to hold unlimited equity stakes in industrial companies, combined with the historical insignificance of public financial markets, has led to high concentrations of ownership in many companies. Banks are controlling shareholders of many German businesses, with representation on the board of directors and effective control over the business's access to debt and equity capital. German managers are thus inclined to think twice before ignoring shareholder interests.

Like their American counterparts, Japanese banks are prohibited from owning more than 5 percent of an industrial company's shares, and Japanese capital markets are more highly developed than German markets. Nonetheless, Japan's *keiretsu* form of organization produces results similar to those in Germany. As noted in the appendix to Chapter 2, a *keiretsu* is a group of companies, usually including a lead bank, that purchase sizable ownership interests in one another as a means of cementing important business relations. When the majority of a company's stock is in the hands of business partners and associates through cross-share holdings, managers ignore shareholder interests only at their peril.

Whether the more direct control exercised by German and Japanese shareholders is any better economically than the more indirect American variety is open to question. For while the German and Japanese models may facilitate a direct shareholder voice in company affairs, they also tend to encourage a clubby, "old-boy" approach to corporate governance that can be inimical to necessary change and innovation. Moreover, evidence is accumulating that both the German and Japanese approaches to corporate governance are in decline. In Germany a growing interest on the part of companies in raising capital on public markets rather than from banks has undermined banks' authority, while in Japan an increasing emphasis on stock price performance as opposed to business relationships as the principal criterion for holding shares has recently led to sharp declines in cross-share holdings.

Common Stock as an Investment

Common stockholders receive two types of investment return: dividends and possible share price appreciation. If d_1 is the dividends per share during the year and p_0 and p_1 are the beginning-of-the-year and end-of-the-year stock price, respectively, the *annual income* a stockholder earns is

$$d_1 + p_1 - p_0$$

Dividing by the beginning-of-the-year stock price, the *annual return* is

$$\frac{\text{Annual}}{\text{return}} = \frac{\text{Dividend}}{\text{yield}} + \frac{\text{Percentage change in}}{\text{share price}}$$

$$= \frac{d_1}{p_0} + \frac{p_1 - p_0}{p_0}$$

Over the 1928–2004 period, equity investors in large-company common stocks received an average dividend yield of 4.0 percent and average capital appreciation of 7.6 percent.

Common stocks are an ownership claim against primarily real, or productive, assets. If companies can maintain profit margins during inflation, real, inflation-adjusted profits should be relatively unaffected by inflation. For years this reasoning led to the belief that common stocks are a hedge against inflation, but this did not prove to be the case during the bout of high inflation during the 1970s. Looking at Table 5.1 again, we see that had an investor purchased a representative portfolio of common stocks in 1899 and reinvested all dividends received in the same portfolio, his average annual return in 2004, over the entire 104 years, would have been 11.7 percent. However, from 1973 through 1981, a period when prices rose an average of 9.2 percent per annum, the average annual nominal return on common stocks was only 5.2 percent. This implies a negative *real*

Do Dividends Increase Annual Return?

It may appear from the preceding equation that annual return rises when dividends rise. But the world is not so simple. An increase in current dividends means one of two things: The company will have less money to invest, or it will have to raise more money from external sources to make the same investments. Either way, an increase in current dividends reduces the stockholders' claim on future cash flow, which reduces share price appreciation. Depending on which effect dominates, annual returns may or may not increase as dividends rise.

---

return of about 4 percent. The comparable figures for corporate bonds over this period were a nominal return of 2.5 percent and a negative real return of about 6.7 percent.

The common stock return of 11.7 percent from 1900 through 2004 compares with a return of 5.3 percent on government bonds over the same period. The difference between the two numbers of 6.4 percent can be thought of as a *risk premium*, the extra return common stockholders earned as compensation for the added risks they bore. Comparing the return on common stocks to the annual percentage change in consumer prices, we see that the *real* return to common stock investors over the period was about 8.6 percent (11.7% − 3.1%).

Figure 5.1 presents much of the same information more dramatically. It shows an investor's wealth at year-end 2004 had she invested $1 in various assets at year-end 1899. Common stocks are the clear winners here. By 2004 the original $1 investment in common stock would have grown to a whopping $17,545. In contrast, $1 invested in long-term government bonds would have been worth only $160 in 2004. Reflecting the pernicious effect of inflation, the corresponding real numbers are $784.3 for common stock and $7.20 for government bonds. Common stocks, however, have proven to be a much more volatile investment than bonds, as Figure 5.2 attests.

Preferred Stock

Preferred stock is a hybrid security: like debt in some ways, like equity in others. Like debt, preferred stock is a fixed-income security. It promises the investor an annual fixed dividend equal to the security's coupon rate times its par value. Like equity, the board of directors need not distribute this dividend unless it chooses. Also like equity, preferred dividend payments are *not* a deductible expense for corporate tax purposes. For the same coupon rate, this makes the *after-tax* cost of bonds about two-thirds that of preferred shares. Another similarity with equity is that although preferred stock may have a call option, it frequently has no maturity. The

FIGURE 5.1 **If Your Grandmother Had Invested Only a Dollar in 1900; Nominal Returns on U.S. Assets, 1900–2004**

(Assumed initial investment of $1 at year-end 1899; includes reinvestment income.)

Source: Elroy Dimson, Paul Marsh, and Mike Staunton, *Global Investment Returns Yearbook 2005* (London: ABN–AMRO, 2005), p. 180.

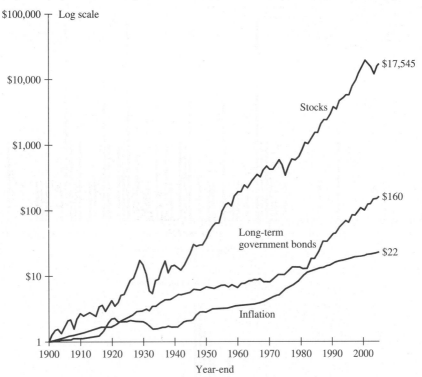

preferred shares are outstanding indefinitely unless the company chooses to call them.

Cumulative Preferred

Company boards of directors have two strong incentives to pay preferred dividends. One is that preferred shareholders have priority over common shareholders with respect to dividend payments. Common shareholders receive no dividends unless preferred holders are paid in full. Second, virtually all preferred stocks are *cumulative*. If a firm passes a preferred dividend, the arrearage accumulates and must be paid in full before the company can resume common dividend payments.

The control preferred shareholders have over management decisions varies. In some instances, preferred shareholders' approval is routinely required for major decisions; in others, preferred shareholders have no voice in management unless dividend payments are in arrears.

FIGURE 5.2 **Distribution of Annual Return on Stocks and Bonds, 1928–2004**

Source: Professor Aswath Damodaran's website: **pages.stern.nyu.edu/~adamodar/.**

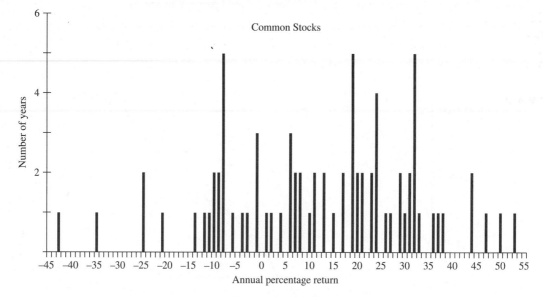

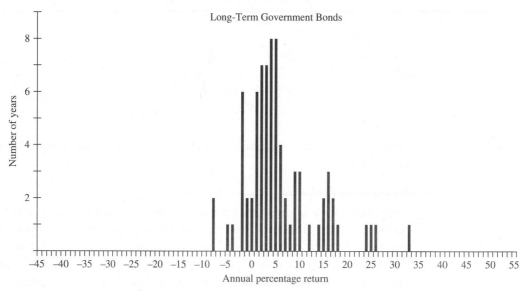

Preferred stock is not a widely used form of financing. Some managers see preferred stock as *cheap equity*. They observe that preferred stock gives management much of the flexibility regarding dividend payments and maturity dates that common equity provides. Yet because preferred shareholders have no right to participate in future growth, they see preferred stock as less expensive than equity. The majority, however, see preferred stock as *debt with a tax disadvantage*. Because few companies would ever omit a preferred dividend payment unless absolutely forced to, most managers place little value on the flexibility of preferred stock. To them the important fact is that interest payments on bonds are tax deductible, whereas dividend payments on preferred stock are not.

Financial Markets

Having reviewed the basic security types, let us now turn to the markets in which these securities are issued and traded. Of particular interest will be the provocative notion of market efficiency.

Broadly speaking, financial markets are the channels through which investors provide money to companies. Because these channels differ greatly depending on the nature of the company and securities involved, they can best be described by considering the financing needs of three representative firms: a startup, a candidate for an initial public offering, and a multinational. Although these brief vignettes certainly do not exhaust the topic, they do offer a useful overview of financial markets and their more important participants.

Private Equity Financing

Janet Holmes has developed a promising new medical device and now wants to start a company to capitalize on her research. Her problem is where to find the financing. After brief inquiry, she learns that conventional financing sources such as bank loans and public stock or bond offerings are out of the question. Her venture is far too risky to qualify for a bank loan and too small to attract public funding. A banker has expressed interest in a small loan collateralized by accounts receivable, machinery, and any personal assets she owns, but this will not be nearly enough. Instead, Janet will have to rely primarily on personal savings, friends and family, strategic investors, or venture capitalists to fund her business. Strategic investors are operating companies—frequently potential competitors—that make significant equity investments in startups as a way to gain access to promising new products and technology. Some strategic investors, including Microsoft, Intel, and Cisco Systems, have come to view new venture investing as a means of outsourcing research and development. Rather than develop all new products in-house, they sprinkle money across a number of promising startups, expecting to acquire any that prove successful.

Venture capitalists come in two flavors: wealthy individuals, often referred to as "angel investors," and professional venture capital companies. Venture capital companies are financial investors who make high-risk equity investments in entrepreneurial businesses deemed capable of rapid growth and high investment returns. They purchase a significant fraction of a company and take an active policy role in management. Their goal is to liquidate the investment in five or six years when the company goes public or sells out to another firm. Venture capital firms routinely consider dozens of candidates for every investment made and expect to suffer a number of failures for each investment success. In return, they expect winners to return 5 to 10 times their initial investment. Most of their investments are in technology firms of one kind or another.

Venture capital companies are prominent examples of what are known as "private equity" firms. Although private equity firms invest in a wide variety of opportunities, including new ventures, leveraged buyouts, and distressed businesses, they all share two important traits: their investments are high-risk, and they employ an unusual organizational form known as a private equity partnership. Instead of the conventional public-company form, private equity investments are structured as limited partnerships with a specified duration, usually of 10 years. Acting as the general partner, the private equity firm raises a pool of money from limited partners, consisting primarily of institutional investors, such as pension funds, college endowments, and insurance companies. As limited partners, these investors enjoy the same limited liability protections afforded conventional shareholders. The private equity sponsor then invests the money raised, actively manages the investments for a period of years, liquidates the portfolio, and returns the proceeds to the limited partners. In return, the private equity firm charges the limited partners handsome fees consisting of an annual management charge equaling 1 to 2 percent of the original investment, plus what is know as *carried interest*, typically 20 percent or more of any capital appreciation earned on the portfolio. For example, the carried interest on a $1 billion portfolio subsequently liquidated for $3 billion would be $400 million ($400 million = 20% × [$3 billion − $1 billion]). At any one time private equity firms may be managing a number of limited partnerships of differing size and years to maturity.

Private equity partnerships are becoming increasingly popular investment vehicles because they appear to address several incentive problems inherent in more conventional investment forms.

- The partnership form minimizes any differences between owners and managers. As knowledgeable, active owners, private equity investors make it clear that management's goal is not to meet artificial short-run earnings targets, but to create value for owners.

- The fixed life of the partnership imposes an aggressive, buy-fix-sell attitude on managers, prompting them to take decisive actions.

FIGURE 5.3   **Venture Capital Investment in U.S. Companies**

Source: PricewaterhouseCoopers/Venture Economics/NVCA. **www.ventureeconomics.com/vec/stats/2005q1/nation_us1.html.**

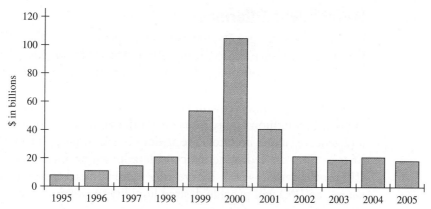

Note: The 2005 amount is the annualized value of the first quarter rate.

- As Dave Barry might put it, the horizon also assures investors that they will eventually get their money back, rather than having to stand by idly while management feeds it to chipmunks.

Reliable data on the volume and growth rate of private equity investments are not available. Private equity firms are not publicly traded and their partnership fundraising does not require SEC registration, so information is anecdotal. Figure 5.3, gathered from industry sources, shows estimated venture capital investment in U.S. companies during the last decade. Note that investment volume exploded from a base of less than $10 billion to more than $100 billion at the height of the dot-com boom. Plagued by the demise of the boom and the following recession, the number fell to an annual rate of just under $20 billion in the first quarter of 2005, still a healthy increase over 1995.

Knowledgeable observers judge that venture capital constitutes about one-third of total private equity financing, which puts the industry total at about $60 billion annually. To fully appreciate this number, it is necessary to realize that while venture capitalists generate high risk by investing in young companies, most other private equity firms accomplish the same feat by using large amounts of debt financing. The debt-to-equity ratio in a typical leveraged buyout is in the range of 3 or 4 dollars of debt for every dollar of equity. This means the $40 billion of private equity not flowing into new ventures probably commands $160 to $200 billion in new investment capital annually. On a more pragmatic level, we might also judge the growing importance of the industry by noting that some commentators

See **www.federalreserve.gov/ pubs/staffstudies/168/default. htm** for an excellent overview of the economics of private equity.

are openly speculating whether private equity firms might take a run at acquiring a crippled General Motors.[3]

Initial Public Offerings

Genomic Devices got its start six years ago when it raised $15 million from three venture capital firms. After two more rounds of venture financing totaling $40 million, Genomic is now a national company with sales of $125 million and an annual growth rate of more than 40 percent. To finance this rapid growth, management estimates the company needs another $25 million equity infusion. At the same time, company founders and venture capital investors are anxious to see some cash from their years of toil. This has led to active consideration of an initial public offering (IPO) of common stock. By creating a public market for the company's shares, an IPO will provide desired liquidity to existing owners as well as supplying necessary funding.

Investment Banking

Genomic Devices' first step toward an IPO will be to conduct what is known in the trade as a "bake-off." This involves reviewing proposals from several investment banks detailing the mechanics of how they would sell the new shares and what a great job each could do for the company. Investment bankers can be thought of as the grease that keeps financial markets running smoothly. They are finance specialists who assist companies in raising money. Other activities include stock and bond brokerage, investment counseling, merger and acquisition analysis, and corporate consulting. Some investment banking companies, such as Merrill Lynch, employ thousands of brokers and have offices all over the world. Others, such as Goldman Sachs, specialize in working with companies or trading securities, and consequently are less in the public eye. As to the range of services provided, H. F. Saint said it best in his Wall Street thriller *Memoirs of an Invisible Man:* "[Investment bankers] perform all sorts of interesting services and acts—in fact any service or act that can be performed in a suit, this being the limitation imposed by their professional ethics."[4]

When a company is about to raise new capital, an investment banker's responsibilities are not unlike his fees: many and varied. (Capital raising techniques differ from one country to another depending on custom and law. In the interest of space, and with apologies to non-American readers, I will confine my comments here to the American scene.) The winner of

---

[3] "Carving up Carmakers?" *BusinessWeek,* May 2, 2005. For an industry overview, see *"Global Private Equity 2004,"* PricewaterhouseCoopers, **www.pwcmoneytree.com.**

[4] H. F. Saint, *Memoirs of an Invisible Man* (New York: Dell, 1987), p. 290.

the bake-off receives the mantle "managing underwriter" and immediately begins advising the company on detailed design of the security to be issued. Then the banker helps the company register the issue with the SEC. This usually takes 30 to 90 days and includes detailed public disclosure of information about the company's finances, its officer compensation, plans, and so on—information some managements would prefer to keep confidential.

While the registration wends its way toward approval, the managing underwriter orchestrates the "road show" during which top company executives market the issue to institutional investors in New York and other financial centers. The managing underwriter also puts together a *selling* and an *underwriting syndicate*. A syndicate is a team of as many as 100 or more investment banking firms that join forces for a brief time to sell new securities. Each member of the selling syndicate accepts responsibility for selling a specified portion of the new securities to investors. Members of the underwriting syndicate in effect act as wholesalers, purchasing all of the securities from the company at a guaranteed price and attempting to sell them to the public at a higher price. The "Rules of Fair Practice" of the National Association of Securities Dealers prohibit underwriters from selling new securities to the public at a price above the original offer price quoted to the company. If necessary, however, the syndicate may sell them at a lower price.

Given the volatility of stock markets and the length of time required to go through registration, it may appear that underwriters bear significant risks when they guarantee the issuer a fixed price for the shares. This is not the way the world works, however. Underwriters do not commit themselves to a firm price on a new security until just hours before the sale, and if all goes as planned, the entire issue will be sold to the public on the first day of offer. It is the company, not the underwriters, that bears the risk that the terms on which the securities can be sold will change during registration.

The life of a syndicate is brief. Syndicates form several months prior to an issue for the purpose of "building the book," or preselling the issue, and disband as soon as the securities are sold. Even on unsuccessful issues, the syndicate breaks up several weeks after the issue date, leaving the underwriters to dispose of their unsold shares on their own. I will have more to say about the issue costs and pricing of IPOs in a few paragraphs.

Seasoned Issues

Our third representative firm in need of financing is Trilateral Enterprises, a multinational consumer products company with annual sales of almost $90 billion. Trilateral wants to raise $200 million in new debt and has narrowed the choices down to a U.S. "shelf registration" or an international issue executed through the company's Netherlands Antilles subsidiary.

Shelf Registration

First authorized in 1982, a shelf registration allows frequent security issuers to avoid the cumbersome traditional registration process by filing a general-purpose registration, good for up to two years, indicating in broad terms the securities the company may decide to issue. Once the registration is approved by the SEC, and provided it is updated periodically, the company can put the registration on the "shelf," ready for use as desired. A shelf registration cuts the time lag between the decision to issue a security and receipt of the proceeds from several months to as little as 48 hours. Because 48 hours is far too little time for investment bankers to throw a syndicate together, shelf registrations tend to be "bought deals" in which a single investment house buys the entire issue in the hope of reselling it piecemeal at a profit. Also, because it is just as easy for the issuer to get price quotes from two investment banks as from one, shelf registrations increase the likelihood of competitive bidding among investment banks. As a result, issue costs for shelf registered issues are as much as 10 percent to 50 percent lower than for traditionally registered issues, depending on the type of security and other factors.[5]

International Markets

Large corporations can raise money on any of three types of markets: *domestic, foreign,* or *international.* A domestic financial market is the market in the company's home country, while foreign markets are the domestic markets of other countries. U.S. financial markets are thus domestic to IBM and General Motors but foreign to Sony Corporation and British Petroleum; Japanese markets are domestic to Sony but foreign to IBM, General Motors, and British Petroleum.

Companies find it attractive to raise money in foreign markets for a variety of reasons. When the domestic market is small or poorly developed, a company may find that only foreign markets are large enough to absorb the contemplated issue. Companies may also want liabilities denominated in the foreign currency instead of their own. For example, when Walt Disney expanded into Japan, it sought yen-denominated liabilities to reduce the foreign exchange risk created by its yen-denominated revenues.

---

[5] Robert J. Rogowski and Eric H. Sorensen, "Deregulation in Investment Banking, Shelf Registrations, Structure, and Performance," *Financial Management,* Spring 1985, pp. 5–15. See also Sanjai Bhagat, M. Wayne Marr, and G. Rodney Thompson, "The Rule 415 Experiment: Equity Markets," *Journal of Finance,* December 1985, pp. 1385–1402.

Finally, issuers may believe foreign-denominated liabilities will prove cheaper than domestic ones in view of anticipated exchange rate changes.

Access to foreign financial markets has historically been a sometime thing. The Swiss and Japanese governments have frequently restricted access to their markets by limiting the aggregate amount of money foreigners may raise in a given time period or imposing firm size and credit quality constraints on foreign issuers. Even U.S. markets, the largest and traditionally most open markets in the world, have not always offered unrestricted access to foreigners. Beginning in the late 1960s and continuing for almost a decade, foreign borrowers in the United States were subject to a surcharge known as the interest equalization tax (IET). The tax was purportedly to compensate for low U.S. interest rates, but most observers saw it as an attempt to bolster a weak dollar in foreign exchange markets by constraining foreign borrowing.

The third type of market on which companies can raise money, international financial markets, is best viewed as a free market response to the regulatory constraints endemic in domestic and foreign markets. A transaction is said to occur in the international financial market whenever the currency employed is outside the control of the issuing monetary authority. A dollar-denominated loan to an American company in London, a euro-denominated loan to a Japanese company in Singapore, and a British pound bond issue by a Dutch company underwritten in Frankfurt are all examples of international financial market transactions. In each instance, the transaction occurs in a locale that is beyond the direct regulatory reach of the issuing monetary authority. Thus, the U.S. Federal Reserve has trouble regulating banking activities in London even when the activities involve American companies and are denominated in dollars. Similarly, the Bundesbank has difficulty regulating euro activities in Singapore.

International financial markets got their start in London shortly after World War II and were originally limited to dollar transactions in Europe. From this beginning, the markets have grown enormously to encompass most major currencies and trading centers around the globe. Today international financial markets give companies access to large pools of capital, at very competitive prices, with minimal regulatory or reporting requirements.

Two important reasons international markets have often been able to offer lower-cost financing than domestic markets are the absence of reserve requirements on international bank deposits and the ability to issue bonds in what is known as *bearer form*. In the United States and many other domestic markets, banks must abide by reserve requirements stipulating that they place a portion of each deposit in a special, often non-interest-bearing account at the central bank. Because these reserves tie up resources without yielding a competitive return, domestic loans must carry a higher interest rate than international loans to yield the same profit.

The chief appeal of bearer bonds is that they make it easier for investors to avoid paying taxes on interest income. The company issuing a bearer bond never knows the bond's owners and simply makes interest and principal payments to anyone who presents the proper coupon at the appropriate time. In contrast, the issuer of a registered security maintains records of the owner and the payments made. Because bearer securities facilitate tax avoidance, they are illegal in the United States. This is why Trilateral Enterprises anticipates issuing their bonds to non-U.S. residents through its Netherlands Antilles subsidiary. The use of bearer bonds in international markets means international bonds can carry lower coupon rates than comparable domestic bonds and still yield the same after-tax returns.

The ability of international financial markets to draw business away from domestic markets has sharply accelerated the deregulation of domestic financial markets. As long as companies and investors can avoid onerous domestic regulations by simply migrating to international markets, regulators face a Hobson's choice: They can either remove the offending regulations or keep the regulations and watch international markets grow at the expense of domestic ones. The interest equalization tax is an apt example. When first imposed, the tax had the desired effect of restricting foreign companies' access to dollar financing. Over time, however, borrowers found they could avoid the tax by simply going to the international markets. The longer-run effect of the IET, therefore, was to shift business away from the United States without greatly affecting the total volume of dollar financing. Indeed, an avowed goal in repealing the IET was to make U.S. markets more competitive with international markets.

Not all regulations are bad, of course. Regulatory oversight of financial markets and the willingness of governments to combat financial panics have greatly stabilized markets and economies for over 70 years. The ongoing question is whether the deregulatory pressures created by international financial markets are improving efficiency by stripping away unwarranted restraints or dangerously destabilizing the world economy. Stay tuned.

Issue Costs

Financial securities impose two kinds of costs on the issuer: annual costs, such as interest expense, and issue costs. We will consider the more important annual costs later. Issue costs are the costs the issuer and its shareholders incur on initial sale. For privately negotiated transactions, the only substantive cost is the fee charged by the investment banker in his or her capacity as agent. On a public issue, there are legal, accounting, and printing fees, plus those paid to the managing underwriter. The managing underwriter states his fee in the form of a *spread*. To illustrate, suppose ABC Corporation is a publicly traded company that wants to sell 10 million new shares of common stock using traditional registration procedures, and its shares presently trade at $20 on the New York Stock Exchange. A few hours prior to public sale, the managing underwriter might inform ABC management, "Given the present tone of the markets, we can sell the new shares at an issue price of $19.00 and a spread of $1.50, for a net to the company of $17.50 per share." This means the investment banker intends to *underprice* the issue $1.00 per share ($20 market price less $19 issue price) and is charging a fee of $1.50 per share, or $15 million, for his services. This fee will be split among the managing underwriter and the syndicate members by prior arrangement according to each bank's importance in the syndicates.

To underprice an issue means to offer the new shares at a price below that of existing shares, or in the case of an IPO, below the market price of the shares shortly after the issue is completed. One obvious motivation investment bankers have for underpricing is to make their own job easier. Selling something worth $20 for $19 is a lot easier than selling for $20. But there appears to be more to the practice than this. In any public sale of securities, well-informed insiders are selling paper of uncertain value to less informed outsiders. One way to quell outsiders' natural concern with being victimized by insiders is to consistently underprice new issues. This gives uninformed buyers the expectation the shares will more likely rise than fall after issue. Underpricing is not an out-of-pocket cost to the company, but it is a cost to shareholders. The greater the underpricing, the more securities a company must issue to raise a given amount of money. If the securities are bonds, this translates into higher interest expense, and if they are shares, it translates into a reduced percentage ownership for existing owners.

Empirical studies of issue costs confirm two prominent patterns. First, equity is much more costly than debt. Representative costs of raising capital in public markets, ignoring underpricing, average about 2.2 percent of proceeds for straight debt, 3.8 percent for convertible bonds, and 7.1 percent for offerings of equity by publicly traded companies. This figure rises to 11.0 percent for IPOs. Second, issue costs for all security types rise rapidly as issue size declines. Issue costs as a percentage of gross proceeds for equity are as low as 3 percent for issues larger than $100 million but rise to more than 20 percent for issues under $500,000. Comparable figures for

Google Goes Dutch

A certain amount of underpricing may be necessary in conventional IPOs, but one has to ask when enough is enough. Between 1990 and 2004, first-day returns to IPO buyers averaged 23.2 percent, reaching a high of 55 percent in 1999![6] If we think of the difference between the amount of money that could have been raised in the absence of underpricing, and the amount actually raised as money left on the table, issuers over the past 15 years have left almost $100 billion on the table, a figure that dwarfs any fees paid to investment bankers.

Largely in reaction to these figures, there has been growing interest in an alternative, and seemingly more democratic, means of pricing and distributing new shares known as a Dutch auction. Rather than rely on investment bankers to pick a price, a Dutch auction invites interested buyers to submit a bid indicating how many shares they want at what price. The issuer then rank-orders the bids from high price to low and proceeds down the list until it identifies the minimum bid price necessary to sell all the intended shares. All bids above this clearing price receive shares, *priced at the clearing price*, while all lower bids are rejected. If the clearing price is $85, a bidder at $100 pays only $85. Dutch auctions appeal to uninformed buyers because, like a political election, they know their bid will probably not determine the outcome. Instead the outcome will be determined by the collective wisdom (or foolishness) of all bidders. Issuers should also like Dutch auctions because they promise to cut underpricing and investment bankers' fees.

In August 2004, search-engine giant Google Inc. tested this theory when it sold 20 million shares to the public via Dutch auction. What were the results? Mixed. Investment banking fees were only 3 percent of proceeds, but the first-day gain in stock price was 18 percent, not far from the 15-year average of 23.2 percent.

debt financing are from below 0.9 percent for large issues to more than 10 percent for very small ones.[7]

Efficient Markets

A recurring issue in raising new capital is *timing*. Companies are naturally anxious to sell new securities when prices are high. Toward this end, managers routinely devote considerable time and money to predicting future price trends in financial markets.

Concern for proper timing of security issues is natural, but there is a perception among many academicians and market professionals that attempts to forecast future prices in financial markets is a loser's game.

---

[6] Jay R. Ritter, "Some Factoids about the 2004 IPO Market," Table 1. **http://bear.cba.ufl.edu/ritter.**

[7] Wayne H. Mikkelson and M. Megan Partch, "Valuation Effects of Security Offerings and the Issuing Process," *Journal of Financial Economics,* January–February 1986; Inmoo Lee, Scott Lockhead, Jay Ritter, and Quanshui Zhao, "The Cost of Raising Capital," *Journal of Financial Research,* Spring 1996; Securities and Exchange Commission, "Report of the Advisory Committee on the Capital Formation and Regulatory Process" (Washington, D.C.: U.S. Government Printing Office, July 24, 1996).

For more on market effi-
ciency, see **www.answers.
com/topic/efficient-market-
hypothesis**.

Such pessimism follows from the notion of *efficient markets*, a much-debated and controversial topic in recent decades. A detailed discussion of efficient markets would take us too far afield, but because the topic has far-reaching implications, it merits some attention. Check the recommended website in the margin and readings at the end of the chapter for more detailed treatments.

Market efficiency is controversial in large part because many proponents have overstated the evidence supporting efficiency and have misrepresented its implications. To avoid this, let us agree on two things right now. First, market efficiency is a question not of black or white but of shades of gray. A market is not efficient or inefficient but *more* or *less* efficient. More-over, the degree of efficiency is an empirical question that can be answered only by studying the particular market under consideration. Second, market efficiency is a matter of perspective. The New York Stock Exchange can be efficient to a dentist in Des Moines who doesn't know an underwriter from an undertaker; at the same time, it can be highly *in*efficient to a specialist on the floor of the exchange who has detailed information about buyers and sellers of each stock and up-to-the-second prices.

What Is an Efficient Market?

Market efficiency describes how prices in competitive markets respond to new information. The arrival of new information at a competitive market can be likened to the arrival of a lamb chop at a school of flesh-eating piranha, where investors are, plausibly enough, the piranha. The instant the lamb chop hits the water, turmoil erupts as the fish devour the meat. Very soon the meat is gone, leaving only the worthless bone behind, and the waters soon return to normal. Similarly, when new information reaches a competitive market, much turmoil erupts as investors buy and sell securities in response to the news, causing prices to change. Once prices adjust, all that is left of the information is the worthless bone. No amount of gnawing on the bone will yield any more meat, and no further study of old information will yield any more valuable intelligence.

How long does this price adjustment process take? Louis Ederington and Jae Ha Lee at the University of Oklahoma provide an answer in their study of market responses to scheduled news releases. Looking at prices in various interest rate and foreign exchange markets on a trade-by-trade basis, they find that price changes begin within 10 seconds of the news release and are basically completed within 40 seconds. If you want to make money in financial markets trading on news, you'd best not dally.[8]

---

[8] Louis H. Ederington and Jae Ha Lee, "The Short-Run Dynamics of the Price Adjustment to New Information," *Journal of Financial and Quantitative Analysis,* March 1995, pp. 117–34.

How Rapidly Do Stock Prices Adjust to New Information?

Figure 5.4 gives an indication of the speed with which common stock prices adjust to new information. It is a result of what is known as an *event study*. In this instance the researcher, Michael Bradley, is studying the effect of acquisition offers on the stock price of the target firm. It is easiest to think of the graph initially as a plot of the daily prices of a single target firm's stock from a period beginning 40 days before the announcement of the acquisition offer and ending 40 days after. An acquisition offer is invariably good news to the target firm's shareholders, because the offer is at a price well above the prevailing market price of the firm's shares; so we expect to see the target company's stock price rise after the announcement. The question is: How rapidly? The answer evident from the graph is: Very rapidly. We see that the stock price drifts upward prior to the announcement, shoots up dramatically on the announcement day, and then drifts with little direction after the announcement. Clearly, if you read about the announcement in the evening paper and buy the stock the next morning, you will miss out on the major price move. The market will already have responded to the new information.

The upward drift in stock price prior to the announcement is consistent with three possible explanations: (1) Insiders are buying the stock in anticipation of the announcement, (2) security analysts are very good at anticipating which firms will be acquisition targets and when the offer will be made, or (3) acquiring firms tend to announce offers after the price of the target firm's stock has increased for several weeks. I have my own views, but will leave it to you to decide which explanation is most plausible.

An old Jewish proverb says, "For example is no proof." If the price pattern illustrated by the graph were for just one firm, it would be only a curiosity. To avoid this problem, Bradley studied the price patterns of 161 target firms involving successful acquisitions that occurred over 15 years. The prices you see are an index composed of the prices of the 161 firms, and the time scale is in "event time," not calendar time. Here the event is the acquisition announcement, defined as day 0, and all other dates are relative to this event date. The pattern observed therefore describes general experience, not an isolated event.

In recent years, academicians have performed a great number of event studies involving different markets and events, and the preponderance of these studies indicates that financial markets in the United States respond to new, publicly available information within one day or sooner. In the Ederington and Lee study mentioned earlier, the response was basically completed within 40 seconds.

An efficient market, then, is one in which prices adjust rapidly to new information and current prices fully reflect available information about the assets traded. "Fully reflect" means investors rapidly pounce on new information, analyze it, revise their expectations, and buy or sell securities accordingly. They continue to buy or sell securities until price changes eliminate the incentive for further trades. In such an environment, current prices reflect the cumulative judgment of investors. They *fully reflect* available information.

The degree of efficiency a particular market displays depends on the speed with which prices adjust to news and the type of news to which they respond. It is common to speak of three levels of informational efficiency:

1. A market is *weak-form* efficient if current prices fully reflect all information about past prices.

FIGURE 5.4   **Time Series of the Mean Price Index of the Shares of 161 Target Firms Involved in Successful Tender Offers**

Source: Michael Bradley, "Interfirm Tender Offers and the Market for Corporate Control," *Journal of Business* 53, no. 4 (1980).

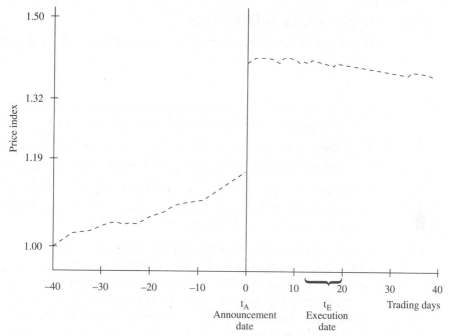

2. A market is *semistrong-form* efficient if current prices fully reflect all publicly available information.

3. A market is *strong-form* efficient if current prices fully reflect all information public or private.

Extensive tests of many financial markets suggest that with limited exceptions, most financial markets are semistrong-form efficient but not strong-form efficient. In other words, you generally cannot make money trading on public information; insider trading, however, based on private information, can be lucrative. This statement needs to be qualified in two respects. First, there is the issue of perspective. The preceding statement applies to the typical investor, who is subject to brokerage fees and lacks special information-gathering equipment. It does *not* apply to market makers. Second, it is impossible to test every conceivable type and combination of public information for efficiency. All we can say is that the most plausible types of information tested with the most sophisticated techniques available indicate efficiency. This does not preclude the possibility that a market will be inefficient with respect to some as yet untested information source. Nor does it preclude researchers who find evidence of profitable market inefficiencies and choose to exploit them rather than publish their findings.

Implications of Efficiency

If financial markets are semistrong-form efficient, the following statements are true:

- Publicly available information is not helpful in forecasting future prices.

- In the absence of private information, the best forecast of future price is current price, perhaps adjusted for a long-run trend.

- Without private information, a company cannot improve the terms on which it sells securities by trying to select the optimal time to sell.

- Without private information or the willingness to accept above-average risk, investors should not expect to consistently earn above the market-average rate of return.

Individuals without private information have two choices: They can admit that markets are efficient and quit trying to forecast security prices, or they can attempt to make the market inefficient from their perspective. This involves acquiring the best available information-gathering system in the hope of learning about events before others do. A variation on this strategy, usually illegal, is to seek inside information. Advance knowledge that the Food and Drug Administration had refused to review ImClone System's new cancer drug, for example, would undoubtedly be useful information to Martha Stewart or any other investor. A third gambit used by some investors is to purchase the forecasts of prestigious consulting firms. The chief virtue of this approach appears to be that there will be someone to blame if things go wrong. After all, if the forecasts were really any good, the consulting firms could make money by trading, thereby eliminating the need to be nice to potential customers.

As the preceding comments suggest, market efficiency is a subtle and provocative notion with a number of important implications for investors as well as companies. Our treatment of the topic here has been necessarily brief, but it should be sufficient to suggest that unless executives have inside information or superior information-gathering and analysis systems, they may have little to gain from trying to forecast prices in financial markets. This conclusion applies to many markets in which companies participate, including those for government and corporate securities, foreign currencies, and commodities.

There is, however, one important caveat to this conclusion. Because managers clearly possess private information about their own companies, they should have some ability to predict future prices of their own securities. This means managers' efforts to time new security issues based on inside knowledge of their company and its prospects may in fact be appropriate. But notice the distinction. The decision to postpone an equity issue because the president believes the company will significantly outperform analysts' expectations in the coming year is fully defensible in a world of semistrong-form-efficient markets, but the decision to postpone an issue because the treasurer believes stocks in general will soon rise is not. The former decision is based on inside information; the latter is not.

APPENDIX

Forward Contracts, Options, and the Management of Corporate Risks

This appendix looks briefly at two weapons in the manager's financial risk management arsenal: forward contracts and options. As a brief diversion, we will also consider the valuation of employee stock options. Forwards and options are members of a class of securities known as *derivatives* because their value derives from, or depends upon, the value of one or more underlying assets. Estimates put the value of derivative contracts outstanding at over $200 *trillion*, with the amount of money at risk totaling almost $8 *trillion*.

These topics merit our attention for several reasons.

- Sharp increases in the volatility of foreign exchange rates, interest rates, and commodity prices beginning in the early 1970s have heightened corporate interest in controlling these risks and led to increased participation in related markets.

- As companies make increasing use of forward and option markets to manage risk, the need for all executives to appreciate what these markets can and cannot do to enhance company performance grows apace. The fact that a number of otherwise sophisticated companies, including Procter & Gamble and Volkswagen, reported multimillion-dollar losses on what were originally intended to be risk-reducing activities highlights the need for all managers to understand derivatives.

- The popularity of employee stock options as a form of compensation, and the challenges companies have encountered in reporting their costs, make it important for executives to understand the basics of option valuation.

In the interest of brevity, I will confine the discussion here to the use of financial markets to manage foreign exchange risks and to the valuation of employee stock options. If you want to study these topics in more depth or to learn about similar techniques for managing interest rate, commodity price, or credit risks, take a look at the book mentioned below.[1]

Forward Markets

Most markets are *spot* markets, in which a price is set today for immediate exchange. In a *forward* market, the price is set today but exchange occurs at some stipulated future date. Buying bread at the grocery store is a spot market transaction, while reserving a hotel room to be paid for later is a forward market transaction. Most assets trading in forward markets also trade spot. To illustrate these markets, the spot price of one euro today in currency markets is $1.2859, meaning payment of this amount will buy one euro for immediate delivery. In contrast, the 180-day forward rate is $1.2941, meaning payment of this slightly greater amount in 180 days will buy one euro for delivery at that time. A forward transaction involves an irrevocable contract, most likely with a bank, in which the parties set the price today at which they will trade euros for dollars at a future date.

Speculating in Forward Markets

Although our focus in this appendix is on risk avoidance, we will begin at the opposite end of the spectrum by looking at forward market speculation. As you will see, speculation—especially the creative use of one speculation to counteract another—is the essence of the risk management techniques to be described. To demonstrate this important fact, imagine that an irresistible impulse has prompted you to remortgage your home and bet $100,000 on the New York Knicks to beat the Boston Celtics in an upcoming basketball game. Your spouse, however, is not amused to learn of your wager and threatens serious consequences unless you immediately cancel the bet. But, of course, bets are seldom canceled without a broken kneecap or two.

So what do you do? You hedge your bet. Acknowledging your mother was wrong all those years ago—that two wrongs may indeed make one right—you place a second wager, but this time on the Celtics to beat the Knicks. Now, no matter who wins, the proceeds from your winning wager will cover the cost of your losing one, and except for the bookie's take, it's just as though you had never made the first bet. You have covered your

---

[1] Steven Allen, *Financial Risk Management: A Practitioner's Guide to Managing Market and Credit Risk* (New York: John Wiley & Sons, 2003).

bet. Companies use financial market "wagers" analogously to manage unavoidable commercial risks.

For a closer look at forward market speculation, suppose the treasurer of American Merchandising Inc. (AMI) believes the euro will weaken dramatically over the next six months.[2] Forward currency markets offer a simple way for the treasurer to bet on his belief by executing a modest variation on the old "buy-low, sell-high" strategy. Here he will sell high first and buy low later: sell euros forward today at $1.2941, wait 180 days as the euro plummets, and then purchase euros in the spot market for delivery on the forward contract. If the treasurer is correct, the forward price at which he sells the euros today will exceed the spot price at which he buys them in six months, and he will profit from the difference. Of course, the reverse is also possible: If the euro strengthens relative to the dollar, the forward selling price could be below the spot buying price, and the treasurer will lose money.

Putting this into equation form, the treasurer's gain or loss on, say, a €1 million forward sale is

$$\text{Gain or loss} = (F - \tilde{S})\, \text{€}1 \text{ million}$$

where F is the 180-day forward price and $\tilde{S}$ is the spot price 180 days hence. The spot price has a tilde over it as a reminder that it is unknown today.

A convenient way to represent such transactions is with a *position diagram* showing the transaction's gain or loss on the vertical axis as a function of the uncertain future spot rate. As Figure 5A.1(a) shows, the treasurer's gamble is a winner when the future spot price is below today's forward rate and a loser when it is above that rate. We will refer to this and similar position diagrams throughout the appendix.

Hedging in Forward Markets

We are now ready to see how currency speculation can reduce the risk of loss on cross-border transactions. Set aside the treasurer's bet on the euro for a moment and suppose AMI has just booked a €1 million sale to a German buyer, with payment to be received in 180 days. The dollar value of this account receivable, of course, depends on the future exchange rate. In symbols,

$$\$ \text{ Value of AMI's receivable} = \tilde{S}(\text{€}1 \text{ million})$$

---

[2] My apologies to non-U.S. readers for making the United States the home country throughout this appendix. Please take solace in the fact that we Americans need all the help we can get when it comes to understanding exchange rates.

FIGURE 5A.1   **Forward Market Hedge**

(a) Forward Sale of €1 Million

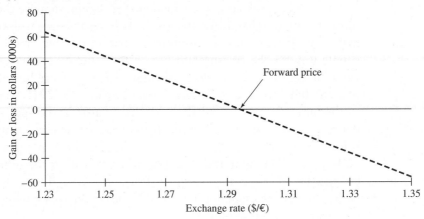

(b) € Account Receivable

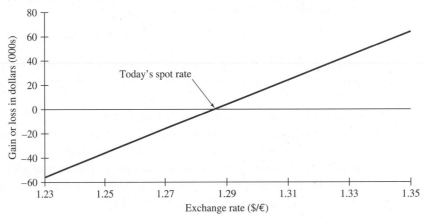

(c) Forward Market Hedge of € Receivable

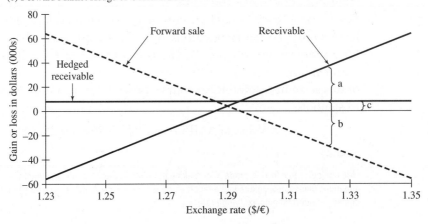

where $\tilde{S}$ is again the spot exchange rate. AMI faces foreign exchange risk, or exposure, because the dollar value of its German receivable in six months depends on the uncertain, future spot rate.

Figure 5A.1(b) is a position diagram for AMI's account receivable. It shows the change in the dollar value of AMI's receivable as the exchange rate changes. If the spot rate remains at $1.2859, the receivable will show neither a gain nor a loss in value, but as the price of the euro changes, so does the value of the receivable. In particular, an unlucky fall in the euro in coming months could turn an expected profit on the German sale into a loss—not exactly a morale booster for the operating folks who worked so hard to make the sale.

By generating the German account receivable, AMI has inadvertently bet that the euro will strengthen. If it wants to shed this risk, it can easily do so by instructing the treasurer to place an offsetting bet in the forward market. In this instance, the treasurer needs to sell €1 million 180 days forward, just as before. Upon adding the gain or loss on the forward sale to the dollar value of the account receivable, we find that AMI has "locked in" a value for the German receivable of $1,294,100:

$$\underset{\text{forward sale}}{\text{Gain or loss on}} + \underset{\text{receivable}}{\text{\$ Value of}}$$

$$(F - \tilde{S})\,€1 \text{ million} + (\tilde{S})\,€1 \text{ million}$$

$$= (F)\,€1 \text{ million}$$

$$= (1.2941)\,€1 \text{ million}$$

$$= \$1,294,100$$

The elimination of $\tilde{S}$ from the equation indicates that the treasurer's judicious combination of two opposing bets eliminates AMI's currency exposure. Now, regardless of what happens to the spot rate, AMI will receive $1,294,100 in 180 days. The treasurer has executed a *forward market hedge*, the effect of which is to replace the unknown future spot rate with the known forward rate in determining the dollar value of the receivable. AMI has locked in the forward rate.

How does the forward market hedge differ from the forward market speculation described earlier? It doesn't; the transactions are identical. The only difference is one of intent. In the speculation, the treasurer intends to benefit from his belief that the euro will fall. In the hedge, the treasurer presumably has no opinion about the euro's future price and intends only to avoid the risk of losing money on the account receivable. When the same transaction can be either a risky speculation or a risk-reducing hedge depending only on the intent of the person rolling the dice, it should come as no surprise to learn that companies frequently have trouble controlling their risk management activities.

Figure 5A.1(c) shows the forward market hedge graphically. The solid, upward-sloping line is the gain or loss on the unhedged receivable from (b), while the dotted, downward-sloping line is the position diagram for the forward sale from (a). The bold horizontal line represents the combined effect of the receivable and the forward sale. When both are undertaken, the *net* outcome is independent of the future spot rate. The forward hedge eliminates risk just as opposing bets on the Celtics–Knicks game did.

Instead of manipulating equations to determine the net effect of hedging, it is usually simpler to do the same thing graphically by adding the position diagram from one bet to that of the other at each exchange rate. For instance, adding the gain on the receivable, denoted by *a* in Figure 5A.1(c), to the loss on the forward sale, *b*, yields the net result, *c*. The fact that the net result at each exchange rate lies on a horizontal line confirms that the value of the hedged receivable does not depend on the future spot rate. In other words, the hedge eliminates exchange risk.[3]

Hedging in Money and Capital Markets

The treasurer eliminated exchange risk on AMI's euro asset by creating a euro liability of precisely the same size and maturity. In the jargon of the trader, he *covered* the company's *long position* by creating an offsetting *short position*, where a long position refers to a foreign-currency asset and a short position corresponds to a foreign-currency liability. By offsetting one against the other, he *squared* the position.

A second way to create a short position in euros is to borrow euros today, promising to repay 1 million euros in 180 days, and sell the euros immediately in the spot market for dollars. Then, in 180 days, the 1 million euros received in payment of the account receivable can be used to repay the loan. After the dust settles, such a *money market* hedge enables AMI to receive a known sum of dollars today in return for 1 million euros in 180 days. As you might expect in efficient markets, the costs of hedging in forward markets and in money and capital markets are almost identical.

Hedging with Options

Options are for those who tire of Russian roulette—unless, of course, the options are one leg of a hedge. An *option* is a security entitling the holder to either buy or sell an underlying asset at a specified price and for a specified

---

[3] The hedged position in Figure 5A.1(c) appears to result in a gain. Strictly speaking, however, this is not necessarily the case. A hedge involves an expected loss only when the forward rate is below the treasurer's *expected* future *spot* rate. The figure implicitly assumes the treasurer's *expected* future spot rate equals the current spot, which clearly need not be true.

time. Options come in two flavors: A *put* option conveys the right to sell the underlying asset, while a *call* is the right to buy it. To illustrate, for a payment of $32,400 today, you can purchase *put* options on the euro giving you the right to sell € 1 million for $1.29 a euro at any time over the next 180 days. As a matter of semantics, $1.29 is known as the option's *exercise*, or *strike*, price, and 180 days is its *maturity*. The $32,400 purchase price, payable today, is referred to as the *premium*.

Figure 5A.2(a) shows the position diagram for these put options at maturity for different exchange rates. The lower, dotted line includes the premium, while the solid line omits it. Concentrating first on the solid line, we see that the puts are worthless at maturity when the spot exchange rate exceeds the option's strike price. The right to sell euros for $1.29 each obviously isn't very enticing when they command a higher price in the spot market. In this event, the options will expire worthless, and you will have spent the $32,400 premium for nothing. The outcome is very different, however, when the spot rate is below the strike price at maturity. If the spot exchange rate falls to $1.25, for instance, the option to sell € 1 million at $1.29 is worth $40,000, and this number rises rapidly as the euro sinks further toward zero. In the best of all possible worlds (provided you're not European), the euro will be worthless, and your puts will garner $1.29 million—not a bad return on an $32,400 bet.

The position diagram for call options is just the reverse of that for puts. Based on today's closing prices, 180-day call options on € 1 million with a strike price of $1.29 are available for a premium of $39,400. As shown in Figure 5A.2(b), these calls will expire worthless unless the spot price rises above the strike price; the right to buy something for more than its spot price has no value. But once above the strike price, the value of the calls rises penny for penny with the spot.

To understand why options appeal to serious speculators, imagine you believe the euro will rise to $1.35 within six months. Using the forward market to speculate on your belief, you can purchase € 1 million forward today for $1.2941 each and sell them in six months for $1.35, thereby generating a return of 4.3 percent [(1.35 − 1.2941)/1.2941 = 4.3%]. Alternatively, you can purchase the call options for $39,400, followed in six months by exercise of the call and immediate sale of the euros for $1.35 each, thereby producing a heart-skipping return of 52 percent ([(1.35 − 1.29 × $1 million) − $39,400]/$39,400 = 52%)—more than 10 times higher than the forward market speculation. Of course, the downside risks are equally stimulating; a fall in the euro to $1.22 would generate a loss of only 5.7 percent in the forward market compared to a 278 percent loss with options.

FIGURE 5A.2 **Option Market Hedge**

(a) Put Option on €1 Million

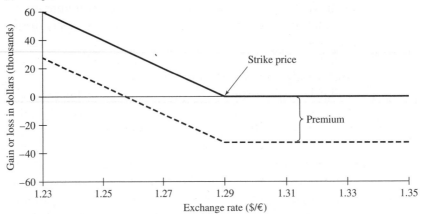

(b) Call Option on €1 Million

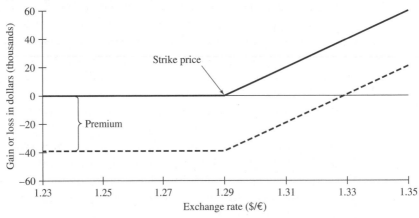

(c) Option Market Hedge of Receivable

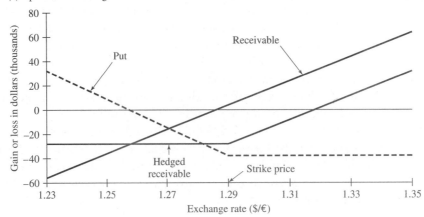

How might AMI use options to reduce exchange risk on the company's German receivable? Because the receivable makes the company long in euros, the treasurer will want to create an offsetting short position; that is, he will want to purchase put options. Calls would only add to AMI's currency risk.

Analyzing the hedge graphically, Figure 5A.2(c) shows the combined effect of AMI's German receivable and purchase of the described put options. As before, the upward-sloping, solid line represents the gain or loss in the dollar value of the receivable, and the bent, dotted line shows the payoff on the puts, including the premium. Adding the two together at each exchange rate yields the kinked solid line, portraying AMI's exchange risk after hedging with options.

Comparing the forward market hedge in Figure 5A.1 with the option hedge, we see that the option works much like an insurance policy, limiting AMI's loss when the euro weakens while still enabling the company to benefit when it strengthens. The cost of this policy is the option's premium.

Options are especially attractive hedging vehicles in two circumstances. One is when the hedger has a view about which way currencies will move but is too cowardly to speculate openly. Options enable the hedger to benefit when her views prove correct but limits losses when they are incorrect. Options are also attractive when the exposure is contingent. When a company bids on a foreign contract, its currency exposure obviously depends on whether the bid is accepted. Hedging this contingent exposure in forward markets results in unintended, and possibly costly, reverse exposure whenever the bid is rejected. The worst possible outcome with an option hedge, however, is loss of the premium.

Limitations of Financial Market Hedging

Because new initiates to the world of hedging frequently overestimate the technique's power, a few cautionary reflections on the severe limitations of financial market hedges are in order.

Two basic conditions must hold before commercial risks can be hedged effectively in financial markets. One is that the asset creating the risk, or one closely correlated with it, must trade in financial markets. In our example, this means euros must be a traded currency. For this reason, an exposure in Indian rupees is much harder to manage than one in euros.

The second necessary condition for effective foreign-currency hedging in financial markets is that the amount and the timing of the foreign cash flow be known with reasonable certainty. This is usually not a problem when the cash flow is a foreign receivable or payable, but when it is an operating cash flow, such as expected sales, cost of sales, or earnings, the

---

Currency and Interest Rate Swaps

Another derivative security, known as a *swap,* has altered the way many financial executives think about issuing and managing company debt. A swap is a piece of paper documenting the trade of future cash flows between two parties in which each commits to pay or receive the other's cash flows. The market value of a swap at any time equals the difference in the value of the underlying cash flows exchanged. A *currency* swap involves the trade of liabilities denominated in different currencies, while an *interest rate* swap entails the trade of fixed-rate payments for floating-rate ones. Swaps do not appear on the participating companies' financial statements, and lenders typically are unaware a swap has occurred. Swaps have become so commonplace that an active market now exists in which standard swaps are bought and sold over the phone much like stocks and bonds. If your company has a 10-year, Swiss franc liability and would prefer one denominated in U.S. dollars, phone a swap dealer for a quote.

Swaps inevitably seem exotic and a bit pathological on first acquaintance, but the underlying concept is really an elementary one. Whenever each of two parties has something the other wants, a trade can benefit both. A swap is such a trade in which the items exchanged are future interest and principal payments. Some swaps, denoted as asset swaps, involve rights to *receive* future payments, while more common liability swaps involve the obligation to *make* future payments.

Swaps have proven to be valuable financing tools for at least two reasons. First, swaps help solve a fundamental problem facing many companies when raising capital. Prior to the advent of swaps, a company's decision about what type of debt to issue often involved a compromise between what the company really wanted and what investors were willing to buy. An issuer might have wanted fixed-rate, French franc debt but settled for floating-rate, Canadian dollar debt because the terms were better. But with swaps, the issuer can have his cake and eat it too. Just issue floating-rate, Canadian dollar debt and immediately swap into fixed-rate, French franc debt. In effect, swaps enable the issuer to separate concerns about what type of debt the company needs from those regarding what type investors want to buy, thereby greatly simplifying the issuance decision and reducing borrowing costs.

A second virtue of swaps is that they are a slick tool for interest rate and currency risk management. Worried the Swiss franc will soon strengthen, increasing the dollar burden of your company's Swiss franc debt? No problem: Swap out of francs into dollars. Worried that interest rates are about to fall, saddling your company with a pile of high-cost, fixed-rate debt? Piece of cake: Swap into floating-rate debt and watch borrowing costs float down with the rates.

---

story is quite different. For example, suppose the treasurer of an American exporter to Germany anticipates earnings next year of 1 million euros, and she wants to lock in the dollar value of these profits today. What should she do? At first glance, the answer is obvious: Sell 1 million euros forward for dollars. But further consideration will reveal severe problems with this strategy. First, the exporter's long position in euros equals not next year's profits but next year's sales, a much larger number. Second, instead of hedging a known future cash flow as in our account receivable example, the exporter must hedge an unknown, expected amount. Moreover, because changes in the dollar-euro exchange rate will affect the competitiveness of the American exporter's products in Germany, we know that expected sales are themselves dependent on the future exchange rate. In terms of a position diagram, this means the foreign cash flow we seek to hedge cannot be represented by a straight line, which greatly complicates any hedging strategy. Third, if the American company expects to continue exporting to Germany into the foreseeable future, its exposure extends far beyond next year's sales. So even if it successfully hedges next year's sales, this represents only a small fraction of the company's total euro exposure. We conclude that hedging the risks of individual transactions such as those generating accounts receivable is a straightforward task, but hedging the much larger risks inherent in operating cash flows in financial markets is a complex, nearly impossible undertaking.

Our final caveat about financial market hedging is more philosophical. Empirical studies suggest that foreign exchange, commodity, and debt markets are all "fair games," meaning the chance of benefiting from unexpected price changes in these markets about equals the chance of losing. If this is so, companies facing repeated exchange exposures, or those with a number of exposures in different currencies, might justifiably dispense with hedging altogether on the grounds that over the long run, losses will about equal gains anyway. According to this philosophy, financial market hedging is warranted only when the company seldom faces currency exposures, when the potential loss is too big for the company to absorb gracefully, or when the elimination of exchange exposure yields administrative benefits such as more accurate performance evaluation or improved employee morale.

Valuing Options

As employee stock options have become more common, so has executives' interest in valuing options. "How much am I worth?" turns out to be a powerful learning incentive. So let us close with a quick primer on valuing options.

Suppose you receive a five-year option to purchase 100 shares of Cisco Systems stock for $20 a share when the stock is selling for $18, and you want to know what the option is worth today. It is apparent that your option would be worthless if you had to exercise it immediately, for the privilege of buying something for $20 when it is freely available elsewhere for $18 is not highly prized. Your option is said to be "out of the money." But fortunately you do not have to exercise the option immediately. You can wait for up to five years before acting and, indeed, may be prohibited from exercising the option for a period of time. Looking to the future, chances are good that sometime before the option matures, Cisco stock will sell for more than $20. The option will then be "in the money," in which case you can exercise it and sell the stock for a profit. We conclude that the value of the option today depends fundamentally on two things: the chance that Cisco's stock will rise above the option's strike price prior to maturity and the potential amount by which it might exceed the strike price. The challenge in valuing an option is to decide what these two things are worth.

Options have been around for many years, but it was not until 1973 that Fisher Black and Myron Scholes offered the first practical solution to this valuation challenge. Their solution is remarkable both for what it contains and for what it omits. Black and Scholes demonstrated that the value of an option depends on five variables, four of which are readily available in the newspaper. They are

- The current price of the underlying asset (which in our example is Cisco stock).
- The option's time to maturity.
- The option's strike price.
- The interest rate.

As you might expect, the value of a call option usually rises with the price of the underlying asset and the option's time to maturity, but falls with the strike price. The Cisco call option is more valuable when Cisco is selling at $50 than at $18 and when the option is good for 10 years as opposed to 5. Conversely, it is worth less when its strike price is $40 as opposed to $20. The value of a call rises as interest rates rise because a call option can be viewed as a delayed purchase of the underlying asset, and the higher the interest rate, the more valuable this deferral privilege becomes.

The one unobservable determinant of an option's value is the expected volatility of return on the underlying asset. In English, the value of the Cisco option depends on how uncertain investors are about the return on Cisco stock over the life of the option. The standard approach to estimating expected volatility is to look at the stock's past volatility, as measured by the standard deviation of past returns. (Standard deviation is a widely used statistical measure of dispersion, which we will consider in more detail in Chapter 8.) If the standard deviation of return on Cisco stock in the recent past has been 20 percent, this is a plausible estimate of its future volatility.

The intriguing thing about volatility is that option value rises with volatility. In other words, a call option on a speculative stock is actually worth more than an identical option on a blue chip. That's right. Options are contrary to intuition and to most of finance, where volatility means risk and risk is bad. With options, volatility is good. To see why, recall that an option allows its owner to walk away unscathed when things go poorly. In our example, if Cisco stock never rises above $20, the worst that can happen is that you will have some new wallpaper. This means that an option owner is only concerned with upside potential, and the greater the volatility, the greater this potential. If you received a dollar every time a batter hit a home run, wouldn't you rather back an erratic slugger than a steady singles hitter? The same is true of options. Uncertainty is good for options.

The input variable that is surprisingly missing from the Black-Scholes formula is the predicted future value of the underlying asset. In our example, there is no need to forecast the value of Cisco stock over the next five years to value the option. The result is much greater precision valuing options.

With the Black-Scholes option-pricing formula in hand, valuing an option is now a straightforward, three-step process. First, find the current values of the four observable variables. Second, estimate the future volatility of the underlying asset's return, usually by extrapolating its past volatility. And third, throw these numbers into the Black-Scholes option pricing formula, or one of its latter-day extensions, and wait for the computer to disgorge an answer. As an example, let's value the Cisco option under the following conditions:

Option strike price	$20
Option maturity	5 years
Current Cisco stock price	$18
Interest rate	3.5%
Volatility of Cisco stock	2.1%

My volatility estimate is from The Option Strategist, a Web-based investment advisory company that provides historical volatilities for many stocks.[4] The number used is Cisco's annualized historical volatility over the prior 100 days as measured on May 4, 2005. Rather than manipulating the Black-Scholes formula myself—a tedious task—I will use Robert's Option Pricer.[5] Plugging the requisite five numbers into the option pricer, we learn that the estimated value of the option on 100 Cisco shares is $389. At a volatility of 35 percent, the value jumps to $595. Receipt of the Cisco options may merit a celebratory dinner, but don't buy the Mercedes just yet.[6]

---

[4] The Option Strategist, McMillan Analysis Corporation, **www.optionstrategist.com/free/analysis/data/index.html**.

[5] Robert's Option Pricer, **www.intrepid.com/~robertl/option-pricer.html**.

[6] I have taken some liberties with the material in this section in the interest of simplicity. First, the pricing formula used in Robert's Option Pricer is an extension of Black-Scholes. In addition to the five variables discussed, the formula requires the dividend yield, which for Cisco is zero. It is also necessary to specify that the Cisco option is an American option because it can be exercised prior to maturity. Finally, I should acknowledge that employee stock options differ in important respects from traded options and that as a result, the calculated option values likely overstate the true value of employee stock options. In particular, conventional valuation formulas assume the option is continuously tradable, which is not true for employee stock options.

Growth of the options industry since introduction of the Black-Scholes pricing model recalls Mark Twain's quip, "If your only tool is a hammer, pretty soon all the world appears to be a nail." The ability to price options with reasonable accuracy has led to a remarkable growth in the volume and variety of options traded, including those on interest rates, stocks, stock indices, foreign exchange, weather, and a wide variety of physical commodities. In addition to traded options, we have discovered the presence of embedded options lurking in many conventional financial instruments such as home mortgages and commercial bank loans. In the past, these options were either ignored or only crudely reflected in the pricing of the instrument. Now it is possible to value each option separately and price it accordingly. From the discovery of embedded options in conventional instruments, it has been a small step to the creation of innovative new instruments that include heretofore unavailable options. Finally, we have recently begun to realize that many corporate investment decisions, such as whether or not to introduce a new product, contain embedded options that, at least in theory, can be priced using the techniques described. Examples of what are known as *real options* include the choice to expand production, to terminate production, or to change the product mix. The ability to price these options promises to greatly improve corporate investment decisions. (We will say more on this topic in Chapter 8.) Once you know how to price them, all the world indeed appears to be an option.

SUMMARY

1. This chapter examined financial instruments and markets. When raising capital, the financial manager acts much like a marketing manager. The product is claims on the firm's cash flow and assets, and the manager's goal is to package and sell these claims in a manner that yields the highest price to the company.

2. Companies are *not* greatly restricted by law or regulation in their ability to select or design a security. The key questions in designing a new security are: What does the investor want, and what meets the company's needs?

3. Fixed-income securities, such as bonds and most preferred stocks, generate a comparatively safe income stream to the investor but do not participate in the growth of the firm. Over the last century, corporate bonds as an investment have done little more than keep up with inflation.

4. Common stock is a residual-income security with claim on all income after payment of prior fixed claims. Common stockholders are the

principal beneficiaries of company growth. They receive income in the form of dividends and share price appreciation. Over the past century, the average *real* return on common stocks has been about 8.6 percent per year.

5. Private equity firms raise capital via limited partnerships to make intermediate-term, high-risk investments. Venture capitalists are members of the private equity industry.

6. Investment bankers play a key role in initial public offerings of common stock acting as advisors, underwriters, and selling agents. Issuing companies do not know the price at which their securities will be sold until immediately before the sale occurs and thus bear all of the price risk during the registration process.

ADDITIONAL RESOURCES

Dimson, Elroy, Paul Marsh, and Mike Staunton. *Triumph of the Optimists: 101 Years of Global Investment Returns*. Princeton, NJ: Princeton University Press, 2002. 302 pages.

   An elegant book by three British academics providing detailed information about returns earned on financial instruments in 16 countries over the twentieth century. An authoritative source of important information. About $100. Updated annually in *Global Investment Returns Yearbook* published by the bank ABN-AMRO.

Fabozzi, Frank J., Franco Modigliani, Frank J. Jones, and Michael G. Ferri. *Foundations of Financial Markets and Institutions*. 3rd ed. Englewood Cliffs, NJ: Prentice Hall, 2002. 663 pages.

   A thorough introduction to financial markets loaded with relevant concepts and institutional details. Authors combine solid academic credentials with practical experience. About $140.

Gladstone, David, and Laura Gladstone. *Venture Capital Handbook: An Entrepreneur's Guide to Raising Venture Capital*, revised edition. London: Financial Times Prentice Hall, 2002. 448 pages.

   If you intend to raise venture capital money or to become a venture capitalist, read this book. About $30.

Malkiel, Burton G. *A Random Walk Down Wall Street*. 8th ed. New York: W.W. Norton & Company, 2004. 416 pages.

   The classic best-selling introduction to market efficiency and personal investing by someone who knows both the academic and professional sides of the story. About $15.

Van Horne, James C. *Financial Market Rates and Flows*. 6th ed. Englewood Cliffs, NJ: Prentice Hall, 2001. 304 pages.

A well-written, informative look at the function of financial markets, the flow of funds through markets, market efficiency, interest rates, and interest rate differentials. An excellent summary of empirical studies of financial markets. Intended as a supplement for courses in financial markets and for practitioners interested in issuing or investing in fixed-income securities. Not a bedtime read. Available in paperback. About $55.

WEBSITES

www.cboe.com
Home of the Chicago Board Options Exchange. Site includes option prices, a dictionary, and online complimentary courses.

www.intrepid.com/~robertl
Robert's Option Pricer. Lots of information on stock options and related topics. You give the option pricer the five bits of information necessary to price an option, and it returns the estimated price. Also contains information on the volatility of stock prices. Check out "About options" at the bottom of the option pricer page for a witty introduction to options. Anyone who answers the question "How are options priced?" with "Usually with great difficulty" deserves a look.

www.investorguide.com
Check out "University" tab for brief articles on a wide variety of investing and personal finance topics.

www.sandhillecon.com/pdf/AcadWhitePaper.pdf
Read "Benchmarking the Returns to Venture," by Susan E. Woodward and Robert E. Hall. Authors conclude, "There is mild evidence in favor of the proposition that venture-type investments have higher returns, risk-adjusted, than does Nasdaq, but the magnitude is not as high as some venture boosters have suggested."

www.ventureeconomics.com
A resource site for venture capital investing including detailed statistics, a glossary, and many downloads.

www.vnpartners.com
Includes an informative primer on venture capital.

PROBLEMS

Answers to odd-numbered problems are at the end of the book. For additional problems with answers, see **www.mhhe.com/higgins8e.**

1. What is more important to investors: the number of a company's shares they own, the price of the company's stock, or the percentage of the company's equity they own? Why?

2. If the stock market in the United States is efficient, how do you explain the fact that some people make very high returns? Would it be more difficult to reconcile very high returns with efficient markets if the same people made extraordinary returns year after year?

3. A company wants to raise $500 million in a new stock issue. The company's investment banker indicates that a sale of new stock will require 8 percent underpricing and a 7 percent spread. (Hint: the underpricing is 8 percent of the current stock price, and the spread is 7 percent of the issue price.)

   a. Assuming the company's stock price does not change from its current price of $75 per share, how many shares must the company sell and at what price to the public?

   b. How much money will the investment banking syndicates earn on the sale?

   c. Is the 8 percent underpricing a cash flow? Is it a cost? If so, to whom?

4. Suppose in Figure 5.4 that the stock prices of target firms in acquisitions responded to acquisition announcements over a three-day period rather than almost instantly.

   a. Would you describe such an acquisition market as efficient? Why, or why not?

   b. Can you think of any trading strategy to take advantage of the delayed price response?

   c. If you and many others pursued this trading strategy, what would happen to the price response to acquisition announcements?

   d. Some argue that market inefficiencies contain the seeds of their own destruction. In what ways does your answer to this problem illustrate the logic of this statement, if at all?

5. The return an investor earns on a bond over a period of time is known as the *holding period return*, defined as interest income plus or minus the change in the bond's price, all divided by the beginning bond price.

   a. What is the holding period return on a bond with a par value of $1,000 and a coupon rate of 6 percent if its price at the beginning of the year was $1,050 and its price at the end was $940? Assume interest is paid annually.

   b. Can you give two reasons the price of the bond might have decreased over the year?

6. Companies generally can borrow money using bank debt or by issuing bonds. Why might a firm choose one method over the other?

7. a. Suppose that Liquid Force's stock price consistently falls by an amount equal to one-half the dividend it pays on the payment date. Ignoring taxes, can you think of an investment strategy to take advantage of this information?

   b. If you and many others pursued this strategy, predict what would happen to Liquid Force's stock price on the dividend payment date.

   c. Suppose that Liquid Force's stock price consistently falls by an amount equal to twice the dividend payment on the payment date. Ignoring taxes, can you think of an investment strategy to take advantage of this information?

   d. If you and many others pursued this strategy, predict what would happen to Liquid Force's stock price on the dividend payment date.

   e. In an efficient market, ignoring taxes and transaction costs, how do you think stock prices will change on dividend payment dates?

   f. Given that investors receive returns from common stock in the form of dividends and capital appreciation, do you think that increasing dividends will benefit investors in efficient markets and in the absence of taxes?

Problems 8 and 9 test your understanding of the chapter appendix.

8. The common shares of Fortune Brands, Inc. (FO), owner of many brands including Knob Creek bourbons, Wild Horse wines, Titleist golf products, and Swingline staplers, are trading today on the NYSE for $80 a share. You have employee stock options to purchase 1,000 FO shares for $75 per share. The options mature in three years. The annualized volatility of FO stock over the past 100 days has been 35 percent. The company's current dividend yield is 1.5 percent, and the interest rate is 6 percent. (Assume the options are American options that may be exercised at any time up to the maturity date.)

   a. Using the option pricer website mentioned in the appendix, estimate the value of your FO options.

   b. What is the estimated value of the options if their maturity is five months instead of three years? Why does the value of the options decline as the maturity declines?

   c. What is the estimated value of the options if their maturity is three years but FO's volatility is 55 percent? Why does the value of the options increase as volatility increases?

9. Some refer to common stock as an option on a company's assets. Do you see any logic to this statement? What is the logic, if any?

10. Use the Standard and Poor's Market Insight website, **www.mhhe. com/edumarketinsight**, for this problem. Assume that as of December 31, 2004, Fortune Brands, Inc., wants to raise $200 million in a new stock issue and that JP Morgan, the company's investment banker, believes the issue will require 6 percent underpricing and a 7 percent spread. (The underpricing is 6 percent of the current stock price, and the spread is 7 percent of the issue price.)

    a. Assuming the company's stock price does not change from its December 31, 2004 price, how many shares must the company sell and at what price to the public? (Consult Excel Analytics, Market Data, Monthly Adj. Prices.)

    b. How much money will the investment banking syndicates earn on the sale?

    c. Based on the company's March, 2005 price, what rate of return did the investors who bought stock approximately 3 months earlier receive?

    d. Based on the number of common shares outstanding as of December 2004 (consult Excel Analytics, Annual Balance Sheet), what proportion of the company's shares were sold in this offering?

CHAPTER SIX

The Financing Decision

Equity Capital: The least amount of money owners can invest in a business and still obtain credit.

Michael Sperry

In the last chapter, we began our inquiry into financing a business by looking at financial instruments and the markets in which they trade. In this chapter, we examine the company's choice of the proper financing instruments.

Selecting the proper financing instruments is a two-step process. The first step is to decide how much external capital is required. Frequently this is the straightforward outcome of the forecasting and budgeting process described in Chapter 3. Management estimates sales growth, the need for new assets, and the money available internally. Any remaining monetary needs must be met from outside sources. Often, however, this is only the start of the exercise. Next comes a careful consideration of financial markets and the terms on which the company can raise capital. If management does not believe it can raise the required sums on agreeable terms, a modification of operating plans to bring them within budgetary constraints is initiated.

Once the amount of external capital to be raised has been determined, the second step is to select—or, more accurately, design—the instrument to be sold. This is the heart of the financing decision. As indicated in the last chapter, an issuer can choose from a tremendous variety of financial securities. The proper choice will provide the company with needed cash on attractive terms. An improper choice will result in excessive costs, undue risk, or an inability to sell the securities. In this context it is important to keep in mind that most operating companies make money by creatively acquiring and deploying assets, not by dreaming up clever ways to finance these assets. This means that the focus of the financing decision should generally be on supporting the company's business strategy, and that care should be taken to avoid financing choices that carry even a modest chance of derailing this strategy. Better to make company financing the passive handmaiden of operating strategy than to jeopardize that strategy in pursuit of marginally lower financing costs. This is especially true for rapidly growing companies where aggressive financing choices can be especially costly.

For simplicity, we will concentrate on a single financing choice: XYZ Company needs to raise $200 million this year; should it sell bonds or stock? But do not let this narrow focus obscure the complexity of the topic. First, bonds and stocks are just extreme examples of a whole spectrum of possible security types. Fortunately, the conclusions drawn regarding these extremes will apply to a modified degree to other instruments along the spectrum. Second, many businesses, especially smaller ones, are often unable or unwilling to sell stock. For these firms, the relevant financing question is not whether to sell debt or equity but how much debt to sell. As will become apparent later in the chapter, the inability to raise equity forces companies to approach financing decisions as part of the broader challenge of managing growth. Third and most important, financing decisions are seldom one-time events. Instead, the raising of money at any point in time is just one event in an evolving financial strategy. Yes, XYZ Company needs $200 million today, but it will likely need $150 million in two years and an undetermined amount in future years. Consequently, a major element of XYZ's present financing decision is the effect today's choice will have on the company's future ability to raise capital. Ultimately, then, a company's financing strategy is closely intertwined with its long-run competitive goals and the way it intends to manage growth.

A word of warning before we begin: Questions of how best to finance a business recall the professor's admonition to students in a case discussion class: "You will find that there are no right answers to these cases, but many wrong ones." In the course of this chapter you will learn there is no single right answer to the question of how best to finance a business, but you will also discover some important guidelines to help you avoid the many wrong answers.

This chapter addresses a central topic in finance known as OPM: other people's money. We look first at how OPM fundamentally affects the risk and return faced by the owners of any risky asset. We then examine several practical tools for measuring these risk-return effects in a corporate setting, and we conclude by reviewing current thinking on the determinants of the optimal use of debt by a business. In the course of our review we will consider the tax implications of various financing instruments, the distress costs a company faces when it relies too heavily on OPM, the incentive effects of high leverage, the challenges faced by companies unable to sell new equity, and what are known as signaling effects. These refer to the way a company's stock price reacts to news that the company intends to sell a particular financing instrument. The chapter appendix takes up a major conceptual building block in finance known variously as the irrelevance proposition or the M&M theorem.

Financial Leverage

In physics, a lever is a device to increase force at the cost of greater movement. In business, OPM, or what is commonly called *financial leverage*, is a device that increases owners' expected return at the cost of greater risk. Mechanically, financial leverage involves the substitution of fixed-cost debt financing for owners' equity, and because this substitution increases fixed interest expenses, it follows that financial leverage increases the variability of returns to owners. Financial leverage is thus the proverbial two-edged sword, increasing owners' risk as well as return.

Table 6.1 illustrates this fundamental point in the form of a very simple risky investment. Ignoring taxes, the investment requires a $1,000 outlay today in return for a 50-50 chance at either $900 or $1,400 in one year. We are interested in how the owners' expected return and risk vary as we alter the type of financing. Panel A at the top of the table assumes all-equity financing. Observe that the investment promises an equal chance at a return of minus 10 percent or plus 40 percent (a $400 profit on a $1,000

TABLE 6.1   Debt Financing Increases Expected Return and Risk to Owners

The Investment: Pay $1,000 today for a 50-50 change at $900 or $1,400 in one year.

Panel A: 100% Equity Financing. Owners Invest $1,000.

Investment Outcome	Probability	To Owners	Return to Owners	Probability Weighted Return
$ 900	0.50	$ 900	−10%	−5%
1,400	0.50	1,400	40	20
			Expected return =	15%

Panel B: 80% Debt Financing; 1-year Loan at 10% Interest. Owners Invest $200.

Investment Outcome	Probability	Due Lender	Residual to Owners	Return to Owners	Probability Weighted Return
$ 900	0.50	$880	$ 20	−90%	−45%
1,400	0.50	880	520	160	80
				Expected return =	35%

investment implies a 40 percent return). Looking at the bold figures in Panel A, we see that these numbers imply an expected return on the investment of 15 percent with a range of possible outcomes between −10 percent and +40 percent.

Now let's pile on the debt and see what happens. Assume we finance 80 percent of the cost of the same investment with an $800, one-year loan at an interest rate of 10 percent. This reduces the owners' investment to $200. Panel B of Table 6.1 shows that while the investment cash flows are unchanged, the residual cash flows to owners change dramatically. Because owners must pay $880 in principal and interest to creditors before receiving anything, they now stand an equal chance of getting back $20 or $520 on their $200 investment. Looking again at the bold numbers in Panel B, this translates into an attractive expected return of 35 percent and a daunting range of possible outcomes between −90 percent and +160 percent.

This example clearly demonstrates that debt financing does two things to owners: It increases their expected return and it increases their risk. The example also illustrates that a single risky investment can be converted into a wide variety of risk-return combinations by simply varying the means of financing. Want to minimize risk and return on an investment? Finance with equity. Willing to take a gamble? Make the same investment, but finance it with some debt? Want to really roll the dice? Crank up the leverage. These same observations apply to companies as well as individual investments: Financial leverage increases expected return and risk to shareholders, and companies are able to generate a wide array of shareholder, risk-return combinations by varying the way they finance the business. (Incidentally, if you are worried about what happens to the $800 owners have leftover in Panel B, don't. The same conclusions follow if we assume owners combine their $1,000 of equity with $4,000 of borrowed money to invest $5,000 in the risky asset. All of the dollar figures in Panel B go up, but the returns remain the same.)

A second way to look at financial leverage is to note that it is a close cousin to *operating leverage*, defined as the substitution of fixed-cost methods of production for variable-cost methods. Replacing hourly workers with a robot increases operating leverage because the robot's initial cost pushes up fixed costs, while the robot's willingness to work longer hours without additional pay reduces variable costs. This produces two effects: Sales required to cover fixed costs rise, but once break-even is reached, profits grow more quickly with additional sales. Analogously, the substitution of debt for equity financing increases fixed costs in the form of higher interest and principal payments, but because creditors do not share in company profits, it also reduces variable costs. Increased financial leverage thus has two effects as well: More operating income is required to cover fixed financial costs, but once breakeven is achieved, profits grow more quickly with additional operating income.

To see these effects more clearly, let's look at the influence of financial leverage on return on equity. Recall from Chapter 2 that despite some problems, ROE is a widely used measure of financial performance defined as profit after tax divided by owners' equity. As shown in the footnote below, ROE can be written for our purposes as

$$ROE = ROIC + (ROIC - i') D/E$$

where ROIC is the company's return on invested capital (defined in Chapter 2 as EBIT after tax divided by all sources of cash on which a return must be earned), i' is the after-tax interest rate, $(1-t)i$, D is interest-bearing debt, and E is the book value of equity.[1] You can think of ROIC as the return a company earns before the effects of financial leverage are considered. Looking at i', recall that because interest is a tax-deductible expense, a company's tax bill declines whenever its interest expense rises; i' captures this effect.

To illustrate this equation, we can write ROE for Harley-Davidson, Inc., in 2004 as

$$ROE = 20.0\% + (20.0\% - 1.2\%) \$1,295.4/\$3,218.5$$

$$27.6\% = 20.0\% + 7.6\%$$

where 1.2 percent is Harley-Davidson's after tax borrowing rate, $1,295.4 million is its interest-bearing debt, and $3,218.5 million is its book value of equity. Harley-Davidson earned a basic return of 20.0 percent on its assets, which it levered into a 27.6 percent return on equity by substituting $1,295.4 million of debt for equity in its capital structure.[2]

This revised expression for ROE is revealing. It shows clearly that the impact of financial leverage on ROE depends on the size of ROIC relative to i'. If ROIC exceeds i', financial leverage, as measured by D/E, increases ROE. The reverse is also true: If ROIC is less than i', leverage reduces ROE. In English, the equation says that when a company earns more on borrowed money than it pays in interest, return on equity will rise, and

---

[1] Write profit after tax as $(EBIT - iD)(1-t)$, where EBIT is earnings before interest and tax, iD is interest expense—written as the interest rate, i, times interest-bearing debt outstanding, D—and t is the firm's tax rate. This equation reflects the steps an accountant goes through to calculate profit after tax from EBIT. The rest is algebra.

$$ROE = \frac{(EBIT - iD)(1 - t)}{E} = \frac{EBIT(1 - t)}{E} - \frac{iD(1 - t)}{E} = ROIC \times \frac{D + E}{E} - i' \frac{D}{E},$$

which equals the above equation.

[2] If 1.2 percent looks like a low interest rate, I agree. Review of footnotes to Harley-Davidson's financial statements suggests that the low rate is due at least in part to favorable interest rate swaps. The company nets the gains on these swap contracts against interest expense on their income statement.

vice versa. Leverage thus improves financial performance when things are going well but worsens performance when things are going poorly. It is the classic fair-weather friend.

And lest you think that earning a return above borrowing cost is an easy target, be aware that in 2004, a pretty good year for corporate profits, only 57 percent of the publicly traded, nonfinancial firms tracked by Standard & Poor's accomplished this feat. Even among larger firms with sales above $200 million, the comparable figure was just 78 percent. In business as in other walks of life, expectations are often unfulfilled.

Figure 6.1 is a graphical representation of the ROE equation above. The steeply pitched, solid curve represents a typical distribution of possible ROEs for an all-equity company. Note that the expected ROE is 10 percent and the range of possible outcomes is from a loss of about 12 percent to gain of 35 percent. The flatter, dotted curve shows the possible ROEs for the same distribution of all-equity returns when the company's debt-to-equity ratio is 2.0 and the after-tax borrowing rate is 4 percent. Debt financing levers the expected ROE from 10 percent up to 22 percent but also greatly broadens the range of possible outcomes. Now a loss of as much as 40 percent or a gain of more than 80 percent can occur.

For at least two reasons, it is appropriate to think of the range of possible ROEs as a measure of risk. First, a larger range of possible outcomes means greater uncertainty about what ROE the company will earn. Second, a

FIGURE 6.1   **Leverage Increases Risk and Expected Return**

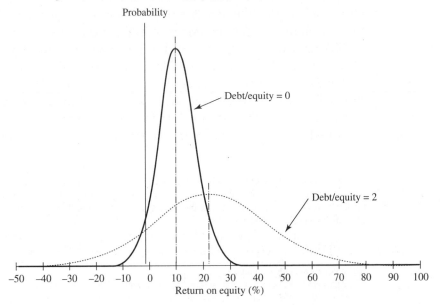

larger range of possible outcomes means a greater chance of bankruptcy. Look at the left-side tails of the two distributions, it is apparent that with zero leverage, the worst the company will do is lose about 12 percent on equity, but with a debt-to-equity ratio of 2 to 1, the same level of operating income generates a loss of about 40 percent, more than a threefold increase. In this situation, operating income is not sufficient to cover interest expense, and debt magnifies the loss. If the loss is large enough or persistent enough, bankruptcy can occur. In sum, we see again that financial leverage increases both expected return to owners and risk.

Measuring the Effects of Leverage on a Business

For a practical look at measuring the risks and returns of debt financing in a corporate setting, consider the challenge faced by Carlos Thompson, financial vice president of Harbridge Elextronix in early 2006. Harbridge Electronix, a manufacturer of electronic parts and subassemblies, was trying to decide how best to raise $300 million to finance completion of a major reorganization and expansion program. The program, which had been under way for two years, was expected to cost a total of $525 million. Thompson's forecasts indicated that Harbridge would be able to fund $225 million of this total out of operating cash flows and excess cash, leaving $300 million to be financed externally.

Historically, the company had sought to limit capital expenditures to an amount that could be financed out of internally generated funds and modest new borrowings. However, the board of directors had deemed the current investments too important to postpone and had directed Thompson to prepare a financing recommendation for consideration at their next board meeting. Complicating Thompson's decision was the fact that several younger members of senior management had recently voiced criticism of what they perceived to be Harbridge's overly timid financing policies. In their words, "We're leaving money on the table and short changing our shareholders by not levering up this business." One source of their enthusiasm for debt financing appeared to be the perception that higher leverage would increase earnings per share, a key determinant of Harbridge's executive bonuses. These executives saw the current situation as an ideal opportunity to right the balance by financing with debt. Thompson was less sure.

Harbridge's investment bankers indicated that the company could raise the needed money in either of two ways:

1. Sell 15 million new shares of common stock at a net price of $20 a share.

2. Sell $300 million, par value bonds at an interest rate of 8 percent. The maturity would be 20 years, and the bonds would carry an annual sinking fund of $15 million.

Looking to the future, Thompson believed the expansion program would increase Harbridge's earnings before interest and taxes (EBIT) to about $300 million in 2006. As shown in the following figures, EBIT had been rather volatile in the recent past. Thompson further anticipated that Harbridge's need for outside capital in the coming years would rise, probably to the $50–$100 million range annually. The company had paid annual dividends of 50 cents per share in recent years, and Thompson believed management intended to continue doing so.

	1999	2000	2001	2002	2003	2004	2005	2006F
EBIT ($ millions)	190	100	270	260	25	15	210	300

F = forecast.

Table 6.2 presents selected information about the two financing options in 2006. It shows that in the absence of any new financing, Harbridge will have $200 million in debt outstanding, interest expenses of $16 million, and a $40 million principal repayment. All of these numbers escalate sharply with $300 million in new debt financing. New stock, on the other hand, will leave these quantities unchanged but will increase common shares outstanding from 50 to 65 million and total dividend payments from $25 to $33 million.

Leverage and Risk

Thompson's first task in analyzing the financing options available to Harbridge Electronix should be to decide if the company can safely carry the financial burden imposed by the debt. The best way to do this is to compare the company's forecasted operating cash flows to the annual financial burden imposed by the debt. There are two ways to do this: construct pro forma financial forecasts of the type discussed in Chapter 3,

TABLE 6.2 Selected Information about Harbridge Electronix's Financing Options in 2006 ($ millions)

	Before New Financing	Stock Financing	Bond Financing
Interest-bearing debt outstanding	$200	$ 200	$500
Interest expense	16	16	40
Principal payments	40	40	55
Shareholders equity (book value)	820	1,120	820
Common shares outstanding	50	65	50
Dividends paid at $0.50 per share	25	33	25

TABLE 6.3   Harbridge Electronix Financial Obligations and Coverage Ratios in 2006 ($ millions)

Expected EBIT = $300; tax rate = 40%

	Stock		Bonds	
	After Tax	**Before Tax**	**After Tax**	**Before Tax**
Financial Obligations				
Interest expense		$16		$40
Principal payment	$40	67	$55	92
Common dividends	33	55	25	42

	Stock		Bonds	
	Coverage	**Percentage EBIT Can Fall**	**Coverage**	**Percentage EBIT Can Fall**
Coverage Ratios				
Times interest earned	18.8	95%	7.5	87%
Times burden covered	3.6	72	2.3	56
Times common covered	2.2	54	1.7	42

perhaps augmented by sensitivity analysis and simulations, or, more simply, calculate several coverage ratios. To provide a flavor of the analysis without repeating much of Chapter 3, I will confine discussion here to coverage ratios on the understanding that if real money were involved, detailed financial forecasting would be the order of the day. Because coverage ratios were treated in Chapter 2, our discussion can be brief.

The before- and after-tax burdens of Harbridge Electronix's financial obligations under the two financing options appear in the top portion of Table 6.3. Recall that because we want to compare these financial obligations to the company's EBIT, a before-tax number, we must gross up the after-tax amounts to their before-tax equivalents. This involves dividing the after-tax numbers by $(1 - t)$ where t is the company's tax rate. For Harbridge $t = 40\%$.

Three coverage ratios, corresponding to the progressive addition of each financial obligation listed in Table 6.3, appear in the bottom portion of the table for an assumed EBIT of $300 million. To illustrate the calculation of these ratios, "times common covered" equals $300 EBIT divided by the sum of all three financial burdens in before-tax dollars. [For bonds, $1.7 = 300/(40 + 92 + 42)$.] Note that our analysis here is not an incremental one. We are interested in the total burden imposed by new and existing debt, not just that of the new borrowings.

The column headed "Percentage EBIT Can Fall" offers a second way to interpret coverage ratios. It is the percentage amount by which EBIT can decline from its expected level before coverage drops to 1.0. For example, interest expense with bond financing is $40 million; thus, EBIT can fall from $300 million to $40 million, or 87 percent, before times interest earned for bond financing equals 1.0. A coverage of 1.0 is critical, because any lower coverage indicates that operating income will be insufficient to cover the financial burden under consideration, and another source of cash must be available.

As expected, these figures confirm the greater risk inherent in debt financing. In every instance, Harbridge's coverage of its financial obligations will be worse with debt financing than with equity. In fact, with debt financing, a decline in EBIT of only 42 percent from the expected level will put the company's dividend in jeopardy. And although missing a dividend payment is admittedly less catastrophic than missing an interest or a principal payment, it is still an eventuality most companies would just as soon avoid.

To put these numbers into context, Thompson will next want to compare them with various industry figures. As an example, Table 6.4 shows debt-to-asset and times-interest-earned ratios for nonfinancial companies in the Standard & Poor's 500 stock index from 1999 through 2004, and for selected industries in 2004. Note that the debt-to-assets ratio for the S&P

TABLE 6.4 **Average Nonfinancial Debt Ratios 1999–2004 and Industry Debt Ratios 2004**

Nonfinancial companies in Standard and Poor's 500 index and industry components, size-weighted averages. (Numbers in parentheses are the number of companies in sample.)

	1999	2000	2001	2002	2003	2004
Nonfinancial Companies in Standard & Poor's 500						
Debt to total assets* (%)	32	31	32	33	31	30
Times interest earned	5.0	4.8	3.9	4.3	4.9	5.9

Industry Debt Ratios 2004		
	Debt to Total Assets (%)	**Times Interest Earned**
Biotechnology (3)	15	31.5
Broadcasting, cable TV (3)	24	2.3
Computer hardware (7)	14	42.2
Electrical components (4)	23	10.1
Electric utilities (20)	37	2.6
Homebuilding (3)	50	5.1
Industrial machinery (8)	16	12.7
Movies and entertainment (4)	19	4.9
Pharmaceuticals (13)	18	26.1
Telecommunications equipment (13)	14	13.3

*All interest-bearing debt; all quantities measured at book value.

TABLE 6.5   Median Values of Key Ratios by Standard & Poor's Rating Category

Source: "CreditStats Final Adjusted Key U.S. Industrial Financial Ratios," RatingsDirect, Standard & Poor's, August 2004.

(Industrial long-term debt, three-year figures, 2001–2003)							
	AAA	**AA**	**A**	**BBB**	**BB**	**B**	**CCC**
Times interest earned (×)	23.8	13.6	6.9	4.2	2.3	0.9	0.4
EBITDA interest coverage (×)	25.3	17.1	9.4	5.9	3.1	1.6	0.9
Funds from operations/total debt (%)	167.8	77.5	43.2	34.6	20.0	10.1	2.9
Pretax return on capital (%)	35.1	26.9	16.8	13.4	10.3	6.7	2.3
Total debt/capital (%)	6.2	34.8	39.8	45.6	57.2	74.2	101.2
Number of companies	6	18	124	207	274	250	43

Variable definitions:
EBITDA = Earnings before interest, taxes, depreciation, and amortization.
Funds from operations = Net income from continuing operations plus depreciation, amortization, deferred income taxes, and other noncash items.
Pretax return on capital = EBIT/Average of beginning and ending capital, including short-term debt, current maturities, long-term debt (including amount for operating lease debt equivalent), noncurrent deferred taxes, and equity.
Long-term debt/capital = Long-term debt (including amount for operating lease debt equivalent)/Long-term debt + shareholders' equity (including preferred stock) plus minority interest.

Note: These figures are not meant to be industry standards. Company data are adjusted to eliminate nonrecurring gains and losses and to include an amount for operating lease debt equivalent.

companies has held steady at about 31 percent, while the coverage ratio dipped during the recession early in the decade before recovering to almost six times by 2004. Thompson will be especially interested in the two industries most similar to Harbridge, computer hardware and electrical components. By comparison Harbridge's prospective 7.5 times-interest-coverage ratio with debt financing will be well below the comparable industry ratios of 42.2 and 10.1 times, respectively.

Table 6.5 offers a somewhat more favorable comparison. It shows the variation in key performance ratios across Standard & Poor's bond-rating categories in the 2001 through 2003 time period. Note that the median times-interest-earned ratio falls steadily across the rating categories, from a high of 23.8 times for AAA companies down to 0.4 times for CCC firms. By this yardstick, Harbridge's prospective interest coverage ratio of 7.5 would put it in the AA to A range, a respectable rating.

Leverage and Earnings

Our brief look at Harbridge's coverage ratios under the two financing schemes suggests that debt financing is at least feasible. Next let's see how the two financing schemes are likely to affect reported income and ROE. Thompson can do this by looking at the company's projected income

TABLE 6.6 Harbridge Electronix Partial Pro Forma Income Statements in 2006 under Bust and Boom Conditions ($ millions except EPS)

	Bust		Boom	
	Stock	**Bonds**	**Stock**	**Bonds**
EBIT	$ 100	$ 100	$ 500	$ 500
Interest expense	16	40	16	40
Earnings before tax	84	60	484	460
Tax at 40%	34	24	194	184
Earnings after tax	$ 50	$ 36	$ 290	$ 276
Number of shares (millions)	65	50	65	50
Earnings per share	$0.78	$0.72	$ 4.47	$5.52
Return on invested capital	4.5%	4.5%	22.7%	22.7%
Return on equity	4.5%	4.4%	25.9%	33.7%

statement under the two plans. Ignoring for the moment the possibility that the company's financing choice might affect its sales or operating income, Thompson can begin his analysis with projected EBIT. Table 6.6 shows the bottom portion of a 2006 pro forma income statement for Harbridge under bust and boom conditions. Bust corresponds to a recessionary EBIT of $100 million, while boom represents a very healthy EBIT of $500 million.

Several noteworthy observations emerge from these figures. One involves the tax advantage of debt financing. Observe that Harbridge's tax bill is always $10 million lower under bond financing than under stock financing, leaving more cash flow to be divided among owners and creditors. It is as if the government pays companies a subsidy, in the form of reduced taxes, to encourage the use of debt financing. Letting t be the company's tax rate and I its interest expense, the subsidy equals tI annually. Many believe this subsidy, frequently known as the *interest tax shield* from debt financing, is the chief benefit of debt financing. It is available to any company using debt financing provided only that the company has sufficient taxable income to shield.

A second observation is that common stock financing always produces higher earnings after tax, simply because it involves no additional interest expense. But the most interesting point is the effect of the financing decision on EPS and ROE, both indicators of returns to shareholders. Looking at the boom conditions in Table 6.6, we see the expected effect of leverage: EPS with debt financing is a robust 23 percent higher than with equity. Under bust conditions, however, the reverse is true: Stock financing produces a higher EPS than debt. This corresponds to our earlier

FIGURE 6.2   **Range of Earnings Chart for Harbridge Electronix**

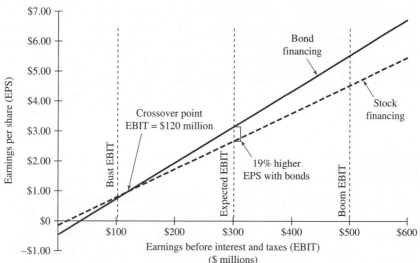

example, when the return on invested capital was less than the after-tax interest rate. Return-on-equity percentages display the same pattern: higher for debt under boom conditions but lower under bust conditions.

To display this information more informatively, Thompson can construct a *range of earnings*, or EBIT, chart. To do so, he need only plot the EBIT-EPS pairs calculated in Table 6.6 on a graph and connect the appropriate points with straight lines. Figure 6.2 shows the resulting range of earnings chart for Harbridge. It presents the earnings per share Harbridge will report for any level of EBIT under the two financing plans. Consistent with our boom-bust pro formas, note that the bond financing line passes through an EPS of $5.52 at $500 million EBIT and $0.72 at $100 million EBIT, while the corresponding figures for stock financing are $4.47 and $0.78, respectively.

Thompson will be particularly interested in two aspects of the range of earnings chart. One is the increase in EPS Harbridge will report at the expected EBIT level if the company selects bonds over stock financing. As the graph shows, this increase will be an attractive 19 percent at an expected EBIT of $300 million. Thompson will also observe that in addition to generating an immediate increase in EPS, bond financing puts Harbridge on a faster growth trajectory. This is represented by the steeper slope of the bond financing line. For each dollar Harbridge adds to EBIT, EPS will rise more with bond financing than with equity. Unfortunately, the reverse is also true: For each dollar EBIT declines, EPS will fall more with bond financing than with equity financing.

The second aspect of the range of earnings chart that will catch Thompson's eye is that bond financing does not always yield a higher EPS. If Harbridge's EBIT falls below a critical crossover value of $120 million, EPS will actually be higher with stock financing than with bonds. Harbridge's expected EBIT is well above the crossover value today, but the historical record presented earlier indicates that EBIT has been volatile in past years, and in fact has been below $120 million in three of the past seven years. Higher EPS with bond financing clearly is not guaranteed.

How Much to Borrow

Coverage ratios, pro forma forecasts, and range of earnings charts yield important information about Harbridge Electronix's ability to support various amounts of debt and about the effect of different debt levels on shareholder earnings. With this foundation, it is now time to address the chapter's central question: How do we determine what level of debt financing is best for a firm? How does Carlos Thompson decide whether Harbridge Electronix should issue debt or equity? There is general agreement that the purpose of a firm's financing decision should be to increase shareholder value. But what does this objective imply for specific financing decisions? As noted earlier, the current state of the art will not enable us to answer these questions with any great precision. We can, however, identify the key decision variables and suggest practical guides to Thompson's deliberations.

Irrelevance

See **www.dfaus.com/reprints/** for a candid interview with Merton Miller on the M&M theory and his philosophy of personal investing. See also interviews with Gene Fama and Rex Sinquefield.

Speaking broadly, there are two possible channels by which financing decisions might affect shareholder value: by increasing the value shareholders attach to a given stream of operating cash flows, or by increasing the level of the cash flows themselves. Some years ago, two economists eliminated the apparently more promising first channel. Franco Modigliani and Merton Miller, known universally today as M&M, demonstrated that when expected operating cash flows are constant, the amount of debt a company carries has no effect on its value and hence should be of no concern to value-maximizing managers or their shareholders. In their words, when cash flows are constant, the capital structure decision is irrelevant. In terms of risk and return, M&M demonstrated that the increased risk to shareholders from higher debt financing precisely offsets the increased return, leaving value unaffected.

Note the irony here. Questions of risk and return are centrally important to individuals. Strongly risk-averse individuals will prefer equity financing, while risk-indifferent ones will prefer debt. And if financing choices are so important at the personal level, it seems natural to conclude they must also be important at the market level. Financing decisions must affect market values. However, this conclusion does not necessarily follow. Indeed, the genius of M&Ms' irrelevance proposition is to demonstrate that under certain conditions, financing choices have no effect on value—despite their importance to individuals. Logicians would say that the irrelevance proposition corrects a fallacy of composition—the act of falsely drawing conclusions about a whole based on the features of its constituents.

The argument that changes in capital structure do not affect shareholder value may seem patently absurd at first glance. When a company substitutes debt for equity in its capital structure, the value of equity must surely decline. True, but that's not the whole story. Suppose a $5 billion all-equity company raises $2 billion in debt and repurchases a like amount of its equity. The repurchase will clearly drive shareholders' investment in the business down to $3 billion. However, because shareholders also receive $2 billion in cash when they sell shares to the company, their total wealth remains $5 billion. Unless the increase in leverage causes firm value to deviate from $5 billion, shareholders can neither gain nor lose from the transaction. Note too that if increased leverage does add to firm value, all the increase will flow to shareholders. Creditors get their contracted $2 billion, no more and no less.

Intuitively, M&M's irrelevance argument comes down to this. Companies own physical assets, such as trucks and buildings, and owe paper liabilities, such as stocks and bonds. A company's physical assets are the real creators of value, and as long as the expected cash flows produced by these assets stay constant, it is hard to imagine how simply reshuffling paper claims to the cash flows could create value. The company is worth no more with one set of paper claims than another. The cash flow M&M have in mind here is the annual after-tax amount available for distribution to owners and creditors, or earnings-after-tax plus interest expense. (See the appendix to this chapter for more on the irrelevance proposition, including a numerical example.)

The chief contribution of M&Ms' irrelevance proposition is to focus attention on the second channel by which financing choices might affect shareholder value. The proposition tells us that financing decisions *are* important to the extent that they affect expected cash flows, and that the best financing choice is the one that maximizes these flows. To decide whether Harbridge Electronix should issue debt or equity, therefore, Carlos Thompson needs to consider how the choice will affect his company's expected after-tax profits plus interest expense.

FIGURE 6.3   **The Higgins 5-Factor Model for Financing Decisions**

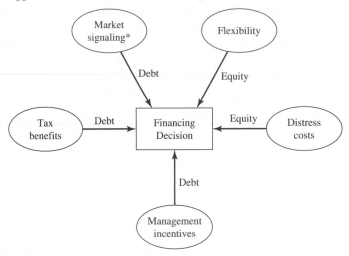

*Technically, market signaling affects investor perceptions of company cash flows, not the cash flows themselves. However, this distinction is not important for present purposes.

In the following pages we examine five ways in which a company's financing decision can affect its cash flows. With a nod to Michael Porter, Figure 6.3 presents these forces as part of what I will modestly call the Higgins 5-Factor Model. The figure also shows each factor's direction of influence when considered in isolation. Thus tax benefits considered alone suggest more debt financing, while distress costs caution more equity. Thompson's job is to consider each of these five factors in light of Harbridge Electronix's specific circumstances, and come to a reasoned judgment about their combined effect on company cash flows.

Tax Benefits

The tax advantages of debt financing are readily apparent. As noted in Table 6.6, Harbridge Electronix's tax bill falls $10 million annually when it increases debt by $300 million—a clear benefit to the firm and its owners. As Warren Buffett so deftly put it back in the days of a 48 percent corporate tax rate, "If you can eliminate the federal government as a 48 percent partner in your business, it's got to be worth more." As the tax bill goes down, the cash flow available for distribution to owners and creditors rises dollar for dollar.

Distress Costs

One popular perspective on selecting an appropriate debt level views the decision as a trade-off between the just-noted tax advantages of debt financing and various costs a company incurs when it uses too much debt.

Collectively, these costs are known as the costs of *financial distress*. According to this view, the tax benefits of debt financing predominate at low debt levels, but as debt increases, the costs of financial distress grow to the point where they outweigh the tax advantages. The appropriate debt level, then, involves a judicious balancing of these offsetting costs and benefits.

The costs of financial distress are more difficult to quantify than the benefits of increased interest tax shields, but they are no less important to financing decisions. These costs come in at least three flavors, which we will review briefly under the headings of bankruptcy costs, indirect costs, and conflicts of interest.

Bankruptcy Costs

The expected cost of bankruptcy equals the probability bankruptcy will occur times the costs incurred when it does. As a glance at Harbridge's coverage ratios attests, an obvious problem with aggressive debt financing is that rising debt levels increase the probability the business will be unable to meet its financial obligations. With high debt, what might otherwise be a modest downturn in profits can turn into a contentious bankruptcy as the company finds itself unable to make interest and principal payments in a timely manner.

While this is not the place for a complete review of bankruptcy laws and procedures, two points are worth making. First, bankruptcy does not necessarily imply liquidation. Many bankrupt companies are able to continue operations while they reorganize their business and are eventually able to leave bankruptcy and return to normal life. Second, bankruptcy in the United States is a highly uncertain process. For once in bankruptcy, a company's fate rests in the hands of a bankruptcy judge and a multitude of attorneys, each representing an aggrieved party and each determined to pursue the best interests of his or her client until justice is done or the money runs out. Bankruptcy today is thus akin to a high-stakes poker game in which the only certain winners are attorneys. And, depending on their luck, managers and owners can come away with a revitalized business or next to nothing.

Increased debt clearly heightens the probability of bankruptcy, but this is not the whole story. The other important consideration is the cost to the business if bankruptcy does occur. If bankruptcy involves only a few amicable meetings with creditors to reschedule debt, there is little need to limit borrowing to avoid bankruptcy. On the other hand, if bankruptcy spells immediate liquidation at fire-sale prices, aggressive borrowing is obviously foolhardy. A key factor in determining the cost of bankruptcy to an individual company is what can be called the "resale" value of its assets. Two simple examples will illustrate this notion.

Changing Attitudes Toward Bankruptcy

In recent decades, the public purpose of the bankruptcy process in the United States has shifted somewhat from protecting the rights of creditors toward protecting those of workers, communities, and society at large. Two things have changed in response. One is that creditors have factored the likelihood of greater losses in bankruptcy into their loan pricing by demanding higher rates. The other is that many managers have changed their attitude toward bankruptcy. Bankruptcy was once seen as a black hole in which companies were clumsily dismembered for the benefit of creditors and shareholders lost everything. Today some executives view it as a quiet refuge where the courts keep creditors at bay while management works on its problems. Manville Corporation was the first company to see the virtues of bankruptcy in August 1982, when, although solvent by any conventional definition, it declared bankruptcy in anticipation of massive product liability suits involving asbestos. Continental Airlines followed in September 1983, using bankruptcy protection to abrogate what it considered ruinous labor contracts. Subsequently, A. H. Robbins and Texaco, among others, have found bankruptcy an inviting haven while wrestling with product liability suits and a massive legal judgment, respectively. In all these instances, the companies expected to emerge from bankruptcy healthier and more valuable than when they entered.

First, suppose ACE Corporation's principal asset is an apartment complex and, due to local overbuilding and overly aggressive use of debt financing, ACE has been forced into bankruptcy. Because apartment complexes are readily salable, the likely outcome of the proceedings will be the sale of the complex to a new owner and distribution of the proceeds to creditors. The cost of bankruptcy in this instance will be correspondingly modest, consisting of the obvious legal, appraisal, and court costs, plus whatever price concessions are necessary to sell the apartments. In substance, because bankruptcy will have little effect on the operating income generated by the apartment complex, bankruptcy costs will be relatively low, and ACE can justify aggressive debt financing.

Note that the cost of bankruptcy here does not include the difference between what ACE and its creditors originally thought the apartments were worth and their value just prior to bankruptcy. This loss is due to overbuilding, not bankruptcy, and is incurred by the firm regardless of how it is financed or whether or not it declares bankruptcy. Even all-equity financing, while it may prevent bankruptcy, will not eliminate this loss.

At the other extreme, Moletek is a genetic engineering firm whose chief assets are a brilliant research team and attractive growth opportunities. If Moletek stumbles into bankruptcy, the cost is likely to be very high. Selling the company's assets individually in a liquidation will generate little cash, because most of the assets are intangible. It will also be difficult to realize value by keeping the company intact, either as an independent firm or in the hands of a new owner, for in such an unsettled environment it will be hard to retain key employees and to raise the funds needed to exploit growth opportunities. In essence, because bankruptcy will adversely affect Moletek's operating income, bankruptcy costs are likely to be high and Moletek would be wise to use debt sparingly.

In sum, our brief overview of bankruptcy costs suggests that they vary with the nature of a company's assets. If the resale value of the assets is high either in liquidation or when sold intact to new owners, bankruptcy costs are correspondingly modest. Such firms should be expected to make liberal use of debt financing. Conversely, when resale value is low because the assets are largely intangible and would be difficult to sell intact, bankruptcy costs are comparatively high. Companies matching this profile should use more conservative financing.

Indirect Costs

In addition to direct bankruptcy costs, companies frequently incur a number of more subtle indirect costs as the probability of bankruptcy grows. These costs are especially troublesome because they can be mutually reinforcing, causing a chain reaction in which one cost feeds on another. Internally, these costs include lost profit opportunities as management cuts back investment, R&D, and marketing to conserve cash. Externally, they include lost sales as customers become concerned about future parts and service availability, higher financing costs as investors worry about future payments, and increased operating costs as suppliers become reluctant to make long-run commitments or to provide trade credit. Lost sales and increased costs, in turn, pressure management to become even more conservative, risking further losses. And if this weren't enough, competitors, tasting blood in the water, are inclined to initiate price wars and to compete more aggressively for the company's customers.

Trade creditors in certain industries show an especially strong propensity to cut and run. With a portfolio of perhaps thousands of small-ticket receivables to manage, these suppliers are unwilling to work with ailing customers and instead rush for the exits at the first sign of trouble. With a conservative management, restless customers, aggressive competitors, and flighty suppliers, the slope between financial health and bankruptcy can be a slippery one.

Conflicts of Interest

Managers, owners, and creditors in healthy companies usually share the same fundamental objective: to see the business prosper. When a company falls into financial distress, however, this harmony can evaporate as the various parties begin to worry more about themselves than the firm. The resulting conflicts of interest are a third potential cost of aggressive

TABLE 6.7   **An Investment That Benefits Owners but Hurts the Firm and Its Creditors ($ millions)**

	Do Nothing	Make Investment		Expected Value
		50–50 Chance		
		Success	Failure	
Owners	$ 0	$ 30	$ 0	$15
Creditors	90	100	30	65
Total	$90	$130	$30	$80

Spend $60 million today for a 50–50 chance at $100 million or $0 in one year.

debt financing. Here is an example of one such conflict, known as the overinvestment problem.

A $60 million investment offering an equal chance of $100 million or $0 million in one year is clearly a bad deal. Paying $60 million now for an expected payoff of $50 million in one year is not the path to riches ($50 million = ½ $100 million + ½ $0 million). No sane manager in a healthy business should even contemplate such an investment. But consider how this investment looks to the owners of a struggling company that has $100 million of debt coming due in one year and only $90 million in assets.

Table 6.7 shows the possible outcomes of this investment as seen by the owners and creditors of such a firm. Consider the owners first. If they do not make the investment, they stand to receive nothing in bankruptcy. If they make the investment, however, they have a 50 percent chance of walking away with $30 million, and the worst they can do is end up where they started: with nothing ($30 million = $90 million firm assets − $100 million due creditors + $100 million investment return − $60 million investment cost). In other words, the owners have nothing to lose and $30 million to gain by making the investment, so why not roll the dice? Creditors, on the other hand, are less fortunate. Absent the investment they will receive $90 million in bankruptcy, but with the investment they stand an equal chance of receiving $100 million or only $30 million ($30 million = $90 million − $60 million investment). The owners' ability to stick creditors with investment losses while capturing much of the gains for themselves encourages self-interested, destructive behavior in the face of bankruptcy. Conflicts of interest such as this constitute yet another potential cost of financial distress.[3]

---

[3] Underinvestment problems can also arise in near-bankrupt companies in which managers knowingly forgo attractive investment opportunities because too much of the benefits accrue to creditors rather than to owners.

Before dismissing the overinvestment problem as an academic artifact, you may be interested to learn that it accurately describes the behavior of many U.S. savings and loan owners prior to the multibillion-dollar government bailout in the late 1980s. A number of savings and loans in this period were known in the trade as the "walking dead" because their liabilities greatly exceeded their assets and only the continued generosity of the government-supported deposit insurance program enabled them to keep their doors open. Faced with the near certainty that their equity would one day be wiped out, many owners took wild risks with depositors' money, hoping a big winner would bail them out.

So what do these musings about the relative importance of taxes and financial distress costs imply about how to finance a business? Our analysis suggests that managers should consider the following three firm-specific factors when making financing choices:

1. The ability of the company to utilize additional interest tax shields over the life of the debt.

2. The increased probability of bankruptcy created by added leverage.

3. The cost to the firm if bankruptcy occurs.

Applying this checklist to Harbridge Electronix, we can say that the first consideration should be no barrier to increased debt inasmuch as the company appears able to utilize whatever tax shields debt creates. On the other hand, the company's past income volatility suggests considerable caution in the use of debt financing. This conclusion is strengthened if we presume that as a manufacturer of electronic parts and subassemblies, Harbridge has substantial intangible assets, including growth opportunities, that would have low resale value in bankruptcy.

Flexibility

The tax benefits–distress costs perspective treats financing decisions as if they were one-time events. Should Harbridge Electronix raise $300 million today by selling bonds or stock? A broader perspective views such individual decisions within the context of a longer-run financing strategy that is shaped in large part by the firm's growth potential and its access to capital markets over time.

At one extreme, if Harbridge has the rare luxury of always being able to raise debt or equity capital on acceptable terms, the decision is straightforward. Thompson can simply select a target capital structure premised on long-run tax benefits and distress costs and then base specific debt–equity choices on the proximity of the company's present capital structure to its target. So if Harbridge's existing debt-to-equity ratio were below target, debt financing would be the obvious choice.

In the more realistic case where continuous access to capital markets is not ensured, the decision becomes more complex. For now Thompson must worry not only about long-run targets but also about how today's decision might affect Harbridge's future access to capital markets. This is the notion of financial flexibility: the concern that today's decision not jeopardize future financing options.

Looking at Harbridge, we know the company anticipates tapping the markets for from $50 million to $100 million annually in coming years. Also, given the company's volatile past earnings and comparatively low coverage ratios, it is possible that selling bonds now will "close off the top," meaning that over the next few years Harbridge may be unable to raise meaningful amounts of additional debt without a proportional increase in equity. (*Top* as used here refers to the top portion of the liabilities side of an American balance sheet. British balance sheets show equity on top of liabilities, but then they drive on the wrong side too.) Having thus reached its debt capacity, Harbridge would find itself dependent on the equity market for any additional external financing over the next few years. This is a precarious position because equity can be a fickle source of financing. Depending on market conditions and recent company performance, equity may not be available at a reasonable price—or indeed any price. And Harbridge would then be forced to forgo attractive investment opportunities for lack of cash. This could prove very expensive, because the inability to make competitively mandated investments can result in a permanent loss of market position. On a more personal note, Thompson's admission that Harbridge must pass up lucrative investment opportunities because he cannot raise the money to finance them will not be greeted warmly by his colleagues. Consequently, a concern for financing future growth suggests that Harbridge issue equity now while it is available, thereby maintaining financial flexibility to meet future contingencies.

The situation is more extreme for most small companies and many larger ones that are unable or unwilling to sell new equity. For these firms the financing decision is not whether to issue debt or equity, but whether to issue debt or restrict growth. Of necessity these companies need to place their financing decision in the larger context of managing growth. Recall from Chapter 4 that when a company is unable or unwilling to sell new equity, its sustainable growth rate is

$$g^* = PRA\hat{T}$$

where P, R, A, and $\hat{T}$ are profit margin, retention ratio, asset turnover ratio, and financial leverage, respectively. In this equation, P and A are determined on the operating side of the business. The financial challenge for these companies is to develop dividend, financing, and growth strategies

---

Reverse Engineering the Capital Structure Decision

Most companies select or stumble into a particular capital structure and then pray the rating agencies will treat them kindly when rating the debt. A growing number of businesses, however, are reverse engineering the process: first selecting the bond rating they want and then working backward to estimate the maximum amount of debt consistent with the chosen rating. Several consulting companies facilitate this effort by selling proprietary models—based on the observed pattern of past rating agency decisions—for predicting what bond rating a company will receive at differing debt levels.

The appeal of reverse engineering the capital structure decision is twofold. First, it reveals how much more debt a company can take on before suffering a rating downgrade. This is important information to businesses concerned about overuse of debt and to those interested in increasing the interest tax shields associated with debt financing. Second, it eliminates all speculation about how creditors will respond to a particular financing decision, enabling executives to focus instead on the more concrete question of what credit rating is appropriate for their company given its current prospects and strategy.

---

that enable the firm to expand at an appropriate rate without using too much debt or resorting to common stock financing.

An executive student of mine once told me I would never do anything entrepreneurial because "you know too much about what could go wrong." In the case of debt financing, I am inclined to agree. Too many entrepreneurs, convinced of the eventual success of their endeavors, appear to view debt as an unmitigated blessing. In their eyes, debt's only attribute is that it enables them to expand the size of their empire beyond their own net worth; thus their growth management strategy becomes simply to borrow as much money as creditors will lend. In other words, they maximize $\hat{T}$ in the above equation. Delegating the financing decision to creditors certainly simplifies life, but it also unwisely puts a critical management decision in the hands of self-interested outsiders. The smarter approach is to select a prudent capital structure and manage the firm's growth rate to lie within this constraint.

Market Signaling

Concern for future financial flexibility customarily favors equity financing today. A persuasive counterargument against equity financing, however, is the stock market's likely response. In Chapter 4, we mentioned that on balance, U.S. corporations do not make extensive use of new equity financing and suggested several possible explanations for this apparent bias. It is time now to discuss another.

Academic researchers have explored the stock market's reaction to various company announcements regarding future financing, and the results make fascinating reading. In one study, Paul Asquith and David Mullins, then of Harvard, were interested in what happens to a company's stock price when the firm announces a new equity sale.[4] To find out, they performed an event study, similar to the one described in the last chapter, on 531 common stock offerings over the period 1963 to 1981. Defining the event date as the day of first public announcement, Asquith and Mullins found that more than 80 percent of the industrial firms sampled experienced a decline in stock price on the event date and that for the sample as a whole, the decline could not reasonably be attributed to random chance. Moreover, the observed decline did not appear to be recouped in subsequent trading; rather, it remained as a permanent wealth loss to existing owners.

The size of the announcement loss was startling, averaging *more than 30 percent* of the size of the new issue. To put this number into perspective, a 30 percent loss means Harbridge Electronix could expect to suffer a permanent loss in the market value of existing equity of about $90 million the day it announced a $300 million equity issue (0.30 × $300 million = $90 million).

To complete the picture, similar studies of debt announcements have not observed the adverse price reactions found for equity financing. Further, it appears that equity announcements work both ways; that is, a company's announcement of its intention to repurchase some of its shares is greeted by a significant increase in stock price.

Why do these price reactions occur? Several explanations exist. One, suggested most often by executives and market practitioners, attributes the observed price reactions to dilution. According to this reasoning, a new equity issue slices the corporate pie into more pieces and reduces the portion of the pie owned by existing shareholders. It is therefore natural that the shares existing shareholders own will be worth less. Conversely, when a company repurchases its shares, each remaining share represents ownership of a larger portion of the company and hence is worth more.

Other observers, including yours truly, remain unconvinced by this reasoning, pointing out that while an equity issue may be analogous to slicing a pie into more pieces, the pie also grows by virtue of the equity issue. And there is no reason to expect that a smaller slice of a larger pie is necessarily worth less; nor is there any reason to expect remaining shareholders to necessarily gain from a share repurchase. True, each post-repurchase share represents a larger percentage ownership claim, but the repurchase also reduces the size of the company.

A more intriguing explanation involves what is known as *market signaling*. Suppose, plausibly enough, that Harbridge Electronix's top managers

[4] Paul Asquith and David W. Mullins, Jr., "Equity Issues and Offering Dilution," *Journal of Financial Economics,* January–February 1986, pp. 61–89.

know much more about their company than do outside investors, and consider again Harbridge's range of earnings chart, Figure 6.2. Begin by reflecting on which financing option you would recommend if, as Harbridge's financial vice president, you were highly optimistic about the company's future. After a thorough analysis of the market for Harbridge's products and its competitors, you are confident that EBIT can only grow over the next decade, most likely at a rapid rate. If you have been awake the last few pages, you will know that the logical choice in this circumstance is debt financing. Debt produces higher EPS today and puts the company on the steeper growth trajectory. Moreover, growing income will make it easy to support the higher financial burden of the debt.

Now reverse the exercise and consider which financing option you would recommend if you were concerned about Harbridge's prospects, fearing that future EBIT might well decline. In this scenario, equity financing is the clear winner because of its superior coverage and higher EPS at low operating levels.

But if those who know the most about a company finance with debt when the future looks bright and with equity when it looks grim, what does an equity announcement tell investors? Right: It signals the market that management is concerned about the future and has opted for the safe financing choice. Is it any wonder, then, that stock price falls on the announcement and that many companies are thus reluctant to even mention the "E" word, much less sell it?

The market signal conveyed by a share repurchase announcement is just the reverse. Top management is optimistic about the company's future prospects and perceives that current stock price is inexplicably low, so low that share repurchase constitutes an irresistible bargain. A repurchase announcement therefore signals good news to investors, and stock price rises.

A more Machiavellian view, which nonetheless comes to the same conclusion, sees management as exploiting investors by opportunistically selling shares when they are overpriced and repurchasing them when they are underpriced. But regardless of whether management elects to sell new equity because it is concerned about the company's future or because it wants to gouge new investors, the signal is the same: New equity announcements are bad news and repurchase announcements are good news.

Stewart Myers of MIT reasons that the adverse market signals associated with new financing announcements encourage companies to adopt what he calls a "pecking order" approach to financing.[5] At the top of the pecking order as the most preferred means of financing are internal sources, retained profits, depreciation, and excess cash accumulated from

[5] Stewart C. Myers, "The Capital Structure Puzzle," *Journal of Finance,* July 1984, pp. 575–592.

past profit retentions. Companies prefer internal financing sources because they avoid market signaling entirely. External sources are second in order of preference, with debt financing dominating equity because it is less likely to generate a negative signal. The financing decision, then, essentially amounts to working progressively down this pecking order in search of the first feasible source. Myers also notes that the observed debt-to-equity ratios of such pecking-order companies are less a product of a rational balancing of advantages and disadvantages of debt relative to equity and more the aggregate result over time of the company's profitability relative to its investment needs. Thus, high-profit-margin, modestly growing companies can get away with little or no debt, while lower-margin, more rapidly expanding businesses may be forced to live with higher leverage ratios.

Management Incentives

Incentive effects are not relevant in most financing decisions, but when relevant, their influence can be dominating.

Managers in many companies enjoy a degree of autonomy from owners. And human nature being what it is, they are inclined to use this autonomy to pursue their own interests rather than those of owners. This separation of ownership and control enables managers to indulge their personal preferences for such things as retaining profits in the business rather than returning them to owners, pursuing growth at the expense of profitability, and settling for satisfactory performance rather than excellence.

A virtue of aggressive debt financing in some instances is that it can reduce the gap between owners' interests and those of managers. The mechanics are simple. When a company's interest and principal repayment burden is high, even the most recalcitrant manager understands that he must generate healthy cash flows or risk losing the business and his job. With creditors breathing down their necks, managers quickly find there is no room for ill-advised investments or less than maximum effort. As discussed in more detail in Chapter 9, leveraged buyout firms have found that aggressive debt financing, especially when combined with significant management ownership, can create powerful incentives to improve performance. Ownership in such highly levered companies serves as a carrot to encourage superior performance, while the high debt level is a stick to punish inferior performance.

The Financing Decision and Growth

We have examined five ways in which a company's financing choices can affect its value. The art of the financing decision is to weigh the relative importance of these five forces for the specific firm. To illustrate the process, let's consider what these forces suggest about how debt levels should vary with firm growth.

Rapid Growth and the Virtues of Conservatism

Review of the likely effect of the five forces on rapidly growing businesses strongly suggests that high growth and high debt are a dangerous combination. First, the most powerful engine of value creation in a rapidly growing business is new investment, not interest tax shields or incentive effects that might accompany debt financing. Better, therefore, to make financing a passive servant to growth by striving to maintain unrestricted access to financial markets. This implies modest debt financing. Second, to the extent that high growth firms generate volatile income streams, chances of financial distress rise rapidly as interest coverage falls. Third, because much of a high-growth firm's value is represented by intangible growth opportunities, expected bankruptcy costs of such firms are large.

These considerations suggest the following financing polices for rapidly growing businesses:

- Maintain a conservative leverage ratio with ample unused borrowing capacity to ensure continuous access to financial markets.

- Adopt a modest dividend payout policy that enables the company to finance most of its growth internally.

- Use cash, marketable securities, and unused borrowing capacity as temporary liquidity buffers to provide financing in years when investment needs exceed internal sources.

- If external financing is necessary, use debt only to the point where the leverage ratio begins to threaten financial flexibility.

- Sell equity rather than restrict access to financial markets, and reduce growth only as a last resort after all other alternatives have been exhausted.

Low Growth and the Appeal of Aggressive Financing

Compared to their rapidly growing brethren, slow-growth companies have a much easier time with financing decisions. Because their chief financial problem is disposing of excess operating cash flow, concerns about financial flexibility and adverse market signaling are largely foreign to them. However, beyond merely eliminating a problem, this situation creates an opportunity that a number of companies have successfully exploited. The logic goes like this. Face the reality that the business has few attractive investment opportunities, and seek to create value for owners

Don't Talk to Deere & Company About Market Signaling

The experiences of Deere & Company, the world's largest farm equipment manufacturer, in the late 1970s and early 1980s provide a vivid object lesson for much of this chapter. Among the lessons illustrated are the value of financial flexibility, the use of finance as a competitive weapon, and the power of market signaling.

Beginning in 1976, rising oil prices, high and increasing inflation rates, and record-high interest rates sent the farm equipment industry into a severe tailspin. Much more conservative financially than its principal rivals, Massey Ferguson and International Harvester, Deere chose this moment to use its superior balance sheet strength as a competitive weapon. While competitors retrenched under the burden of high interest rates and heavy debt loads, Deere borrowed liberally to finance a major capital investment program and support financially distressed dealers. The strategy saw Deere's three-company market share rise from 38 percent in 1976 to 49 percent by 1980; such was the value of Deere's superior financial flexibility.

But by late 1980, with its borrowing capacity dwindling and the farm equipment market still depressed, Deere faced the difficult choice between curtailing its predatory expansion program and issuing new equity into the teeth of an industry depression. On January 5, 1981, the company announced a $172 million equity issue and watched the market value of its existing shares immediately fall by $241 million. So powerful was the announcement effect that Deere's existing shareholders lost more value than Deere stood to raise from the issue.

Despite the negative market response, Deere managers were so strongly convinced of the long-run virtues of their strategy that they gritted their teeth, issued the equity, and used the proceeds to reduce indebtedness. Deere thus regained the borrowing capacity and the financial flexibility it needed to continue expanding, while its rivals remained mired in financial distress.

through aggressive use of debt financing. Use the company's healthy operating cash flow as the magnet for borrowing as much money as is feasible, and use the proceeds to repurchase shares.

Such a strategy promises at least three possible payoffs to owners. First, increased interest tax shields reduce income taxes, leaving more money for investors. Second, the share repurchase announcement should generate a positive market signal. Third, the high financial leverage may significantly improve management incentives. Thus, the burden high financial leverage imposes on management to make large, recurring interest and principal payments or face bankruptcy may be just the elixir needed to encourage them to squeeze more cash flow out of the business.

In summary, an old saw among bank borrowers is that the only companies banks are willing to lend money to are those that don't need it. We see now that much the same dynamic may be at work on the borrowers' side. Slow-growth businesses that don't need external financing may find it attractive to finance aggressively, while rapidly growing businesses in need of external cash find it appealing to maintain conservative capital structures.

Empirical work supports the wisdom of this perspective. In their study of the ties between company value and the use of debt financing, John

Colt Industries' Experience with Aggressive Financing

Colt Industries' late 1986 recapitalization illustrates the potential of aggressive financing in mature businesses. Facing increasing cash flows from its aerospace and automotive operations and a dearth of attractive investment opportunities, Colt decided to recapitalize its business by offering shareholders $85 in cash plus one share of stock in the newly recapitalized company in exchange for each old share held.

To finance the $85 cash payment, Colt borrowed $1.4 billion, raising total long-term debt to $1.6 billion and reducing the book value of shareholders' equity to *minus* $157 million. In other words, after the recapitalization, Colt's liabilities exceeded the book value of its assets by $157 million, yielding a negative book value of equity. We are talking serious leverage here. But book values are of secondary importance to lenders when the borrower has the cash flow to service its obligations, and this is where Colt's healthy operating cash flows were critical. Management's willingness to commit virtually all of its future cash flow to debt service enabled the company to secure the needed financing.

How did the shareholders make out? Quite well, thank you. Just prior to the announcement of the exchange offer, Colt's shares were trading at $67, and immediately after the exchange was completed, shares in the newly recapitalized company were trading for $10. So the offer came down to this: $85 cash plus one new share of stock worth $10 in exchange for each old share worth $67. This works out to a windfall gain to owners of $28 a share, or 42 percent ($28 = $85 + $10 − $67).

McConnell and Henri Servaes have found that for high-growth businesses increasing leverage reduces firm value, while precisely the reverse is true for slow-growth businesses.[6]

What does all this imply for Harbridge Electronix's decision? It's a tough call, but based on the information available, my advice is to sell equity. Debt financing's $10 million annual tax benefit would be nice, and equity's $90 million signaling cost would hurt, but these factors are outweighed in my mind by the increased distress costs and loss of flexibility that accompany debt financing. The company's volatile income stream and modest interest coverage relative to competitors suggest that debt financing will materially increase the probability of financial distress, while the intangible growth opportunities characteristic of the industry imply high costs if distress occurs. In addition, the company's projected continuing need for external financing speaks to the importance of maintaining flexibility via a conservative capital structure. In my judgment, expected cash flows to capital providers will be maximized with equity financing. Granted, the company's price-to-earnings multiple based on 2005 earnings is only about ten times, but equity is at least available. My advice is to grab it while they can.

[6] John J. McConnell and Henri Servaes, "Equity Ownership and the Two Faces of Debt," *Journal of Financial Economics,* September 1995, pp. 131–57.

Selecting a Maturity Structure

When a company decides to raise debt, the next question is: What maturity should the debt have? Should the company take out a 1-year loan, sell 7-year notes, or market 30-year bonds? Looking at the firm's entire capital structure, the minimum-risk maturity structure occurs when the maturity of liabilities equals that of assets, for in this configuration, cash generated from operations over coming years should be sufficient to repay existing liabilities as they mature. In other words, the liabilities will be self-liquidating. If the maturity of liabilities is less than that of assets, the company incurs a refinancing risk because some maturing liabilities will have to be paid off from the proceeds of newly raised capital. Also, as noted in Chapter 5, the rollover of maturing debt is not an automatic feature of capital markets. When the maturity of liabilities is greater than that of assets, cash provided by operations should be more than sufficient to repay existing liabilities as they mature. This provides an extra margin of safety, but it also means the firm may have excess cash in some periods.

If maturity matching is minimum risk, why do anything else? Why allow the maturity of liabilities to be less than that of assets? Companies mismatch either because long-term debt is unavailable on acceptable terms or because management anticipates that mismatching will reduce total borrowing costs. For example, if the treasurer believes interest rates will decline in the future, an obvious strategy is to use short-term debt now and hope to roll it over into longer-term debt at lower rates in the future. Of course, efficient-markets advocates criticize this strategy on the grounds that the treasurer has no basis for believing she can forecast future interest rates.

Inflation and Financing Strategy

An old adage in finance is that it's good to be a debtor during inflation because the debtor repays the loan with depreciated dollars. It is important to understand, however, that this saying is correct only when the inflation is unexpected. When creditors expect inflation, the interest rate they charge rises to compensate for the expected decline in the purchasing power of the loan principal. This means it is not necessarily advantageous to borrow during inflation. In fact, if inflation unexpectedly declines during the life of a loan, it can work to the disadvantage of the borrower. The proper statement of the old adage, therefore, is that it's good to be a borrower during unexpected inflation.

APPENDIX

The Irrelevance Proposition

This appendix demonstrates the irrelevance of capital structure proposition mentioned in the chapter and illustrates in greater detail why the tax deductibility of interest favors debt financing. The irrelevance proposition says that holding expected cash flows constant, the way a company finances its operations has no effect on firm or shareholder value. As far as owners are concerned, a company might just as well use 90 percent debt financing as 10 percent.

The irrelevance proposition is significant not because it describes reality, but because it directs attention to what's important about financing decisions: understanding how financing choices affect firm cash flows. The proposition is also an interesting intellectual puzzle in its own right.

No Taxes

Legend has it that a waitress once asked Yogi Berra how many pieces he'd like his pizza cut into, and he replied, "You'd better make it six; I don't think I'm hungry enough to eat eight." Absent taxes, a company's financing decision can be likened to slicing Yogi's pizza: No matter how you slice up claims to the firm's cash flow, it is still the same firm with the same earning power and hence the same market value. The benefits of increased return to shareholders from higher leverage are precisely offset by the increased risks so that market value is unaffected by leverage.

Here is an example demonstrating this assertion. Your stockbroker has come up with two possible investments, Timid Inc. and Bold Company. The two firms happen to be identical in every respect except that Timid uses no debt financing while Bold relies on 80 percent debt financing at an annual interest cost of 10 percent. Each has $1,000 of assets and generates expected annual earnings before interest and tax of $400 in perpetuity. For simplicity, we will suppose that both companies distribute all their earnings every year as dividends.

The first two columns of Table 6A.1 show the bottom portion of pro forma income statements for the two companies in the absence of taxes. Note that Timid, Inc., shows higher earnings because it has no interest expense. Comparing Timid's $400 annual earnings to your prospective investment of $1,000 suggests a 40 percent annual return. Not bad! However, your broker recommends Bold Company, pointing out that because

TABLE 6A.1 In the Absence of Taxes, Debt Financing Affects Neither Income nor Firm Value; In the Presence of Taxes, Prudent Debt Financing Increases Income and Firm Value

	No Taxes		Corporate Taxes at 40%	
	Timid Inc.	Bold Co.	Timid Inc.	Bold Co.
Corporate Income				
EBIT	$ 400	$ 400	$ 400	$ 400
Interest expense	0	80	0	80
Earnings before tax	400	320	400	320
Corporate tax	0	0	160	128
Earnings after tax	$ 400	$ 320	$ 240	$ 192
Investment	$1,000	$ 200	$1,000	$ 200
Rate of return	40%	160%	24%	96%
Personal Income				
Dividends received	400	320	240	192
Interest expense	80	0	80	0
Total income	$ 320	$ 320	$ 160	$ 192
Equity invested	$ 200	$ 200	$ 200	$ 200
Rate of return	160%	160%	80%	96%
Personal Taxes at 33%				
Income before tax			160	192
Personal taxes			53	63
Income after tax			$ 107	$ 129
Equity invested			$ 200	$ 200
Rate of return			54%	64%

of the company's aggressive use of debt financing, you can purchase its entire equity for only $200. Comparing Bold Company's annual income of $320 to a $200 investment produces an expected annual return of 160% ($320/$200 = 160%). Wow!

But you have studied enough finance to know that the expected return to equity almost always rises with debt financing, so this result is not especially surprising. Moreover, a moment's reflection should convince you that it is incorrect to compare returns on two investments with different risk. If the return on investment A is greater than the return on investment B and they have the same risk, A is the better choice. But if A has a higher return and higher risk, as in the present case, all bets are off. Poker players and fighter pilots might prefer investment A despite its higher risk, while we more timid souls might reach the opposite conclusion.

More to the point, it is important to note that you are not dependent on Bold Company for financial leverage. You can borrow on your own account to help pay for your purchase of Timid's shares and in so doing precisely replicate Bold's numbers. The bottom portion of the left two columns in Table 6A.1, labeled Personal Income, show the results of your borrowing $800 at 10 percent interest to finance purchase of Timid's shares. Subtracting $80 interest and comparing your total income to your $200 equity investment, we find that your levered return on Timid stock is now also 160 percent. You can generate precisely the same return on either investment provided you are willing to substitute personal debt for corporate debt.

So what have we proven? We have shown that when investors can substitute homemade leverage for corporate leverage in the absence of taxes, the way a business is financed does not affect the total return to owners. And if total return is unaffected, neither is the value of the business. Firm value is independent of financing. If investors can replicate the leverage effects of corporate borrowing on their own account, there is no reason for them to pay more for a levered firm than an unlevered one. (If the logic here seems a bit counterintuitive, you will be heartened to learn that Franco Modigliani and Merton Miller won Nobel Prizes largely for explaining it.)

Taxes

Let us now repeat our saga in a more interesting world that includes taxes. The figures in the upper-right corner of Table 6A.1 show Timid and Bold's earnings after taxes in the presence of a 40 percent corporate tax rate. As before, absent any borrowing on your part, Bold continues to offer the more attractive return of 96 percent versus 24 percent for Timid. But contrary to the no-taxes case, the substitution of personal borrowing for corporate borrowing does not eliminate the differential. Even after borrowing $800 to help finance purchase of Timid, your return is only 80 percent versus 96 percent on Bold's stock. The levered business now offers a higher return and thus is more valuable than its unlevered cousin.

Why does debt financing increase the value of a business in the presence of taxes? Look at the tax bills of the two companies. Timid's taxes are $160, while Bold's are only $128, a saving of $32. Three parties share in the fruits of a company's success: creditors, owners, and the tax collector. Our example shows that debt financing, with its tax-deductible interest expense, reduces the tax collector's take in favor of the owners'. In other words, the financing decision increases expected cash flow to owners.

The bottom portion of Table 6A.1 is for suspicious readers who think these results might hinge on the omission of personal taxes. There you will note that imposition of a 33 percent personal tax on income reduces the annual after-tax advantage of debt financing from $32 to $22, but does not eliminate it. Note too that this conclusion holds at any personal tax rate, as long as it is the same for both firms. Because many investors, such as mutual funds and pension funds, do not pay taxes, the convention is to dodge the problem of defining an appropriate personal tax rate by concentrating on earnings after corporate taxes but before personal taxes. We will gratefully follow that convention here.

I should note that our finding of a tax law bias in favor of debt financing is largely an American result. In most other industrialized countries, corporate and personal taxes are at least partially integrated, meaning dividend recipients receive at least partial credit on their personal tax bills for corporate taxes paid on distributed profits. As in our no-tax example, there are no tax benefits to debt financing when corporate and personal taxes are fully integrated.

In the presence of American-style corporate taxes, then, the reshuffling of paper claims to include more debt does create value—at least from the shareholders' perspective, if not from that of the U.S. Treasury—because it increases the cash flow available to private investors. The amount of the increase in annual income to shareholders created by debt financing equals the corporate tax rate times the interest expense, or what we referred to earlier as the interest tax shield. In our example, annual company earnings after tax plus interest expense increases $32 a year ($192 + $80 − $240 = $32), which also equals the tax rate of 40 percent times the interest expense of $80.

Saying the same thing in symbols, if V_L is the value of the company when levered and V_U is its value unlevered, our example says that

$$V_L = V_U + \text{Value} \, (tI)$$

where t is the corporate tax rate, I is annual interest expense in dollars, and Value (tI) represents the value today of all future interest tax shields. In the next chapter, we will refer to this last term as the present value of future tax shields. In words, then, our equation says the value of a levered company equals the value of the same company unlevered plus the present value of the interest tax shields.

Taken at face value, this appendix suggests a disquieting conclusion: The value of a business is maximized when it is financed entirely with debt. But you know after reading the chapter that this is just the beginning of our story. For just as the tax deductibility of interest causes firm value to rise with leverage, the costs of financial distress cause it to fall. Add concerns about financial flexibility, market signaling, and incentive effects; season with a pinch of sustainable growth; and you have the recipe for the modern view on corporate financing decisions. Not a feast, perhaps, but certainly a hearty first course.

SUMMARY

1. This chapter studied corporate financing decisions, particularly the advantages and disadvantages of financial leverage.

2. A company's fundamental goal when evaluating financing options should be to support its business strategy.

3. Financial leverage increases owners' expected returns at the cost of greater risk.

4. Pro forma financial forecasts and coverage ratios are valuable for evaluating the added risks of debt financing, while range of earnings charts are useful for looking at the expected returns.

5. M&Ms' irrelevance proposition argues that the value shareholders assign to a given cash flow stream is independent of the way the stream is financed. Financing decisions are thus important to the extent that they change the expected cash flows generated by the firm, and the best financing choice is the one that maximizes expected cash flows.

6. Financing decisions can affect firm cash flows, and hence value, in at least five ways: tax benefits, distress costs, flexibility, market signaling, and management incentives. The heart of the financing decision is estimating the net effect of these forces for a specific firm.

7. Review of these forces for rapidly growing firms suggests they follow conservative financing policies. Conversely, mature, slow-growth businesses may find aggressive leverage ratios appealing.

8. New equity announcements appear to signal investors that management is concerned about the future or that it believes the firm's shares are overpriced. On average new equity announcements cause stock price to fall by an amount equal to about 30 percent of the equity to be raised. Repurchase announcements generate positive signals, while debt announcements are neutral.

9. New equity financing is not always available on agreeable terms. A major concern in most financing decisions is the effect of today's financing choice on tomorrow's options. Decisions that constrain future financing options reduce financial flexibility.

ADDITIONAL RESOURCES

Asquith, Paul, and David W. Mullins, Jr. "Signaling with Dividends, Stock Repurchases, and Equity Issues." *Financial Management*, Autumn 1986, pp. 27–44.

A well-written summary of empirical work on measuring the capital market's reaction to major equity-related announcements. An excellent introduction to and overview of market signaling.

Hovakimian, Armen, Tim Opler, and Sheridan Titman, "The Debt-Equity Choice," *Journal of Financial and Quantitative Analysis*, March 2001.

Presents evidence that capital structure choices are consistent with the pecking-order theory in the short run but that the tax benefits–distress costs trade-off theory is more important in the long run.

Stern, Joel M., and Donald H. Chew, Jr., ed., *The Revolution in Corporate Finance*, 4th ed. Malden, MA: Blackwell Publishing, 2003. 631 pages.

A collection of practitioner-oriented articles, many by leading academics, originally appearing in the *Journal of Applied Corporate Finance*. See especially "The Modigliani-Miller Proposition after 30 Years," by Merton Miller; "Raising Capital: Theory and Evidence," by Clifford W. Smith, Jr.; and "Still Searching for Optimal Capital Structure," by Stewart C. Myers. $60.

WEBSITES

www.abiworld.org
The American Bankruptcy Institute's website with news and statistics about many aspects of corporate and personal bankruptcy.

www.sia.com
The Securities Industry Association's website. Check out Research/Statistics/Surveys and On Capitol Hill, where you will find primers on securities and securities law.

PROBLEMS

Answers to odd-numbered problems are at the end of the book. For additional problems with answers, see **www.mhhe.com/higgins8e.**

1. Headquartered in Germany, SAP Ag is a leader in the enterprise application software business. General Motors is the world's largest car manufacturer. Which company do you think would bear heavier costs in the event of financial difficulties? Why? What does this imply for their respective capital structures?

2. Explain how a company can incur costs of financial distress without ever going bankrupt. What is the nature of these costs?

3. One recommendation in the chapter is that companies with promising investment opportunities should strive to maintain a conservative capital structure. Yet many promising small businesses are heavily indebted.

   a. Why should companies with promising investment opportunities strive to maintain conservative capital structures?

   b. Why do you suppose that many promising small businesses apparently do not follow this recommendation?

4. Why might it make sense for a mature, slow-growth company to have a high debt ratio?

5. The chapter discusses potential conflicts of interest between shareholders and bondholders. Some argue that bondholders can protect themselves against stockholder expropriation by writing bond covenants. Covenants are provisions in the loan contract requiring or prohibiting firm actions, such as prohibiting investments in certain industries or repurchasing shares. Well-written covenants, they argue, can eliminate any costs associated with conflicts between shareholders and bondholders. Do you agree? Why or why not?

6. You can access Playtex Products Inc.'s SEC filings, including 10-Ks (annual reports) at **www.edgarscan.pwcglobal.com.**

   a. What were Playtex's debt-to-assets and times-interest-earned ratios in 2000 and 2001?

   b. How much could EBIT have fallen in 2001 before Playtex would have been unable to make its interest payments out of operating income?

   c. How volatile has Playtex's operating income been over the period 1996–2001?

   d. Playtex is a family of well-known retail brands. It is number 1 or 2 in each of its three main businesses: tampons, suntan lotion, and infant care. In general terms, how costly do you think financial trouble would be to Playtex if it began to appear the company might default on its debt? Why?

   e. Based on your analysis, is Playtex heavily or modestly indebted? Should the company acquire more debt, or shed existing debt? Why?

7. Explain how each of the following changes will affect Harbridge Electronix's range of earnings chart, Figure 6.2. Which changes would make debt financing more attractive, which less attractive?

   a. An increase in the interest rate on debt.

   b. An increase in Harbridge's stock price.

    c. Increased uncertainty about Harbridge's future earnings.

    d. Increased common stock dividends.

    e. An increase in the amount of debt Harbridge already has outstanding.

8. FARO Technologies, whose products include portable 3-D measurement equipment, has 400 million shares outstanding trading at $5 a share. The company announces its intention to raise $200 million by selling new shares.

    a. What do market signaling studies suggest will happen to FARO's stock price on the announcement date? Why?

    b. How large a gain or loss in aggregate dollar terms do market signaling studies suggest existing FARO shareholders will experience on the announcement date?

    c. What percentage of the amount of money FARO intends to raise is this expected gain or loss?

    d. What percentage of the value of FARO's existing equity prior to the announcement is this expected gain or loss?

    e. At what price should FARO expect its existing shares to sell immediately after the announcement?

9. This is a more difficult but informative problem. James Brodrick & Sons, Inc., is growing rapidly and, if at all possible, would like to finance its growth without selling new equity. Selected information from the company's five-year financial forecast follows.

Year	1	2	3	4	5
Earnings after tax (millions)	$100	$130	$170	$230	$300
Investment (millions)	$175	$300	$300	$350	$440
Book value debt-to-equity ratio (%)	120	120	120	120	120
Marketable securities (millions)	$200	$200	$200	$200	$200
(Year 0 marketable securities = $200 million)					

    a. According to this forecast, what dividends will the company be able to distribute annually without raising new equity? What will the annual dividend payout ratio be?

    b. Assume the company wants a stable payout ratio over time and plans to use its marketable securities portfolio as a buffer to absorb year-to-year variations in earnings and investments. Set the annual payout ratio equal to the five-year sum of total dividends paid in question *a* divided by total earnings. Then solve for the size of the company's marketable securities portfolio each year.

    c. Suppose earnings fall below forecast every year. What options does the company have for continuing to fund its investments?

d. What does the pecking-order theory say about how management will rank these options?

e. Why might management be inclined to follow this pecking order?

10. The equity of Enterprise Holds Inc. has a market value of $3 million. It currently has 300,000 shares outstanding, and a book value of equity of $1,095,000. An unexpected cash windfall has prompted management to consider either a special dividend of $6.00 per share or a stock repurchase for cash.

a. If management estimates that a stock repurchase announcement will increase stock price by 5 percent, how many shares should they be prepared to repurchase?

b. Can you think of any reasons a share repurchase might be preferable to a special dividend?

11. As the financial vice president for Aether Media, you have the following information:

Expected net income after tax next year before new financing	$40 million
Sinking-fund payments due next year on existing debt	$14 million
Interest due next year on existing debt	$15 million
Company tax rate	36%
Common stock price, per share	$20
Common shares outstanding	18 million

a. Calculate Aether's times-interest-earned ratio for next year assuming the firm raises $40 million of new debt at an interest rate of 7 percent.

b. Calculate Aether's times-burden-covered ratio for the next year assuming annual sinking-fund payments on the new debt will equal $8 million.

c. Calculate next year's earnings per share assuming Aether raises the $40 million of new debt.

d. Calculate next year's times-interest-earned ratio, times-burden-covered ratio, and earnings per share if Aether sells 2 million new shares at $20 a share instead of raising new debt.

12. This problem asks you to evaluate a major increase in financial leverage on the part of Avon Products Inc. The company's financial statements for 2001–2003 and specific questions are available for download at **www.mhhe.com/higgins8e.** (Select Student Edition > Choose a Chapter > Excel Spreadsheets.) You will also find it useful to consult the company's past annual reports (10-Ks) available at **edgarscanpwcglobal.com.**

13. Problem 13, part f. in Chapter 3 asks you to construct a five-year financial projection for Jasmine Apparel beginning in 2006. Based on your forecast, or the suggested answer in C3_Problem_13.xls, answer the questions below. The file is available at **www.mhhe.com/higgins8e.** (Select Student Edition > Choose a Chapter > Excel Spreadsheets.)

    a. Calculate the company's annual times-interest-earned ratio over the forecast period.

    b. Calculate the percentage EBIT can fall before interest coverage dips below 1.0 for each year in the forecast.

    c. Consulting Table 6.5 in the text, what bond rating would Jasmine Apparel have in 2005 if the rating were based solely on the firm's interest coverage ratio?

    d. Based on this rating, would a significant increase in financial leverage be a prudent strategy for Jasmine Apparel?

STANDARD
&POOR'S

14. Use the Standard and Poor's Market Insight website, **www.mhhe.com/ edumarketinsight,** for this problem.

    a. For fiscal year 2004, compare several coverage and leverage ratios of The Boeing Company with those of Oracle Corp. (Excel Analytics, Annual Ratio Report). Which company has the higher financial leverage?

    b. Given the nature of these companies' operations and assets, which company would you expect to exhibit higher leverage, and why?

PART FOUR

Evaluating Investment Opportunities

CHAPTER SEVEN

Discounted Cash Flow Techniques

A nearby penny is worth a distant dollar.

Anonymous

The chief determinant of what a company will become is the investments it makes today. The generation and evaluation of creative investment proposals is far too important a task to be left to finance specialists; instead, it is the ongoing responsibility of all managers throughout the organization. In well-managed companies, the process starts at a strategic level with senior management specifying the businesses in which the company will compete and determining the means of competition. Operating managers then translate these strategic goals into concrete action plans involving specific investment proposals. A key aspect of this process is the financial evaluation of investment proposals, or what is frequently called *capital budgeting*. The achievement of an objective requires the outlay of money today in expectation of increased future benefits. It is necessary to decide, first, whether the anticipated future benefits are large enough, given the risks, to justify the current expenditure, and second, whether the proposed investment is the most cost-effective way to achieve the objective. This and the following chapter address these questions.

Viewed broadly, the discounted cash flow techniques considered here and in the following chapters are relevant whenever a company contemplates an action entailing costs or benefits that extend beyond the current year. This covers a lot of ground, including such disparate topics as valuing stocks and bonds, analyzing equipment acquisitions or sales, choosing among competing production technologies, deciding whether to launch a new product, valuing divisions or whole companies for purchase or sale, assessing marketing campaigns and R&D programs, and even designing a corporate strategy. Indeed, it is not an exaggeration to say that discounted cash flow analysis is the backbone of modern finance and even modern business.

Figures of Merit

The financial evaluation of any investment opportunity involves three discrete steps:

1. Estimate the relevant cash flows.

2. Calculate a figure of merit for the investment.

3. Compare the figure of merit to an acceptance criterion.

A *figure of merit* is a number summarizing an investment's economic worth. A common figure of merit is the rate of return. Like the other figures of merit to be discussed, the rate of return translates the complicated cash inflows and outflows associated with an investment into a single number summarizing its economic worth. An *acceptance criterion*, on the other hand, is a standard of comparison that helps the analyst determine whether an investment's figure of merit is attractive enough to warrant acceptance. It's like a fisher who can keep only fish longer than 10 inches. To the fisher, the length of the fish is the relevant figure of merit, and 10 inches is the acceptance criterion.

Although determining figures of merit and acceptance criteria appears to be difficult on first exposure, the first step, estimating the relevant cash flows, is the most challenging in practice. Unlike the basically mechanical problems encountered in calculating figures of merit and acceptance criteria, estimating relevant cash flows is more of an art form, often requiring a thorough understanding of a company's markets, competitive position, and long-run intentions. Difficulties range from commonplace concerns with depreciation, financing costs, and working capital investments to more arcane questions of shared resources, excess capacity, and contingent opportunities. And pervading the whole topic is the fact that many important costs and benefits cannot be measured in monetary terms and so must be evaluated qualitatively.

In this chapter, we will initially set aside questions of relevant cash flows and acceptance criteria to concentrate on figures of merit. Later we will return to the estimation of relevant cash flows. Acceptance criteria will be addressed in the following chapter under the general heading "Risk Analysis in Investment Decisions."

To begin our discussion of figures of merit, let's consider a simple numerical example. Pacific Rim Resources, Inc., is contemplating construction of a container-loading pier in Seattle. The company's best estimate of the cash flows associated with constructing and operating the pier for a 10-year period appears in Table 7.1.

Figure 7.1 presents the same information in the form of a *cash flow diagram*, which is simply a graphical display of the pier's costs and benefits

TABLE 7.1   **Cash Flows for Container-Loading Pier ($ millions)**

Year	0	1	2	3	4	5	6	7	8	9	10
Cash flow	($40)	7.5	7.5	7.5	7.5	7.5	7.5	7.5	7.5	7.5	17

FIGURE 7.1   **Cash Flow Diagram for Container-Loading Pier**

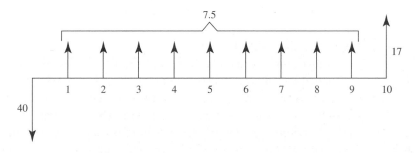

distributed along a time line. Despite its simplicity, I find that many common mistakes can be avoided by preparing such a diagram for even the most elementary investment opportunities. We see that the pier will cost $40 million to construct and is expected to generate cash inflows of $7.5 million annually for 10 years. In addition, the company expects to salvage the pier for $9.5 million at the end of its useful life, bringing the 10th-year cash flow to $17 million.

The Payback Period and the Accounting Rate of Return

Pacific's management wants to know whether the anticipated benefits from the pier justify the $40 million cost. As we will see shortly, a proper answer to this question must reflect the *time value of money*. But before addressing this topic, let's consider two commonly used, back-of-the-envelope-type figures of merit that, despite their popularity, suffer from some glaring weaknesses. One, known as the *payback period*, is defined as the time the company must wait before recouping its original investment. The pier's payback period is 5⅓ years, meaning the company will have to wait this long to recoup its original investment (5⅓ = 40/7.5).

The second widely used, but nonetheless deficient, figure of merit is the *accounting rate of return*, defined as

$$\text{Accounting rate of return} = \frac{\text{Annual average cash inflow}}{\text{Total cash outflow}}$$

The pier's accounting rate of return is 21.1 percent ([(7.5 × 9 + 17) /10]/40).

The problem with the accounting rate of return is its insensitivity to the timing of cash flows. For example, a postponement of all of the cash inflows from Pacific's container-loading pier to year 10 obviously reduces the value of the investment but does not affect the accounting rate of return. In addition to ignoring the timing of cash flows within the payback date, the payback period is insensitive to all cash flows occurring beyond this date. Thus, an increase in the salvage value of the pier from $9.5 million to $90.5 million clearly makes the investment more attractive. Yet it has no effect on the payback period, nor does any other change in cash flows in years 6 through 10.

In fairness to the payback period, I should add that although it is clearly an inadequate figure of investment merit, it has proven to be useful as a rough measure of investment risk. In most settings, the longer it takes to recoup an original investment, the greater the risk. This is especially true in high-technology environments where management can forecast only a few years into the future. Under these circumstances, an investment that does not promise to pay back within the forecasting horizon is equivalent to a night in Las Vegas without the floor show.

The Time Value of Money

An accurate figure of merit must reflect the fact that a dollar today is worth more than a dollar in the future. This is the notion of the time value of money, and it exists for at least three reasons. One is that inflation reduces the purchasing power of future dollars relative to current ones; another is that in most instances, the uncertainty surrounding the receipt of a dollar increases as the date of receipt recedes into the future. Thus, the promise of $1 in 30 days is usually worth more than the promise of $1 in 30 months, simply because it is customarily more certain.

A third reason money has a time value involves the important notion of opportunity costs. By definition, the *opportunity cost* of any investment is the return one could earn on the next best alternative. A dollar today is worth more than a dollar in one year because the dollar today can be productively invested and will grow into more than a dollar in one year. Waiting to receive the dollar until next year carries an opportunity cost equal to the return on the forgone investment. Because there are always productive opportunities for investment dollars, all investments involve opportunity costs.

Compounding and Discounting

Because money has a time value, we cannot simply combine cash flows occurring at different dates as we do in calculating the payback period and the accounting rate of return. To adjust investment cash flows for their differing time value, we need to use the ideas of compounding and discounting. Anyone who has ever had a bank account knows intuitively what compounding is. Suppose you have a bank account paying 10 percent annual interest, and you deposit $1 at the start of the year. What will it be worth at the end of the year? Obviously, $1.10. Now suppose you leave the dollar in the account for two years. What will it be worth then? This is a little harder, but most of us realize that because you earn interest on your interest, the answer is $1.21. *Compounding* is the process of determining the future value of a present sum. The following simple cash flow diagrams summarize the exercise.

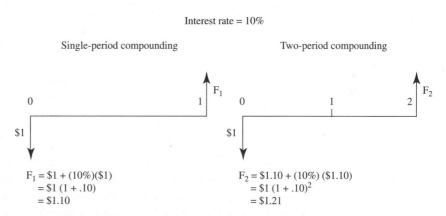

Discounting is simply compounding turned on its head: It is the process of finding the present value of a future sum. Yet despite the obvious similarities, many people find discounting somehow mysterious. And as luck would have it, the convention has become to use discounting rather than compounding to analyze investment opportunities.

Here is how discounting works. Suppose you can invest money to earn a 10 percent annual return and you are promised $1 in one year. What is the value of this promise today? Clearly, it is worth less than $1, but the exact figure is probably not something that pops immediately to mind. In fact, the answer is $0.909. This is the *present value* of $1 to be received in one year, because if you had $0.909 today, you could invest it at 10 percent interest, and it would grow into $1 in one year [$1.00 = 0.909(1 + 0.10)].

Now, if we complicate matters further and ask what is the value of one dollar to be received in two years, intuition fails most of us completely. We know the answer must be less than $0.909, but beyond that things are a fog. In fact, the answer is $0.826. This sum, invested for two years at 10 percent interest, will grow, or compound, into $1 in two years. The following cash flow diagrams illustrate these discounting problems. Note the formal similarity to compounding. The only difference is that in compounding we know the present amount and seek the future sum, whereas in discounting we know the future sum and seek the present amount.

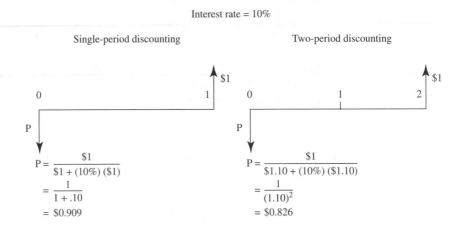

Interest rate = 10%

Single-period discounting   Two-period discounting

Present Value Calculations

How did I know the answers to these discounting problems? I could have done the arithmetic in any of three ways: use a computer to solve the formulas appearing below the cash flow diagrams; look up the answers in Appendix A at the back of the book; or punch the appropriate numbers into a financial calculator. In this instance I opted for a calculator, but the choice is largely a matter of convenience.

Appendix A, appearing at the end of the book, is known as a *present value table*. It shows the present value of $1 to be received at the end of any number of periods from 1 to 50 and at interest rates ranging from 1 to 50 percent per period. The present values appearing in the table are generated from repeated application of the above formulas for differing time periods and interest rates. It might be useful to consult Appendix A for a moment to confirm the present values just mentioned.

As a matter of semantics, the interest rate in present value calculations is frequently called the *discount rate*. It can be interpreted two ways. If a company already has cash in hand, the discount rate is the rate of return available on alternative, similar-risk investments. In other words, it is the company's *opportunity cost of capital*. If a firm must raise the cash by selling securities, the discount rate is the rate of return expected by buyers of the securities. In other words, it is the investors' *opportunity cost of capital*. As we will see in the next chapter, the discount rate is frequently used to adjust an investment's cash flows for risk and hence is also known as a *risk-adjusted discount rate*.

Appendix B at the end of the book is a close cousin to Appendix A. It shows the present value of $1 to be received at the end of *each period* for anywhere from 1 to 50 periods and at discount rates ranging from 1 to 50 percent. When cash flows are the same for a number of periods, as in this appendix, they are known as *annuities*. To illustrate both appendices, suppose the Cincinnati Reds sign a new, young catcher to a contract promising $2 million a year for four years. Let us calculate what the contract is worth today if the ballplayer has similar-risk investment opportunities yielding 15 percent a year.

The cash flow diagram for the contract is as follows:

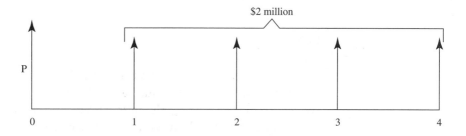

To find the present value, *P*, using Appendix A, we must find the present value at 15 percent of each individual payment. The arithmetic is

$$\text{Present value of contract} = 0.870 \times \$2 \text{ million} + 0.756 \times \$2 \text{ million} + 0.658 \times \$2 \text{ million} + 0.572 \times \$2 \text{ million} = \$5,710,000$$

A much simpler approach is to recognize that since the dollar amount is an annuity, Appendix B can be used. Consulting Appendix B, we learn that the present value of $1 per period for four periods at a 15 percent discount rate is $2.855. Thus, the present value of $2 million per year is

$$\text{Present value of contract} = 2.855 \times \$2 \text{ million} = \$5,710,000$$

Although the baseball player expects to receive a total of $8 million over the next four years, the present value of these payments is barely over $5.7 million. Such is the power of compound interest.

A financial calculator is basically a family of automated present value tables where you provide the information and the calculator does the arithmetic. Five keys are of interest for discounted cash flow calculations: *n*, the number of periods; *i*, the interest rate; *PV*, a present cash flow;

PMT, an annuity stream of cash flows; and *FV*, a future cash flow. The diagram below shows how these quantities relate to one another.

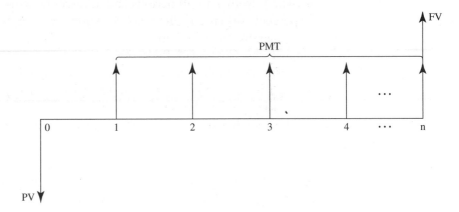

Here is a simple schematic illustrating the use of a financial calculator to find the present value of the catcher's contract. Begin by punching in the length of the contract, the interest rate, and the annual cash to be received, in any order. Then ask the calculator to find the present value, and it immediately returns the answer. The answer has a minus sign indicating this is the amount one should be willing to pay to receive the contract today.

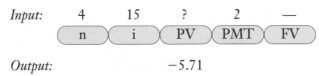

Input: 4   15   ?   2   —

n   i   PV   PMT   FV

Output: −5.71

For convenience, I will use this schematic to describe subsequent discounted cash flow calculations, without suggesting this is the only way to perform them.

Equivalence

The important fact about the present value of future cash flows is that the present sum is *equivalent* in value to the future cash flows. It is equivalent because if you had the present value today, you could transform it into the future cash flows simply by investing it at the discount rate. To confirm this important fact, the following table shows the cash flows involved in transforming $5.71 million today into the baseball player's contract of $2 million a year for four years. We begin by investing the present value at 15 percent interest. At the end of the first year, the investment grows to over $6.5 million, but the first $2 million salary payment reduces the principal to just over $4.5 million. In the second year, the investment grows to over $5.2 million, but the second salary installment brings the principal down to just over $3.2 million. And so it goes until at the end of four years, the $2 million salary payment just exhausts the account. Hence, from the baseball player's perspective, $5.71 million today is equivalent in value to $2 million a year for four years because he can readily convert the former into the latter by investing it at 15 percent.

Year	Beginning-of-Period Principal	Interest at 15%	End-of-Period Principal	Withdrawal
1	$5,710,000	$856,500	$6,566,500	$2,000,000
2	4,566,500	684,975	5,251,475	2,000,000
3	3,251,475	487,721	3,739,196	2,000,000
4	1,739,196	260,879	2,000,075	2,000,000

Note: The $75 remaining in the account after the last withdrawal is due to round-off error.

The Net Present Value

Now that you have mastered compounding, discounting, and equivalence, let's use these concepts to analyze the container pier investment. More specifically, let us replace the future cash flows appearing in Figure 7.1 with a single cash flow of equivalent worth occurring today. Because all cash flows will then be in current dollars, we will have eliminated the time dimension from the decision and can proceed to a direct comparison of present value cash inflows against present value outflows.

Here is the arithmetic. Assuming other similar-risk investment opportunities are available yielding 10 percent annual interest, the present value of the cash inflows from the pier investment is $49.75 million.

Input: 10   10   ?   7.5   9.5

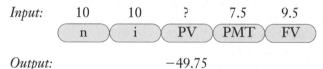

Output: −49.75

Note that the cash flow in year 10 here is composed of a $7.5 million annuity and a $9.5 million future amount, totaling $17 million.

The cash flow diagrams that follow provide a schematic representation of this calculation. The present value calculation transforms the messy original cash flows on the left into two cash flows of equivalent worth on the right, each occurring at time zero. And our decision becomes elementary. Should Pacific invest $40 million today for a stream of future cash flows with a value today of $49.75 million? Yes, obviously. Paying $40 million for something worth $49.75 million makes eminent sense.

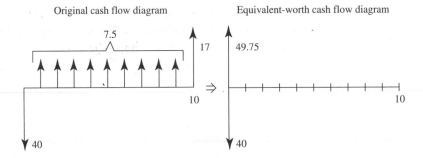

What we have just done is calculate the pier's *net present value*, or *NPV*, an important figure of investment merit:

$$\text{NPV} = \frac{\text{Present value of}}{\text{cash inflows}} - \frac{\text{Present value of}}{\text{cash outflows}}$$

The NPV for the container pier is $9.75 million.

NPV and Value Creation

The declaration that an investment's NPV is $9.75 million may not generate a lot of enthusiasm around the water cooler, so it is important to provide a more compelling definition of the concept. An investment's NPV is nothing less than a measure of how much richer you will become by undertaking the investment. Thus, Pacific's wealth rises $9.75 million when it builds the pier because it pays $40 million for an asset worth $49.75 million.

This is an important insight. For years, a common mantra among academics, management gurus, and an increasing number of senior executives has been that managers' purpose in life should be to create value for owners. A crowning achievement of finance has been to transform value creation from a catchy management slogan into a practical decision-making tool that not only indicates which activities create value but also estimates the amount of value created. Want to create value for owners? Here's how: Embrace positive-NPV activities—the higher the NPV, the better—and eschew negative-NPV activities. Treat zero-NPV activities as marginal because they neither create nor destroy wealth.

In symbols, when

NPV > 0, accept the investment.

NPV < 0, reject the investment.

NPV = 0, the investment is marginal.

The Benefit-Cost Ratio

The net present value is a perfectly respectable figure of investment merit, and if all you want is one way to analyze investment opportunities, feel free to skip ahead to the section "Determining Relevant Cash Flows." On the other hand, if you want to be able to communicate with people who use different but equally acceptable figures of merit, and if you want to reduce the work involved in analyzing certain types of investments, you will need to slog though a few more pages.

A second time-adjusted figure of investment merit popular in government circles is the *benefit-cost ratio (BCR)*, also known as the *profitability index*, defined as

$$\text{BCR} = \frac{\text{Present value of cash inflows}}{\text{Present value of cash outflows}}$$

The container pier's BCR is 1.24 ($49.75/$40). Obviously, an investment is attractive when its BCR exceeds 1.0 and is unattractive when its BCR is less than 1.0.

The Internal Rate of Return

Without doubt the most popular figure of merit among executives is a close cousin to the NPV known as the investment's *internal rate of return*, or *IRR*. To illustrate the IRR and show its relation to the NPV, let's follow the fanciful exploits of the Seattle area manager of Pacific Rim Resources as he tries to win approval for the container pier investment. After determining that the pier's NPV is positive at a 10 percent discount rate, the manager forwards his analysis to the company treasurer with a request for approval. The treasurer responds that she is favorably impressed with the manager's methodology but believes that in today's interest rate environment, a discount rate of 12 percent is more appropriate. So the Seattle manager calculates a second NPV at a 12 percent discount rate and finds it to be $5.44 million—still positive but considerably lower than the original $9.75 million ($5.44 million = $45.44 million, as shown below, −$40 million).

Input: 10   12   ?   7.5   9.5

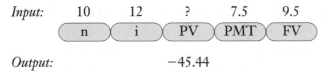

Output: −45.44

Confronted with this evidence, the treasurer reluctantly agrees that the project is acceptable and forwards the proposal to the chief financial officer. (That the NPV falls as the discount rate rises here should come as no surprise, for all of the pier's cash inflows occur in the future, and a higher discount rate reduces the present value of future flows.)

The chief financial officer, who is even more conservative than the treasurer, also praises the methodology but argues that with all the risks involved and the difficulty in raising money, an 18 percent discount rate is called for. After doing his calculations a third time, the dejected Seattle manager now finds that at an 18 percent discount rate, the NPV is −$4.48 million (−$4.48 million = $35.52 million, as shown below, −$40 million).

Input: 10   18   ?   7.5   9.5

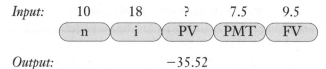

Output: −35.52

Because the NPV is now negative, the chief financial officer, betraying his former career as a bank loan officer, gleefully rejects the proposal. The manager's efforts prove unsuccessful, but in the process he has helped us to understand the IRR.

Table 7.2 summarizes the manager's calculations. From these figures, it is apparent that something critical happens to the investment merit of the container pier as the discount rate increases from 12 to 18 percent. Somewhere within this range, the NPV changes from positive to negative and the investment changes from acceptable to unacceptable. The critical discount rate at which this change occurs is the investment's IRR.

Formally, an investment's IRR is defined as

IRR = Discount rate at which the investment's NPV equals zero

The IRR is yet another figure of merit. The corresponding acceptance criterion against which to compare the IRR is the opportunity cost of capital for the investment. If the investment's IRR exceeds the opportunity cost of capital, the investment is attractive, and vice versa. If the IRR equals the cost of capital, the investment is marginal.

In symbols, if K is the percentage cost of capital, then if

IRR > K, accept the investment.

IRR < K, reject the investment.

IRR = K, the investment is marginal.

TABLE 7.2   **NPV of Container Pier at Different Discount Rates**

Discount Rate	NPV
10%	$9.75 million
12	5.44
	← ——— IRR = 15%
18	−4.48

You will be relieved to learn that in most, but regrettably not all, instances, the IRR and the NPV yield the same investment recommendations. That is, in most instances, if an investment is attractive based on its IRR, it will also have a positive NPV, and vice versa. Figure 7.2 illustrates the relation between the container pier's NPV and its IRR by plotting the information in Table 7.2. Note that the pier's NPV = 0 at a discount rate of about 15 percent, so this by definition is the project's IRR. At capital costs below 15 percent, the NPV is positive and the IRR also exceeds the cost of capital, so the investment is acceptable on both counts. When the cost of capital exceeds 15 percent, the reverse is true, and the investment is unacceptable according to both criteria.

Figure 7.2 suggests several informative ways to interpret an investment's IRR. One is that the IRR is a break-even return in the sense that at capital costs below the IRR the investment is attractive, but at capital costs greater than the IRR it is unattractive. A second, more important interpretation is that the IRR is the rate at which money remaining in an investment grows, or compounds. As such, an IRR is comparable in all respects to the interest rate on a bank loan or a savings deposit. This means you can compare the IRR of an investment directly to the annual percentage cost of the capital to be invested. We cannot say the same thing about other, simpler measures of return, such as the accounting rate of return, because they do not properly incorporate the time value of money.

FIGURE 7.2   **NPV of Container Pier at Different Discount Rates**

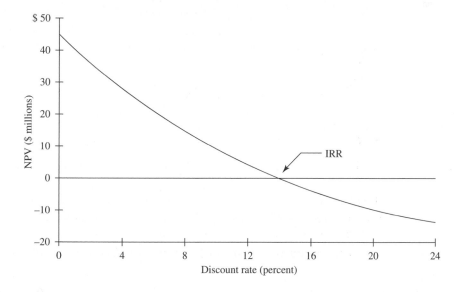

The Container Pier Investment Is Economically Equivalent to a Bank Account Paying 15 Percent Annual Interest

To confirm that an investment's IRR is equivalent to the interest rate on a bank account, suppose that instead of building the pier, Pacific Rim Resources puts the $40 million cost of the pier in a bank account earning 15 percent annual interest. The table below demonstrates that Pacific can then use this bank account to replicate precisely the cash flows from the pier and that, just like the investment, the account will run dry in 10 years. In other words, ignoring any differences in risk, the fact that the pier's IRR is 15 percent means the investment is economically equivalent to a bank savings account yielding this rate.

	($ millions)			
Year	Beginning-of-Period Principal	Interest Earned at 15%	End-of-Period Principal	Withdrawals = Investment Cash Flows
1	$40.0	$6.0	$46.0	$ 7.5
2	38.5	5.8	44.3	7.5
3	36.8	5.5	42.3	7.5
4	34.8	5.2	40.0	7.5
5	32.5	4.9	37.4	7.5
6	29.9	4.5	34.4	7.5
7	26.9	4.0	30.9	7.5
8	23.4	3.5	26.9	7.5
9	19.4	2.9	22.3	7.5
10	14.8	2.2	17.0	17.0

Calculating an IRR typically involves a bit of trial-and-error searching for the right number. This can cause problems when using present value tables but presents no difficulties when using a computer or a calculator—although you may notice a pronounced pause with a calculator as it searches for the correct value. The calculation below confirms that the container pier's IRR is 15 percent.

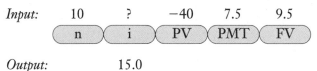

Input: 10   ?   −40   7.5   9.5

            n   i   PV   PMT   FV

Output: 15.0

Table 7.3 illustrates the container pier calculations on an Excel spreadsheet. The three entries in the column labeled "Equation" would not normally appear on a spreadsheet. They are the equations I entered to coax the computer into calculating the figures of merit shown in the "Answer" column. Each equation takes advantage of the fact that spreadsheets contain a number of built-in functions for performing various financial

TABLE 7.3 Calculating Container Pier's Estimated NPV, IRR, and BCR with a Computer Spreadsheet

	A	B	C	D	E	F	...	K	L
1	ESTIMATED ANNUAL CASH FLOWS ($ millions)								
2	Year	0	1	2	3	4	...	9	10
3	Cash flow	($40)	7.5	7.5	7.5	7.5	...	7.5	17
4									
5	Discount rate:		10%						
6									
7						Equation		Answer	
8	Net present value (NPV)				= NPV (C5, C3:L3) + B3			$9.75	
9									
10	Benefit-Cost Ratio (BCR)				= NPV (C5, C3:L3)/−B3			1.24	
11									
12	Internal Rate of Return (IRR)				= IRR (B3: L3, 0.12)			15%	

calculations. The NPV function calculates the net present value of the cash flows appearing in the range C3 through L3, at the interest rate specified in cell C5. From this present value, I have subtracted the initial $40 million expense in cell B3 to calculate the desired net present value. The IRR function calculates the internal rate of return of the numbers appearing in cells B3 through L3. To aid in the iterative search for the IRR, the function requests an initial guess of what the IRR might be. I have used 12 percent.

A common mistake to avoid: The NPV function calculates the net present value of an indicated range of numbers *as of one period before the first cash flow occurs.* This means that had I entered "npv(C5,B3:L3)," the computer would have calculated the NPV at time -1. To avoid this, I calculated the NPV of the cash flows in years 1 through 10, and then added the time 0 cash flow.

A Few Applications and Extensions

Discounted cash flow concepts are the foundation for much of finance. To demonstrate their versatility, to sharpen your mastery of the concepts, and to introduce some topics we will refer to later in the book, I want to consider several useful applications and extensions.

Bond Valuation

Investors regularly use discounted cash flow techniques to value bonds. For example, suppose ABC Corporation bonds have an 8 percent coupon rate paid annually, a par value of $1,000, and nine years to maturity. An investor wants to determine the most she can pay for the bonds if she wants to earn at least 7 percent on her investment. The relevant cash flow diagram is:

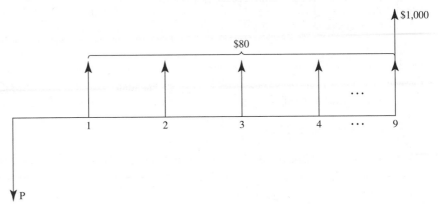

In essence, the investor wants to find *P* such that it is equivalent in value to the future cash receipts discounted at 7 percent. Calculating the present value, we find it equals $1,065.15, meaning her return over nine years will be precisely 7 percent when she pays this amount for the bond.

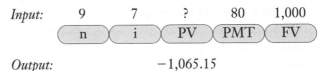

Input: 9   7   ?   80   1,000

Output: −1,065.15

Moreover, we know her return will fall below 7 percent when she pays above this price, and rise above 7 percent when she pays less.

More commonly an investor knows the price of a bond and wants to know what return it implies. If ABC Corp. bonds are selling for $1,030, the investor wants to know the return she will earn if she buys the bonds and holds them to maturity. In the jargon of the trade, she wants to know the bond's *yield to maturity*. Performing the necessary calculation, we learn the bond's yield to maturity, or IRR, is 7.53 percent.

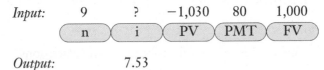

Input: 9   ?   −1,030   80   1,000

Output: 7.53

The IRR of a Perpetuity

Some British and French government bonds have no maturity date and simply promise to pay the stated interest every year forever. Annuities that last forever are called *perpetuities*. Many preferred stocks are perpetuities.

Later in Chapter 9 when valuing companies, we will occasionally find it convenient to think of company cash flows as perpetuities.

How can we calculate the present value of a perpetuity? It turns out to be embarrassingly easy. Begin by noting that the present value of an annuity paying $1 a year for 100 years discounted at, say, 12 percent is only $8.33!

Input: 100   12   ?   1   —

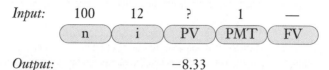

Output: −8.33

Think of it: Although the holder will receive a total of $100, the present value is less than $9. Why? Because if the investor put $8.33 in a bank account today yielding 12 percent a year, he could withdraw approximately $1 in interest every year *forever* without touching the principal (12% × $8.33 = $0.9996). Consequently, $8.33 today has approximately the same value as $1 a year forever.

This suggests the following simple formula for the present value of a perpetuity. Letting A equal the annual receipt, r the discount rate, and P the present value,

$$P = \frac{A}{r}$$

and

$$r = \frac{A}{P}$$

To illustrate, suppose a share of preferred stock sells for $480 and promises an annual dividend of $52 forever. Then its IRR is 10.8 percent (52/480). Because the equations are so simple, perpetuities are often used to value long-lived assets and in many textbook examples.

Equivalent Annual Cost

In most discounted cash flow calculations we seek a present value or an internal rate of return, but this is not always the case. Suppose, for example, that Pacific Rim Resources is considering leasing its $40 million container pier to a large Korean shipping company for a period of 12 years. Pacific Rim believes the pier will have a $4 million continuing value at the end of the lease period. To consummate the deal, the company needs to know the annual fee it must charge to recover its investment, including the opportunity cost of the funds used. In essence, Pacific Rim needs a number that converts the initial expenditure and the salvage value into an equal value annual payment. At a 10 percent interest rate and ignoring taxes, the required annual lease payment is $5.68 million.

A Note on Differing Compounding Periods

For simplicity, I have assumed that the compounding period for all discounted cash flow calculations is one year. Of course, this is not always the case. In the United States and Britain, bond interest is calculated and paid semi-annually; many credit card issuers use monthly compounding; and some savings instruments advertise daily compounding.

The existence of different compounding intervals forces us to distinguish between two interest rates: a quoted interest rate, often called the *annual percentage rate* or APR, and a true rate, known as the *effective annual rate,* or EAR.

To appreciate the distinction, you know that $1 put to work at 10 percent interest, compounded annually, will be worth $1.10 in one year. But what will it be worth when the compounding period is semi-annual? To find out we need to divide the stated interest rate by 2 and double the number of compounding periods. Thus, at the end of six months, the investment will be worth $1.05, and at the end of the year it will be worth $1.1025 ($1.05 + .05 × $1.05). With semi-annual compounding, the interest earned in the first compounding period earns interest in the second, leading to a slightly higher ending value. So although the stated interest rate is 10 percent, semi-annual compounding boosts the effective return to 10.25 percent. The account's APR is 10 percent, but its EAR is 10.25 percent.

Letting *m* equal the number of compounding periods in a year, we can generalize this example to the following expression.

$$EAR = \left(1 + \frac{APR}{m}\right)^m - 1$$

Thus, the effective annual interest rate on a 6 percent savings account with daily compounding is $(1 + .06/365)^{365} - 1 = 6.18\%$, while the effective annual rate on a credit card loan charging 18 percent, compounded monthly, is $(1 + .18/12)^{12} - 1 = 19.56\%$.

There are two morals to this story. First, when an instrument's compounding period is less than one year, its true interest rate is its EAR, not its APR. And second, when comparing instruments with different compounding periods, you must look at their EARs, not their APRs. This might all be of only minor interest were it not for the fact that common practice, strongly supplemented by Federal Truth in Lending laws, emphasizes APRs to the virtual exclusion of EARs.

Input:

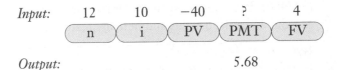

12	10	−40	?	4
n	i	PV	PMT	FV

Output: 5.68

This quantity, known as the investment's *equivalent annual cost*, is the effective, time-adjusted annual cost of the pier. The calculation tells us that if Pacific Rim sets the lease payment equal to the pier's equivalent annual cost, it will earn an IRR of precisely 10 percent on the investment. We will say more about equivalent annual costs in the chapter appendix.

Mutually Exclusive Alternatives and Capital Rationing

We now consider briefly two common occurrences that often complicate investment selection. The first is known as *mutually exclusive alternatives*. Frequently, there is more than one way to accomplish an objective, and the investment problem is to select the best alternative. In this case, the investments are said to be mutually exclusive. Examples of mutually exclusive alternatives abound, including the choice of whether to build a concrete or a wooden structure, whether to drive to work or take the bus, and whether to build a 40-story or a 30-story building. Even though each option gets the job done and may be attractive individually, it does not make economic sense to do more than one. If you decide to take the bus to work, driving to work as well could prove a difficult feat. When confronted with mutually exclusive alternatives, then, it is not enough to decide if each option is attractive individually; you must determine which is best. Mutually exclusive investments are in contrast to independent investments, where the capital budgeting problem is simply to accept or reject a single investment.

When investments are independent, all three figures of merit introduced earlier—the NPV, BCR, and IRR—will generate the same investment decision, but this is no longer true when the investments are mutually exclusive. In all of the preceding examples, we implicitly assumed independence.

A second complicating factor in many investment appraisals is known as *capital rationing*. So far we have implicitly assumed that sufficient money is available to enable the company to undertake all attractive opportunities. In contrast, under capital rationing, the decision maker has a fixed investment budget that may not be exceeded. Such a limit on investment capital may be imposed externally by investors' unwillingness to supply more money, or it may be imposed internally by senior management as a way to control the amount of investment dollars each operating unit spends. In either case, the investment decision under capital rationing requires the analyst to *rank* the opportunities according to their investment merit and accept only the best.

Both mutually exclusive alternatives and capital rationing require a ranking of investments, but here the similarity ends. With mutually exclusive investments, money is available, but for technological reasons only certain investments can be accepted; under capital rationing, a lack of money is the complicating factor. Moreover, even the criteria used to rank the investments differ in the two cases, so the best investment among mutually exclusive alternatives may not be best under conditions of capital rationing. The appendix to this chapter discusses these technicalities and indicates which figures of merit are appropriate under which conditions.

The IRR in Perspective

Before turning to the determination of relevant cash flows in investment analysis, I want to offer a few concluding thoughts about the IRR. The

IRR has two clear advantages over the NPV and the BCR. First, it has considerably more intuitive appeal. The statement that an investment's IRR is 45 percent is more likely to get the juices flowing than the exclamation that its NPV is $12 million or its BCR is 1.41. Second, the IRR sometimes makes it possible to sidestep the challenging task of determining the appropriate discount rate for an investment. Thus when a normal-risk opportunity's IRR is 80 percent, we can be confident that it is a winner at any reasonable discount rate. And when the IRR is 2 percent, we can be equally certain it is a loser regardless of the rate. The only instances in which we have to worry about coming up with an accurate discount rate are when the IRR is in a marginal range of, say, 5 to 25 percent. This differs from the NPV and the BCR, where we have to know the discount rate before we can even begin the analysis.

Unfortunately, the IRR also suffers from several technical problems that compromise its use, and while this is not the place to describe these problems in detail, you should know they exist. (See one of the books recommended at the end of this chapter for further information.) One difficulty is that on rare occasions an investment can display multiple IRRs; that is, its NPV can equal zero at two or more different discount rates. Other investments can have no IRR; their NPVs are either positive at all discount rates or negative at all rates. A second, more serious problem to be discussed in the appendix is that the IRR is an invalid yardstick for analyzing mutually exclusive alternatives and under capital rationing.

On balance then the IRR is much like Bill Clinton: appealing but flawed. And although a diligent technician can circumvent each of the problems mentioned, I have to ask if it is worth the effort when the NPV offers a simple, straightforward alternative. In my view the appropriate watchword for the IRR is to appreciate its intuitive appeal but read the warning label before applying.

Determining the Relevant Cash Flows

It's time now to put down the calculator and confront the really difficult part of evaluating investment opportunities. Calculating a figure of merit requires an understanding of the time value of money and equivalence, and it necessitates a modicum of algebra. But these difficulties pale to insignificance compared to those arising in estimating an investment's relevant cash flows. Calculating figures of merit requires only technical competence; determining relevant cash flows demands business judgment and perspective.

Two principles govern the determination of relevant cash flows. Both are obvious when stated in the abstract but can be devilishly difficult to apply in practice:

1. *The cash flow principle:* Because money has a time value, record investment cash flows when the money actually moves, not when the accountant using accrual concepts says they occur. And if the money doesn't move, don't count it.
2. *The with-without principle:* Imagine two worlds, one in which the investment is made and one in which it is rejected. All cash flows that are different in these two worlds are relevant to the decision, and all those that are the same are irrelevant.

The following extended example illustrates the practical application of these principles to a number of commonly recurring cash flow estimation problems.

Nina Sanders, newly appointed general manager of the Handheld Devices Division of Plasteel Communications, has a problem. Prior to her appointment, division executives had put together a proposal to introduce an exciting new line of cellular telephones. The numbers spun out by division analysts looked excellent, but when the proposal was presented to the company's Capital Expenditure Review Committee, it was attacked from all sides. One committee member called it "plain amateurish"; another accused Sanders' division of "trying to steal" his assets. Surprised by the strong emotions expressed and anxious to avoid further confrontation, the committee chair quickly tabled the proposal pending further review and likely revision by Sanders. Her task now was to either substantiate or correct the work of her subordinates.

Table 7.4 shows the projected costs and benefits of the new product as presented to the committee, with the most contentious issues highlighted. The top part of the table shows the initial investment and anticipated salvage value in five years. The cellular phone business was changing so rapidly that executives believed improved new phones would make the contemplated product obsolete within about five years. The center portion of the table is essentially a projected income statement for the new product, while the bottom portion, beginning with "Free Cash Flow," contains the financial analysis. According to these figures, the new line costs $46 million and promises a 37 percent internal rate of return.

Free cash flow (FCF) is the "bottom line" of investment projections. It is the estimated total cash consumed or generated each year by the investment, and as such is the cash flow stream we discount to calculate the investment's NPV or IRR. A generic definition is

$$\text{FCF} = \text{Earnings after tax} + \text{Noncash charges} - \text{Investment}$$

TABLE 7.4 Division Financial Analysis of New Line of Cellular Telephones ($ millions)

	0	1	2	3	4	5
				Year		
Plant and equipment	$(30)					$ 15
Increased working capital	(14)					
Preliminary engineering	(2)					
Excess capacity	0					
Total investment	$(46)					
Total salvage value						$ 15
Sales		$60	$82	$140	$157	$120
Cost of sales		26	35	60	68	52
Gross profit		34	47	80	89	68
Interest expense		5	4	4	3	3
Allocated expenses		0	0	0	0	0
Selling and administrative expenses		10	13	22	25	19
Total operating expenses		14	17	26	28	22
Operating income		20	29	54	61	46
Depreciation		3	3	3	3	3
Income before tax		17	26	51	58	43
Tax at 40 percent		7	11	20	23	17
Income after tax		$10	$16	$ 30	$ 35	$ 26
Free cash flow	$(46)	$10	$16	$ 30	$ 35	$ 41
Net present value @ 15%	$ 35					
Benefit-cost ratio	1.76					
Internal rate of return	37%					

Totals may not add due to rounding.

where we think of a project's salvage value as a negative investment. We will say more about FCF in later chapters.

Depreciation

The first point of contention at the meeting was the division's treatment of depreciation. As shown in Table 7.4, division analysts had followed conventional accounting practice by subtracting depreciation from gross profit to calculate profit after tax. Upon seeing this, one committee member asserted that depreciation was a noncash charge and therefore irrelevant to the decision, while other participants agreed that depreciation was relevant but maintained the division's approach was incorrect. Sanders needed to determine the correct approach.

Accountants' treatment of depreciation is reminiscent of the Swiss method of counting cows: Count the legs and divide by four. It gets the job done, but not always in the most direct manner. Division analysts are correct in noting that the physical deterioration of assets is an economic fact of life that must be included in investment evaluation. However, they did this when they forecasted that the salvage value of new plant and equipment would be less than its original cost. Thus, new plant and equipment constructed today for $30 million and salvaged five years later for $15 million is clearly forecasted to depreciate over its life. Having included depreciation by using a salvage value below initial cost, it would clearly be double-counting to also subtract an annual amount from operating income as accountants would have us do.

And here our story would end were it not for the tax collector. Although annual depreciation is a noncash charge and hence irrelevant for investment analysis, annual depreciation does affect a company's tax bill, and taxes *are* relevant. So we need to use the following two-step procedure: (1) Use standard accrual accounting techniques, including the treatment of depreciation as a cost, to calculate taxes due; then (2) add depreciation back to income after tax to calculate the investment's after-tax cash flow (ATCF). ATCF is the correct measure of an investment's operating cash flow. Note that ATCF equals the first two terms in the free cash flow expression just defined, where depreciation is the most common noncash charge.

Table 7.4 reveals that division analysts did step 1 but not step 2. They neglected to add depreciation back to income after tax to calculate ATCF. Given their estimates, the appropriate number for year 1 is

$$\text{After-tax cash flow} = \text{Earnings after tax} + \text{Depreciation}$$
$$\$13 \quad = \quad \$10 \quad + \quad \$3$$

I should hasten to add that in the course of the next few pages, we will make further corrections to the table, resulting in additional changes in after-tax cash flow. But focusing now solely on depreciation, $13 million is the correct number.

The following table shows the full two-step process for calculating year 1 after-tax cash flow:

Operating income	$20
Less: Depreciation	3
Profit before tax	17
Less: Tax at 40%	7
Income after tax	10
Plus: Depreciation	3
After-tax cash flow	$13

Note the subtraction of depreciation to calculate taxable income and the subsequent addition of depreciation to calculate after-tax cash flow.

Depreciation as a Tax Shield

Here is yet another way to view the relation between depreciation and after-tax cash flows.

The recommended way to calculate an investment's after-tax cash flow is to add depreciation to profit after tax. In symbols,

$$\text{ATCF} = (R - C - D)(1 - T) + D$$

where R is revenue, C is cash costs of operations, D is depreciation, and T is the firm's tax rate. Combining the depreciation terms, this expression can be written as

$$\text{ATCF} = (R - C)(1 - T) + TD$$

where the last term is known as the *tax shield from depreciation.*

This expression is interesting in several respects. First, it shows unambiguously that were it not for taxes, annual depreciation would be irrelevant for estimating an investment's after-tax cash flow. Thus, if T is zero in the expression, depreciation disappears entirely.

Second, the expression demonstrates that after-tax cash flow rises with depreciation. The more depreciation a profitable company can claim, the higher its after-tax cash flow. On the other hand, if a company is not paying taxes, added depreciation has no value.

Third, the expression is useful for evaluating a class of investments known as *replacement decisions,* in which a new piece of equipment is being considered as a replacement for an old one. In these instances, cash operating costs and depreciation may vary among equipment options, but not revenues. Because revenues do not change among equipment options, the with/without principle tells us they are not relevant to the decision. Setting R equal to zero in the above equation,

$$\text{ATCF} = (-C)(1 - T) + TD$$

In words, the relevant cash flows for replacement decisions are operating costs after tax plus depreciation tax shields.

The table also suggests a second way to calculate ATCF:

$$\text{After-tax cash flow} = \text{Operating income} - \text{Taxes}$$

$\$13$	=	$\$20$	$-$	$\$7$

This formulation shows clearly that depreciation is irrelevant for calculating after-tax cash flow except as it affects taxes.

Working Capital and Spontaneous Sources

In addition to increases in fixed assets, many investments, especially those for new products, require increases in working-capital items such as inventory and receivables. According to the with-without principle, changes in working capital that are the result of an investment decision are relevant to the decision. Indeed, in some instances, they are the largest cash flows involved.

Division analysts thus are correct to include a line item in their spreadsheet for changes in working capital. However, working capital investments have several unique features not captured in the division's numbers. First, working-capital investments usually rise and fall with the new product's sales volume. Second, they are reversible in the sense that at the end of the investment's life, the liquidation of working-capital items usually generates cash inflows approximately as large as the original outflows. Or, said differently, working-capital investments typically have large salvage values. The third unique feature is that many investments requiring working-capital increases also generate *spontaneous sources* of cash that arise in the natural course of business and have no explicit cost. Examples include increases in virtually all non-interest-bearing short-term liabilities such as accounts payable, accrued wages, and accrued taxes. The proper treatment of these spontaneous sources is to subtract them from the increases in current assets when calculating the project's working-capital investment.

To illustrate, the following table shows a revised estimate of the working-capital investment required to support the division's new product assuming (1) new current assets, net of spontaneous sources, equal 20 percent of sales and (2) full recovery of working capital at the end of the product's life. Note that the annual investment equals the year-to-year change in working capital so that it rises and falls with sales.

Year	0	1	2	3	4	5
New-phone sales	$0	$ 60	$ 82	$ 140	$ 157	$120
Working capital @ 20% of sales	0	12	16	28	31	24
Change in working capital	0	12	4	12	3	−7
Recovery of working capital						24
Total working capital investment	$0	$(12)	$(4)	$(12)	$ (3)	$ 31

Sunk Costs

A *sunk cost* is one that has already been incurred and that, according to the with-without principle, is not relevant to present decisions. By this criterion, the division's inclusion of $2 million in already incurred preliminary engineering expenses is clearly incorrect and should be eliminated. The division's response that "we need to record these costs somewhere or the engineers will spend preproduction money like water" has merit. But the proper place to recognize them is in a separate expense budget, not in the new-product proposal. When making investment decisions, it is important to remember that we are seekers of truth, not auditors controlling costs or managers measuring performance. We are thus not captives of the particular reporting or performance appraisal systems used by the company.

This seems easy enough, but here are two examples where ignoring sunk costs is psychologically harder to do. Suppose you purchased some common stock a year ago at $100 a share and it is presently trading at $70. Even though you believe $70 is an excellent price for the stock given its current prospects, would you be prepared to admit your mistake and sell it now, or would you be tempted to hold it in the hope of recouping your original investment? The with-without principle says the $100 price is sunk and hence irrelevant, except for possible tax effects, so sell the stock. Natural human reluctance to admit a mistake and the daunting prospect of having to justify the mistake to a skeptical boss or spouse frequently muddy our thinking.

As another example, suppose the R&D department of a company has devoted 10 years and $10 million to perfecting a new, long-lasting light bulb. Its original estimate was a development time of two years at a cost of $1 million, and every year since R&D has progressively extended the development time and increased the cost. Now it is estimating only one more year and an added expenditure of only $1 million. Since the present value of the benefits from such a light bulb is only $4 million, there is strong feeling in the company that the project should be killed and whoever had been approving the budget increases throughout the years should be fired.

In retrospect, it is clear the company should never have begun work on the light bulb. Even if successful, the cost will be well in excess of the benefits. Yet at any point along the development process, including the current decision, it may have been perfectly rational to continue work. Past expenditures are sunk, so the only question at issue is whether the anticipated benefits exceed the *remaining* costs required to complete development. Past expenditures are relevant only to the extent that they influence one's assessment of whether the remaining costs are properly estimated. So if you believe the current estimates, the light bulb project should continue for yet another year.

Allocated Costs

The proper treatment of depreciation, working capital, and sunk costs in investment evaluation is comparatively straightforward. Now things get a bit murkier. According to Plasteel Communications' *Capital Budgeting Manual,*

> New investments that increase sales must bear their fair share of corporate overhead expenses. Therefore, all new-product proposals must include an annual overhead charge equal to 14 percent of sales, without exception.

Yet, as Table 7.4 reveals, division analysts ignored this directive in their analysis of the new phone. They did so on the grounds that the manual is simply wrong, that allocating overhead expenses to new products violates the with-without principle and stifles creativity. In their words, "If exciting projects like this one have to bear the deadweight costs of corporate overhead, we'll never be competitive in this business."

The point at issue here is whether expenses not directly associated with a new investment, such as the president's salary, legal department expenses, and accounting department expenses, are relevant to the decision. A straightforward reading of the with-without principle says that if the president's salary will not change as a result of the new investment, it is not relevant, nor are legal and accounting department expenses, if they will not change. This is clear enough. If they won't change, they aren't relevant.

But who is to say these expenses will not change with the new investment? Indeed, it appears to be an inexorable fact of life that over time, as companies grow, presidents' salaries become larger while legal and accounting departments expand. The issue therefore is not whether expenses are allocated but whether they vary with the size of the business. Although we may be unable to see a direct cause-effect tie between such expenses and increasing sales, a longer-run relation likely exists between the two. Consequently, it does make sense to require all sales-increasing investments to bear a portion of those allocated costs that grow with sales. Remember, allocated costs are not necessarily fixed costs.

A related problem arises with cost-reducing investments. To illustrate, many companies allocate overhead costs to departments or divisions in proportion to the amount of direct labor expense the unit incurs. Suppose a department manager in such an environment has the opportunity to invest in a labor-saving asset. From the department's narrow perspective, such an asset offers two benefits: (1) a reduction in direct labor expense and (2) a reduction in the overhead costs allocated to the department. Yet from the total-company perspective and from the correct economic perspective, only the reduction in direct labor is a benefit because the total-company overhead costs are unaffected by the decision. They are simply reallocated from one cost center to another.

Excess Capacity

The most acrimonious debate over the proposed new product involved the Handheld Division's plan to use another division's excess production capacity. Three years earlier, the Switching Division had added a new production line that was presently operating at only 50 percent capacity. Handheld analysts reasoned that they could put this idle capacity to good use by manufacturing several subcomponents of their new phone there. As they saw it, using idle capacity avoided a major capital expenditure and saved the corporation money. They therefore had assigned zero cost to use of the excess capacity. The general manager of the Switching Division saw things rather differently. He argued vehemently that those assets were his, he had paid for them, and he damned sure wasn't going to give them away. He demanded that the Handheld Division either purchase his idle capacity for a fair price or build their own production line. He estimated that the excess capacity was worth at least $20 million. Handheld analysts responded that this was nonsense. The excess capacity had already been paid for and was thus a sunk cost for the current decision.

For technological reasons, it is frequently necessary to acquire more capacity than needed to accomplish a task, and the question arises of how to handle the excess. In this instance, as is often the case, the answer depends on the company's future plans. If the Switching Division has no alternative use for the excess capacity now or in the future, no cash flows are triggered when the Handheld Division uses it. The idle capacity thus is a free good with zero cost. On the other hand, if the Switching Division has alternative uses for the capacity now, or if it is likely to need the capacity in the future, there are costs associated with its use by the Handheld Division, and they should appear in the new-product proposal.

As a concrete example, suppose the Switching Division estimates that it will need the excess capacity in two years to accommodate its own growth. In this event, it is appropriate to assign zero cost to the capacity for the first two years but to require the Handheld Division's new product to bear the cost of new capacity at the end of year 2. Even though the Handheld Division may not ultimately occupy the new capacity, its acquisition is contingent on today's decision and therefore relevant to that decision. After the dust settles, the Handheld Division benefits from the temporarily idle capacity by deferring expenditures on new capacity for two years.

Sharing resources among divisions in this way raises a host of practical accounting questions such as whether the first division should compensate the second for resources used, how the transaction will affect divisional performance measures, and how the cost of new capacity in two years will be recorded. However, because these questions do not involve the movement of cash to or from the firm, they are not germane to the investment decision. The watchword thus should be to make the correct investment choice today and worry about accounting issues such as these later.

The reverse excess capacity problem also arises: A company is contemplating acquisition of an asset that is too large for its present needs and must decide how to treat the excess capacity created. For example, suppose a company is considering the acquisition of a hydrofoil boat to provide passenger service across a lake, but effective use of the hydrofoil will require construction of two very expensive special-purpose piers. Each pier will be capable of handling 10 hydrofoils, and for technical reasons it is impractical to construct smaller piers. If the full cost of the two piers must be borne by the one boat presently under consideration, the boat's NPV will be large and negative, suggesting rejection of the proposal; yet if only $\frac{1}{10}$ of the pier costs is assigned to the boat, its NPV will be positive. How should the pier costs be treated?

The proper treatment of the pier costs again depends on the company's future plans. If the company does not anticipate acquiring any additional hydrofoils in the future, the full cost of the piers is relevant to the present decision. On the other hand, if this boat is but the first of a contemplated fleet of hydrofoils, it is appropriate to consider only a fraction of the pier's costs today. More generally, the problem the company faces is that of defining the investment. The relevant question is not whether the company should acquire a boat but whether it should enter the hydrofoil transportation business. The broader question forces the company to look at the investment over a longer time span and consider explicitly the number of boats to be acquired.

Financing Costs

Financing costs refer to any dividend, interest, or principal payments associated with the particular means by which a company intends to finance an investment. As shown in Table 7.4, Handheld Division analysts anticipate financing a significant fraction of the new product's cost with debt and have included a line item in their projections for the interest cost on the debt. Nina Sanders realized that according to the with-without principle, financing costs of some sort are relevant to the decision; money is seldom free. But she was not sure her analysts had treated them properly.

Sanders' intuition is correct. Financing costs are relevant to investment decisions, but care must be taken not to double-count them. As the next chapter will clarify, the most common discount rate used in calculating any of the recommended figures of merit equals the annual percentage cost of capital to the company. It would obviously be double-counting to subtract financing costs from an investment's annual cash inflows and expect the investment to also generate a return greater than the cost of the capital employed. The standard procedure, therefore, is to reflect the cost of money in the discount rate and ignore all financing costs when estimating an investment's cash flows. We will revisit this problem in the next chapter.

TABLE 7.5 Revised Financial Analysis of New Line of Cellular Telephones ($ millions)

			Year			
	0	**1**	**2**	**3**	**4**	**5**
Assumptions:						
Increased working capital	20 percent of sales, full recovery at end of year 5					
Preliminary engineering	Already spent—sunk cost					
Excess capacity	$20 million cost of new capacity in year 2,					
	$2 million annual depreciation					
Interest expense	Subsumed in discount rate					
Allocated expenses	Variable allocated costs equal to 14% of sales					
Plant and equipment	$(30)					15
Increased working capital	0	(12)	(4)	(12)	(3)	31
Preliminary engineering	0					
Excess capacity			(20)			14
Total costs	$(30)	$(12)	$(24)	$(12)	$ (3)	
Total salvage value						$ 60
Sales		$ 60	$ 82	$140	$157	$120
Cost of sales		26	35	60	68	52
Gross profit		34	47	80	89	68
Interest expense		0	0	0	0	0
Allocated expenses		8	11	20	22	17
Selling and administrative expenses		10	13	22	25	19
Total operating expenses		18	25	42	47	36
Operating income		16	22	38	42	32
Depreciation		3	3	5	5	5
Income before tax		13	19	33	37	27
Tax at 40 percent		5	8	13	15	11
Income after tax		$ 8	$ 11	$ 20	$ 22	$ 16
Add back depreciation		3	3	5	5	5
After-tax cash flow		$ 11	$ 14	$ 25	$ 27	$ 21
Free cash flow	$(30)	$ (1)	$(10)	$ 13	$ 24	$ 82
Net present value @ 15%	$ 25					
Benefit-cost ratio	1.67					
Internal rate of return	30%					

Totals may not add due to rounding.

Table 7.5 presents Sanders' revised figures for her division's new-product proposal. The new line of cell phones still looks attractive, with an IRR of 30 percent, and Sanders now has reason to expect a more cordial welcome from her colleagues on the Capital Budget Review Committee.

From these examples, I hope you have gained an appreciation for the challenges executives face in identifying relevant costs and benefits in new investment opportunities and why this is a job for operating managers, not finance specialists.

APPENDIX

Mutually Exclusive Alternatives and Capital Rationing

We noted briefly in the chapter that the presence of mutually exclusive alternatives or capital rationing complicates investment analysis. This appendix explains how investments should be analyzed in these cases.

Two investments are mutually exclusive if accepting one precludes further consideration of the other. The choices between building a steel or a concrete bridge, laying a 12-inch pipeline instead of an 8-inch one, or driving to Boston instead of flying are all mutually exclusive alternatives. In each case, there is more than one way to accomplish a task, and the objective is to choose the best way. Mutually exclusive investments stand in contrast to independent investments, where each opportunity can be analyzed on its own without regard to other investments.

When investments are independent and the decision is simply to accept or reject, the NPV, the BCR, and the IRR are equally satisfactory figures of merit. You will reach the same investment decision regardless of the figure of merit used. When investments are mutually exclusive, the world is not so simple. Let's consider an example. Suppose Petro Oil and Gas Company is considering two alternative designs for new service stations and wants to evaluate them using a 10 percent discount rate. As the cash flow diagrams in Figure 7A.1 show, the inexpensive option involves a present investment of $522,000 in return for an anticipated $100,000 per year for 10 years; the

FIGURE 7A.1   **Cash Flow Diagrams for Alternative Service Station Designs**

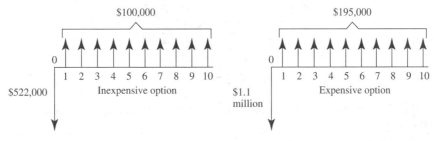

TABLE 7A.1 **Figures of Merit for Service Station Designs**

	NPV at 10%	BCR at 10%	IRR
Inexpensive option	$92,500	1.18	14%
Expensive option	98,200	1.09	12

expensive option costs $1.1 million but, because of its greater customer appeal, is expected to return $195,000 per year for 10 years.

Table 7A.1 presents the three figures of merit for each investment. All of the figures of merit signal that both options are attractive, the NPVs are positive, the BCRs are greater than 1.0, and the IRRs exceed Petro's opportunity cost of capital. If it were possible, Petro should make both investments, but because they are mutually exclusive, this does not make technical sense. So rather than just accepting or rejecting the investments, Petro must rank them and select the better one. When it comes to ranking the alternatives, however, the three figures of merit no longer give the same signal, for although the inexpensive option has a higher BCR and a higher IRR, it has a lower NPV than the expensive one.

To decide which figure of merit is appropriate for mutually exclusive alternatives, we need only remember that the NPV is a direct measure of the anticipated increase in wealth created by the investment. Since the expensive option will increase wealth by $98,200, as opposed to only $92,500 for the inexpensive option, the expensive option is clearly superior.

The problem with the BCR and the IRR for mutually exclusive alternatives is that they are insensitive to the scale of the investment. As an extreme example, would you rather have an 80 percent return on a $1 investment or a 50 percent return on a $1 million investment? Clearly, when investments are mutually exclusive, scale is relevant, and this leads to the use of the NPV as the appropriate figure of merit.

What Happened to the Other $578,000?

Some readers may think the preceding reasoning is incomplete because we have said nothing about what Petro can do with the $578,000 it would save by choosing the inexpensive option. It would seem that if this saving could be invested at a sufficiently attractive return, the inexpensive option might prove to be superior after all. We will address this concern in the section titled "Capital Rationing." For now, it is sufficient to say that the problem arises only when there is a fixed limit on the amount of money Petro has available to invest. When the company can raise enough money to make all investments promising positive NPVs, the best use of any money saved by selecting the inexpensive option will be to invest in zero-NPV opportunities. And because zero-NPV investments do not increase wealth, any money saved by selecting the low-cost option does not alter our decision.

Unequal Lives

The Petro Oil and Gas example conveniently assumed that both service station options had the same 10-year life. This, of course, is not always the case. When the alternatives have different lives, a simple comparison of NPVs is usually inappropriate. Consider the problem faced by a company trying to decide whether to build a wooden bridge or a steel one:

- The wooden bridge has an initial cost of $125,000, requires annual maintenance expenditures of $15,000, and will last 10 years.

- The steel bridge costs $200,000, requires $5,000 annual maintenance, and will last 40 years.

Which is the better buy? At a discount rate of, say, 15 percent, the present value cost of the wooden bridge over its expected life of 10 years is $200,282 ($125,000 initial cost + $75,282 present value of maintenance expenditures as shown below).

Input:

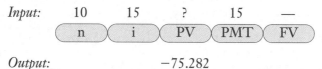

Output: −75.282

This compares with a figure for the steel bridge over its 40-year life of $233,209 ($200,000 initial cost + $33,209 present value of maintenance expenditures as shown below).

Input:

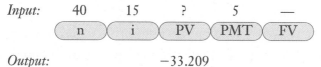

Output: −33.209

So if the object is to minimize the cost of the bridge, a simple comparison of present values would suggest that the wooden structure is a clear winner. However, this obviously overlooks the differing life expectancy of the two bridges, implicitly assuming that if the company builds the wooden bridge, it will not need a bridge after 10 years.

The message is clear: when comparing mutually exclusive alternatives having different service lives, it is necessary to reflect this difference in the analysis. One approach is to examine each alternative over the same common investment horizon. For example, suppose our company believes it will need a bridge for 20 years; due to inflation, the wooden bridge will cost $200,000 to reconstruct at the end of 10 years; and the salvage value of the steel bridge in 20 years will be $90,000. The cash flow diagrams for the two options are thus as follows:

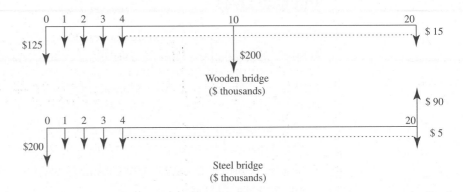

Wooden bridge
($ thousands)

Steel bridge
($ thousands)

Now the present value cost of the wooden bridge is $268,327 ($125,000 initial cost + $93,890 present value of maintenance expenditures as shown below + $49,437 present value cost of new bridge in 10 years as shown below).

Input: 20   15   ?   15   —

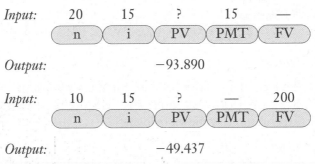

Output: −93.890

Input: 10   15   ?   —   200

Output: −49.437

And the cost of the steel bridge is $225,798 ($200,000 initial cost + $25,798 present value of maintenance expenditures net of salvage value).

Input: 20   15   ?   5   −90

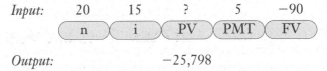

Output: −25,798

Compared over a common 20-year investment horizon, the steel bridge has the lower present value cost and is thus superior.

A second way to choose among mutually exclusive alternatives with differing lives is to calculate the equivalent annual cost of each. Here's the arithmetic for the two bridges.

Wooden bridge

Input: 10   15   200,282   ?   —

n	i	PV	PMT	FV

Output: −39.9

Steel bridge

Input: 40   15   233,209   ?   —

n	i	PV	PMT	FV

Output: −35.1

Spreading the $200,282 present value cost of the wooden bridge over its 10-year life expectancy, we find that the bridge's equivalent annual cost is $39,900, while the analogous figure over a 40-year life for the steel bridge is only $35,100. Looking at the decision over a 40-year horizon, and assuming no change in the cost of a new wooden bridge every 10 years, our decision is now obvious. Because we can have the steel bridge at an equivalent annual cost below that of the wooden bridge, the steel bridge is the better choice.

But notice the assumption necessary to reach this conclusion. If due to technological improvements, we believe the replacement cost of the wooden bridge will fall over time, its higher equivalent annual cost in the first decade might well be offset by lower annual costs in subsequent decades, tipping the balance in favor of the wooden bridge. Similarly, if we believe inflation will cause the replacement cost of the wooden bridge to rise over time, its equivalent annual cost in the first decade is again insufficient information on which to base an informed decision. We conclude that equivalent annual costs are a slick way to analyze mutually exclusive alternatives with differing lives when prices are constant. However, the technique is more difficult to apply in the face of changing prices.

Capital Rationing

Implicit in our discussion to this point has been the assumption that money is readily available to companies at a cost equal to the discount rate. The other extreme is capital rationing. Under *capital rationing*, the company has a fixed investment budget that it may not exceed. As was true with mutually exclusive alternatives, capital rationing requires us to rank investments rather than simply accept or reject them. Despite this similarity, however, you should understand that the two conditions are fundamentally different. With mutually exclusive alternatives, the money is

TABLE 7A.2 Four Independent Investment Opportunities under Capital Rationing (capital budget = $200,000)

Investment	Initial Cost	NPV at 12%	BCR at 12%	IRR
A	$200,000	$10,000	1.05	14.4%
B	120,000	8,000	1.07	15.1
C	50,000	6,000	1.12	17.6
D	80,000	6,000	1.08	15.5

available but, for technical reasons, the company cannot make all investments. Under capital rationing, it may be technically possible to make all investments, but there is not enough money. This difference is more than semantic, for, as the following example illustrates, the nature of the ranking process differs fundamentally in the two cases.

Suppose Sullivan Electronics Company has a limited investment budget of $200,000 and management has identified the four independent investment opportunities appearing in Table 7A.2. According to the three figures of merit, all investments should be undertaken, but this is impossible because the total cost of the four investments exceeds Sullivan's budget. Looking at the investment rankings, the NPV criterion ranks A as the best investment, followed by B, C, and D in that order, while the BCR and IRR rank C best, followed by D, B, and A. So we know that A is either the best investment or the worst.

To make sense of these rankings, we need to remember that the underlying objective in evaluating investment opportunities is to increase wealth. Under capital rationing, this means the company should undertake that *bundle* of investments generating the highest *total* NPV. How is this to be done? One way is to look at every possible bundle of investments having a total cost less than the budget constraint and select the bundle with the highest *total* NPV. A shortcut is to rank the investments by their BCRs and work down the list, accepting investments until either the money runs out or the BCR drops below 1.0. This suggests that Sullivan should accept projects C, D, and $\frac{7}{12}$ of B, for a total NPV of $16,670 $[(6,000 + 6,000 + \frac{7}{12} \times 8,000)]$. Only $\frac{7}{12}$ of B should be undertaken because the company has only $70,000 remaining after accepting C and D.

Why is it incorrect to rank investments by their NPVs under capital rationing? Because under capital rationing, we are interested in the payoff per dollar invested—the bang per buck—not just the payoff itself. The Sullivan example illustrates the point. Investment A has the largest NPV, equal to $10,000, but it has the smallest NPV per dollar invested. Since investment dollars are limited under capital rationing, we must look at the benefit per dollar invested when ranking investments. This is what the BCR does.

Two other details warrant mention. In the preceding example, the IRR provides the same ranking as the BCR, and although this is usually the case, it is not always so. It turns out that when the two rankings differ, the BCR ranking is the correct one. Why the rankings differ and why the BCR is superior are not worth explaining here. It is sufficient to remember that if you rank by IRR rather than BCR, you might occasionally be in error. A second detail is that when fractional investments are not possible—when it does not make sense for Sullivan Electronics to invest in $\frac{7}{12}$ of project B—rankings according to any figure of merit are unreliable, and one must resort to the tedious method of looking at each possible bundle of investments in search of the highest total NPV.

The Problem of Future Opportunities

Implicit in the preceding discussion is the assumption that as long as an investment has a positive NPV, it is better to make the investment than to let the money sit idle. However, under capital rationing, this may not be true. To illustrate, suppose the financial executive of Sullivan Electronics believes that within six months, company scientists will develop a new product costing $200,000 and having an NPV of $60,000. In this event, the company's best strategy is to forgo all of the investments presently under consideration and save its money for the new product.

This example illustrates that investment evaluation under capital rationing involves more than a simple appraisal of current opportunities; it also involves a comparison between current opportunities and future prospects. The difficulty with this comparison at a practical level is that it is unreasonable to expect a manager to have anything more than a vague impression of what investments are likely to arise in the future. Consequently, it is impossible to decide with any assurance whether it is better to invest in current projects or wait for brighter future opportunities. This means practical investment evaluation under capital rationing necessarily involves a high degree of subjective judgment.

A Decision Tree

Mutually exclusive investment alternatives and capital rationing complicate an already confusing topic. To provide a summary and an overview, Figure 7A.2 presents a capital budgeting decision tree. It indicates the figure or figures of merit that are appropriate under the various conditions discussed in the chapter. For example, following the lowest branch in the tree, we see that when evaluating investments under capital rationing that are independent and can be acquired fractionally, ranking by

FIGURE 7A.2 **Capital Budgeting Decision Tree**

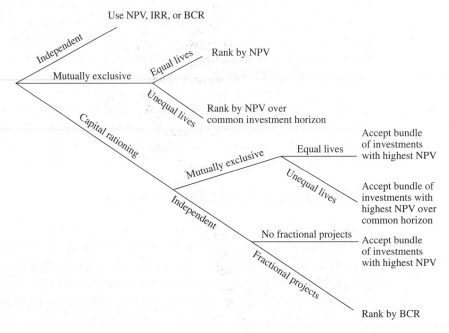

the BCR is the appropriate technique. To review your understanding of the material, see if you can explain why the recommended figures of merit are appropriate under the various conditions indicated, whereas the others are not.

SUMMARY

1. This chapter examined the use of discounted cash flow techniques and the estimation of relevant cash flows in investment appraisal.

2. The three steps in financial evaluation of investment opportunities are (a) estimate the relevant cash flows, (b) calculate a figure of merit, and (c) compare it with an acceptance criterion. The first step is the hardest in practice.

3. Money has a time value because risk customarily increases with the futurity of an event, because inflation reduces the purchasing power of future cash flows, and because waiting for future cash flows involves a lost opportunity to make interim investments.

4. The payback period and the accounting rate of return ignore the time value of money and hence are inferior figures of merit. The payback period, however, is a useful indicator of investment risk.

5. Cash flows at two dates are equivalent if it is possible to transform the near-term cash flow into the later cash flow by investing it at the prevailing interest rate. Discounting uses equivalence to convert a messy stream of future receipts and disbursements into equal-value cash flows occurring today.

6. A valid figure of merit is the net present value, defined as the difference between the present value of cash inflows and outflows. Projects with a positive net present value are acceptable. They increase the decision maker's wealth by an amount equal to the opportunity's NPV. NPV transforms the value creation slogan into a practical guide for decision making.

7. A second popular, valid figure of merit is the internal rate of return, defined as the discount rate that makes the investment's NPV equal to zero. It is also the rate at which money left in a project is compounding and therefore is comparable to the interest rate on a bank loan. Investments with an internal rate of return greater than the cost of capital are acceptable.

8. The guiding principles in deciding what cash flows are relevant for an investment decision are the with-without principle and the cash flow principle.

9. Recurring problems in determining relevant cash flows involve depreciation, working-capital changes, allocated costs, sunk costs, temporary excess capacity, and financing costs.

ADDITIONAL RESOURCES

Peterson, Pamela P., and Frank J. Fabozzi. *Capital Budgeting: Theory and Practice.* New York: John Wiley & Sons, 2002. 243 pages.

A thorough treatment by two solid academics. Advertised as "Advanced enough for the practitioners yet accessible enough for the novice…" $35.

Shapiro, Alan C. *Capital Budgeting and Investment Analysis.* Englewood Cliffs, NJ: Prentice Hall, 2004. 264 pages.

Topics include the basics, the estimation of project cash flows, the cost of capital, risk analysis, and the ties between capital budgeting and corporate strategy. Written by a respected senior professor. $42.

SOFTWARE

Written to accompany this text, DCF performs a discounted cash flow analysis of user-supplied cash flows. Output consists of six figures of merit, including NPV and IRR, a present value profile graph, and a cash flow diagram. For a complimentary copy see **www.mhhe.com/higgins8e.**

WEBSITES

hadm.sph.sc.edu/courses/econ/tutorials.html

A series of well-prepared interactive lectures, including quizzes, on a range of business topics including discounting future income, the internal rate of return, and perils of the internal rate of return.

www.berkshirehathaway.com

More than 20 years of Warren Buffett's legendary letters to shareholders, and an opportunity to purchase a Berkshire Hathaway golf shirt. Check out Buffett's "Owner's Manual," a succinct explanation of Berkshire's broad economic principles of operations. When I grow up, I want to write like Warren Buffett.

PROBLEMS

Answers to odd-numbered problems are at end of book. For additional problems with answers, see **www.mhhe.com/higgins8e.**

1. Answer the following questions assuming the interest rate is 10 percent.
   a. What is the present value of $1,000 to be received in 4 years?
   b. What is the present value of $1,000 in 8 years? Why does the present value fall as the number of years increases?
   c. How much would you pay for the right to receive $5,000 at the end of year 1, $4,000 at the end of year 2, and $8,000 at the end of year 10?
   d. How much would you pay for a 10-year bond with a par value of $1,000 and a 7 percent coupon rate? Assume interest is paid annually.
   e. How much would you pay for a share of preferred stock paying a $5-per-share annual dividend forever?
   f. What will be the value in 7 years of $12,000 invested today?
   g. How long will it take for a $2,000 investment to double in value?
   h. What will be the value in 20 years of $500 invested at the end of each year for the next 20 years?
   i. A couple wishes to save $250,000 over the next 18 years for their child's college education. What uniform annual amount must they deposit at the end of each year to accomplish their objective?
   j. What return do you earn if you pay $22,470 for a stream of $5,000 payments lasting ten years? What does it mean if you pay less than $22,470 for the stream? More than $22,470?
   k. How long must a stream of $600 payments last to justify a purchase price of $ 6,000.00? Suppose the stream lasted only five years. How large would the salvage value (liquidating payment) need to be to justify the investment of $6,000.00?

l. An investment of $1,300 today returns $61,000 in 50 years. What is the internal rate of return on this investment?

m. A company is planning to set aside money to repay $150 million in bonds that will be coming due in 8 years. How much money would the company need to set aside at the end of each year for the next 8 years to repay the bonds when they come due? How would your answer change if the money were deposited at the beginning of each year?

2. An individual wants to borrow $100,000 from a bank and repay it in five equal annual end-of-year payments, including interest. If the bank wants to earn a 10 percent rate of return on the loan, what should the payments be? Ignore taxes and default risk.

3. Your mother is buying a house for $500,000 and intends to pay $100,000 down, and borrow the remaining $400,000 (including all closing costs). She is evaluating two loan options: borrow $400,000 at 10 percent on a 30-year term loan (i.e., a mortgage, with monthly payments), or borrow the same amount at 9 percent, but with a loan fee equal to 3 percent of the loan amount. This fee is payable upon closing and cannot be financed. Her opportunity cost on her money is 9 percent, and she has asked your assistance. Please ignore any tax effects.

   a. How much will her monthly payments be if she chooses the 10 percent loan? (Hint: the monthly interest rate equals the annual rate divided by 12.)

   b. How much will her monthly payments be if she chooses the 9 percent loan?

   c. Your mother expects to stay in this house for only 5 years, at which time she plans to sell her house. Ignoring any differences in the principal values of the loans in five years, which mortgage would you advise her to take? Why?

4. If National HealthCare Corp. reported earnings per share of $7.58 in 1996 and $19.38 in 2005, at what annual rate did earnings per share grow over this period?

5. A developer offers lots for sale at $50,000, $10,000 to be paid down and $10,000 to be paid at the end of each of the next four years with "no interest to be charged." In discussing a possible purchase, you find that you can get the same lot for $42,700 cash. You also find that on a time purchase there will be a service charge of $1,000 at the date of purchase to cover legal and handling expenses and the like. Approximately what rate of interest before income taxes will actually be paid if the lot is purchased on this time payment plan?

6. Times are tough for Auger Biotech. Having raised $75 million in an initial public offering of its stock early in the year, the company is poised to launch its product. If Auger engages in a promotional campaign costing $50 million this year, its annual after-tax cash flow over the next five years will be only $500,000. If it does not undertake the campaign, it expects its after-tax cash flow to be *minus* $15 million annually for the same period. Assuming the company has decided to stay in its chosen business, is this campaign worthwhile when the discount rate is 10 percent? Why or why not?

7. One year ago, Caffe Vita Coffee Roasting Co. (CVCRC) purchased three small-batch coffee roasters for $3.3 million. The company now finds that new roasters are available that offer significant advantages. The new roasters can be purchased for $4.5 million, have an economic life of 10 years, and have no salvage value. It is expected that the new roasters will produce a gross margin of $1.2 million per year, so that, using straight-line depreciation, the annual taxable income will be $750,000.

   The current roasters are expected to produce a gross profit of $600,000 per year and, assuming a total economic life of 11 years and straight-line depreciation, a profit before tax of $300,000. The current market value of the old roasters is $1.5 million. CVCRC's tax rate is 45 percent, and its cost of capital after tax is 10 percent.

   Ignoring possible taxes on sale of used equipment and assuming zero salvage values at the end of the roasters' economic lives, should CVCRC replace its year-old roasters?

8. (Read the chapter appendix before attempting this problem.) A company is considering the following investment opportunities.

Investment	A	B	C
Initial cost ($ millions)	$5.5	$3.0	$2.0
Expected life	10 yrs	10 yrs	10 yrs
NPV @ 15%	$340,000	$300,000	$200,000
IRR	20%	30%	40%

a. If the company can raise large amounts of money at an annual cost of 15 percent, and if the investments are independent of one another, which should it undertake?

b. If the company can raise large amounts of money at an annual cost of 15 percent, and if the investments are mutually exclusive, which should it undertake?

    c. If the company has a fixed capital budget of $5.5 million, and if the investments are independent of one another, which should it undertake?

9. In 1987, a Van Gogh painting *Sunflowers* (not reputed to be one of his best) sold at auction, net of fees, for $36 million. In 1889, 98 years earlier, the same painting sold for $125. Calculate the rate of return to the seller on this investment. What does this suggest about the merits of fine art as an investment?

eXcel

10. Read the information regarding a possible new investment presented at **www.mhhe.com/higgins8e**. (Select Student Edition > Choose a Chapter > Excel Spreadsheets.)

    a. Complete the spreadsheet to estimate the project's annual after-tax cash flows.

    b. What is the investment's net present value at a discount rate of 10 percent?

    c. What is the investment's internal rate of return?

    d. How does the internal rate of return change if the discount rate equals 20 percent?

    e. How does the internal rate of return change if the growth rate in EBIT is 8 percent instead of 3 percent?

eXcel

11. The spreadsheet for this problem provides a brief overview of selected financial functions in Excel and poses several questions regarding mortgage loans requiring monthly payments. The spreadsheet is available at **www.mhhe.com/higgins8e**. (Select Student Edition > Choose a Chapter > Excel Spreadsheets.)

eXcel

12. This problem asks you to evaluate two mutually exclusive investment alternatives with differing life expectancies under various conditions including capital rationing. Relevant information about the investments and specific questions are available at **www.mhhe.com/higgins8e**. (Select Student Edition > Choose a Chapter > Excel Spreadsheets.)

eXcel

13. You work for Mattel and you are negotiating with Lucasfilm for the rights to manufacture and sell Star Wars lunchboxes (you already sell related action figures). Your marketing department estimates that you can sell $500 million worth of lunchboxes per year for 3 years, starting next year. At the end of year 3, you will liquidate the assets of the business. Additional information appears at **www.mhhe.com/higgins8e**. (Select Student Edition > Choose a Chapter > Excel Spreadsheets.) Given this information, identify the relevant cash flows, and calculate the investment's net present value, benefit-cost ratio, and internal rate of return.

CHAPTER EIGHT

Risk Analysis in Investment Decisions

A man's gotta make at least one bet a day, else he could be walking around lucky and never know it.

Jimmy Jones, horse trainer

Most thoughtful individuals and some investment bankers know that all interesting financial decisions involve risk as well as return. By their nature, business investments require the expenditure of a known sum of money today in anticipation of uncertain future benefits. Consequently, if the discounted cash flow techniques discussed in the last chapter are to be useful in evaluating realistic investments, they must incorporate considerations of risk as well as return. Two such considerations are relevant. At an applied level, risk increases the difficulty of estimating relevant cash flows. More importantly at a conceptual level, risk itself enters as a fundamental determinant of investment value. Thus, if two investments promise the same expected return but have differing risks, most of us will prefer the low-risk alternative. In the jargon of economics, we are *risk averse*, and as a result, risk reduces investment value.

Risk aversion among individuals and corporations creates the common pattern of investment risk and return shown in Figure 8.1. The figure shows that for low-risk investments, such as government bonds, expected return is modest, but as risk increases, so too must the anticipated return. I say "must" because the risk-return pattern shown is more than wishful thinking. Unless higher-risk investments promise higher returns, you and I, as risk-averse investors, will not hold them.

This risk-return trade-off is fundamental to much of finance. Over the past four decades, researchers have demonstrated that under idealized conditions, and with risk defined in a specific way, the risk-return trade-off is a straight-line one as depicted in the figure. The line is known as the *market line* and represents the combinations of risk and expected return one can anticipate in a properly functioning economy.

FIGURE 8.1 **The Risk-Return Trade-Off**

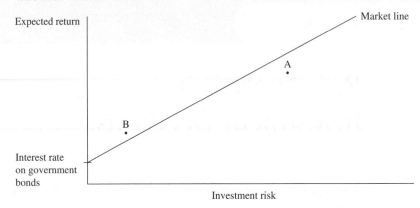

The details of the market line need not detain us here. What is important is the realization that knowledge of an investment's expected return is not enough to determine its worth. Instead, investment evaluation is a two-dimensional task involving a balancing of risk against return. The appropriate question when evaluating investment opportunities is not "What's the rate of return?" but "Is the return sufficient to justify the risk?" The investments represented by A and B in Figure 8.1 illustrate this point. Investment A has a higher expected return than B; nonetheless, B is the better investment. Despite its modest return, B lies above the market line, meaning it promises a higher expected return for its risk than available alternatives, whereas investment A lies below the market line, meaning alternative investments promising a higher expected return for the same risk are available.[1]

This chapter examines the incorporation of risk into investment evaluation. Central to our discussion of discounted cash flow techniques in the last chapter was a quantity variously referred to as the interest rate, the discount rate, and the opportunity cost of capital. While stressing that this quantity somehow reflected investment risk and the time value of money, I was purposely vague about its origins. It is time now to correct this omission by explaining how to incorporate investment risk into the discount rate. After defining investment risk in more detail, we will estimate the cost of capital to Harley-Davidson, Inc., the company profiled in earlier chapters, and will examine the strengths and weaknesses of the cost of capital as

[1] Saying the same thing more analytically, we know from our earlier study of financial leverage that owners of asset B need not settle for safe, low returns. Rather, they can use debt financing to lever B's expected return and risk to higher values. In fact, the market line tells us that with just the right amount of debt financing, owners of asset B can attain A's higher expected return, and more, with no greater risk. B is therefore the better investment.

Are You Risk Averse?

Here is a simple test to find out. Which of the following investment opportunities do you prefer?

1. You pay $10,000 today and flip a coin in one year to determine whether you will receive $50,000 or *pay* another $20,000.

2. You pay $10,000 today and receive $15,000 in one year.

If investment 2 sounds better than 1, join the crowd; you are risk averse. Even though both investments cost $10,000 and promise an expected one-year payoff of $15,000, or a 50 percent return, studies indicate that most people, when sober and not in a casino, prefer the certainty of option 2 to the uncertainty of option 1. The presence of risk reduces the value of 1 relative to 2.

For a simple, self-test of your risk tolerance from a leading provider of analytic risk tools, see **www.riskgrades.com**, select "Grade Yourself."

a risk-adjusted discount rate. The chapter concludes with a look at several important pitfalls to avoid when evaluating investment opportunities and at economic value added, a hot topic in the world of performance appraisal. The appendix considers two logical extensions to the chapter material known as asset-betas and adjusted present value analysis, or APV.

You should know at the outset that the topics in this chapter are not simple, for the addition of a whole second dimension to investment analysis in the form of risk introduces a number of complexities and ambiguities. The chapter therefore will offer a general road map for how to proceed and an appreciation of available techniques rather than a detailed set of answers. But look on the bright side: If investment decisions were simple, there would be less demand for well-educated managers and aspiring financial writers.

Risk Defined

Speaking broadly, there are two aspects to investment risk: The *dispersion* of an investment's possible returns, and the *correlation* of these returns with those available on other assets. Looking first at dispersion, Figure 8.2 shows the possible rates of return that might be earned on two investments in the form of bell-shaped curves. According to the figure, the expected return on investment A is about 12 percent, while the corresponding figure for investment B is about 20 percent.

Dispersion risk captures the intuitively appealing notion that risk is tied to the range of possible outcomes, or alternatively to the uncertainty surrounding the outcome. Thus because investment A shows considerable bunching of possible returns about the expected return, its risk is low. Investment B, on the other hand, evidences considerably less clustering,

FIGURE 8.2   **Illustration of Investment Risk: Investment A Has a Lower Expected Return and a Lower Risk Than B**

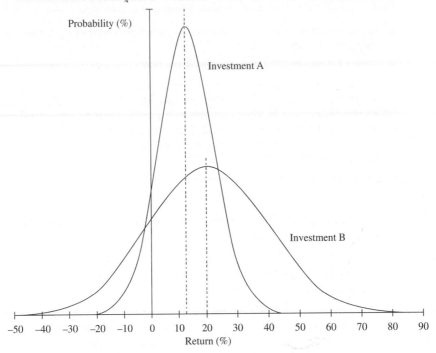

and is thus higher risk. Borrowing from statistics, one way to measure this clustering tendency is to calculate the standard deviation of return. The details of calculating an investment's expected return and standard deviation of return need not concern us here.[2] It is enough to know that risk relates to the dispersion, or uncertainty, in possible outcomes and that techniques exist to measure this dispersion.

[2] An investment's expected return is the probability-weighted average of possible returns. If three returns are possible—8, 12, and 18 percent—and if the chance of each occurring is 40, 30, and 30 percent, respectively, the investment's expected return is

$$\text{Expected return} = 0.40 \times 8\% + 0.30 \times 12\% + 0.30 \times 18\% = 12.2\%$$

The standard deviation of return is the probability-weighted average of the deviations of possible returns from the expected return. To illustrate, the differences between the possible returns and the expected return in our example are $(8\% - 12.2\%)$, $(12\% - 12.2\%)$, and $(18\% - 12.2\%)$. Because some of these differences are positive and others are negative, they would tend to cancel one another out if we added them directly. So we square them to ensure the same sign, calculate the probability-weighted average of the squared deviations, and then find the square root.

$$\begin{aligned}\text{Standard} \atop \text{deviation} &= [0.4(8\% - 12.2\%)^2 + 0.3(12\% - 12.2\%)^2 + 0.3(18\% - 12.2\%)^2]^{1/2} \\ &= 4.1\%\end{aligned}$$

The probability-weighted average difference between the investment's possible returns and its expected return is 4.1 percentage points.

TABLE 8.1 **Diversification Reduces Risk**

Investment	Weather	Probability	Return on Investment	Weighted Outcome
Ice cream stand	Sun	0.50	60%	30%
	Rain	0.50	−20	−10
				20
Umbrella shop	Sun	0.50	−30	−15
	Rain	0.50	50	25
				10
Portfolio:				
1/2 Ice cream stand and umbrella shop	Sun	0.50	15	7.5
	Rain	0.50	15	7.5
				15%

Risk and Diversification

Dispersion risk, as just described, is often known as an investment's *total risk*, or more fancifully its Robinson Crusoe risk. It is the risk an owner would face if he were alone on a desert island unable to buy any other assets. The story changes dramatically, however, once the owner is off the desert island and again able to hold a diversified portfolio. For then the risk from holding a given asset is customarily less than the asset's total risk—frequently a lot less. In other words, there is more—or perhaps I should say less—to risk than simply dispersion in possible outcomes.

To see why, Table 8.1 presents information about two very simple risky investments: purchase of an ice cream stand and an umbrella shop.[3] For simplicity, let's suppose tomorrow's weather will be either rain or sun with equal probability. Purchase of the ice cream stand is clearly a risky undertaking, since the investor stands to make a 60 percent return on his investment if it is sunny tomorrow but lose 20 percent if it rains. The umbrella shop is also risky, since the investor will lose 30 percent if tomorrow is sunny but will make 50 percent if it rains.

Yet despite the fact that these two investments are risky when viewed in isolation, they are not risky when seen as members of a portfolio containing both investments. In a portfolio consisting of half ownership of the ice cream stand and of the umbrella shop, the losses and gains from the two investments precisely counterbalance one another in each state, so that

---

[3] I used to think this was a fanciful example until I noticed how quickly street vendors in Washington D.C. switched between selling soft drinks and umbrellas depending on the weather.

regardless of tomorrow's weather, the outcome is a certain 15 percent. (For example, if it is sunny tomorrow, the ice cream stand makes 60 percent on half of the portfolio and the umbrella shop loses 30 percent on the other half for a net of 15 percent [$15\% = 0.5 \times 60\% + 0.5 \times -30\%$].) The expected outcome from the portfolio is the average of the expected outcomes from each investment, but the risk of the portfolio is zero. Owning both assets eliminates the dispersion in possible returns. Despite what you may have heard, there really is a free lunch in finance. It is called diversification.

This is an extreme example, but it does illustrate an important fact about risk: When it is possible to own a diversified portfolio, the relevant risk is not the investment's risk in isolation—its Robinson Crusoe risk—but its risk as part of the portfolio. And, as the example demonstrates, the difference between these two perspectives can be substantial.

An asset's risk in isolation is greater than its risk as part of a portfolio whenever the asset's returns and the portfolio's returns are less than perfectly correlated. In this commonplace situation, some of the asset's return variability is offset by variability in the portfolio's returns, and the effective risk borne by the investor declines. Look again at Table 8.1. The return on the ice cream stand is highly variable, but because it hits a trough precisely when the umbrella shop return hits a peak, return variability for the two investments combined disappears. The portfolio will earn 15 percent rain or shine. In other words, when assets are combined in a portfolio an "averaging out" process occurs that reduces risk.

Because most business investments depend to some extent on the same underlying economic forces, it is unusual to find investment opportunities with perfectly inversely correlated returns as in the ice cream stand–umbrella shop example. However, the described diversification effect still exists. Whenever investment returns, or cash flows, are less than perfectly positively correlated—whenever individual investments are unique in some respects—an investment's risk as part of a portfolio is less than the dispersion of its possible returns.

Saying the same thing more formally, it is possible to partition an investment's total risk into two parts as follows:

$$\text{Total risk} = \text{Systematic risk} + \text{Unsystematic risk}$$

Systematic risk reflects exposure to economywide events, such as interest rate changes and business cycles, and cannot be reduced by diversification. Unsystematic risk, on the other hand, reflects investment-specific events, such as fires and lawsuits, which can be eliminated through diversification. Because savvy shareholders own diversified investment portfolios, only systematic risk is relevant for evaluating investment opportunities. The rest can be diversified away.

FIGURE 8.3   **The Power of Diversification in Common Stock Portfolios**

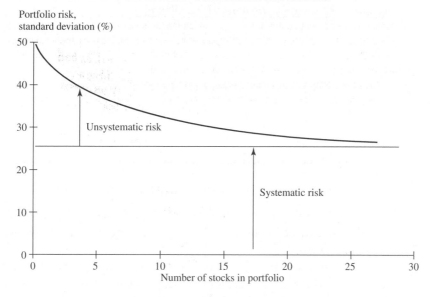

Figure 8.3 demonstrates the power of diversification in common stock portfolios. It shows the relationship between the variability of portfolio returns, as measured by the standard deviation of return, and the number of randomly chosen stocks in the portfolio. Note that variability is high when the number of stocks is low but declines rapidly as the number increases. As the number of stocks in the portfolio grows, the "averaging out" effect takes place, and unsystematic risk declines. Studies suggest that unsystematic risk all but vanishes when portfolio size exceeds about 30 randomly chosen stocks, and that diversification eliminates approximately one-half of total risk.[4]

Estimating Investment Risk

Having defined risk and risk aversion in at least a general way, let us next consider how we might estimate the amount of risk present in a particular investment opportunity. In some business situations, an investment's risk can be calculated objectively from scientific or historical evidence. This is true, for instance, of oil and gas development wells. Once an exploration company has found a field and mapped out its general configuration,

[4] Meir Statman, "How Many Stocks Make a Diversified Portfolio?" *Journal of Financial and Quantitative Analysis* 22 (September 1987), pp. 353–63.

Systematic Risk and Conglomerate Diversification

Some executives seize on the idea that diversification reduces risk as a justification for conglomerate diversification. Even when a merger promises no increase in profitability, it is said to be beneficial because the resulting diversification reduces the risk of company cash flows. Because shareholders are risk averse, this reduction in risk is said to increase the value of the firm.

Such reasoning is at best incomplete. If shareholders wanted the risk reduction benefits of such a conglomerate merger, they could achieve them much more simply by just owning shares of the two independent companies in their own portfolios. Shareholders do not depend on company management for such benefits. Executives intent on acquiring other firms must look elsewhere to find a rationale for their actions.

the probability that a development well drilled within the boundaries of the field will be commercially successful can be determined with reasonable accuracy.

Sometimes history can be a guide. A company that has opened 1,000 fast-food restaurants around the world should have a good idea about the expected return and risk of opening the 1,001st. Similarly, if you are thinking about buying IBM stock, the historical record of the past variability of annual returns to IBM shareholders is an important starting point when estimating the risk of IBM shares. I will say more about measuring the systematic risk of traded assets, such as IBM shares, in a few pages.

These are the easy situations. More often, business ventures are one-of-a-kind investments for which the estimation of risk must be largely subjective. When a company is contemplating a new-product investment, for example, there is frequently little technical or historical experience on which to base an estimate of investment risk. In this situation, risk appraisal depends on the perceptions of the managers participating in the decision, their knowledge of the economics of the industry, and their understanding of the investment's ramifications.

Three Techniques for Estimating Investment Risk

Three previously mentioned techniques—sensitivity analysis, scenario analysis, and simulation—are useful for making subjective estimates of investment risk. Although none of the techniques provides an objective measure of investment risk, they all help the executive to think systematically about the sources of risk and their effect on project return. Reviewing briefly, an investment's IRR or NPV depends on a number of uncertain economic factors, such as selling price, quantity sold, useful life, and so on.

Sensitivity analysis involves an estimation of how the investment's figure of merit varies with changes in one of these uncertain factors. One commonly used approach is to calculate three returns corresponding to an optimistic, a pessimistic, and a most likely forecast of the uncertain variables. This provides some indication of the range of possible outcomes. Scenario analysis is a modest extension that changes several of the uncertain variables in a mutually consistent way to describe a particular event.

We looked at simulation in some detail in Chapter 3 as a tool for financial planning. Recall that simulation is an extension of sensitivity and scenario analysis in which the analyst assigns a probability distribution to each uncertain factor, specifies any interdependence among the factors, and asks a computer repeatedly to select values for the factors according to their probability of occurring. For each set of values chosen, the computer calculates a particular outcome. The result is a graph, similar to Figure 3.1, plotting project return against frequency of occurrence. The chief benefits of sensitivity analysis, scenario analysis, and simulation are that they force the analyst to think systematically about the individual economic determinants of investment risk, indicate the sensitivity of the investment's return to each of these determinants, and provide information about the range of possible returns.

Including Risk in Investment Evaluation

Once you have an idea of the degree of risk inherent in an investment, the second step is to incorporate this information into your evaluation of the opportunity.

Risk-Adjusted Discount Rates

The most common way to do this is to add an increment to the discount rate; that is, discount the expected value of the risky cash flows at a discount rate that includes a premium for risk. Alternatively, you can compare an investment's IRR, based on expected cash flows, to a required rate of return that again includes a risk premium. The size of the premium naturally increases with the perceived risk of the investment.

To illustrate the use of such risk-adjusted discount rates, consider a $10 million investment promising risky cash flows with an expected value of $2 million annually for 10 years. What is the investment's NPV when the risk-free interest rate is 5 percent and management has decided to use a 7 percent risk premium to compensate for the uncertainty of the cash flows?

An Example of Sensitivity Analysis

A standard option in many software programs for analyzing investment opportunities is the ability to analyze the sensitivity of the results to changes in key assumptions. Below is representative output from such an analysis.

Relative Impact of Key Variables on Net Present Value (Investment NPV = $21,259)

A 1% Increase in:	Increases NPV by:	Percent Increase
Sales growth rate	$2,240	10.5
Operating profit margin	2,462	11.6
Capital investment	−1,249	−5.9
Working-capital investment	−1,143	−5.4
Discount rate	−1,996	−9.4

A quick look at these numbers indicates that, of the five variables tested, the NPV is most sensitive to changes in the projected profit margin and sales growth rate. This suggests that management would be smart to pay special attention to their estimates of these two variables, and once the investment is undertaken, to manage these quantities closely.

The cash flow diagram for the investment follows. The bell-shaped curve above the diagram shows the distribution of uncertain annual cash flows. At a 12 percent risk-adjusted discount rate, the project's NPV is $1.3 million ($10 million initial cost + $11.3 million present value of future cash flows as shown below).

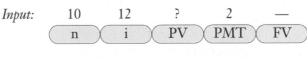

Input: 10   12   ?   2   —

    (n) (i) (PV) (PMT) (FV)

Output: −11.3

Because the investment's NPV is positive, the investment is attractive even after adjusting for risk. An equivalent approach is to calculate the investment's IRR, using expected cash flows, and compare it to the risk-adjusted rate. Because the project's IRR of 15.1 percent exceeds 12 percent, we again conclude that the investment is attractive despite its risk.

Note how the risk-adjusted discount rate reduces the investment's appeal. If the investment were riskless, its NPV at a 5 percent discount rate would be $5.4 million, but because a higher risk-adjusted rate is deemed appropriate, NPV falls by over $4 million. In essence, management requires an inducement of at least this amount before it is willing to make the investment.

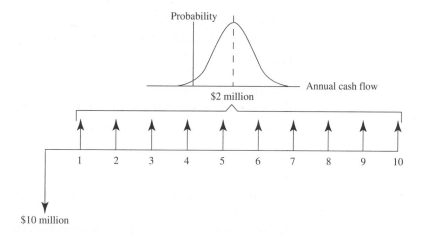

A virtue of risk-adjusted discount rates is that most executives have at least a rough idea of how an investment's required rate of return should vary with risk. Stated differently, they have a basic idea of the position of the market line in Figure 8.1. For instance, they know from the historical data in Table 5.1 of Chapter 5 that over many years, common stocks have yielded an average annual return about 6.4 percentage points higher than the return on government bonds. If the present return on government bonds is 6 percent, it is plausible to expect an investment that is about as risky as common stocks to yield a return of about 12.4 percent. Similarly, executives know that an investment promising a return of 40 percent is attractive unless its risk is extraordinarily high. Granted, such reasoning is imprecise; nonetheless, it does lend some objectivity to risk assessment.

The Cost of Capital

Now that we introduced risk-adjusted discount rates and illustrated their use, the remaining challenge is to identify the appropriate rate for a specific investment. Do we just add 7 percentage points to the risk-free rate, or is there a more objective process?

There is a more objective process, and it rests on the notion of the *cost of capital*. When creditors and owners invest in a business, they incur opportunity costs equal to the returns they could have earned on alternative, similar-risk investments. Together these opportunity costs define the minimum rate of return the company must earn on existing assets to meet the expectations of its capital providers. This is the firm's cost of capital. If we can estimate this minimum required rate of return, we have an objectively determined risk-adjusted discount rate suitable for evaluating typical, or average risk, investments undertaken by a firm. Rather than relying on managers "gut feelings" about investment risk, the cost of capital methodology enables us to look to financial markets for valuable information about the appropriate risk-adjusted discount rate.

Moreover, once we know how to estimate one company's cost of capital, we can use the technique to estimate the risk-adjusted discount rate applicable to a wide variety of project risks. The trick is to reason by analogy as follows. If Project A appears to be about as risky as investments undertaken by Company 1, use Company 1's cost of capital as the required return for Project A, or better yet, use an average of the cost of capital to Company 1 and all its industry peers. Thus, if a traditional landline telephone company is contemplating an investment in the cell phone industry, a suitable required rate of return for the decision is the average cost of capital to existing cell phone providers. In the following paragraphs we define the cost of capital more precisely, estimate Harley-Davidson's cost of capital, and discuss its use as a risk-adjustment vehicle.

The Cost of Capital Defined

Suppose we want to estimate the cost of capital to XYZ Corporation and we have the following information:

	XYZ Liabilities and Owners' Equity	Opportunity Cost of Capital
Debt	$100	10%
Equity	200	20

We will discuss the origins of the opportunity costs of capital in a few pages. For now just assume we know that given alternative investment opportunities, creditors expect to earn at least 10 percent on their loans and shareholders expect to earn at least 20 percent on their ownership of XYZ shares. With this information, we need answer only two simple questions to calculate XYZ's cost of capital:

1. *How much money must XYZ earn annually on existing assets to meet the expectations of creditors and owners?*

The creditors expect a 10 percent return on their $100 loan, or $10. However, because interest payments are tax deductible, the effective after-tax cost to a profitable company in, say, the 50 percent tax bracket is only $5. The owners expect 20 percent on their $200 investment, or $40. So in total, XYZ must earn $45 [$45 = (1 − 0.5)(10%) $100 + (20%)$200].

2. *What rate of return must the company earn on existing assets to meet the expectations of creditors and owners?*

A total of $300 is invested in XYZ on which the company must earn $45, so the required rate of return is 15 percent ($45/$300). This is XYZ's cost of capital.

Let's repeat the above reasoning using symbols. The money XYZ must earn annually on existing capital is

$$(1 - t)K_D D + K_E E$$

where t is the tax rate, K_D is the expected return on debt or the cost of debt, D is the amount of interest-bearing debt in XYZ's capital structure, K_E is the expected return on equity or the cost of equity, and E is the amount of equity in XYZ's capital structure. Similarly, the annual return XYZ must earn on existing capital is

$$K_W = \frac{(1 - t)K_D D + K_E E}{D + E} \tag{8.1}$$

where K_W is the cost of capital.

From the preceding example,

$$15\% = \frac{(1 - 50\%)10\% \times \$100 + \$20\% \times \$200}{\$100 + \$200}$$

In words, a company's cost of capital is the cost of the individual sources of capital, weighted by their importance in the firm's capital structure. The subscript W appears in the expression to denote that the cost of capital is a weighted-average cost. This is also why the cost of capital is often denoted by the acronym WACC for weighted-average cost of capital. To demonstrate that K_W is a weighted-average cost, note that one-third of XYZ's capital is debt and two-thirds is equity, so its WACC is one-third the cost of debt plus two-thirds the cost of equity:

$$15\% = (1/3 \times 5\%) + (2/3 \times 20\%)$$

The Cost of Capital and Stock Price

An important tie exists between a company's cost of capital and its stock price. To see the linkage, ask yourself what happens when XYZ Corporation earns a return on existing assets greater than its cost of capital. Because the return to creditors is fixed by contract, the excess return accrues entirely to shareholders. And because the company can earn more than shareholders' opportunity cost of capital, XYZ's stock price will rise as new investors are attracted by the excess return. Conversely, if XYZ earns a return below its cost of capital on existing assets, shareholders will not receive their expected return, and its stock price will fall. The price will continue falling until the prospective return to new buyers again equals equity investors' opportunity cost of capital. Another definition of the cost of capital, therefore, is *the return a firm must earn on existing assets to keep its stock price constant.* Finally, from a shareholder value perspective, we can say that management creates value when it earns returns above the firm's cost of capital and destroys value when it earns returns below this target.

Cost of Capital for Harley-Davidson, Inc.

To use the cost of capital as a risk-adjusted discount rate, we must be able to measure it. This involves assigning values to all of the quantities on the right side of equation 8.1. To illustrate the process, let's estimate Harley-Davidson's cost of capital at year-end 2004.

The Weights

We begin by measuring the weights, D and E. There are two common ways to do this, only one of which is correct: Use the book values of debt and equity appearing on the company's balance sheet, or use the market values. By *market value*, I mean the price of the company's bonds and common shares in securities markets multiplied by the number of each security type outstanding. As Table 8.2 shows, the book values of Harley-Davidson's debt and equity at the end of 2004 were $1,295.4 million and $3,218.5 million, respectively. The figure for debt includes only interest-bearing debt because other liabilities are either the result of tax accruals that are subsumed in the estimation of after-tax cash flow or spontaneous sources of cash that are part of working capital in the investment's cash flows. The table also indicates that the market value of Harley-Davidson's debt and equity on the same date were $1,295.4 million and $17,879.9 million, respectively.

TABLE 8.2 Book and Market Values of Debt and Equity for Harley-Davidson, Inc. (December 31, 2004)

Source	Book Value		Market Value	
	Amount ($ millions)	Percentage of Total	Amount ($ millions)	Percentage of Total
Debt	$1,295.4	28.7%	$ 1,295.4	6.8%
Equity	3,218.5	71.3	17,879.9	93.2
Total	$4,513.9	100.0%	$19,175.3	100.0%

Consistent with common practice, I have assumed here that the market value of Harley-Davidson's debt equals its book value. This assumption is almost certainly incorrect, but just as certainly the difference between the book and market values of debt is quite small compared to that for equity. The market value of Harley-Davidson's equity is its price per share at year-end of $60.75 times 294.32 million common shares outstanding. The market value of equity exceeds the book value by a ratio of 5.6 to 1 because investors are optimistic about the company's future prospects.

To decide whether book weights or market weights are appropriate for measuring the cost of capital, consider the following analogy. Suppose that 10 years ago you invested $20,000 in a portfolio of common stocks that, through no doing of your own, is now worth $50,000. After talking to stockbrokers and investment consultants, you believe a reasonable return on the portfolio, given present market conditions, is 10 percent a year. Would you be satisfied with a 10 percent return on the original $20,000 cost of the portfolio, or would you expect to earn 10 percent on the current $50,000 market value? Obviously the current market value is relevant for decision making; the original cost is sunk and therefore irrelevant. Similarly, Harley-Davidson's owners and creditors have investments worth $17,879.9 million and $1,295.4 million, respectively, on which they expect to earn competitive returns. Thus, the market values of debt and equity are appropriate for measuring the cost of capital.

The Cost of Debt

This is an easy one. Bonds with risk and maturity similar to Harley-Davidson were yielding a return of approximately 5.5 percent in December 2004, and the company's marginal tax rate is about 35 percent. Consequently, the aftertax cost of debt to Harley-Davidson was 3.6 percent $[(1 - 35\%) \times 5.5\%]$. Some financial neophytes are tempted to use the coupon rate on the debt rather than the prevailing market rate in this calculation. But the coupon rate is, of course, a sunk cost. Moreover, because we want to use the cost of capital to evaluate new investments, we want the cost of new debt.

The Cost of Equity

Estimating the cost of equity is as hard as estimating debt was easy. With debt, or preferred stock, the company promises the holder a specified stream of future payments. Knowing these promised payments and the current price of the security, it is a simple matter to calculate the expected return. This is what we did in the last chapter when we calculated the yield to maturity on a bond. With common stock, the situation is more complex. Because the company makes no promises about future payments to shareholders, there is no simple way to calculate the return expected.

The following cash flow diagrams illustrate the problem, displaying the cash flows first to a bond investor and then to a stock investor. Finding K_D is a simple discounted cash flow problem. Finding K_E would be just as simple, except we do not know the future cash receipts shareholders expect. This calls for some ingenuity.

Investor's Cash Flow Diagram for a Bond

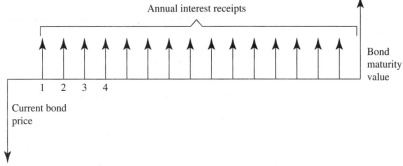

K_D = Discount rate that makes present value of cash inflows equal to current price.

Investor's Cash Flow Diagram for Common Stock

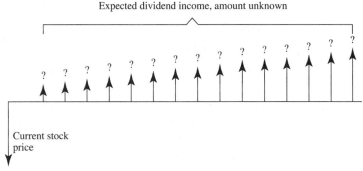

K_E = Discount rate that makes present value of unknown expected dividend income equal current price.

Assume a Perpetuity

One way out of this dilemma recalls the story of the physicist, the chemist, and the economist trapped at the bottom of a 40-foot pit. After failing with a number of schemes based on their knowledge of physics and chemistry to extract themselves from the pit, the two finally turn to the economist in desperation and ask if there isn't anything in his professional training that might help them devise a means of escape. "Why, yes," he replies. "The problem is really quite elementary. Simply assume a ladder." Here our "ladder" is an assumption about the future payments shareholders expect. From this heroic beginning, the problem really does become quite elementary. To illustrate, suppose equity investors expect to receive an annual dividend of d per share forever. The cash flow diagram then becomes

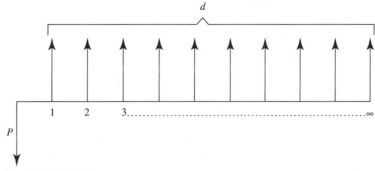

Current price of stock

Because we know P and have assumed a future payment stream, all that remains is to find the discount rate that makes the present value of the payment stream equal the current price. From the last chapter, we know that the present value of such a perpetuity at a discount rate of K_E is

$$P = \frac{d}{K_E}$$

and, solving for the discount rate,

$$K_E = \frac{d}{P}$$

In words, if you are willing to assume investors expect a company's stock to behave like a perpetuity, the cost of equity capital is simply the dividend yield.

Perpetual Growth

A somewhat more plausible assumption is that shareholders expect a per share dividend next year of d and expect this dividend to grow at the rate of g percent per annum *forever.* In this case, the cash flow diagram becomes

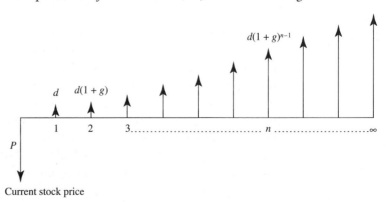

Current stock price

Fortunately, it turns out that this discounted cash flow problem also has an unusually simple solution. Without boring you with the arithmetic details, the present value of the assumed payment stream at a discount rate of K_E is

$$P = \frac{d}{K_E - g}$$

and, solving for the discount rate,

$$K_E = \frac{d}{P} + g$$

This equation says that if the perpetual growth assumption is correct, the cost of equity capital equals the company's dividend yield (d/P), plus the growth rate in dividends. This is known as the *perpetual growth equation* for K_E.

The problem with the perpetual growth estimate of K_E is that it is only as good as the assumption on which it is based. For mature companies such as railroads, electric utilities, and steel mills, it may be reasonable to assume that observed growth rates will continue indefinitely. And in these cases, the perpetual growth equation yields a plausible estimate of the cost of equity capital. The equation would be difficult to apply to Harley-Davidson, however, because the company's present growth rate cannot be maintained in perpetuity.

Let History Be Your Guide

A second and generally more fruitful approach to estimating the cost of equity capital looks at the determinants of expected returns on risky investments. In general, the expected return on any risky asset is composed of three factors:

$$\text{Expected return on risky asset} = \text{Risk-free interest rate} + \text{Inflation premium} + \text{Risk premium}$$

The equation says that the owner of a risky asset should expect to earn a return from three sources. The first is compensation for the opportunity cost incurred in holding the asset. This is the risk-free interest rate. The second is compensation for the declining purchasing power of the currency over time. This is the inflation premium. The third is compensation for bearing the asset's systematic risk. This is the risk premium. Fortunately, we do not need to treat the first two terms as separate factors because together they equal the expected return on a default-free bond such as a government bond. In other words, owners of government bonds expect a return from the first two sources but not the third. Consequently,

$$\frac{\text{Expected return}}{\text{on risky asset}} = \frac{\text{Interest rate on}}{\text{government bond}} + \frac{\text{Risk}}{\text{premium}}$$

Since we can readily determine the government bond interest rate, the only challenge is to estimate the risk premium.

When the risky asset is a common stock, it is useful to let history be our guide and recall from Table 5.1 that on average over the last century, the annual return on U.S. common stocks exceeded that on government bonds by 6.4 percentage points. As a reward for bearing the added systematic risk, common stockholders earned a 6.4 percentage point higher annual return than government bondholders. Treating this as a risk premium and adding it to a 2004 long-term government bond rate of 4.2 percent yields an estimate of 10.6 percent as the cost of equity capital for a typical company.

What is the logic of treating the 6.4 percentage point historical excess return as a risk premium? Essentially it is that over a long enough time, the return investors receive and what they expect to receive should approximate each other. For example, suppose investors expect a 20-percentage-point excess return on common stocks but the actual return keeps turning out to be 3 percentage points. Then two things should happen: Investors should lower their expectations, and selling by disappointed investors should increase subsequent realized returns. Eventually expectations and reality should come into rough parity.

We now have an estimate of the cost of capital to an "average-risk" company, but of course few companies are precisely average-risk. How, then, can we customize our average cost expression to reflect the risk of a specific firm? The answer is to insert a "fudge factor," known as the company's *equity beta*, into the expression so that it becomes

$$\frac{\text{Cost of equity}}{\text{capital}} = \frac{\text{Interest rate on}}{\text{government bond}} + \beta_e \left(\begin{array}{c} \text{Historical excess return} \\ \text{on common stocks} \end{array} \right)$$

or in symbols,

$$K_E = i_g + \beta_e \times Rp \tag{8.2}$$

where i_g is a government bond rate, β_e is the equity beta of the target company, and Rp is the excess return on common stocks. You can think of β_e as a scale factor reflecting the systematic risk of a specific company's shares relative to that of an average share. When the stock's systematic risk equals that of an average share, β_e equals 1.0, and the historical risk premium applies directly. But for above-average risk shares, β_e exceeds 1.0, and the risk premium grows accordingly. Conversely, for below-average

FIGURE 8.4 **Harley-Davidson's Beta Is the Slope of the Best-Fit Line Below**
Monthly Returns of Harley-Davidson, Inc., v. S&P 500, 60 Months through April 2005

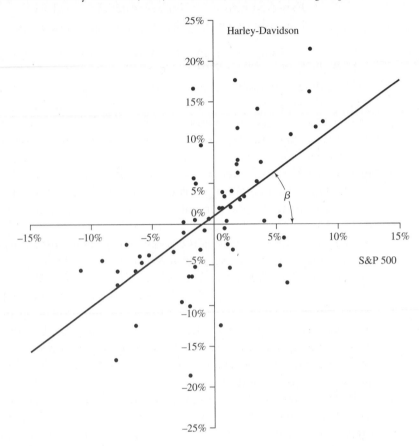

risk shares, β_e is below 1.0, and only a fraction of the historical risk premium applies.

Estimating Beta

But, you might well ask, how do we estimate a company's beta? Actually, it's pretty simple. Figure 8.4 provides everything required to estimate Harley-Davidson's beta. It shows the monthly realized returns, including dividends, on Harley-Davidson's common stock relative to returns on the Standard & Poor's 500 Stock Index over the past 60 months. For example, in April 2004, the S&P index fell 2 percent, while Harley-Davidson stock rose 6 percent. This return pair constitutes one point on the graph. The S&P 500 index is a broadly diversified portfolio containing many common shares; so its systematic risk is a reasonable surrogate for the systematic risk of an average share, and of the market as a whole. Also appearing in the figure is a best-fit,

A Virtue of Statistics

Many of the concepts in this chapter can be described quite simply with the aid of a little statistics. As already noted, an investment's *total risk* refers to its dispersion in possible returns, commonly represented by the standard deviation of returns, while its *systematic risk* depends on the extent to which the investment's returns correlate with those on a broadly diversified portfolio. We can thus represent the systematic risk of investment *j* as

$$\text{Systematic risk} = \rho_{jm}\sigma_j$$

where ρ_{jm} is the correlation coefficient between investment *j* and well-diversified portfolio *m*, and σ_j is the standard deviation of returns on investment *j*. The correlation coefficient is, of course, a dimensionless number ranging between $+1$ and -1, with $+1$ characterizing perfectly positively correlated returns and -1 perfectly inversely correlated returns. For most business investments, ρ_{jm} is in the range of 0.5 to 0.8, meaning that 20 to 50 percent of the investment's total risk can be diversified away.

A common stock's *equity beta* equals its systematic risk relative to that of a well-diversified portfolio, or in symbols, stock *j*'s equity beta is

$$\beta_j = \frac{\rho_{jm}\sigma_j}{\rho_{mm}\sigma_m}$$

But because any variable must be perfectly positively correlated with itself, this expression reduces to

$$\beta_j = \frac{\rho_{jm}\sigma_j}{\sigma_m}$$

In addition to representing stock *j*'s equity beta, this expression also equals the slope coefficient of the regression of r_j on r_m, where r_j and r_m are realized returns on stock *j* and the diversified portfolio, respectively.

straight line indicating the average relationship among the paired returns. (If you are familiar with regression analysis, this is a simple regression line.)

The slope of this line is the beta estimate we seek. It measures the sensitivity of Harley-Davidson's equity returns to movements in the S&P index. The indicated slope of 1.11 means that on average, the return on Harley-Davidson's equity rises or falls 1.11 percent for every one percent change in the index, indicating that Harley-Davidson's equity is higher risk than average. Clearly if this line were less steeply sloped, Harley-Davidson's stock would be less sensitive to market movements, or alternatively to economy-wide events, and thus less risky. A more steeply sloped line would, of course, imply just the reverse. The fact that all of the return pairs plotted in the figure do not lie precisely on the straight line reflects the importance of unsystematic risk in determining Harley-Davidson's monthly returns. Remember that because unsystematic risk can be eliminated through diversification, it should play no role in determining required returns or prices.

TABLE 8.3 **Representative Company Betas**

Source: Standard & Poor's Compustat.

Company	Beta	Company	Beta
Adobe Systems	1.71	General Electric	0.91
American Express	1.13	Hewlett-Packard	1.99
Analog Devices	2.78	Intel	2.35
Apple Computer	1.87	Int'l Flavors & Fragrances	0.46
Bank of America	0.62	Kroger	0.50
Bell South	1.07	Lilly	0.41
Black & Decker	1.04	Merck	0.41
Boeing	0.80	Metlife	0.49
Comcast	0.75	Microsoft	1.35
Computer Sciences	1.65	Molson Coors Brewing	0.42
Costco	0.87	Monsanto	1.01
Deere	0.64	Oracle	1.62
Dell	1.51	Safeway	0.49
Du Pont	0.89	Starbucks	0.49
Duke Energy	0.66	Union Pacific	0.40
eBay	2.08	Yahoo	3.00

Fortunately you do not need to worry about calculating betas yourself. Beta risk is so important a factor in security analysis that many stockbrokerage companies and investment advisors regularly publish the betas of virtually all publicly traded common stocks. Table 8.3 presents recent betas for a representative sample of firms. Observe that beta ranges from a low of 0.40 for Union Pacific Railroad to a high of 3.00 for Yahoo. Note too that the numbers are intuitively plausible, with high-risk businesses such as technology and Internet companies having high betas, while low-risk companies such as railroads, food processors, and grocery stores have lower betas.

Inserting Harley-Davidson's estimated equity beta of 1.11 into equation 8.2 yields the following cost of equity capital:

$$K_E = 4.2\% + 1.11 \times 6.4\% = 11.3\%$$

Harley-Davidson's Weighted-Average Cost of Capital

All that remains now is the figure work. Table 8.4 presents my estimate of Harley-Davidson's cost of capital in tabular form. Harley-Davidson's weighted-average cost of capital is 10.8 percent. This means that at year-end 2004, Harley-Davidson needed to earn at least this percentage return on the market value of existing assets to meet the expectations of creditors and

TABLE 8.4   Calculation of Harley-Davidson's Cost of Capital*

Source	Amount ($ millions)	Percentage of Total	Cost after Tax	Weighted Cost
Debt	$ 1,295.4	6.8%	3.6%	0.2%
Equity	17,879.9	93.2	11.3	10.5
			Cost of capital =	10.8%

*Totals may not add due to rounding.

shareholders and, by inference, to maintain its stock price. In equation form,

$$K_W = \frac{(1 - 0.35)(5.5\%)(\$1,295.4 \text{ million}) + (11.3\%)(\$17,879.9 \text{ million})}{\$1,295.4 \text{ million} + \$17,879.9 \text{ million}}$$
$$= 10.8\%$$

Before leaving our discussion of beta, I should note that while the motivation offered for equation 8.2 has been largely intuitive, the equation actually rests on a solid conceptual foundation known as the Capital Asset Pricing Model, or the CAPM. According to the CAPM, equation 8.2 is nothing less than the equation of the market line shown earlier in Figure 8.1. As such, it describes the equilibrium relationship between the expected return on any risky asset and its systematic risk. Said differently, Equation 8.2 defines the minimum acceptable rate of return an investor should demand on any risky asset.

The Cost of Capital in Investment Appraisal

The fact that the cost of capital is the return a company must earn on *existing assets* to meet creditor and shareholder expectations is an interesting detail, but we are after bigger game here: We want to use the cost of capital as an acceptance criterion for *new investments*.

Are there any problems in applying a concept derived for existing assets to new investments? Not if one critical assumption holds: The new investment must have the same risk existing assets do. If it does, the new investment is essentially a "carbon copy" of existing assets, and the cost of capital is the appropriate risk-adjusted discount rate. If it does not, we must proceed more carefully.

The market line in Figure 8.5 clearly illustrates the importance of the equal-risk assumption. It emphasizes that the rate of return risk-averse individuals anticipate rises with risk. This means, for example, that management should demand a higher expected return when introducing a new product than when replacing aged equipment, because the new product is presumably riskier and therefore warrants a higher return. The figure also

FIGURE 8.5   **An Investment's Risk-Adjusted Discount Rate Increases with Risk**

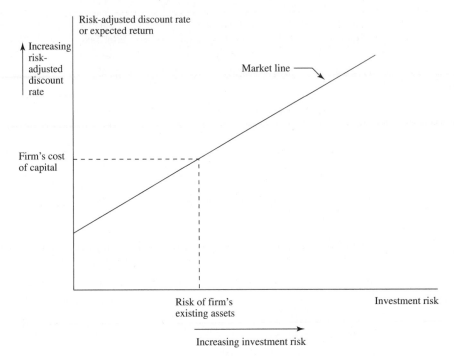

shows that a company's cost of capital is but one of many possible risk-adjusted discount rates, the one corresponding to the risk of the firm's existing assets. We conclude that the cost of capital is an appropriate acceptance criterion only when the risk of the new investment equals that of existing assets. For all other investments, the cost of capital is inappropriate. But do not despair, for even when inappropriate itself, the cost of capital concept is central to identifying a correct risk-adjusted rate.

Multiple Hurdle Rates

Companies adjust their hurdle rates for differing investment risks in at least three ways. The first two are straightforward extensions of the cost of capital. For large projects the approach is to identify an industry in which the contemplated investment would be considered average risk, estimate the weighted-average cost of capital for several companies in the industry, and use an average of these estimates as the project's required rate of return. For example, when a pharmaceutical company contemplates a biotechnology investment, a reasonable hurdle rate for the decision is an average of the capital costs to existing biotechnology companies.

The Cost of Capital to a Private Company

Two hurdles exist to estimating a private company's cost of capital. The first is conceptual. Some owners of private companies argue that because their company's securities do not trade on public markets, any cost of capital based on these markets is not relevant to them. This reasoning is incorrect. Financial markets define the opportunity costs incurred by all individuals when they make investment decisions regardless of whether those investments are publicly traded or privately held. A private business owner would obviously be foolish to make a business investment promising a 5 percent return when comparable-risk investments promising 15 percent are available in public markets.

The second hurdle is one of measurement. Without market values for the company's debt and equity and without equity returns on which to base a beta estimate, what do we do? I recommend the strategy described above for estimating project and divisional capital costs. Identify one or more public competitors, estimate their capital costs, and use the resulting average to represent the private firm's cost of capital. In instances where the private business has a much different capital structure from the public competitors, it may be necessary to do some further adjusting of the kind described in the appendix. When the private firm is much smaller than the public competitors, it may also be appropriate to make an upward adjustment in the cost of capital, amounting to perhaps two percentage points, to reflect the added risks faced by small firms.

A challenge when applying this approach is deciding which companies to include in the sample. The cost of capital to a diversified firm is the weighted-average of the capital costs prevailing in each of its businesses. This means that even when a diversified company is a major competitor in the target business, its cost of capital may not accurately reflect the risk of that business. As a result, the best sample candidates are "pure-plays," undiversified firms that compete only in the target business. However, pure-plays are not always available, and in their absence considerable judgment and a certain amount of art must be applied when selecting sample companies and deciding how best to weight their numbers.

A second risk adjustment technique used by multidivision companies is to calculate a separate cost of capital for each division. As just noted, the cost of capital to a multidivision company will be an average of the costs of capital appropriate to each business line. When such companies use a single, corporatewide cost of capital across all divisions, they risk committing two types of errors. In low-risk divisions they are inclined to reject some worthwhile, low-risk investments for lack of expected return, while in their high-risk divisions, they are inclined to do just the opposite: accept uneconomic, high-risk investments because of their prospective returns. Over time such companies find their lower-risk divisions withering for lack of capital, while their higher-risk divisions are force-fed too much capital.

To avoid this dilemma, many multidivision companies use the methods just described to estimate a different hurdle rate for each division. They begin by identifying several primary division competitors—hopefully including a few pure-plays. They then estimate the weighted-average cost of capital of these competitors, and use an average of these numbers as the division's cost of capital.

The third approach is more *ad hoc*. Many companies adjust for differing project risks by defining several risk buckets and assigning a different hurdle rate to each bucket. For example, Harley-Davidson might use the following four buckets.

Type of Investment	Discount Rate (%)
Replacement or repair	7.0
Cost reduction	9.0
Expansion	10.8
New product	16.0

Investments to expand capacity in existing products are essentially carbon-copy investments, so their hurdle rates equal Harley-Davidson's cost of capital. Other types of investments have a higher or lower hurdle rate, depending on their risk relative to expansion investments. Replacement or repair investments are the safest because virtually all of the cash flows are well known from past experience. Cost reduction investments are somewhat riskier, because the magnitude of potential savings is uncertain. New-product investments are the riskiest type of all, because both revenues and costs are uncertain.

Multiple hurdle rates are consistent with risk aversion and with the market line, but the amount by which the hurdle rate should be adjusted for each level of risk is largely arbitrary. Whether the hurdle rate for cost reduction investments should be 1 or 3 percentage points below Harley-Davidson's cost of capital cannot be determined objectively.

Four Pitfalls in the Use of Discounted Cash Flow Techniques

You now know the basics of investment appraisal: Estimate the opportunity's annual, expected after-tax cash flows and discount them to the present at a risk-adjusted discount rate appropriate to the risk of the cash flows. When the opportunity is a "carbon-copy" investment, the firm's weighted-average cost of capital is the appropriate discount rate. In other instances, an upward or downward adjustment to the firm's cost of capital is necessary.

In the interest of full disclosure, I will now gingerly mention four pitfalls in the practical application of discounted cash flow techniques. The first two are easily avoided once you are aware of them; the last two

The Fallacy of the Marginal Cost of Capital

Some readers, especially engineers, look at equation 8.1 and naively conclude that it is possible to reduce a company's weighted-average cost of capital by using more of the cheap source of financing, debt, and less of the expensive source, equity. In other words, they conclude that increasing leverage will reduce the cost of capital. This reasoning, however, evidences an incomplete understanding of leverage. As we observed in Chapter 6, increasing leverage increases the risk borne by shareholders. Because they are risk averse, shareholders react by demanding a higher return on their investment. Thus, K_E and, to a lesser extent, K_D rise as leverage increases. This means that increasing leverage affects a company's cost of capital in two opposing ways: Increasing use of cheap debt reduces K_W, but the rise in K_E and K_D that accompanies added leverage increases it.

To review this reasoning, ask yourself how you would respond to a subordinate who made the following argument in favor of an investment: "I know the company's cost of capital is 12 percent and the IRR of this carbon-copy investment is only 10 percent. But at the last directors' meeting, we decided to finance this year's investments with new debt. Since new debt has a cost of only about 4 percent after tax, it is clearly in our shareholders' interest to invest 4 percent money to earn a 10 percent return."

The subordinate's reasoning is incorrect. Financing with debt means increasing leverage and increasing K_E. Adding the change in K_E to the 4 percent interest cost means the true *marginal* cost of the debt is well above the interest cost. In fact, it is probably quite close to K_W.

highlight important limitations of discounted cash flow techniques as conventionally applied. Collectively these pitfalls mean you need to master several more topics before attempting to pass as an expert.

The Enterprise Perspective versus the Equity Perspective

Any corporate investment partially financed with debt can be analyzed from either of two perspectives: that of the company, commonly known as the *enterprise* perspective, or that of its owners, often referred to as the *equity* perspective. As the following example demonstrates, these two perspectives are functionally equivalent in the sense that when properly applied they yield the same investment decision—but woe be to him who confuses the two.

Suppose ABC Industries has a capital structure composed of 40 percent debt, costing 5 percent after tax, and 60 percent equity, costing 20 percent. Its WACC is therefore

$$K_W = 5\% \times 0.40 + 20\% \times 0.60 = 14\%$$

The company is considering an average-risk investment costing $100 million and promising an after-tax cash flow of $14 million a year in perpetuity. If undertaken, ABC plans to finance the investment with $40 million in new borrowings and $60 million in equity. Should ABC make the investment?

The Enterprise Perspective

The left side of the following diagram shows the investment's cash flows from the enterprise perspective. Applying our now standard approach, the investment is a perpetuity with a 14 percent internal rate of return. Comparing this return to ABC's weighted-average cost of capital, also 14 percent, we conclude that the investment is marginal. Undertaking it will neither create nor destroy shareholder value.

The Equity Perspective

The right side of the diagram shows the same investment from the owners' viewpoint, or the equity perspective. Because $40 million of the initial cost will be financed by debt, the equity outlay is only $60 million. Similarly, because $2 million after-tax must be paid to creditors each year as interest, the residual cash flow to equity will be only $12 million. The investment's internal rate of return from the equity perspective is therefore 20 percent.

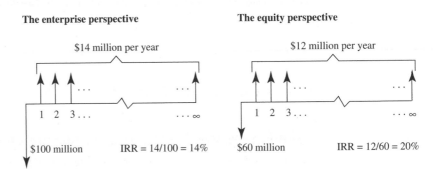

Does the fact that the return is now 20 percent mean the investment is suddenly an attractive one? Clearly, no. Because the equity cash flows are levered, they are riskier than the original cash flows and hence require a higher risk-adjusted discount rate. Indeed, the appropriate acceptance criterion for these equity cash flows is ABC's cost of equity capital, or 20 percent. (Remember, the discount rate should reflect the risk of the cash flows to be discounted.) Comparing the project's 20 percent IRR to equity with ABC's cost of equity, we again conclude that the investment is only marginal.

It is not an accident that the enterprise and equity perspectives yield the same result. Because the weighted-average cost of capital is defined to ensure that each supplier of capital receives a return equal to her opportunity cost, we know that an investment by ABC earning 14 percent, from the enterprise perspective, will earn just enough to service the debt and generate a 20 percent IRR on invested equity. Problems arise only when you mix the two perspectives, using K_E to discount enterprise cash flows or, more commonly, using K_W to discount equity cash flows.

Which perspective is better? Some of my best friends use the equity perspective, but I believe the enterprise perspective is easier to apply in practice. The problem with the equity perspective is that both the IRR to equity and the appropriate risk-adjusted discount rate vary with the amount of leverage used. The IRR to equity on ABC Industries' investment is 20 percent with $40 million of debt financing but jumps to 95 percent with $90 million of debt and rises to infinity with all-debt financing.

The interdependency between the means of financing and the risk-adjusted discount rate is easily handled in a classroom, but when real money is on the line, we often become so enthralled by the return-enhancing aspect of debt that we forget the required rate of return rises as well. Moreover, even when we remember that leverage increases risk as well as return, it is devilishly hard to estimate exactly how much the cost of equity should change with leverage.

Life is short. I recommend that you avoid unnecessary complications by using the enterprise perspective whenever possible. Assess the economic merit of the investment without regard to how it will be financed or how you will divvy up the spoils. If the investment meets this fundamental test, you can then turn to the nuances of how best to finance it.

Inflation

The second pitfall involves the improper handling of inflation. Too often managers ignore inflation when estimating an investment's cash flows but inadvertently include it in their discount rate. The effect of this mismatch is to make companies overly conservative in their investment appraisal, especially with regard to long-lived assets. Table 8.5 illustrates the point. A company with a 15 percent cost of capital is considering a $10 million, carbon-copy investment. The investment has a four-year life and is expected to increase production capacity by 10,000 units annually. Because the product sells for $900, the company estimates that annual revenues will rise $9 million ($900 × 10,000 units), which, after subtracting production costs, yields an increase in annual after-tax cash flows of $3.3 million. The IRR of the investment is calculated to be 12.1 percent, which is below the firm's cost of capital.

Did you spot the error? By assuming a constant selling price and constant production costs over four years, management has implicitly estimated real, or constant-dollar, cash flows, whereas the cost of capital as calculated earlier in the chapter is a nominal one. It is nominal because both the cost of debt and the cost of equity include a premium for expected inflation.

TABLE 8.5   When Evaluating Investments under Inflation, Always Compare Nominal Cash Flows to a Nominal Discount Rate or Real Cash Flows to a Real Discount Rate ($ millions)

(a) Incorrect Investment Evaluation Comparing Real Cash Flows to a Nominal Discount Rate

	2006	2007	2008	2009	2010
After-tax cash flow	($10.0)	$3.3	$3.3	$3.3	$3.3
		IRR = 12.1%			
		K_W = 15%			
		Decision: Reject			

(b) Correct Investment Evaluation Comparing Nominal Cash Flows to a Nominal Discount Rate

	2006	2007	2008	2009	2010
After-tax cash flow	($10.0)	$3.5	$3.8	$4.0	$4.3
		IRR = 20.0%			
		K_W = 15%			
		Decision: Accept			

The key to capital budgeting under inflation is to always compare like to like. When cash flows are in nominal dollars, use a nominal discount rate. When cash flows are in real, or constant, dollars, use a real discount rate. The bottom portion of Table 8.5 illustrates a proper evaluation of the investment. After including a 5 percent annual increase in selling price and in variable production costs, the expected nominal cash flows from the investment are as shown. As one would expect, the nominal cash flows exceed the constant-dollar cash flows by a growing amount in each year. The IRR of these flows is 20 percent, which now exceeds the firm's cost of capital.[5]

Real Options

The third pitfall involves the possible omission of important managerial options inherent in many corporate investment opportunities. These options seldom arise in simple textbook illustrations because most textbooks, with their emphasis on mechanics, implicitly assume that managers' only task in investment appraisal is to pick winners and that, having done so, they play no subsequent role in determining an investment's success or failure. It is as if managers, having selected their favorite projects, stand idly by while Dame Fate rolls the dice.

[5]An alternative approach would have been to calculate the firm's real cost of capital and compare it to a real IRR. But because this approach is more work and is fraught with potential errors, I recommend working with nominal cash flows and a nominal discount rate instead.

Such passivity may be an appropriate assumption when the investments under review are stocks and bonds, but it can be dangerously inappropriate in other instances when managers have the ability to alter a project during its life. Examples of what are often called *real options*, in recognition of their formal equivalence to traded financial options, include the option to defer the investment to a later date, the option to abandon an investment if cash flows do not meet expectations, the option to modify the scale of operations as demand varies, the option to alter the mix of inputs as raw materials prices change, and the option to make follow-on investments if the initial investment is successful. In each case, management can change the nature or the scope of the investment in response to information not known at the time of the original decision. Such options enhance investment value because they give management the right, but not the obligation, to undertake a future activity. The importance of real options in valuing certain investments can be appreciated by noting that a pure R&D investment could never be justified were it not for the option such expenditures give management to exploit positive research results with follow-on investments.

Here is an example of how real options can affect the value of an investment.[6] General Design Corporation is considering investing $100 million to develop a new line of high-speed semiconductors based on an emerging diamond film technology. Part *a* of Table 8.6 shows that the investment's anticipated life is five years and annual cash flows are expected to be $60 million if the project succeeds and −$40 million if it fails. Management pegs the chance of success at only 50 percent. If General Design requires an 8 percent return on low-risk investments, 15 percent on moderate-risk investments, and 25 percent on high-risk investments, what should it do?

The Option to Abandon

Calculating expected cash flows and discounting at a 25 percent rate reflecting the venture's high risk, the net present value is large and negative, −$73 million. The diamond film project is clearly unacceptable. But on reflection, is it likely that General Design will passively incur losses for five years if the technology is found to be unworkable early on? Having once shot themselves in the foot, will managers continue shooting for another four years, or have they the sense to quit? Assuming more realistically that management has the option to abandon the venture after two years at a salvage value of, say, $20 million, the revised cash flows

---

[6]Strictly speaking, the discounted cash flow approach used in this example is only approximately correct. The correct approach relies on option pricing theory, which is beyond the scope of this book. See Lenos Trigeorgis, *Real Options: Managerial Flexibility and Strategy in Resource Allocation* (Cambridge, MA: MIT Press, 2000), for a more rigorous exposition.

TABLE 8.6 **General Design's Diamond Film Project ($ millions)**

(a) Stage 1: Ignoring Option to Abandon, Probability of Success = 50%

	Expected After-Tax Cash Flows in Year					
	0	**1**	**2**	**3**	**4**	**5**
Success	($100)	$ 60	$ 60	$ 60	$ 60	$ 60
Failure	($100)	−40	−40	−40	−40	−40
Expected	($100)	$ 10	$ 10	$ 10	$ 10	$ 10
NPV at 25% =	($ 73)					

(b) Stage 1: Including Option to Abandon, Probability of Success = 50%

	Expected After-Tax Cash Flows in Year					
	0	**1**	**2**	**3**	**4**	**5**
Success	($100)	$ 60	$ 60	$ 60	$ 60	$ 60
Failure	($100)	−40	−40	20	0	0
Expected	($100)	$ 10	$ 10	$ 40	$ 30	$ 30
NPV at 25% =	($ 43)					

(c) Stage 2: Option to Expand, Probability of Success (Assuming Stage 1 Successful) = 90%

	Expected After-Tax Cash Flows in Year							
0	**1**	**2**	**3**	**4**	**5**	**6**	**7**
Success		($500)	$ 300	$ 300	$300	$300	$300
Failure		($500)	−200	−200	100	0	0
Expected		($500)	$ 250	$ 250	$280	$270	$270

NPV at 25% = $130
Total NPV at 25% (Stage 1 + 0.50 × Stage 2) = $22

appear in part *b* of Table 8.6. Note that the abandonment option is worth $30 million, bringing the NPV up to −$43 million.

The Option to Grow

A chief attraction of many new-technology investments is that success today creates the option to make highly profitable follow-on investments tomorrow, investments that are possible only because management took an intelligent gamble today. In this vein, suppose General Design believes initial success in diamond films will open the door to a stage 2, follow-on investment in two years that is precisely five times the size of today's stage 1 investment.

The probability assigned to a stage 2 success is critical. In management's eyes, if the stage 2 investment were made today, it would probably be no more likely to succeed than would stage 1; after all, stage 2 is the same technology, only five times as large. Consequently if made today, stage 2's NPV would just be five times as negative as stage 1's. But management does not have to make a decision on stage 2 today. It has the option to defer the decision until the initial results from stage 1 are in, and thus will be able to make a more informed choice. Supposing stage 2 will be undertaken only if stage 1 succeeds and that the chance of a stage 2 success given that stage 1 succeeded is 90 percent, part *c* in Table 8.6 shows that the NPV of the stage 2 investment at time zero is $130 million. Because General Design stands only a 50 percent chance of making the stage 2 investment, its expected NPV is half this amount, or $65 million. Adding the expected NPVs of both stages, the total NPV is now a healthy $22 million, and this ignores any stage 3 or stage 4 investments that might logically follow a stage 2 success. Proper consideration of the options embedded in General Design's investment transforms it from a clunker into a winner.

In summary, the complete expression for the net present value of an investment with imbedded options is

$$\begin{matrix} \text{NPV} \\ \text{of investment} \end{matrix} = \begin{matrix} \text{NPV} \\ \text{ignoring real options} \end{matrix} + \begin{matrix} \text{Value of} \\ \text{real options} \end{matrix}$$

And it is entirely possible that the value of the options will more than compensate for a negative conventional NPV. The moral should be clear: Failure to recognize and value real options implicit in corporate investments will make executives inappropriately timid in the face of high-risk, high-payoff opportunities.

Excessive Risk Adjustment

Our last pitfall is a subtle one concerning the proper use of risk-adjusted discount rates. Adding an increment to the discount rate to adjust for an investment's risk makes intuitive sense. You need to be aware, however, that as you apply this discount rate to more distant cash flows, the arithmetic of the discounting process compounds the risk adjustment. Table 8.7 illustrates

TABLE 8.7 **Use of a Constant Risk-Adjusted Discount Rate Implies That Risk Increases with the Remoteness of a Cash Flow (risk-free rate = 5%; risk-adjusted rate = 10%)**

	Present Value of $1	
	Received in 1 Year	Received in 10 Years
Risk-free	$0.95	$0.61
Risk-adjusted	0.91	0.39
Reduction in present value due to risk	$0.04	$0.23

the effect. It shows the present value of $1 in 1 year and in 10 years, first at a risk-free discount rate of 5 percent and then at a risk-adjusted rate of 10 percent. Comparing these present values, note that addition of the risk premium knocks a modest 4 cents off the value of a dollar in 1 year but a sizable 23 cents off in 10 years. Clearly, use of a constant risk-adjusted discount rate is appropriate only when the risk of a cash flow grows as the cash flow recedes farther into the future.

For many, if not most, business investments, the assumption that risk increases with the remoteness of a cash flow is quite appropriate, but as we will see by looking again at General Design's diamond film project, this is not always the case.

Recall that General Design is contemplating a possible two-stage investment. The first stage, costing $100 million, is attractive chiefly because it gives management the option to make a much more lucrative follow-on investment. Because both stages depend on a new, untested diamond film technology, the discount rate used throughout the analysis was General Design's high-risk hurdle rate of 25 percent.

Given the speculative nature of this investment, many executives would argue that it is entirely appropriate to use a high risk-adjusted discount rate throughout. But is it really? The investment clearly involves high risk, but because most of the risk will be resolved in the first two years, use of a constant risk-adjusted discount rate is overly conservative.

To see the logic, suppose you are at time 2, stage 1 has been successful, and the company is about to launch stage 2. Because the stage 2 cash flows are now relatively certain, their value *at time 2* is their expected values, as shown in part *c* of Table 8.6, *discounted at 15 percent*, the rate applicable to moderate-risk investments. This amounts $379 million.

As seen from the present, therefore, General Design's decision to invest in stage 1 gives it a 50 percent chance at a follow-on investment worth $379 million in two years. And because the next two years are high risk, we can find the present value of stage 2 today by discounting the $379 million time 2 value to the present at 25 percent:

$$\text{Expected present value of stage 2 investment} = 0.50 \times \$379 \text{ million} \times 0.640$$

$$= \$121 \text{ million}$$

Adding this sum to the stage 1 NPV of −$43 million yields a total NPV of $78 million. Explicit recognition of the two risk phases in General Design's investment adds another $56 million to its present worth.

To recap, whenever you encounter an investment with two or more distinct risk phases, be careful about using a constant risk-adjusted discount rate, for although such investments may be comparatively rare, they are also frequently the type of opportunities companies can ill afford to waste.

Economic Value Added

In late 1993, *Fortune* magazine ran a cover story entitled "The Real Key to Creating Wealth," which trumpeted, "Rewarded by knockout results, managers and investors are peering into the heart of what makes businesses valuable by using a tool called Economic Value Added."[7] With publicity like this and a steady stream of laudatory articles since, it is little wonder that many otherwise placid executives and investors are interested in what *Fortune* called "today's hottest financial idea and getting hotter."

Having mastered the intricacies of the cost of capital, you will find economic value added, or EVA, to be little more than a restatement of what you already know. The central message of this and the preceding chapter has been that an investment creates value for its owners only when its expected return exceeds its cost of capital. In essence, EVA simply extends the cost of capital imperative to performance appraisal. It says that a company or a business unit creates value for owners only when its operating income exceeds the cost of capital employed. In symbols,

$$EVA = EBIT(1 - \text{Tax rate}) - K_W C$$

where $EBIT(1 - \text{Tax rate})$ is the unit's after-tax operating income, K_W is its WACC, and C is the capital employed by the unit. $K_W C$, then, represents an annual capital charge. The capital-employed variable, C, equals the money invested in the unit over time by creditors and owners. As a first approximation, C is the sum of interest-bearing debt plus the book value of equity or, more generally, all sources of capital to the business on which it must earn a return.[8]

Plugging Harley-Davidson's 2004 numbers into this expression, we find that

$$EVA_{04} = \$1,402.3 \text{ million}(1 - 35.5\%)$$
$$- 10.8\%(\$1,295.4 \text{ million} + \$3,218.5 \text{ million})$$
$$= \$407.0 \text{ million.}$$

Although estimating economic values from accounting data is always problematic, these numbers suggest that Harley-Davidson earned more than enough in 2004 to cover the cost of capital employed and created $407.0 million in new value for its owners—an excellent performance.

[7]Shawn Tully, "The Real Key to Creating Wealth," *Fortune,* September 20, 1993, p. 38.
[8]For details, see G. Bennett Stewart III, *The Quest for Value* (New York: HarperBusiness, 1991).

TABLE 8.8 Discounting an Investment's Annual EVA Stream Is Equivalent to Calculating the Investment's NPV

(a) Standard NPV Analysis

			Year		
	0	1	2	3	4
Initial investment	−$100.00				
Revenue		$80.00	$80.00	$80.00	$80.00
Cash expenses		13.33	13.33	13.33	13.33
Depreciation		25.00	25.00	25.00	25.00
Income before tax		41.67	41.67	41.67	41.67
Tax at 40%		16.67	16.67	16.67	16.67
Income after tax		25.00	25.00	25.00	25.00
Depreciation		25.00	25.00	25.00	25.00
After-tax cash flow	−$100.00	$50.00	$50.00	$50.00	$50.00
NPV at 10%	$ 58.50				

(b) Discounted EVA Analysis

			Year		
	0	1	2	3	4
Capital employed		$100.00	$75.00	$50.00	$25.00
K_W		0.10	0.10	0.10	0.10
$K_W \times$ Capital		10.00	7.50	5.00	2.50
EBIT$(1 - t)$		25.00	25.00	25.00	25.00
$- K_W \times$ Capital		10.00	7.50	5.00	2.50
EVA		$ 15.00	$17.50	$20.00	$22.50
EVA discounted at 10%	$ 58.50				

EVA and Investment Analysis

An important attribute of economic value added is that the present value of an investment's annual EVA stream equals the investment's NPV. This makes it possible to talk about investment appraisal in terms of EVA rather than NPV—provided, of course, there is something to be gained by doing so. The numerical example in Table 8.8 demonstrates this equality. Part *a* of the table is a conventional net present value analysis of a very simple investment. The investment requires an initial outlay of $100, which will be depreciated on a straight-line basis to zero over four years. Adding depreciation to prospective income after tax and discounting the resulting after-tax cash flow at 10 percent yields an NPV of $58.50.

Part *b* of the table presents a discounted EVA treatment of the same investment. To calculate EVA, we need a figure for the annual opportunity cost of capital employed. This equals the percentage cost of capital times the book value of the investment at the beginning of each year. Subtracting this quantity from EBIT after-tax yields annual project EVA, which, discounted at 10 percent, yields a discounted EVA of $58.50—precisely the NPV calculated in part *a*. Thus, another way to evaluate investment opportunities, which is equivalent to NPV analysis, is to calculate the present value of the investment's annual EVA. Still to be answered is why one might want to calculate discounted EVA instead of NPV.[9]

EVA's Appeal

If EVA looks vaguely familiar, it should. The fact that capital provided by creditors and owners is costly and this cost is relevant for measuring economic performance has been recognized for many years. Indeed, we made the point in Chapter 1 when we noted that accounting income overstates true, economic income because it ignores the cost of equity. So novelty cannot explain EVA's sudden appeal, nor can EVA's superiority to return on investment, ROI, as a measure of business performance. For the problems with ROI, defined as operating income over operating assets, have also been widely known for a long while.[10] So why the sudden appeal of EVA after all these years?

The answer, I think, is that EVA, in its present incarnation, addresses a pervasive business problem, one that has greatly undermined many managers' acceptance of modern finance. EVA's appeal is that it integrates three crucial management functions: capital budgeting, performance appraisal, and incentive compensation. Together these functions are intended to positively influence management behavior, but too often they work at cross-purposes, giving managers confusing and apparently conflicting signals about what to do. Thus, in the absence of EVA, managers are told to use NPV, IRR, or BCR to analyze investment opportunities but to look at ROE, ROI, or earnings per share growth when assessing

---

[9] Why the equality? The difference between the two approaches lies in the treatment of the initial investment. NPV records the full cost of the investment at time zero. EVA ignores the initial cost but records an annual depreciation charge plus a carrying cost equal to the WACC times the undepreciated asset value. It turns out that the present value of these two annual charges always equals the initial cost of the investment, regardless of the method of depreciation employed. Therefore, the two methods must yield the same result.

[10] Here is one problem with ROI. Imagine a division with an ROI of only 2 percent and ask what type of investments the division manager is apt to favor. Charged with the task of raising division ROI, the manager will naturally look favorably on any investment promising an ROI above 2 percent regardless of the investment's NPV. Conversely, managers in divisions with high ROIs will be quite conservative in their investment decisions for fear of lowering ROI. A company in which unsuccessful divisions invest aggressively while successful ones invest conservatively is probably not what shareholders want to see.

business unit performance. And all the while, the company's incentive compensation plan relies on still other metrics, requires an advanced degree to fully comprehend, and changes more often than the Italian government. Is it any wonder, then, that many operating managers faced with this apparent confusion take none of it very seriously and rely instead on common sense to muddle through?

Contrast this with EVA-based management. The business goal is to create EVA. Capital budgeting decisions are based on discounted EVA at an appropriate cost of capital. Unit EVA, or change in EVA, measures business unit performance, and incentive compensation depends on unit EVA relative to an appropriate target—clean, simple, and straightforward. Consultants Stern Stewart & Company have even developed a clever method of distributing a manager's bonus over several periods, known as the bonus bank, that puts middle managers at risk much as though they were owners and also helps to discourage myopic, single-period decision making.[11]

EVA certainly has its own problems, and some of its virtues are more cosmetic than real. But it does address an important barrier to the acceptance of the financial way of thinking in many companies, and for this reason alone deserves our attention. Or, as *Fortune's* purple prose might put it, "EVA promises to complete the transformation of value creation from a mere slogan into a powerful management tool, one that may at last move modern finance out of the classroom and into the boardroom—perhaps even onto the shop floor!"

A Cautionary Note

An always present danger when using analytic or numerical techniques in business decision making is that the "hard facts" will assume exaggerated importance compared to more qualitative issues and that the manipulation of these facts will become a substitute for creative effort. It is important to bear in mind that numbers and theories don't get things done; people do. And the best investments will fail unless capable workers are committed to their success. As Barbara Tuchman put it in another context, "In military as in other human affairs will is what makes things happen. There are circumstances that can modify or nullify it, but for offense or defense its presence is essential and its absence fatal."[12]

---

[11] See Stewart, *The Quest for Value*, Chapter 6.
[12] Barbara W. Tuchman, *Stilwell and the American Experience in China 1911–1945* (New York: Bantam Books, 1971), pp. 561–62.

APPENDIX

Asset Beta and Adjusted Present Value

Most companies have two betas: An observable equity beta, discussed at some length in the chapter, and an unobservable asset beta. Equity beta measures the systematic risk of a company's shares, while asset beta measures the systematic risk of its assets. In rare instances when a company is all-equity financed, the risk of its common stock equals that of its assets, and equity beta equals asset beta. For this reason, asset beta is also commonly referred to as the firm's *unlevered* beta. It is the equity beta a firm would report if it were all-equity financed.

One important use of asset betas is to improve the accuracy by which equity betas are measured. To illustrate, when I estimated Harley-Davidson's equity beta by regressing the company's monthly, realized returns against those of the Standard & Poor's 500 Stock Index, I calculated an equity beta of 1.11, as reported in the chapter. But I also found a standard error of estimate equal to 0.20. Standard error is a statistical indicator of the precision of the beta estimate. As a benchmark, when the deviations of the individual observations from the regression line are distributed in a normal, bell-shaped pattern, we know there is a two-thirds chance that the true slope of the regression line is within plus or minus one standard error of the observed slope. This means we can state with some confidence that Harley-Davidson's equity beta is somewhere in the range of 0.91 to 1.31—not an especially comforting conclusion.

A second important use of asset beta is in conjunction with a net present value technique called *Adjusted Present Value*, or *APV.* Together asset beta and APV offer a flexible alternative to the standard WACC-based approach to investment appraisal described in the chapter. This alternative is especially attractive when evaluating complex investment opportunities.

Beta and Financial Leverage

Our starting point in the consideration of asset beta and adjusted present value is the effect of financial leverage on equity beta. Recalling our discussion of company financing decisions in Chapter 6, you know that shareholders face two distinct risks: the basic business risk inherent in the markets in which the firm competes, plus the added financial risk created by the use of debt financing. Asset beta measures the business risk, while equity beta reflects the combined effect of business and financial risks. To appreciate the tie between equity beta and financial leverage, recall from Chapter 6 that debt financing increases the dispersion in possible returns to shareholders, which in turn increases the firm's equity beta.

Because most businesses are levered, it is generally impossible to observe asset beta directly. However, with the aid of the following formula, we can easily calculate asset beta given equity beta, and vice versa.[1]

$$\beta_A = \frac{E}{V}\beta_E$$

where β_A is asset beta, β_E is equity beta, and $\frac{E}{V}$ is the equity-to-firm value ratio, measured at market. This equation says that $\beta_A = \beta_E$ when debt is zero and that β_E rises above β_A by a growing amount as leverage increases. Plugging Harley-Davidson's numbers into the equation, we learn that if the company's equity beta is 1.11, its asset beta must be 1.04 [1.04 = ($17,879.9 million/$19,175.3 million) × 1.11]. Calculating asset beta from equity beta in this manner is known in the trade as *unlevering* beta, while applying the equation in reverse to calculate equity beta from asset beta is referred to as *relevering* beta.

Using Asset Beta to Estimate Equity Beta

The ability to unlever and relever betas is the key to improving equity beta estimates. Three steps are required:

- Identify industry competitors of the target company, and calculate each competitor's asset beta by unlevering its observed equity beta.

---

[1] We can express the market value of a levered firm in two ways: as the market value of its debt plus equity, and as the value of the same firm unlevered plus the present value of the tax shields from debt financing. Equating these two expressions,

$$D + E = V_u + tD$$

where D is interest-bearing debt, E is the market value of equity, V_u is the value of the firm without any debt, and t is the marginal tax rate.

An important property of beta is that the beta of a portfolio is the weighted-average of the betas of the individual assets comprising the portfolio. Applying this insight to both sides of the equation above,

$$\frac{D}{D+E}\beta_D + \frac{E}{D+E}\beta_E = \frac{V_u}{V_u+tD}\beta_A + \frac{tD}{V_u+tD}\beta_{ITS}$$

where β_D is the beta of debt, β_E is the beta of equity, β_A is the beta of the unlevered firm, or equivalently, the firm's asset beta, and β_{ITS} is the beta of the firm's interest tax shields.

Assuming for simplicity (1) the firm's debt is risk free, so $\beta_D = 0$, and (2) the risk of interest tax shields equals the risk of the firm's unlevered asset cash flows, so $\beta_{ITS} = \beta_A$, the above equation simplifies to the equation in the text.

A possible alternative assumption is $\beta_{ITS} = \beta_D = 0$, which yields a more complex expression. For details, see Richard S. Ruback, "Capital Cash Flows: A Simple Approach to Valuing Risky Cash Flows," *Financial Management*, Summer 2002, pp. 85–103.

TABLE 8A.1   **Estimate of Industry Asset Beta for Harley-Davidson, Inc.**

Company	Equity Beta	Equity/Firm Value	Asset Beta	Market Value Equity	Percentage of Total Market Value	Weighted-Asset Beta
Arctic Cat	0.89	100.0%	0.89	$ 317	1.4%	0.01
Brunswick	0.89	84.6	0.75	4,069.9	18.4	0.14
Harley-Davidson	1.11	93.2	1.04	13,734.3	62.2	0.64
Marine Products	1.12	100.0	1.12	513.6	2.3	0.03
Polaris Industries	0.88	99.3	0.87	2,476.2	11.2	0.10
Winnebago Industries	1.46	100.0	1.46	972.7	4.4	0.06
					Industry asset beta	**0.98**

- Average these asset betas, or use their median value, to estimate an industry asset beta.

- Relever this industry asset beta to the target company's capital structure.

The logic of this approach is that firms in the same industry should face the same or similar business risks and should therefore have similar asset betas. Unlevering the observed equity betas removes the differential effects of financial leverage for each company, allowing us to estimate an industry asset beta based on observations from several firms. Then relevering this asset beta to the target's capital structure produces an equity beta consistent with the target's unique structure. The payoff from this approach is that an equity beta estimate based on data from a number of firms should reduce the unavoidable noise inherent in the conventional, single-firm approach.

Table 8A.1 illustrates the mechanics. It presents an estimate of Harley-Davidson's industry asset beta based on numbers for Harley-Davidson and five competitors. To avoid giving undue weight to smaller firms, I weighted the firm asset betas by relative market value of equity in calculating the industry figure. The resulting industry asset beta is 0.98. Relevering this industry beta to reflect Harley-Davidson's unique capital structure yields an estimated equity beta of 1.05, about five percent below the number reported in the chapter.

Asset Beta and Adjusted Present Value

In the standard WACC-based approach to investment appraisal described in the chapter, we ask the weighted average cost of capital to do double duty: to adjust for the risk of the cash flows being discounted, and to capture the tax-shield advantages of the debt financing used by the firm.

We reflect these tax shield advantages by using the after-tax cost of debt in the weighted-average calculation. In most instances this creates no problem; however, difficulties can arise when the firm's capital structure is changing over time, or when the project's debt capacity differs from that implicit in the WACC.

In these situations it becomes advantageous to use an Adjusted Present Value approach, or what is sometimes called "valuation by parts." First, abstract entirely from anything to do with debt financing by estimating the project's NPV assuming all-equity financing. Then capture the tax shield effects of debt financing, and any other "side effects," in separate add-on terms. If the sum of these separate present value terms is positive, the opportunity is financially attractive, and vice versa. In symbols,

$$APV = NPV_{\text{all–equity financing}} + PV_{\text{interest tax shields}} + PV_{\text{any other side effects}}$$

At its root, APV is nothing more than a formalization of the idea that when evaluating investment opportunities, the whole should equal the sum of the parts.

Asset beta and APV fit hand in glove because asset beta enables us to estimate the appropriate discount rate for valuing investments that are all-equity financed. A moment's review of the WACC equation in the chapter will convince you that in the absence of debt financing, WACC collapses to the cost of equity. The discount rate for evaluating all-equity financed investments is therefore represented by Equation 8.2 in the chapter, with β_A replacing β_E

$$K_A = i_g + \beta_A \times Rp$$

where i_g is a government bond rate, β_A is the investment's asset beta, and Rp is the risk premium, usually approximated by the excess return on common stocks over government bonds.

To illustrate the combined use of APV and asset beta, consider the investment opportunity under review by Delaney Pumps. Delaney Pumps manufactures and distributes an extensive line of agricultural irrigation systems. In recent years, computerized control systems used to automate irrigation and to conserve water have become increasingly important in selling high-end systems. And Delaney management is actively considering investing $160 million to develop a state-of-the-art, computerized controller that promises to leapfrog competition. Development work would be contracted to a software development company on a cost-plus basis. Revenue would come from a new product line featuring the controller and from license fees from selected competitors who elected to include the controller in their products. Projected cash flows for the investment appear in Table 8A.2. The projections extend for only four years

TABLE 8A.2 **Adjusted Present Value Analysis of Automated Irrigation Controller ($ in millions)**

	Year				
	0	1	2	3	4
Earnings before interest and taxes		$50.0	$150.0	$80.0	$30.0
Expected free cash flow	$(160.0)	30.0	120.0	60.0	70.0
Interest expense		5.0	15.0	8.0	3.0
Interest tax-shield @ 40% tax rate		2.0	6.0	3.2	1.2
Asset beta	2.41				
NPV all-equity	$ 18.3				
PV tax-shields	8.3				
APV	**$ 26.6**				

because management anticipates that other, more advanced controllers will be available by this time.

Two challenges confronted Delaney management as they began their deliberations. Because the digital controller appeared much riskier than the company's usual capital expenditures, managers were uncomfortable using the company's 10 percent weighted-average cost of capital as the hurdle rate. In addition, Delaney had traditionally financed its business with the goal of maintaining a target times-interest-earned ratio of about 3 to 1. But because this project consisted almost entirely of intangible computer code and because its cash flows were quite uncertain, Delaney's treasurer thought it prudent to target a higher interest coverage of 10 to 1 on this project.

To address these challenges, the treasurer decided to do an APV analysis. Reasoning that the digital controller would probably be an average-risk investment for software companies, she identified five smaller, publicly traded firms specializing in business automation software. She then unlevered the equity betas of these firms and calculated an industry average asset beta equal to 2.41, confirming her intuition that business automation software is indeed a risky business. Combining this asset beta with a 4.2 percent riskless borrowing rate and a 6.4 percent historical risk premium in the equation above, she calculated a hurdle rate for unlevered, business automation software investments equal to 19.6 percent (19.6% = 4.2% + 2.41 × 6.4%). Using this rate to discount the expected free cash flows in Table 8A.2, she found the project's NPV assuming all-equity financing to be $18.3 million.

The investment's principal side effect was the interest-tax shields it would generate over time. At a target times-interest-earned ratio of 10 to 1 and a 40 percent tax rate, the annual interest expense appearing in the table equals one-tenth of projected EBIT, while the corresponding tax shield is 40 percent of this amount. The discount rate used to calculate the present value of these tax shields should, of course, reflect the risk of the cash flows being discounted. Some executives argue that because interest tax shields are debtlike in terms of risk, they should be discounted at a corporate debt rate. Others maintain that while individual debt contracts may generate predictable cash flows, the total debt a business carries varies with its size and cash flows, in which case a discount rate more like K_A is appropriate. Here, because the tax shields are tied mechanically to operating income, K_A is the proper rate. Discounting at this rate, the tax shields are worth $8.3 million, so the investment's APV is an attractive $26.6 million.

$$APV = NPV_{\text{all-equity financing}} + PV_{\text{interest tax shields}}$$
$$\$26.6 \text{ million} = \$18.3 \text{million} + \$8.3 \text{million}$$

Note carefully in this analysis that the treasurer's tax shield calculations had nothing to do with the way Delaney intended to finance the investment and everything to do with how much debt the treasurer believed the project could prudently support. For tactical reasons, companies routinely finance some investments entirely with debt and others entirely with retained profits, but this information is irrelevant to judging an investment's debt capacity and its consequent claim to interest tax shields. To think otherwise would be to commit a variation of the "marginal cost of capital fallacy."

This example deals with a straightforward investment possessing one simple side effect, but I hope it hints at the power of the technique. APV's divide-and-conquer perspective makes it possible to break even very complex problems into a series of tractable, smaller problems, and to solve the complex problem by stringing together solutions to the smaller ones. We can thus analyze a cross-border investment involving several currencies and subsidized financing as the sum of separate NPV calculations for cash flows in each currency translated into the home currency at prevailing exchange rates, plus a separate term capturing the value of the subsidized finance. And we can even apply a separate, customized hurdle rate to each cash flow stream. In a complicated world, APV and its cousin, asset beta, are indeed welcome additions to our tool kit.

SUMMARY

1. This chapter incorporated risk into investment evaluation, with particular emphasis on risk-adjusted discount rates and the cost of capital.
2. Investments involve a trade-off between risk and return. The appropriate question when evaluating investment opportunities is not "What's the rate of return?" but "Is the return sufficient to justify the risk?"

3. Risk refers to the range of possible outcomes for an investment and the correlation of the outcomes with those of other investments. Risk can be estimated objectively for traded assets, but for other assets the estimate must often be largely subjective.

4. An asset's total risk equals its systematic risk, which cannot be eliminated through diversification, plus its unsystematic risk, which can be eliminated. Only systematic risk is relevant for evaluating investment opportunities.

5. The most popular, practical technique for incorporating risk into investment decisions uses a risk-adjusted discount rate in which the analyst adds a premium to the discount rate that reflects the perceived risk of the project.

6. A firm's cost of capital equals the opportunity costs incurred by creditors and owners, weighted by their relative importance in the firm's capital structure. It is a suitable risk-adjusted discount rate for evaluating average-risk investments by the firm. Average-risk investments yielding returns above the firm's cost of capital create value for owners and increase stock price.

7. Equity beta measures the systematic risk of an asset relative to that of a well-diversified portfolio, or equivalently to that of an average-risk share.

8. Estimating the cost of equity is the most difficult step in measuring the cost of capital. For most businesses, the best estimate is the current cost of government borrowing plus the company's equity beta times a risk premium based on historical experience of about 6.9 percentage points.

9. It is necessary to raise or lower the discount rate relative to the cost of capital, depending on whether a specific project is above or below average risk for the business.

10. Leveraged investments can be analyzed from the perspective of the firm making the investment (the entity perspective) or from that of the equity owner (the equity perspective). Used properly, the two perspectives yield the same investment decisions, but for practical reasons, I recommend use of the entity perspective whenever possible.

11. Under inflation, one must always use nominal cash flows and a nominal discount rate or real cash flows and a real discount rate. Never mix the two.

12. Do not overlook real options, such as the option to abandon or the option to expand, when evaluating corporate investment opportunities.

13. A constant risk-adjusted discount rate should not be used to evaluate investments with two or more distinct risk phases. To evaluate such investments, begin with the most distant phase and use a risk-adjusted rate that is appropriate to each phase.

14. Economic value added equals a business unit's operating income after tax less a charge for the opportunity cost of the capital employed. EVA has the potential to integrate capital budgeting, performance appraisal, and incentive compensation.

15. Proper technique is never a substitute for thought, work, or leadership. People, not analysis, get things done.

ADDITIONAL RESOURCES

Bernstein, Peter L. *Against the Gods: The Remarkable Story of Risk.* New York: John Wiley and Sons, 1998. 383 pages.

A stimulating history of man's attempt to cope with risk in human affairs from the 13th century to the present. Bernstein does a great job of explaining the principal tools of risk management in nonmathematical terms and putting them in a historical context. Believe it or not, an excellent read. Available in paperback for about $15.

Bruner, Robert F., Kenneth M. Eades, Robert S. Harris, and Robert C. Higgins. "Best Practices in Estimating the Cost of Capital: Survey and Synthesis." *Financial Practice and Education*, Spring–Summer 1998, pp. 13–27.

A look at the practical challenges of estimating capital costs and how some of America's best companies and investment banks address them.

Dixit, A. K. and R. S. Pindyck. "The Options Approach to Capital Investment." *Harvard Business Review*, May–June 1995, pp. 105–115.

An overview of the practical implications of the real options perspective for capital budgeting.

Copeland, Tom, and Vladimir Antikarov. *Real Options: A Practitioner's Guide.* New York: Texere, 2001. 372 pages.

Despite its many errors and typos, an excellent practical introduction to real options with emphasis on binomial decision trees. About $45.

Luehrman, Timothy A. "Using APV: A Better Tool for Valuing Operations." *Harvard Business Review*, May–June 1997, pp. 132–54.

A practical introduction to adjusted present value, a simple variant of NPV useful for analyzing complex investments.

Visit us at www.mhhe.com/higgins8e

WEBSITES

Finance.yahoo.com

The Yahoo! Finance website contains a wealth of information, if you can find it. This page offers one of the few sources of company betas on the Web. To find an estimate of a company's equity beta, enter the company's stock ticker symbol and select "key statistics."

www.real-options.com

Skip the book ad and go directly to "additional resources."

www.riskgrades.com

An excellent resource on risk and risk management, including a tutorial on risk and a description of riskmetrics, a sophisticated risk measurement tool. Estimate the risk of an asset or portfolio and how portfolio changes affect risk. Requires free registration.

PROBLEMS

Answers to odd-numbered problems are at the end of the book. For additional problems with answers, see **www.mhhe.com/higgins8e**.

1. Is each of the following statements true or false? Explain your answers.

   a. Using the same risk-adjusted discount rate to discount all future cash flows ignores the fact that the more distant cash flows are often more risky than cash flows occurring sooner.

   b. The cost of capital, or WACC, is *not* the correct discount rate to use for all projects undertaken by a firm.

   c. If you can borrow all of the money you need for a project at 6 percent, the cost of capital for this project is 6 percent.

2. Your company's weighted-average cost of capital is 11 percent. You believe the company should make a particular investment, but its internal rate of return is only 9 percent. What logical arguments would you use to convince your boss to make the investment despite its low rate of return? Is it possible that making investments with returns below capital cost will create value? If so, how?

3. Looking at Figure 8.1, explain why a company should reject investment opportunities lying below the market line and accept those lying above the line.

4. You have the following information about Burgundy Basins, a sink manufacturer.

Equity shares outstanding	15 million
Stock price per share	$25.00
Yield to maturity on debt	7%
Book value of interest-bearing debt	$255 million
Coupon interest rate on debt	5%
Market value of debt	$250 million
Book value of equity	$200 million
Cost of equity capital	12%
Tax rate	35%

Burgundy is contemplating what for the company is an average-risk investment costing $25 million and promising an annual after-tax cash flow of $3.5 million in perpetuity.

a. What is the internal rate of return on the investment?

b. What is Burgundy's weighted-average cost of capital?

c. If undertaken, would you expect this investment to benefit shareholders? Why or why not?

5. How will an increase in financial leverage affect a company's cost of equity capital, if at all? How will it affect a company's equity beta?

6. What is the present value of a cash flow stream of $1,000 per year annually for 16 years that then grows at 5 percent per year forever when the discount rate is 12 percent?

7. You are a commercial real estate broker eager to sell an office building. An investor is interested but demands a 20 percent return on her equity investment. The building's selling price is $10 million, and it promises after-tax cash flows of $1 million annually in perpetuity. Interest-only financing is available at 8 percent interest; that is, the debt requires no principal payments. The tax rate is 50 percent.

a. Propose an investment-financing package that meets the investor's return target.

b. Propose an investment-financing package that meets the investor's target when she demands an 80 percent return on equity.

c. Why would an investor settle for a 20 percent return on this investment when she can get as high as 80 percent?

8. (You will need a computer for this problem.) The following information is available about an investment opportunity. Investment will occur at time 0 and sales will commence at time 1.

Initial cost	$10 million
Unit sales	100,000
Selling price per unit, this year	$50.00
Variable cost per unit, this year	$20.00
Life expectancy	10 years
Salvage value	$0
Depreciation	Straight-line
Tax rate	34%
Nominal discount rate	10.0%
Real discount rate	10.0%
Inflation rate	0.0%

a. Prepare a spreadsheet to estimate the project's annual after-tax cash flows.

b. Calculate the investment's internal rate of return and its NPV.

c. How do your answers to questions (a) and (b) change when you assume a uniform inflation rate of 8 percent a year over the next 10 years? (Use the following equation to calculate the nominal discount rate: $i_n = (1 + i_r)(1 + p) - 1$, where i_n is the nominal discount rate, i_r is the real discount rate, and p is expected inflation.)

d. How do you explain the fact that inflation causes the internal rate of return to increase and the net present value to decrease?

e. Does inflation make this investment more attractive or less attractive? Why?

9. The chapter discusses General Design's option to expand its diamond film project.

a. Is the option a call or a put?

b. What is the option's strike price?

10. (This problem tests your understanding of the chapter appendix.) Sweat Equity Appliance, Inc., a private firm that manufactures home appliances, has hired you to estimate the company's beta. You have obtained the following equity betas for publicly traded firms that also manufacture home appliances.

		($ millions)	
Firm	**Beta**	**Debt**	**Market Value of Equity**
Black & Decker	1.40	$2,500	$3,000
Fedders Corp.	1.20	5	200
Maytag Corp.	1.20	540	2,250
Salton, Inc.	2.20	200	100
Whirlpool	1.50	2,900	4,000

The publicly traded firms all have a marginal tax rate of 40 percent.

a. Estimate an asset beta for Sweat Equity.

b. What concerns, if any, would you have about using the betas of these firms to estimate Sweat Equity's asset beta?

STANDARD
&POOR'S

11. Use the Standard & Poor's Market Insight website **(www.mhhe.com/edumarketinsight)** for this problem. Assume Starbucks Corporation is reviewing the cost of equity and the WACC it uses to evaluate new investments. Management collected the following information as of September 30, 2004:

Yield to maturity on debt	8%
Coupon interest rate on debt	9%
Tax rate	40%
Long-term government bond rate	4.5%
Historical excess return on common stocks	6.4%

a. Use Starbucks' September 2004 beta (β) to calculate the company's cost of equity capital. (To find beta go to Excel Analytics, Valuation Data, Profitability.)

b. As of September 2004, calculate Starbucks' WACC. (Hint: For purposes of this exercise, use Total Liabilities as the company's book value of debt. You can find Total Liabilities on Starbucks' Annual Balance Sheet under Excel Analytics. The common shares outstanding are there as well. For the closing market price check Profitability.)

STANDARD
&POOR'S

12. Use the Standard & Poor's Market Insight website **(www.mhhe.com/edumarketinsight)** for this problem. Assume that Starbucks contemplates selling music online over a website, via existing wireless hotspots in its stores. The estimated initial investment in technology and cost of implementation is $36 million, and the expected net increase in annual after-tax cash flow is $4 million in the first year, growing 2 percent a year in perpetuity. Management estimates that this project carries moderately more risk than Starbucks' average project, and believes that the project's risk is roughly comparable to that faced on typical investments made by Apple Computer Inc.

a. Calculate the appropriate discount rate to evaluate this project. You may assume that Starbucks correctly chose the comparable company, and that differences in leverage between Starbucks and Apple have a negligible effect on the analysis. Assume a 40 percent tax rate, 10 percent interest rate on Apple's debt, and other information as presented in Problem 11, above. (Use Apple's financial statements for September 30, 2004.)

b. Based on management's projections, should Starbucks invest in this enhancement?

c. What would be the consequences of Starbucks using its WACC (computed in Problem 11) to evaluate this project?

d. Based on your answers to the preceding questions, what advice would you give Starbucks' management?

eXcel

13. The Excel file C8_Problem_13.xls available at **www.mhhe.com/ higgins8e** (Select Student Edition > Choose a Chapter > Excel Spreadsheets) provides key facts and assumptions concerning Ametek, Inc. Using this information,

a. Estimate Ametek's cost of equity capital.

b. Estimate Ametek's weighted-average cost of capital. Prepare a spreadsheet or table showing the relevant variables.

eXcel

14. The Excel file C8_Problem_14.xls at **www.mhhe.com/higgins8e** (Select Student Edition > Choose a Chapter > Excel Spreadsheets) gives information regarding Ametek, Inc., and five industry competitors. Using this information,

a. Estimate the industry asset beta, weighting each company by its proportion of total market value of equity.

b. Relever the industry asset beta to reflect Ametek's capital structure, and to make another (industry-informed) estimate of Ametek's equity beta.

CHAPTER NINE

Business Valuation and Corporate Restructuring

To complete our merger negotiations, my attorneys will now mark scent your office.

Fortune

On May 7, 1998, after five months of increasingly intimate courtship, Germany's Daimler-Benz AG and America's Chrysler Corporation announced their intention to combine forces in a friendly, exchange-of-shares merger. Although billed initially as a merger of equals, the transaction is generally acknowledged today to have been a Daimler takeover. Valued at $53 billion, the Daimler acquisition of Chrysler was the largest combination of industrial companies in history.

Although it will be years and perhaps decades before we can say categorically whether Daimler's buy was a wise one, there can be little doubt about the initial outcome. Among the early winners were Chrysler shareholders and senior executives. In intense, last-hour, one-on-one negotiations between Chrysler chief executive, Robert Eaton, and his Daimler counterpart, Jürgen Schrempp, Eaton wrested a 28 percent premium for Chrysler shareholders.[1] With the stock selling in the mid-40s and some 648 million Chrysler shares outstanding, this translates into a payoff of $8.2 billion ($8.2 = 28\% \times \$45 \times 648$). In addition, Chrysler's top 30 executives received a total of $395 million in cash and stock on closing (that's an average of $13 million a head if you're keeping score). Eaton alone stood to receive $70 million, plus generous options on the new company's common stock. And to make certain he didn't go away angry, Eaton also negotiated a "golden parachute" of $24 million, which would be his if he were fired or quit "for good reason" within two years. And then there are the investment bankers. In return for representing Chrysler's interests in the negotiations, CS First Boston would receive $15 million on announcement of a transaction and

[1] Much of the information about the Daimler-Chrysler merger in this chapter comes from Bill Vlasic and Bradley A. Stertz, *Taken for a Ride* (New York: HarperBusiness, 2001).

another $20 million on closing, plus an incentive fee pegged to the premium received by Chrysler shareholders and worth as much as $20 million. Daimler shareholders also benefited initially from the acquisition, albeit to a lesser degree, as their shares rose 6 percent on the merger announcement. The stock market's clear initial verdict was that the transaction made economic sense but that most of the spoils were going to Chrysler.

The Daimler-Benz takeover of Chrysler aptly illustrates an important phenomenon in business known broadly as *corporate restructuring*. Guided presumably by the financial principles examined in earlier chapters, senior executives make major, episodic changes in their company's asset mix, capital structure, or ownership composition in pursuit of increased value. In addition to friendly mergers of the Daimler-Chrysler variety, corporate restructuring encompasses hostile acquisitions, purchases or sales of operating divisions, large repurchases of common stock, major changes in financial leverage, spin-offs, carveouts, and leveraged buyouts, or LBOs. (In a spin-off, the parent company distributes shares of a subsidiary to its stockholders much like a dividend, and the subsidiary becomes an independent company. In a carveout, the parent sells all or part of a subsidiary to the public for cash. An LBO is characterized by extensive use of debt financing, often the acquired entity's debt, to help finance an acquisition.)

The Daimler-Chrysler deal and many other restructurings pose several important questions to students of finance, and indeed to all executives. In terms of the Chrysler purchase, they include the following:

1. What led Jürgen Schrempp to believe that Chrysler was worth as much as $57.50 a share?

2. If Schrempp was willing to pay as much as $57.50 a share for Chrysler stock, why was the market price during negotiations only in the mid-40s? Does the stock market misprice companies this drastically, or is something else at work?

3. If Chrysler stock really was worth $57.50, why didn't Chrysler executives, who certainly knew more about their company than Schrempp did, realize this fact and do something to ensure that the value was reflected in Chrysler's stock price?

4. Ultimately, who should decide the merits of corporate restructurings, management or owners? In the Daimler-Chrysler merger, shareholders of both companies voted to approve the deal, but not all restructurings are put up to shareholder vote. More broadly, who really controls today's large corporations, and who should control them? Is it the shareholders, who collectively bear the financial risk, or is it the managers, who at least nominally work for the shareholders?

This chapter addresses these questions and, in the process, examines the principal financial dimensions of corporate restructuring. We begin by looking at business valuation, a family of techniques for estimating the value of a company or division. We then turn to what is known as "the market for corporate control," where we consider why one company might rationally pay a premium to acquire another and how to estimate an aspiring buyer's maximum acquisition price. Next, we examine three primarily financial motives for business restructuring predicated on the virtues of increased tax shields, enhanced management incentives, and shareholder control of free cash flow. The chapter closes with a brief review of the evidence on the economic merits of mergers and leveraged buyouts and a closer look at the Daimler-Chrysler marriage. The chapter appendix examines the venture capital method of valuation.

Valuing a Business

Business valuation merits our serious attention because it is the underlying discipline for a wide variety of important financial activities. In addition to their use in structuring mergers and leveraged buyouts, business valuation principles guide security analysts in their search for undervalued stocks. Investment bankers use the same concepts to price initial public stock offerings, and venture capitalists rely on them to evaluate new investment opportunities. Companies intent on repurchasing their stock also frequently use valuation skills to time their purchases. Business valuation principles are even creeping into corporate strategy under the banner of value-based management, a consultant-spawned philosophy urging executives to evaluate alternative business strategies according to their predicted effect on the market value of the firm. It is thus not an exaggeration to say that although the details and the vocabulary differ from one setting to another, the principles of business valuation are integral to much of modern business.

The first step in valuing any business is to decide precisely what is to be valued. This requires answering three basic questions:

- Do we want to value the company's assets or its equity?

- Shall we value the business as a going concern or in liquidation?

- Are we to value a minority interest in the business or controlling interest?

Let us briefly consider each question in turn.

Assets or Equity?

When one company acquires another, it can do so by purchasing either the seller's assets or its equity. When the buyer purchases the seller's equity, it must assume the seller's liabilities. Thus, when Daimler-Benz acquired Chrysler, it paid $37.3 billion for Chrysler's equity and assumed another $15.5 billion in Chrysler interest-bearing debt, making the total purchase price for Chrysler's assets $52.8 billion. Although it is all too common to speak of Daimler paying $37.3 billion for Chrysler, this is incorrect, or at best misleading. For the true economic cost of the acquisition to Daimler shareholders is $52.8 billion, $37.3 billion incurred in the form of newly printed stock certificates and $15.5 billion in the form of a legal commitment to honor Chrysler's existing liabilities. The effect on Daimler shareholders of assuming Chrysler's debt is the same as paying $52.8 billion for Chrysler's assets and financing $15.5 billion of the purchase price with new debt. In both cases, Chrysler's assets had better generate future cash flows worth at least $52.8 billion or Daimler's shareholders will have made a bad investment. Here's a down-home analogy. If you purchased a house for $100,000 cash and assumption of the seller's $400,000 mortgage, you presumably would never say you bought the house for $100,000. You bought it for $500,000 with $100,000 down. Analogously, Daimler bought Chrysler for $52.8 billion with $37.3 billion down.

Most acquisitions involving companies of any size are structured as an equity purchase; so the ultimate objective of the valuation, and the focus of negotiations, is the value of the seller's equity. However, never lose sight of the fact that the true cost of the acquisition to the buyer is the cost of the equity plus the value of all liabilities assumed.

Dead or Alive?

Companies can generate value for owners in either of two states: in liquidation or as going concerns. *Liquidation value* is the cash generated by terminating a business and selling its assets individually, while *going-concern value* is the present worth of expected future cash flows generated by a business. In most instances, we will naturally be interested in a business's going-concern value.

It will be helpful at this point to define an asset's *fair market value (FMV)* as the price at which the asset would trade between two rational individuals, each in command of all of the information necessary to value the asset and neither under any pressure to trade. Usually the FMV of a business is the higher of its liquidation value and its going-concern value. Figure 9.1 illustrates the relationship. When the present value of expected future cash flows is low, the business is worth more dead than alive, and FMV equals the company's liquidation value. At higher levels of expected future cash flows, liquidation value becomes increasingly irrelevant, and FMV depends almost entirely on going-concern value. It can also be the case that some of a company's assets, or divisions, are worth

FIGURE 9.1   **The Fair Market Value of a Business Is Usually the Higher of Its Liquidation Value and Its Going-Concern Value**

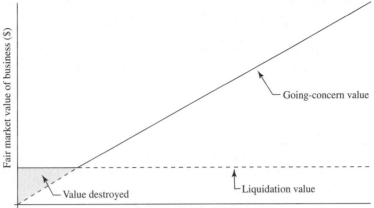

more in liquidation, while others are more valuable as going concerns. In this instance, the firm's FMV is a combination of liquidation and going-concern values as they apply to individual assets.

An exception to the general rule that FMV is the higher of a company's liquidation value and going-concern value occurs when the individuals controlling the company—perhaps after reflecting on their alternative employment opportunities and the pleasures afforded by the corporate yacht—choose not to liquidate, even though the business is worth more dead than alive. Then, because minority investors cannot force liquidation, the FMV of a minority interest can fall below the liquidation value. This is represented in the figure by the shaded triangle labeled "value destroyed." Additional latent value exists, but because minority owners cannot get their hands on it, the value has no effect on the price they are willing to pay for the shares. As minority shareholders see it, the individuals controlling the business are destroying value by refusing to liquidate. Later in the chapter, we will consider other instances in which price, as determined by minority investors, does not reflect full value.

When speaking of control, it is important to note that ownership of a company's shares and control of the company are two vastly different things. Unless a shareholder owns or can influence at least 51 percent of a company's voting stock, there is no assurance he or she will have any say at all in company affairs. Moreover, in most large American public companies, no shareholder or cohesive group of shareholders owns enough stock to exercise voting control, and effective control devolves to the board of directors and incumbent management. In these instances, shareholders are just along for the ride.

Minority Interest or Control?

Oscar Wilde once observed that "Economists know the price of everything and the value of nothing." And in a very real sense he is correct, since to an economist the value of an asset is nothing more or less than the price at which informed buyers and sellers are willing to trade it. The question of whether an asset has value beyond its selling price is one economists are content to leave to philosophers.

If value is synonymous with selling price, one obvious indicator of the worth of a business is its market value, the aggregate price at which its equity and debt trade in financial markets. Thus, just before Daimler and Chrysler announced their intention to merge in May 1998, Chrysler had about 648 million shares outstanding, each selling for $44.88, and $15.5 billion in debt; so its market value was $44.6 billion ($44.6 billion = 648 million × $44.88 + $15.5 billion).

As noted in earlier chapters, the market value of a business is an important indicator of company performance and a central determinant of a company's cost of capital. However, you need to realize that market value measures the worth of the business to *minority* investors. The stock price used to calculate the market value of a business is the price at which small numbers of shares have traded and is thus an unreliable indicator of the price at which a controlling interest might trade. The distinction between minority interest and controlling interest is sharply apparent in Chrysler's case, where the market value of the firm was only $44.6 billion, yet controlling interest fetched a price of $52.8 billion.

Other instances in which market value is inadequate to the business valuation task include the following: The target is privately held, so market value does not exist. The target's stock trades so infrequently or in such modest volume that price is not a reliable indicator of value. The target's stock trades actively, but the analyst wants to compare market value to an independent estimate of value in search of mispriced stocks.

In sum, we can say that market value is directly relevant in business valuation only when the goal is to value a minority interest in a public company. In all other instances, market value may provide a useful frame of reference, but cannot by itself answer most interesting valuation questions. For this we need to think more carefully about the determinants of business value.

Discounted Cash Flow Valuation

Having examined business valuation in the large, we turn now to the specific task of estimating a company's going-concern value. For simplicity, we will begin by considering the value of a minority interest in a privately held firm.

Absent market prices, the most direct way to estimate going-concern value, if not always the most practical, is to think of the target company as if it were nothing more than a giant capital expenditure opportunity. Just as with any piece of capital equipment, investing in a company requires the expenditure of money today in anticipation of future benefits, and the central issue is whether tomorrow's benefits justify today's costs. As in capital expenditure analysis, we can answer this question by calculating the present value of expected future cash flows accruing to owners and creditors. When this number exceeds the acquisition price, the purchase has a positive net present value and is therefore attractive. Conversely, when the present value of future cash flows is less than the acquisition price, the purchase is unattractive.

In equation form,

$$\text{FMV of firm} = \text{PV \{Expected cash flows to owners and creditors\}}$$

This formula says that the maximum price one should pay for a business equals the present value of expected future cash flows to capital suppliers discounted at an appropriate risk-adjusted discount rate. Moreover, as in any other application of risk-adjusted discount rates, we know the rate should reflect the risk of the cash flows being discounted. Because the cash flows here are to owners and creditors of the target firm, it follows that the discount rate should be the target company's weighted-average cost of capital.

A legitimate question at this point is: Why waste energy estimating firm value when the ultimate goal of the exercise is usually to value equity? The answer is simple once you recall that the value of equity is closely tied to the value of the firm. In equation form, we have our old friend

$$\text{Value of equity} = \text{Value of firm} - \text{Value of debt}$$

To determine the value of a company's equity, therefore, we need only estimate firm value and subtract interest-bearing debt. Moreover, because the market value and the book value of debt are usually about equal to each other, estimating the value of debt amounts to nothing more than grabbing a few numbers off the company's balance sheet.[2] If the fair market value of a business is $4 million and the firm has $1.5 million in debt outstanding, its equity is worth $2.5 million. It's that simple.[3] (We ignore

---

[2] There are two instances in which the market value and the book value of debt will differ significantly: Default risk has changed significantly since issue, and the debt is fixed rate and interest rates have changed significantly since issue. In these instances, it pays to estimate the market value of the debt independently.

[3] An alternative approach to equity valuation is to estimate the present value of expected cash flows to equity discounted at the target's cost of equity capital. Executed correctly, this equity approach yields the same answer as the enterprise approach described above; however, I find it more difficult to apply in practice. See the section "The Enterprise Perspective versus the Equity Perspective" in Chapter 8 for details.

non-interesting-bearing debt such as accounts payable and deferred taxes here because they are treated as part of free cash flow, to be described momentarily.)

Free Cash Flow

As in all capital expenditure decisions, the biggest practical challenge in business valuation is estimating the relevant cash flows to be discounted. In Chapter 7 we said the relevant cash flows are the project's annual free cash flows (FCF), defined as EBIT after tax plus depreciation, less investment. When valuing a company, this translates into the following:

$$\frac{\text{Free}}{\text{cash flow}} = \text{EBIT}(1 - \text{Tax rate}) + \text{Depreciation} - \frac{\text{Capital}}{\text{expenditures}} - \frac{\text{Working capital}}{\text{investments}}$$

where EBIT is earnings before interest and taxes.

The rationale for using free cash flow goes like this. EBIT is the income the company earns without regard to how the business is financed; so EBIT(1 − Tax rate) is income after tax excluding the effects of debt financing. Adding depreciation and any other noncash items yields after-tax cash flow. If management were prepared to run the company into the ground, it could distribute this cash flow to owners and creditors, and that would be the end of it. But in most companies, management retains some or all of this cash flow in the business to pay for new capital expenditures and additions to short-term assets. The annual cash flow available for distribution to owners and creditors is thus operating cash flow after tax less capital expenditures and working capital investments.

The working capital term in this expression can be tricky. Working capital investment equals the increase in current assets necessary to support operations, less any accompanying increases in noninterest-bearing current liabilities, or what I referred to in Chapter 7 as "spontaneous sources." This difference equals the net investment in current assets that must be financed by creditors and owners. A second challenge is how to treat any excess cash a company accumulates over and above the amount necessary to support operations. My advice is to omit excess cash from the discounted cash flow valuation and treat it as a separate add-on term. I will demonstrate this process in a few pages.

The Terminal Value

We now come to a serious practical problem. Our equation says that the FMV of a business equals the present value of all future free cash flows. Yet because companies typically have an indefinitely long life expectancy, the literal application of this equation would have us estimating free cash flows for perhaps hundreds of years into the far distant future—a clearly unreasonable task.

The standard way around this impasse is to think of the target company's future as composed of two discrete periods. During the first period, of some 5 to 15 years, we presume the company has a unique cash flow pattern and growth trajectory that we seek to capture by estimating individual, annual free cash flows just as the equation suggests. However, by the end of this forecast period, we assume the company has lost its individuality—has grown up, if you will—and become a stable, slow-growth business. From this date forward, we cease worrying about annual cash flows and instead estimate a single *terminal value* representing the worth of all subsequent free cash flows. If the initial forecast period is, say, 10 years, our valuation equation becomes

FMV of firm = PV(FCF years 1–10 + Terminal value at year 10)

Introduction of a terminal value, of course, only trades one problem for another, for now we need to know how to estimate a company's terminal value. I wish I could assure you that financial economists have solved this problem and present a simple, accurate expression for a company's terminal value, but I can't. Instead, the best I can offer are several plausible alternative estimates and some general advice on how to proceed.

Following are five alternative ways to estimate a company's terminal value with accompanying explanatory comments and observations. To use these estimates effectively, note first that no single estimate is always best; rather, each is more or less appropriate depending on circumstances. Thus, liquidation value may be highly relevant when valuing a mining operation with 10 years of reserves but quite irrelevant when valuing a rapidly growing software company. Second, resist the natural temptation to pick what appears to be the best technique for the situation at hand, ignoring all others. Avoid too the simple averaging of several estimates. Instead, calculate a number of terminal value estimates and begin by asking why they differ. In some instances, the differences will be readily explainable; in others, you may find it necessary to revise your assumptions to reconcile the differing values. Then, once you understand why remaining differences exist and feel comfortable with the magnitude of the differences, select a terminal value based on your assessment of the relative merits of each estimate for the target company.

Five Terminal Value Estimates

Liquidation Value   Highly relevant when liquidation at the end of the forecast period is under consideration, liquidation value usually grossly understates a healthy business's terminal value.

Book Value   Popular perhaps among accountants, book value usually yields a quite conservative terminal value estimate.

Warranted Price-to-Earnings Multiple   To implement this approach, multiply the target firm's estimated earnings to common stock at the end of the forecast horizon by a "warranted" price-to-earnings ratio; then add projected interest-bearing liabilities to estimate the firm's terminal value. As a warranted price-to-earnings ratio, consider the multiples of publicly traded firms that you believe represent what the target will become by the end of the forecast period.[4] If, for example, the target company is a startup but you believe it will be representative of other, mature companies in its industry by the end of the forecast period, the industry's current price-to-earnings multiple may be a suitable ratio. Another strategy is to bracket the value by trying multiples of, say, 10 and 20 times. The approach generalizes easily to other "warranted" ratios, such as market value to book value, price to cash flow, or price to sales.

No-Growth Perpetuity   We saw in Chapter 7 that the present value of a no-growth perpetuity is the annual cash flow divided by the discount rate. This suggests the following terminal value estimate:

$$\frac{\text{Terminal value of}}{\text{no-growth firm}} = \frac{\text{FCF}_{T+1}}{K_W}$$

where FCF_{T+1} is free cash flow in the first year beyond the forecast horizon and K_W is the target's weighted-average cost of capital. As further refinement, we might note that when a company is not growing, its capital expenditures should about equal its annual depreciation charges and its net working capital should neither increase nor decrease over time, both of which imply that free cash flow should simplify to EBIT(1 − Tax rate).

Because most businesses expand over time, if due only to inflation, many analysts believe this equation understates the terminal value of a typical business. I am more skeptical. For, as noted repeatedly in earlier chapters, growth creates value only when it generates returns above capital costs; and in competitive product markets over the long run, such performance is more the exception than the rule. Hence, even if many companies are capable of expanding, they may be worth no more than their no-growth brethren. The implication is that the no-growth equation is applicable to more firms than might first be supposed. I am also mindful of economist Kenneth Boulding's observation that, "Anyone who believes that exponential growth can go on forever in a finite world is either a madman or an economist."

---

[4] For industry price-to-earnings ratios, see **www.stern.nyu.edu/~adamodar/**. Select "Updated Data" and under "Data Sets" go to "multiples."

Perpetual Growth   In Chapter 8, we saw that the present value of a perpetually growing stream of cash equals next year's cash flow divided by the difference between the discount rate and the growth rate. Thus, another terminal value estimate is

$$\text{Terminal value of perpetually growing firm} = \frac{\text{FCF}_{T+1}}{K_W - g}$$

where g is the perpetual-growth rate of free cash flow.

A few words of caution are in order about this popular expression. It is a simple arithmetic fact that any business growing faster than the economy *forever* must eventually become the economy. (When I made this point recently at a Microsoft seminar, the immediate response was "Yeah! Yeah!") The intended conclusion for mere mortal firms is that the absolute upper limit on g must be the long-run growth rate of the economy, or about 2 to 3 percent a year, plus expected inflation. Moreover, because even inflationary growth invariably requires higher capital expenditures and increases in working capital, free cash flow falls as g rises. This implies that unless this inverse relation is kept in mind, the preceding expression may well overstate a company's terminal value—even when the perpetual growth rate is kept to a low figure.[5]

The Forecast Horizon

Terminal values of growing businesses can easily exceed 60 percent of firm value, so it goes without saying that proper selection of the forecast horizon and terminal value are critical to the successful application of discounted cash flow approaches to business valuation. Because most tractable terminal value estimates implicitly assume the firm is a mature, slow-growth, or no-growth perpetuity from that date forward, it is important to extend the forecast horizon far enough into the future that this assumption plausibly applies. When valuing a rapidly growing business, this perspective suggests estimating how long the company can be expected to sustain its supernormal growth before reaching maturity and setting the forecast horizon at or beyond this date.

---

[5] Here is a modestly more complex version of the perpetual-growth expression, to which I am partial:

$$\text{Terminal value} = \frac{\text{EBIT}(1 - \text{Tax rate})(1 - g/r)}{K_W - g}$$

where r is the rate of return on new investment. One virtue of this expression is that growth does not add value unless returns exceed capital cost. To confirm this, set $r = K_W$ and note that the expression collapses to the no-growth equation. A second virtue is that growth is not free, for as growth rises, so must capital expenditures and net working capital. In the equation, higher g reduces the numerator, which is equivalent to reducing free cash flow. See pages 269–70 in the Copeland, Koller, and Murrin book referenced at the end of this chapter for a demonstration that this expression is mathematically equivalent to the earlier perpetual-growth equation.

A Numerical Example

Table 9.1 offers a quick look at a discounted cash flow valuation of our friend from earlier chapters, Harley-Davidson, Inc. It goes without saying that if I were being paid by the hour to value Harley-Davidson and you were being similarly compensated to read about it, we would both proceed much more thoroughly and deliberately. In particular, we would want to know a great deal more about the company's products, markets, and competitors, for a discounted cash flow valuation is only as good as the projections on which it is based. Nonetheless, the table should give you a basic understanding of how to execute a discounted cash flow valuation.

The valuation date is December 31, 2004. In my judgment Harley-Davidson has over a billion dollars in marketable securities that are not necessary to support operations, so I will exclude marketable securities from the discounted cash flow analysis and consider them later as a separate source of value. The free cash flows appearing in the table are

TABLE 9.1   Discounted Cash Flow Valuation of Harley-Davidson, Inc. ($ millions except per share)

	Year					
	2005	**2006**	**2007**	**2008**	**2009**	**2010**
EBIT	$1,528	$1,666	$1,816	$1,979	$2,157	$2,243
Tax at 35%	535	583	635	693	755	785
Earnings after tax	993	1,083	1,180	1,286	1,402	1,458
+ Depreciation	232	253	276	300	327	341
− Capital expenditures	342	357	389	424	462	481
− Increase in NWC	144	157	171	186	203	211
Free cash flow	$ 739	$ 822	$ 896	$ 976	$1,064	$1,107
$PV_{@\,10.8\%}$ of FCFs 05–09	**$3,552**					

Terminal value estimates:		Terminal value 2009
Perpetual growth at 4% $[FCF_{10}/(K_w - g)]$		$16,280
Warranted MV firm/EBIT(1 − tax rate) = 20×		28,043
Projected book value of debt & equity '09		6,549
Best-guess terminal value		21,000
PV of terminal value	**$12,575**	
Estimated value of operations	$16,127	
Value of excess marketable securities	1,337	
Value of firm	**$17,464**	
Value of liabilities	1,295	
Value of equity	$16,168	
Shares outstanding	294.32 million	
Value per share	**$ 54.93**	

based on a five-year pro forma projection. The projection assumes Harley-Davidson's earnings before interest and taxes (EBIT) grow nine percent a year through 2009. The present value of these free cash flows discounted at Harley-Davidson's 10.8 percent cost of capital as estimated in the last chapter, amounts to $3,552 million.

The valuation considers three terminal value estimates. The first relies on the perpetual-growth equation and assumes that beginning in 2010 Harley-Davidson's free cash flows will commence growing at 4 percent a year into the indefinite future. Free cash flow in 2010 will thus be $1,107 million [$1,107 million = $1,064 million (1 + 0.04)]. This amount is less than earnings after tax in the same year because capital expenditures will need to exceed depreciation and net current assets must increase to support the anticipated growth. Plugging these values into the perpetual-growth equation, one estimate of Harley-Davidson's terminal value at the end of 2009 is

$$\text{Terminal value} = \frac{\text{FCF in 2010}}{K_W - g} = \frac{\$1,107 \text{ million}}{0.108 - 0.04} = \$16,280 \text{ million}$$

The second terminal value estimate assumes that at the end of the forecast horizon, Harley-Davidson will command a price-to-earnings multiple of 20 times EBIT after tax, a figure reflecting current valuations of comparable firms. I will say more about this multiple in a few pages. Applying this warranted price-to-earnings ratio to Harley-Davidson's earnings in 2009 yields a second terminal value estimate:

$$\text{Terminal value} = 20 \times \$1,402 \text{ million} = \$28,043 \text{ million}$$

Finally, Harley-Davidson's projected book value of interest-bearing debt and equity in 2009 is $6,549 million. This constitutes a third estimate of the company's terminal value, although certainly a low one.

After reflecting on the relative merits of these three estimates, my best guess is that Harley-Davidson will be worth $21,000 million in 2009. In making this estimate, I put somewhat more weight on the perpetual growth value than on the warranted price-to-earnings figure, while largely ignoring the book value. Discounting $21,000 million back to 2004 and adding it to the present value of free cash flows in the first five years, plus the company's marketable securities, suggests Harley-Davidson is worth $17,464 million at year-end 2004:

$$\text{FMV}_{\text{firm}} = \$3,552 \text{ million} + \$12,575 \text{ million} + \$1,337 \text{ million}$$
$$= \$17,464 \text{ million}$$

The rest is just arithmetic. Harley-Davidson's equity is worth $17,464 million less $1,295 million in interest-bearing debt presently outstanding,

The Problem of Growth and Long Life

In many investment decisions involving long-lived assets, it is common to finesse the problem of forecasting far distant cash flows by ignoring all flows beyond some distant horizon. The justification for this practice is that the present value of far distant cash flows will be quite small. When the cash flow stream is a growing one, however, growth offsets the discounting effect, and even far distant cash flows can contribute significantly to present value. Here is an example.

The present value of $1 a year in perpetuity discounted at 10 percent is $10 ($1/0.10). The present value of $1 a year for 20 years at the same discount rate is $8.51. Hence, ignoring all of the perpetuity cash flows beyond the 20th year reduces the calculated present value by only about 15 percent ($8.51 versus $10.00).

But things change when the income stream is a growing one. Using the perpetual-growth equation, the present value of $1 a year, growing at 6 percent per annum forever, is $25 [$1/(0.10 − 0.06)], while the present value of the same stream for 20 years is only $13.08. Thus, ignoring growing cash flows beyond the 20th year reduces the present value by almost half ($13.08 versus $25.00).

The Sensitivity Problem

At a 10 percent discount rate, the fair market value of a company promising free cash flows next year of $1 million, growing at 5 percent a year forever, is $20 million [$1 million/(0.10 − 0.05)].

Assuming the discount rate and the growth rate could each be in error by as much as 1 percentage point, what are the maximum and minimum possible FMVs for the company? What do you conclude from this?

Answer: The maximum is $33.3 million [$1 million/(0.09 − 0.06)], and the minimum is $14.3 million [$1 million/(0.11 − 0.04)]. It is difficult to charge a client very high fees for advising that a business is worth somewhere between $14.3 and $33.3 million.

or $16,168 million. With 294.32 million shares outstanding, this equates to an estimated price per share of $54.93.

Our discounted cash flow valuation thus indicates that Harley-Davidson is worth $54.93 a share provided the projected free cash flows accurately reflect expected future performance. I take the fact that the company's actual price on the valuation date was $60.75 as evidence that investors were somewhat more optimistic about Harley-Davidson's future than I.

Problems with Present Value Approaches to Valuation

If you are a little hesitant at this point about your ability to apply these discounted cash flow techniques to anything but simple textbook examples, welcome to the club. While DCF approaches to business valuation are conceptually correct, and even rather elegant, they are devilishly difficult to apply in practice. Valuing a business may be conceptually equivalent to any other capital expenditure decision, but there are several fundamental differences in practice:

1. The typical investment opportunity has a finite—usually brief—life, while the life expectancy of a company is indefinite.

2. The typical investment opportunity promises stable or perhaps declining cash flows over time, while the ability of a company to reinvest earnings customarily produces a growing cash flow.

3. The cash flows from a typical investment belong to the owner, while the cash flows generated by the company go to the owner only when management chooses to distribute them. If management decides to invest in Mexican diamond mines rather than pay dividends, a minority owner can do little other than sell out.

As the problems in the accompanying boxes illustrate, these practical differences introduce potentially large errors into the valuation process and can make the resulting FMV estimates quite sensitive to small changes in the discount rate and the growth rate employed.

Valuation Based on Comparable Trades

Granting that discounted cash flow approaches to business valuation are conceptually correct but difficult to apply, are there alternatives? One popular technique involves comparing the target company to similar, publicly traded firms. Imagine shopping for a used car. The moment of truth comes when the buyer finds an interesting car, looks at the asking price, and ponders what to offer the dealer. One strategy, analogous to a discounted cash flow approach, is to estimate the value of labor and raw materials in the car, add a markup for overhead and profit, and subtract an amount for depreciation. A more productive approach is comparison shopping: Develop an estimate of fair market value by comparing the subject car to similar autos that have recently sold or are presently available. If three similar-quality 1982 T-Birds have sold recently for $3,000 to $3,500, the buyer has reason to believe the target T-Bird has a similar value. Of course, comparison shopping provides no information about whether 1982 T-Birds are really worth $3,000 to $3,500 in any fundamental sense; it indicates only the going rate. This was amply demonstrated in the dot-com bubble when knowledge that Infospace was fairly priced relative to AOL, Amazon, and Webvan did not prevent Infospace shareholders from losing their shirts when the whole industry cratered. However, in many other instances knowing relative value is sufficient.

(Another tactic recommended by some is to skip the valuation process altogether and proceed directly to bargaining by asking the dealer what he wants for the car and responding, "B———t, I'll give you half of that." This probably works better for cars than for companies, but don't rule it out entirely.)

Use of comparable trades to value businesses requires equal parts art and science. First, it is necessary to decide which publicly traded companies are most similar to the target and then to determine what the share prices of the publicly traded companies imply for the FMV of the firm in question. The discounted cash flow valuation equations just considered offer a useful starting point. They suggest that comparable companies should offer similar future cash flow patterns and similar business and financial risks. The risks should be similar so that roughly the same discount rate would apply to all of the firms.

In practice, these guidelines suggest we begin our search for comparable companies by considering firms in the same, or closely related, industries with similar growth prospects and capital structures. With luck, the outcome of this exercise will be several more or less comparable publicly traded companies. Considerable judgment will then be required to decide what the comparable firms as a group imply for the fair market value of the target.

As an illustration, Table 9.2 presents a comparable trades valuation of Harley-Davidson. The valuation date is again December 31, 2004, and the chosen comparable companies are the five representative competitors in the "leisure travel" industry introduced in Chapter 2. One of the companies, Brunswick Corporation, is almost Harley-Davidson's size, while the others are a good bit smaller. The first set of numbers in the table looks at Harley-Davidson's growth and financial risk relative to the comparable firms. The numbers indicate that Harley-Davidson's growth in sales and earnings per share has been excellent, at or near the top in both categories and well above average. However, security analysts' expectations for future earnings growth tell a different story, placing the company fourth among the six and close to the average. This is consistent with the fact that Harley-Davidson's sales growth declined noticeably in the past two years. None of the companies, save perhaps Brunswick, carries much debt, so differences in financial risk are not an issue here. Incidentally, I chose not to use the analysts' projected growth rate in my discounted cash flow valuation of Harley-Davidson a few pages back because I find their numbers are frequently overly optimistic.

The second set of numbers in the table shows six possible indicators of value for the comparable firms. Broadly speaking, each indicator expresses how much investors are paying per dollar of current income, sales, or

TABLE 9.2 **Using Comparable Public Companies to Value Harley-Davidson, Inc.**
(December 31, 2004)

	Harley-Davidson	Arctic Cat	Brunswick	Polaris Industries	Marine Products	Winnebago Industries	Excluding Harley-Davidson Median	Excluding Harley-Davidson Mean
Comparison of Harley-Davidson with Comparable Companies: Growth Rates, Financial Risks, Size								
5-year growth rate in sales (%)	15.5	6.2	4.1	6.1	15.5	10.8	6.2	8.5
5-year growth rate in eps (%)	28.1	11.1	47.1	15.9	25.1	17.2	17.2	23.3
I/B/E/S mean 5-yr. growth (%)**	16.2	9.1	16.6	17.9	20.0	14.0	16.6	15.5
Interest coverage ratio (×)	60.9	*	8.9	85.1	*	*	47.0	47.0
Total liabilities to assets (×)	0.4	0.3	0.6	0.5	0.2	0.5	0.5	0.4
Total assets ($ millions)	5,483	286	4,346	793	110	395	395	1,186
Indicators of Value								
Price/earnings (×)		16.9	17.8	27.8	28.6	18.6	18.6	21.9
MV firm/EBIT(1 − Tax rate) (×)		17.3	19.4	24.3	29.0	17.6	19.4	21.5
Price/sales (×)		0.8	0.9	1.6	2.7	1.2	1.2	1.4
MV firm/sales (×)		0.8	1.1	1.7	2.7	1.2	1.2	1.5
MV equity/BV equity (×)		2.8	2.8	8.0	7.7	6.5	6.5	5.6
MV firm/BV firm (×)		2.8	2.3	7.7	7.7	6.5	6.5	5.4
My Estimated Indicators of Value for Harley-Davidson, Inc.								
Price/earnings (×)	23.0							
MV firm/EBIT(1 − Tax rate) (×)	23.0							
Price/sales (×)	3.0							
MV firm/sales (×)	3.0							
MV equity/BV equity	5.6							
MV firm/BV firm	5.0							
Implied Value of Harley-Davidson, Inc.'s, Common Stock per Share								
Price/earnings (×)	$69.54	(= 23 × Net income/# shares)						
MV firm/EBIT(1 − Tax rate) (×)	$66.30	(= [23 × EBIT(1 − Tax rate) − Debt]/# shares)						
Price/sales (×)	$54.23	(= 3.0 × Sales/# shares)						
MV firm/sales (×)	$49.83	(= [3.0 × Sales − Debt]/# shares)						
MV equity/BV equity	$61.24	(= 5.6 × BV equity/# shares)						
MV firm/BV firm	$72.28	(= [5.0 × BV firm − Debt]/# shares)						
My best guess	**$67.00**							
Actual stock price	$60.75							

*These companies have little or no interest-bearing debt outstanding.
**The Institutional Brokers Estimate System (I/B/E/S) is a database of earnings expectations data obtained from more than 2,500 security analysts.
MV = Market value; BV = Book value. Market value is estimated as book value of interest-bearing debt + market value of equity. Earnings are fiscal year earnings.

invested capital for each comparable firm. Thus, the first indicator says that $1.00 of Arctic Cat's current income costs $16.90, while $1.00 of Marine Products' income goes for $28.60. Similarly, the third indicator tells us that $1.00 of Brunswick's sales costs $0.90; while the last indicator says that $1.00 of Polaris Industries' assets, measured at book value, costs \$7.70. Odd-numbered indicators focus on equity values, while even-numbered indicators concentrate on enterprise value.

Reflecting on how Harley-Davidson stacks up against comparable firms in terms of growth and risk, the valuation challenge is to decide what indicators of value are appropriate for Harley-Davidson. The third set of numbers in Table 9.2 are my necessarily subjective estimates. In coming to these estimates, I considered several factors. First, I believe the first two indicators of value are generally better than the others because they relate market value to income as opposed to sales or assets. With rare exceptions, investors are interested in a company's income potential when they buy its shares, not its sales or the assets it owns. Asset-based indicators of value are more relevant when liquidation is contemplated. Sales-based ratios tend to be of interest when current earnings do not represent long-run earning power or when investors lose faith in the accuracy of reported earnings. This is not to say that sales are immune to manipulation, but only that they are somewhat less manipulable than earnings.

Second, when choosing between indicators focusing on equity value as opposed to enterprise value, I prefer the enterprise value ratios because they are less affected by the way a business is financed. This observation is not important here because none of the companies uses much financial leverage.

Third, it makes sense to assign more importance to those indicators of value that are relatively more stable across companies. If the calculated value of one indicator were 10.0 for every comparable company, I would deem it a more reliable indicator of value than if it varied from 1.0 to 30.0. Here the first two ratios, those based on earnings, are noticeably more stable than the others, varying in a range of 1.7 to 1 from highest to lowest.

Fourth, Harley-Davidson's outstanding historical growth, large size, and iconic brand all suggest the company should be at the top of the range for the first two earnings-based ratios. However, the recent slow-down coupled with analysts' diminished projections for future earnings growth caution a lower number. I selected multiples for the first two ratios about 20 percent above the sample median and 5 percent above the mean. Because Harley-Davidson has much higher profit margins than comparable firms, as noted in Chapter 2, I know that a dollar of Harley-Davidson sales will generate more profit than a dollar of any other firm's sales. Consequently, my multiples for the sales-based indicators of value are higher than those for other firms and about twice the sample average. Finally, I know from Chapter 2 that Harley-Davidson is more capital intensive than comparable firms, which leads me to select numbers for the last two, asset-based ratios, about equal to sample averages.

The bottom set of numbers in the table presents the price of Harley-Davidson's stock implied by each chosen indicator of value. To the right of each stock price is an equation illustrating how I translated the chosen indicator of value into an implied stock price. To illustrate the second equation, I estimated that Harley-Davidson's enterprise market value should be 23 times its EBIT after tax. Harley-Davidson's EBIT after tax in 2004 was $904.7 million, so its implied enterprise value is $20,808.1 million. Subtracting interest-bearing debt of $1,295.4 million and dividing by 294.32 million shares yields a stock price of $66.30. The other implied share prices are calculated similarly. The results fall within a range of $49.83 to $72.28, with a mean of $62.24. Reflecting on the observations made above, my best guess of a fair price of Harley-Davidson shares on the valuation date is $67.00, or about 10 percent above the actual price of $60.75. Does this mean that Harley-Davidson was undervalued at year-end 2004? Not necessarily, for I believe the observed price difference to be well within the tolerances inherent in a comparable trades valuation, or indeed any other business valuation technique.[6]

Lack of Marketability

An important difference between owning stock in a publicly traded company and owning stock in a private one is that the publicly traded shares are more liquid; they can be sold quickly for cash without significant loss of value. Because liquidity is a valued attribute of any asset, it is necessary to reduce the FMV of a private company estimated by reference to publicly traded comparable firms. Without boring you with details, a representative lack of marketability discount is on the order of 25 percent.[7] Of course, if the purpose of the valuation is to price an initial public offering of common stock, the shares will soon be liquid, and no discount is required.

A second possible adjustment when using the comparable-trades approach to valuation is a premium for control. Quoted prices for public companies are invariably for a minority interest in the firm, while many valuations involve transactions in which operating control passes from

[6] I chose not to value Harley-Davidson's marketable securities separately here, as I did in the discounted cash flow valuation, because the comparable trades approach makes it difficult to assign a separate value to operations in the absence of excess cash.

[7] Shannon P. Pratt, Robert F. Reilly, and Robert P. Schweihs. *Valuing a Business: The Analysis and Appraisal of Closely Held Companies,* 4th ed. (New York: Irwin/McGraw-Hill, 2000).

seller to buyer. Because control is valuable, it is necessary in these instances to add a premium to the estimated value of the target firm to reflect the value of control. Estimating the size of this control premium is our next task. (A variation on comparable-trades valuation, known as comparable-*transactions*, substitutes prices struck in recent mergers or acquisitions for publicly quoted stock prices. Transactions prices are obviously much less common than quoted prices and are often proprietary. However, in most instances they are probably a better reflection of the value inherent in an acquisition than are quoted prices. In particular, transactions prices already include a premium for control.)

The Market for Control

We have noted on several occasions that buying a minority interest in a company differs fundamentally from buying control. With a minority interest, the investor is a passive observer; with control, she has complete freedom to change the way the company does business and perhaps increase its value significantly. Indeed, the two situations are so disparate that it is appropriate to speak of stock as selling in two separate markets: the market in which you and I trade minority claims on future cash flows and the market in which Daimler-Benz and other acquirers trade the right to control the firm. The latter, the *market for control*, involves a two-in-one sale. In addition to claims on future cash flows, the buyer in this market also gains the privilege of structuring the company as he or she wishes. Because shares trading in the two markets are really different assets, they naturally sell at different prices.

The Premium for Control

Figure 9.2 illustrates this two-tier market. From the perspective of minority investors, the fair market value of a company's equity, represented in the figure by m, is the present value of cash flows to equity given current management and strategy. To a corporation or an individual seeking control, however, the FMV is c, which may be well above m. The difference, $(c - m)$, is the value of control. It is the maximum premium over the minority fair market value an acquirer should pay to gain control. It is also the expected increase in shareholder value created by acquisition. When an acquirer pays FMV_c for a target, all of the increased value will be realized by the seller's shareholders, while at any lower price, part of the increased value will accrue to the acquirer's shareholders. FMV_c is therefore the maximum acquisition price a buyer can justify paying. Said differently, it is the price at which the net present value of the acquisition to the buyer is zero.

FIGURE 9.2 **FMV of a Corporation to Investors Seeking Control May Exceed FMV to Minority Investors**

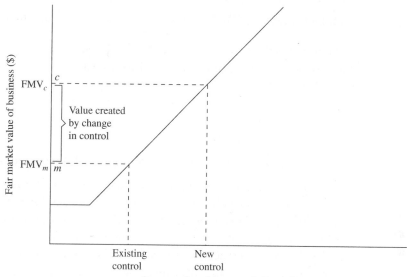

What Price Control?

There are two ways to determine how large a control premium an acquirer can afford to pay. The brute force approach values the business first assuming the merger takes place and then assuming it does not. The difference between these values is the maximum premium an acquirer can justify paying. The second, often more practical approach focuses on the anticipated gains from the merger. In equation form,

$$FMV_c = FMV_m + \text{Enhancements}$$

where c and m again denote controlling and minority interest, respectively. This expression says the value of controlling interest in a business equals the business's FMV under the present stewardship, or what is often called the business's *stand-alone value*, plus whatever enhancements to value the new buyer envisions. If the buyer intends to make no changes in the business now or in the future, the enhancements are zero, and no premium over stand-alone value can be justified. On the other hand, if the buyer believes the merging of two businesses will create vast new profit opportunities, enhancements can be quite large.

Putting a price tag on the value of enhancements resulting from an acquisition is a straightforward undertaking conceptually: Make a detailed list of all the ways the acquisition will increase free cash flows, estimate the magnitude and timing of the cash flows involved, calculate their present values, and sum:

Enhancements = PV{All value-increasing changes due to acquisition}

Controlling Interest in a Publicly Traded Company

An important simplification of our expression for FMV_c is possible when the seller is publicly traded. If we are willing to assume that the preacquisition stock price of the target company reasonably approximates its FMV_m, or at least that we are unable to detect when the approximation is unreasonable, the expression reduces to

$$FMV_c = \text{Market value of business} + \text{Enhancements}$$

where the market value of the business is our old friend the stock market value of equity plus debt. A particular virtue of this formula for valuing acquisition candidates is that it forces attention on the specific improvements anticipated from the acquisition and the maximum price one should pay to get them, a perspective that reduces the possibility that an exuberant buyer will get carried away during spirited bidding and overpay. In other words, it helps to keep animal spirits in check during the negotiation process.

That animal spirits might need an occasional reining in is suggested by Table 9.3. It shows the number of mergers in the United States from 1992 through 2003 and the median premiums paid. Note that the number of acquisitions rose from a cyclical low in 1992 to an all-time high of more than 9,500 in 2000. In addition, the number of big-ticket purchases of more than $1 billion jumped about tenfold to 206 in the same year. Merger volume tailed off significantly in 2001 due to a soft economy and falling stock prices but began to rise again in 2003. Looking at the acquisition premiums, we see that the median purchase price was 30 to 40 percent above the seller's share price five days before the announcement. Evidently acquirers are quite confident of their ability to wring large enhancements out of their acquisitions.

Financial Reasons for Restructuring

We conclude (or at least I conclude) that the best way to value a public company for acquisition purposes is to add the present value of all benefits attributable to the acquisition to the target's current market value. "So," you ask perceptively, "what types of benefits might motivate an acquisition or other form of restructuring?" The list is truly lengthy, ranging from anticipated savings in manufacturing, marketing, distribution, or overhead to better access to financial markets to enhanced investment opportunities; and the perceived sources of value vary from merger to merger. So instead

TABLE 9.3 Number of Mergers and Median Acquisition Premiums, 1992–2003

Source: *2004 Mergerstat Review*, FactSet Mergerstat, LLC, Santa Monica, 2004.

Year	Number of Transactions*	Number over $1 Billion	Median 5-Day Premium**
1992	2,574	18	34.7
1993	2,663	27	33.0
1994	2,997	51	35.0
1995	3,510	74	29.2
1996	5,848	94	27.3
1997	7,800	120	27.5
1998	7,809	158	30.1
1999	9,278	195	34.6
2000	9,566	206	41.1
2001	8,290	121	40.5
2002	7,303	72	34.4
2003	7,983	88	31.6

* Net number of transactions announced.
** Five-day premiums paid are only for those transactions revealing sufficient information to calculate the premium. This is usually about 10 percent of all transactions.

of trying to catalog the myriad possible benefits to a restructuring, I will concentrate on three finance-driven potential enhancements that are sufficiently common and controversial to warrant inquiry. I will refer to them as *tax shields*, *incentive effects*, and *controlling free cash flow*.

Tax Shields

A number of takeovers and restructurings, especially those involving mature, slow-growth businesses, are driven in part by the desire to make more extensive use of interest tax shields. As noted in Chapter 6, the tax deductibility of interest expense reduces a company's tax bill and hence may add to value.

To illustrate the appeal of interest tax shields, consider the following restructuring of Mature Manufacturing, Inc. (2M). Pertinent data for 2M, a publicly traded company, follows.

Mature Manufacturing, Inc. ($ millions)	
Annual EBIT	$25
Market value of equity	200
Interest-bearing debt	0
Tax rate	40%

Kissing Toads

The Oracle of Omaha, Warren Buffett, attributes corporate executives' willingness to pay large control premiums to three very human factors: an abundance of animal spirits, an unwarranted emphasis on company size as opposed to profitability, and overexposure during youth to "the story in which the imprisoned handsome prince is released from a toad's body by a kiss from a beautiful princess. [From this tale, executives] are certain their managerial kiss will do wonders for the profitability of Company T(arget)." Why else, Buffett asks, would an acquiring company pay a premium to control another business when it could avoid the premium altogether by simply purchasing a minority interest?

"In other words, investors can always buy toads at the going price for toads. If investors instead bankroll princesses who wish to pay double for the right to kiss the toad, those kisses had better pack some real dynamite. We've observed many kisses but very few miracles. Nonetheless, many managerial princesses remain serenely confident about the future potency of their kisses—even after their corporate backyards are knee-deep in unresponsive toads."

Source: Warren Buffett, Berkshire Hathaway, Inc. 1981 annual report.

Global Investing Partners believes 2M's management may be interested in a leveraged buyout (LBO) and has approached it with a proposal to form a new corporation, invariably called NEWCO, to purchase all of 2M's equity in the open market. Because 2M's cash flows are very stable, Global figures it can finance most of the purchase price by borrowing $190 million on a 10-year loan at 10 percent interest. The loan will be interest only for the first five years. In the longer run, Global believes 2M can easily support annual interest expenses of $10 million. The value of the anticipated interest tax shields to NEWCO, discounted at a 12 percent rate, is as follows:

Year	Interest Expense	Tax Shield at 40% Tax Rate
1	$19.00	$7.60
2	19.00	7.60
3	19.00	7.60
4	19.00	7.60
5	19.00	7.60
6	19.00	7.60
7	15.89	6.36
8	12.46	4.98
9	10.00	4.00
10	10.00	4.00

Present value of tax shields years 1 – 10 at 12%	= $38.87
Present value of tax shields years 10 and beyond at 12%	= 10.73
Total	$49.60 million

Ignoring the increased costs of financial distress that customarily accompany higher financial leverage, these figures suggest that NEWCO can bid up to $249.60 million to purchase Mature Manufacturing, a 25 percent premium over the current market price ($249.60 million = $200 million stand-alone value + $49.60 million of enhancements). Moreover, Global's required equity investment at this price would be only $59.60 million ($249.60 million acquisition price − $190 million in new debt), implying a post acquisition debt-to-assets ratio of 76 percent. This, believe it or not, is representative financing by LBO standards. LBOs are indeed aptly named.

A final judgment on the value of interest tax shields in leveraged restructurings, of course, rests on a qualitative weighting of the indicated tax savings against the costs of financial distress as discussed in Chapter 6. A reduced tax bill isn't especially attractive when the added debt frightens customers, drives away creditors, and emboldens competitors.

Note that if increased interest tax shields are the objective, an LBO is not the only way to obtain them. 2M can generate much the same effect by simply issuing debt and distributing the proceeds to owners as a large dividend or by a share repurchase. This was Colt Industries' strategy (described in Chapter 6) when it floated a huge debt issue to finance distribution of a special dividend and ended up with $1.6 billion in long-term debt and a negative net worth of $1 billion. But what's to fear from a mountain of debt as long as you have the cash flow to service it? And if you don't, your creditors have so much at stake in your company that they are more likely to behave like partners than police.

Nor must a leveraged buyout necessarily involve a takeover. Many LBOs are initiated by incumbent management who teams up with outside investors to purchase all of the company's stock and take it private. Management risks its own money in return for a sizable equity position in the restructured company.

Incentive Effects

Tax shield enhancements are clearly just a game: To the extent that shareholders win, "we, the people" (in the form of the U.S. Treasury) lose. If this were the only financial gain to takeovers and restructurings, the phenomena would not command serious public attention. Best that we eliminate the tax benefits and get back to producing goods and services instead of stocks and bonds.

The other two potential enhancements are not so easily dismissed. Both involve free cash flow, and both are premised on the belief that restructuring powerfully affects the performance incentives confronting senior management. To examine the incentive effects of restructuring in more detail, let's return to Mature Manufacturing, Inc.

Avoiding Dilution in Earnings per Share

An all-too-popular alternative approach to determining how much one company can afford to bid for another looks at the impact of the acquisition on the acquirer's earnings per share (EPS). Popularity is about all this approach has to recommend it, for it grossly oversimplifies the financial effects of an acquisition, and it rests on an inappropriate decision criterion.

Suppose the following data apply to an acquiring firm, A, and its target, T, in an exchange-of-shares merger; that is, A will give T's shareholders newly printed shares of A in exchange for their shares of T.

	Company A	Company T	Merged Company
Earnings ($ millions)	$ 100	$ 20	$130
Number of shares (millions)	20	40	26
Earnings per share	$ 5	$0.50	$ 5 (minimum)
Stock price	$ 70	$ 5	
Market value of equity (millions)	$1,400	$ 200	

The suggested decision criterion is that A should avoid dilution in EPS. If earnings of the merged firm are forecasted to be $130 million, the figures above indicate that A can issue as many as 6 million shares without suffering dilution [6 million shares = ($130 million/$5) − 20 million]. At $70 a share, this implies a maximum price of $420 million for T ($70 × 6 million), or a 110 percent premium [(420 − 200)/200]. It also suggests a maximum exchange ratio of 0.15 shares of A for each share of T (6 million/40 million).

The obvious shortcomings of this simplistic approach are, first, that earnings are not the cash flows that determine value and, second, that it is grossly inappropriate to base an acquisition decision on only one year's results. Doing so is comparable to making investments because they promise to increase next year's profits. If T's growth prospects are sufficiently bright, it may be perfectly reasonable to sacrifice near-term EPS in anticipation of long-run gains.

Academics have been stamping on this weed for decades, but it never seems to die. Witness the following from *The Wall Street Journal* announcing the Daimler-Chrysler merger. "[T]he cross-border union is actually typical of the stock-for-stock deals that have made the 1990s merger boom so fertile: a combination using favorable accounting in which the buyer has a high price-to-earnings ratio that can make a deal 'accretive' because the seller has a low P/E. Chrysler's price-to-earnings ratio has long been around eight times earnings, analysts say, and has only recently crept up to nine times. Daimler's P/E, meanwhile, is more like 20 times profits, giving the buyer the financial firepower to pay 11 to 12 times earnings and still have the transaction 'accretive,' or beneficial to the earnings of the new DaimlerChrysler."* Business valuation is tough in practice, but there is no reason to use flawed techniques just because they are tractable.

* Steven Lipin and Brandon Mitchener, "Daimler-Chrysler Merger to Produce $3 Billion in Savings, Revenue Gains Within 3 to 5 Years," *The Wall Street Journal*, May 8, 1998.

Before restructuring, the life of a senior manager at Mature Manufacturing, Inc., may well have been an enviable one. With very stable cash flows, a mature business, and no debt, managers had no pressing reason to improve performance. They could pay themselves and their employees generously, make sizable corporate contributions to charity, and, if the president was so inclined, sponsor an Indy race car or an unlimited hydroplane. Alternatively, if they wanted 2M to grow, the company could acquire other firms. This might involve some uneconomical investments, but hey—as long as cash flows are strong, almost anything is possible.

Samuel Johnson once observed, "The certainty of hanging in a fortnight focuses the mind wonderfully." Restructuring can have a similar effect, for it fundamentally changes the world of 2M senior executives. Because they probably have invested much of their own resources in the equity of the newly restructured company, their own material well-being is closely tied to that of the business. Moreover, the huge debt service burden restructuring frequently creates forces management to generate healthy cash flows or face bankruptcy—no more "corpocracy" at 2M. The carrot of ownership and the stick of possible financial ruin create significant incentives for management to maximize free cash flow and spend it for the benefit of owners.

Controlling Free Cash Flow

In addition to interest tax shields and incentive effects of high leverage, a third possible enhancement in restructurings rests on the perception that public companies are not always run solely for the benefit of owners. In this view, value can be created by gaining control of such firms and refocusing the business on the single goal of creating shareholder value. Adherents of this view see shareholder-manager relations as an ongoing tug-of-war for control of the firm's free cash flow. When shareholders have the upper hand, companies are run to maximize shareholder value; but when management is in the driver's seat, increasing value is only one of a number of competing corporate goals. After more than 50 years on the losing end of this tug-of-war, the emergence of the hostile raider in the mid-1980s enabled shareholders to gain the ascendancy and force companies to restructure. According to this view, the hostile acquisitions and restructurings during the latter half of the 1980s were a boon not only to shareholders but to the entire economy; for to the extent that shareholders can force management to increase firm value, the economy's resources are allocated more efficiently.

Consistent with this adversarial view of corporate governance, many takeovers and restructurings occur in mature or declining industries. Because investment opportunities in these industries are low, affected businesses often have large free cash flows. At the same time, industry decline creates real concern in the minds of executives about the continued survival of their organization. And although the proper strategy from a purely financial perspective may be to shrink or terminate the business, management often takes another tack. Out of a deep commitment to the business and concern for employees, the community, and their own welfare, some managers continue to fight the good fight by reinvesting in the business despite its poor returns, or by entering new businesses despite any convincing reasons to expect success. The purpose of restructuring in these instances is brutally basic: Wrest control of free cash flow away from management and put it in the hands of owners.

How, you might ask, does incumbent management ever gain control of a business in the first place? In theory, managers should be incapable of acting in opposition to owners for at least two reasons. First, if a company operates in highly competitive markets, management has very little discretion; it must maximize value or the firm will be driven from the industry. Second, all corporations have boards of directors with the power to hire and fire management and the responsibility to represent owners' interests.

Theory, however, often differs from reality. Many corporations operate in less than perfectly competitive markets, and many corporate boards are not an effective, independent shareholder voice. One possible reason is the process by which directors are chosen. In the great majority of instances, the company's slate of proposed directors runs unopposed. And even then, shareholders may not vote against a candidate, but can only withhold their approval. The only way disaffected shareholders can contest a board seat is to propose their own slate of candidates and use their own money to campaign against management's slate in a proxy contest. Meanwhile, management can use corporate funds to defeat rival candidates.

Indeed, a common view among executives and the courts is that a board's primary responsibility is to help incumbent management run the business, not solely to represent shareholder interests. As a result, boards are often more closely affiliated with management than with owners. Directors are often company insiders; other directors have important ties to the enterprise other than ownership and are more beholden to the chief executive than to shareholders for their seat on the board. Consequently, while such boards may help keep the shelves stocked, they are not about to recommend selling the store.

But change is occurring. Having tasted the fruits of control in the form of unusually high returns during the hostile takeover era, a growing number of institutional investors are choosing to fight rather than switch. Among the tactics employed are lobbying the SEC for liberalization of rules governing voting and shareholder communications, commissioning and publicizing studies to identify underperforming managements, and meeting with underperformers to discuss their plans for improvement. And although company boards have generally opposed these public assaults, a growing number have chosen to meet their critics halfway by initiating several basic procedural reforms intended to increase the board's independence from the chief executive. These include a written job description for the chief executive, regular performance reviews of the chief executive conducted by outside directors, regular meeting of outside directors, a board nominating committee controlled by outside directors, and full board access to all employees without necessary approval or knowledge of the boss. Passage of the Sarbanes-Oxley Act of 2002 in response to accounting scandals at Enron, WorldCom, and elsewhere has accelerated this trend.

As debate topics go, the question of whether management should have broader social responsibilities than simply creating shareholder value is among the more intriguing. Like many important societal questions, however, the issue tends to be resolved more on the basis of power than of logic. Throughout most of the twentieth century, incumbent management retained the power to interpret its responsibilities broadly and to treat shareholders as only one of several constituencies possessing a claim on the corporation. The balance of power shifted abruptly in shareholders' favor during the era of the hostile takeover. And although corporations have largely neutralized the threat of hostile takeover, the rise of the activist shareholder and his ally, the activist board member, suggests that the battle is far from over.

The Empirical Evidence

A final question remains: Do corporate restructurings create value? Do they provide any benefit to society? In the aggregate, the answer is yes. Looking first at mergers, the median five-day acquisition premiums of 30 to 40 percent reported in Table 9.3 leave no doubt that owners of acquired firms benefit handsomely from mergers. Whether the owners of acquiring firms also benefit is more problematic. Using the event study methodology described in Chapter 5, one academic study found that on average, the price of an acquiring firm's shares rises a statistically significant 2.8 percent on the merger announcement.[8] A more recent study of all successful acquisitions involving public tender offers in the period 1963 to 1984 reports similar findings.[9] Investigators found that the combined market value of buyers' and sellers' shares rose an average of 7.4 percent on the announcement. However, they also found that virtually all of the

[8] Paul Asquith, Robert F. Bruner, and David W. Mullins, Jr., "The Gains to Bidding Firms from Merger," *Journal of Financial Economics,* April 1983, pp. 121–39.

[9] Michael Bradley, Anand Desai, and E. Han Kim, "Synergistic Gains from Corporate Acquisitions and Their Division Between the Stockholders of Target and Acquiring Firms," *Journal of Financial Economics,* May 1988, pp. 3–40.

Icahn v. Blockbuster

The recent dust-up between video rental giant Blockbuster, Inc., and dissident shareholders, led by Carl Icahn, is one example of the ongoing contest for control between owners and managers. In May 2005, Icahn and friends sent tremors through boardrooms across America when they won a proxy contest for three seats on Blockbuster's board, including the one held by company chairman and chief executive officer John Antioco. A similar story unfolded the same month in Europe when disaffected institutional investors forced Deutsche Börse, one of Europe's leading stock exchanges, to abandon efforts to acquire the London Stock Exchange, and pressured the company's top two officers to resign.

The most unnerving aspect of these events to executives was the alacrity with which institutional shareholders, primarily hedge funds, joined forces to oppose management. If this became a habit, shareholders would soon have a much stronger and more direct voice in corporate affairs—for better or worse. Hedge funds are lightly regulated, private equity partnerships that have grown rapidly in the past decade, to the point there are now thought to be as many as 8,000 funds in existence.

The Icahn–Blockbuster dispute was a straightforward contest for free cash flow. Like AOL, Kodak, and many other companies, Blockbuster found itself to be a profitable, dominant player in a declining industry. Faced with the difficult choice of growing old gracefully or looking for a younger horse to ride, Blockbuster diligently began looking for a new mount. Among other costly changes, management eliminated the hated, but highly profitable, late fees on rentals, and initiated an online rental business despite the threat it posed to existing operations. Icahn characterized these initiatives as "gambling with shareholders' money" and instead counseled Blockbuster to return excess cash flows to shareholders. When the company demurred, Icahn began calling his hedge fund friends.

---

increased stock market value flowed to selling shareholders, who saw their stock rise just over 30 percent on average. Buyers' shares, on the other hand, rose only about 1 percent. Moreover, most of the buyers' gains occurred in the early years of the study when tender offers were largely unregulated. In the last four years of the study, the price of acquiring firms' shares fell some 3 percent on the announcement.

Michael Porter looked at the same issue from a different perspective when he tracked the acquisition activity of 33 diversified companies over a 35-year period ending in 1986.[10] He found that these active acquirers divested or shuttered more than half of their acquisitions in following years and that the more unrelated the seller's business was to that of the buyer, the greater the chance of failure. He concluded quite naturally from these findings that many, if not most, acquisitions are unsuccessful from the buyer's perspective.

[10] Michael E. Porter, "From Competitive Advantage to Corporate Strategy," *Harvard Business Review*, May–June 1987, pp. 43–59. For a more optimistic view of the attractiveness of mergers, see Patricia L. Anslinger and Thomas E. Copeland, "Growth Through Acquisitions: A Fresh Look," *Harvard Business Review*, January–February 1996, pp. 126–35.

The best study to date on whether leveraged buyouts create value is by Steven Kaplan of the University of Chicago, who examined 48 large management buyouts executed between 1980 and 1986.[11] (A management buyout, or MBO, is an LBO in which prebuyout management plays an active role in taking the company private.)

Looking first at return on operating assets, Kaplan found that relative to overall industry performance, the median buyout firm increased return on operating assets a healthy 36.1 percent in the two years following the buyout. A similar look at capital expenditures revealed that on an industry-adjusted basis, the typical buyout firm reduced its ratio of capital expenditures to assets by a statistically *in*significant 5.7 percent over the same period. Reflecting both improved operating performance and reduced investment, Kaplan found that the typical buyout firm increased an industry-adjusted measure of free cash flow to total assets an enormous 85.4 percent in the two years following the buyout. Evidently the carrot of increased ownership and the stick of heavy debt service really do focus management's attention.

Realized returns to investors were equally impressive. Of the 48 firms in his sample, Kaplan was able to find post-buyout valuation data on 25 because they either issued stock to the public, repurchased stock, were liquidated, or were sold. Recognizing that these 25 may be the cream of the crop, he nonetheless observed impressive performance. The median, market-adjusted return to all sources of capital over the 2.6 years from the buyout date to the valuation date was 28 percent. Moreover, the median internal rate of return to equity on these firms was a staggering 785.6 percent; such is the power of extensive financial leverage when things go well. Is it any wonder that LBO investment firms have been wildly successful?

Kaplan's study tracks LBO performance during one of the longest business expansions in American economic history, so there is no guarantee that such performance could be repeated today. However, the data do suggest that LBOs are not just tax gimmicks. Rather, the increased managerial incentives that accompany LBO restructurings apparently were strong enough to stimulate sharp improvements in operating performance and in shareholder value. The data also pose a stark challenge to those who argue that management alone should control America's corporations.

The Daimler-Chrysler Merger

Daimler's takeover of Chrysler should no longer hold much mystery. Chrysler's $44.88 premerger stock price was the value to minority investors given Chrysler's potential as a stand-alone entity, while the $57.50

---

[11] Steven Kaplan, "The Effects of Management Buyouts on Operating Performance and Value," *Journal of Financial Economics,* October 1989, pp. 217–54.

price paid by Daimler included a sizeable premium for control. Clearly neither price was necessarily incorrect or irrational. Although one might wonder whether Daimler paid too much or too little for Chrysler, I can assure you that having paid more than $40 million in fees to investment banks, both companies had numerous valuation studies of the type described here supporting the acquisition pricing. Whether the assumptions and forecasts underlying those studies were accurate remains to be seen.

To many observers the original business case for merging Daimler-Benz and Chrysler was rock solid. Chrysler, the smallest of Detroit's big three auto makers, had gone through three near-death experiences in the recent past, most colorfully in 1980 when flamboyant chief executive Lee Iacocca, armed with unprecedented federal loan guarantees, saved the company from near certain bankruptcy. By the mid-1990s Chrysler had turned things around completely, riding the minivan craze—where it owned a 47 percent market share—and savvy exploitation of its Jeep brand to new heights. Despite this recent success, however, Chrysler boss Robert Eaton was deeply concerned about the future. Rapid penetration of the U.S. market by Asian and European competitors and increasing industry globalization were creating overcapacity, dampening domestic prices, and increasing pressures toward industry consolidation. Eaton feared that Chrysler did not have the heft to be a long-run survivor in such a market. In addition, auto manufacturers were looking increasingly to developing countries such as Brazil and China as sources of future growth, places where Chrysler was especially weak. Finally, Eaton foresaw a day in the not too distant future when the internal combustion engine would give way to new, energy-saving technologies, and he worried that Chrysler would be unable to afford the huge investments necessary to implement such a change. If Chrysler could not be a long-term survivor, Eaton reasoned it was better to find a partner from a position of strength than to wait for the inevitable decline.

Daimler-Benz certainly had the necessary resources. As Germany's largest company, Daimler employed 300,000 people in a variety of businesses including cars, trucks, aerospace, and broadly related services. Since gaining the top spot in 1995, Daimler's mercurial boss, Jürgen Schrempp, had devoted most of his attention to cleaning up a disastrous diversification effort launched by his predecessor and to defending the company's crown jewel, Mercedes, from the Japanese competitive onslaught. After posting the largest peacetime loss in German history in 1995, Daimler returned to profitability the following year. But like his American counterpart, Schrempp was worried. To remain competitive, Schrempp believed that Mercedes needed to increase volume, enhance labor productivity, and expand offshore manufacture, especially in the

United States. In his mind, this meant that Mercedes needed to go down-market. In addition, Schrempp had long been frustrated by Daimler's hierarchical, bureaucratic management culture and was attracted by the more entrepreneurial, value-based cultures of many American companies. Chrysler's acknowledged product design skills and its image as a feisty, tough competitor appealed to Schrempp.

Daimler's takeover of Chrysler promised to create value in at least three ways. First, the sheer size of the merged company would assure Chrysler access to needed resources and promised efficiencies in purchasing, vehicle design, and manufacture. Second, Chrysler was then one of the most efficient auto manufacturers in the world, and Schrempp anticipated that some of Chrysler's production skills would rub off on Mercedes. Third, the two companies' product lines were highly complementary. A combination thus promised to sharply expand the new company's product offerings, to increase Daimler's U.S. manufacturing capacity, and to greatly enhance Chrysler's offshore presence, especially in Europe. In the eyes of its creators DaimlerChrysler promised to be nothing less than the world's first truly global enterprise and an archetype for the corporation of the twenty-first century.

Unfortunately, results have yet to approach expectations. When news of the merger first became public in May 1998, Daimler's stock traded on the New York Stock Exchange at $98.88 a share. It rose briefly immediately after the merger to $110, and then commenced a long steady decline to the low 40s in June 2005, a decline of about 60 percent during a period in which the market as a whole was up about 6 percent. Why the sharp decline? The initial answer in a word was Chrysler. In 1998 Chrysler recorded an operating profit of $4.2 billion, fully half of the combined company's total profits. Yet by 2001 Chrysler management was projecting a *loss* of more than $2 billion, a truly stunning collapse during a period when North American vehicle sales were hitting all-time highs. More recently problems at Mercedes have undercut a nascent turnaround at Chrysler.

There are at least two credible theories of what went wrong. The more popular sees the Daimler-Chrysler marriage as a cautionary tale of the pitfalls of globalization. Daimler was a huge, proud, Teutonic conglomerate that moved ponderously but precisely. In the German tradition, its executives were used to large staffs, modest salaries, liberal expense accounts, and dress codes. Chrysler was just the opposite, an informal, agile, single-purpose company whose executives operated with modest staffs, tight expense controls, and generous salaries. According to the "pitfalls of globalization" view, the merging of two such contrasting cultures in a purported marriage of equals was a recipe for disaster. The fact that within three years of the merger fully two-thirds of Chrysler senior executives had resigned or been fired lends credence to this clash-of-cultures perspective.

The second, minority view is more intriguing. Soon after the merger was announced, Robert Eaton came under intense fire for having given Chrysler away to a foreign acquirer. To these observers the charming, charismatic Jürgen Schrempp had duped the laconic, introspective engineer into sacrificing Chrysler's independence under the false banner of "a marriage of equals." The minority view, which grows as Chrysler struggles, is that perhaps Eaton knew precisely what he was doing when he took the money and ran. Cognizant of the disaster that was about to befall his company, Eaton took the 28 percent premium and left Daimler to pick up the pieces. According to this view, if anyone was taken for a ride in the Daimler-Chrysler merger, it was Daimler-Benz.

APPENDIX

The Venture Capital Method of Valuation

Venture capitalists are the carrier pilots of corporate finance. They make high-risk, high-return investments in new or early stage companies thought capable of growing rapidly into sizeable enterprises. Their investment horizon is typically five or six years, at which time they expect to cash out as the target company goes public or sells out to a competitor. To manage risk, venture capitalists typically make staged investments in which the company must meet a stated business milestone before qualifying for the next financing round. Venture capitalists also commonly specialize in a particular financing round, such as startup, early stage, or mezzanine. The mezzanine round is the company's last private financing round prior to going public, or merging. In most instances, the risk to new investors and, hence, the return demanded, diminishes from one financing round to the next.

The standard discounted cash flow valuation technique discussed in the chapter is ill-suited to venture investing for several reasons. First, the cash infusions from venture investors are intended to cover near-term, negative free cash flows, so projecting and discounting annual free cash flows is not relevant. Second and more fundamentally, the standard approach to business valuation does not gracefully accommodate multiple financing rounds at different required rates of return.

Rather than use the standard approach, venture capitalists employ a specialized discounted cash flow technique that is better suited to their needs. Our purpose here is to illustrate the venture capital method of valuation, to indicate the level of target returns used in the industry, and to offer several explanations of why these targets appear so outlandishly high. We begin with a simple example of a company in need of only one financing round. We then build on this example to consider a more realistic situation involving multiple financing rounds.

The Venture Capital Method—One Financing Round

Jerry Cross and Greg Robinson, two veteran computer programmers, have what they believe is a pathbreaking idea for a new product. Soon after incorporating as ZMW Enterprises and arbitrarily awarding themselves 2,000,000 shares of common stock, Cross and Robinson prepared a detailed business plan and began talking to venture capitalists about funding their company. The business plan envisions an immediate $5 million venture capital investment, profits of $8 million in year 5, and rapid growth thereafter. The plan indicates that $5 million will be sufficient to commence operations and to cover all anticipated cash needs until the company begins generating positive cash flows in year 5.

After hearing the entrepreneurs' pitch, a senior partner at Touchstone Ventures, a local venture capital company, expressed interest in financing ZMW but demanded 1.552 million shares in return for his firm's $5 million investment. He also mentioned in passing that his offer implied a pre-money valuation for ZMW of $6.4 million and a post-money value of $11.4 million. Determined not to be intimidated, Greg Robinson challenged the venture capitalist to justify his numbers, hoping in the process to learn what he meant by pre- and post-money.

Panel A of Table 9A.1 presents a valuation of ZMW using the venture capital method. Three steps are involved.

1. Estimate ZMW's value at some future date, often based on a conventional comparable trades or comparable transactions analysis.

2. Discount this future value to the present at the venture capitalist's target internal rate of return.

3. Divide the venture capitalist's investment by ZMW's present value to calculate the venture capitalist's required percentage ownership.

As shown in Panel A, Touchstone accepted the entrepreneurs' projection that ZMW would earn $8 million in year 5. They then multiplied this amount by a "warranted" price-to-earnings ratio of 15 to calculate a firm value of $120 million. The price-to-earnings ratio used here typically reflects the multiples implied by other recent venture financings or the

TABLE 9.A1 The Venture Capital Method of Valuation

Panel A: One Financing Round						
Facts and Assumptions (000 omitted)						
Net income year 5	$ 8,000					
Price-to-earnings ratio in year 5	15					
Investment required at time 0	$ 5,000					
Touchstone Ventures' target rate of return	60%					
Time 0 shares outstanding	2,000					
Cash Flow and Valuation						
	0	**1**	**2**	**3**	**4**	**5**
Investment	$ 5,000					
ZMW value in year 5						$120,000
Time 0 value of ZMW at 60% discount rate	$11,444					
Time 5 Touchstone ownership to earn target return	**43.7%**					
Shares purchased by Touchstone*	1,552					
Price per share	$ 3.22					
Pre-money value of ZMW	$ 6,444					
Post-money value of ZMW	$11,444					

Panel B: Two Financing Rounds	
Facts and Assumptions (000 omitted)	
Net income year 5	$ 8,000
Price-to-earnings ratio in year 5	15
Investment required at time 0	$ 5,000
Investment required at time 2	$10,000
Touchstone Ventures' target rate of return	60%
Second-round investor's target rate of return	40%
Time 0 shares outstanding	2,000

TABLE 9.A1 (*concluded*) The Venture Capital Method of Valuation

Cash Flow and Valuation						
	0	**1**	**2**	**3**	**4**	**5**
Investment	$ 5,000		$10,000			
Terminal value year 5						$120,000
Second-Round Investor						
Time 2 value of ZMW at 40% discount rate			$43,732			
Time 5 ownership to earn target return			22.9%			
Touchstone Ventures						
Time 0 value of ZMW at 60% discount rate	$11,444					
Time 5 Touchstone ownership to earn target return	43.7%					
Retention ratio[†]	0.771					
Time 0 Touchstone ownership to earn target return	56.6%					
Shares purchased by Touchstone*	2,613					
Price per share	$ 1.91					
Pre-money value of ZMW	$ 3,827					
Post-money value of ZMW	$ 8,827					
Second-Round Investor						
Shares purchased by second round investor*			1,368			
Price per share			$ 7.31			
Pre-money value of ZMW			$33,732			
Post-money value of ZMW			$43,732			

*If x equals the number of shares purchased by new investors, y is the number of shares currently outstanding, and p is the percentage of the firm purchased by new investors, then $x/(y + x) = p$, and $x = py/(1 - p)$.
[†]Retention ratio = (1 − second round investor's percentage ownership) = (1 − 22.9%). In general, the retention ratio = $(1 - d_1)(1 - d_2) \ldots (1 - d_n)$, where d_n is the percent of ownership given to the nth subsequent round of investors.

multiples presently commanded by public companies in the same or related industries.

Discounting the year 5 value to the present at Touchstone's 60 percent target rate of return yields a present value for ZMW of $11.4 million [$11.4 million = $120 million/$(1 + 0.60)^5$]. This, in turn, implies a percentage ownership for Touchstone of 43.7 percent. The logic here is that if the company is worth $11.4 million after the investment, and if Touchstone contributes $5 million to this total, its fractional ownership should be $5 million/$11.4 million, or 43.7 percent. To confirm this logic, note that if ZMW is worth $120 million in five years, Touchstone's 43.7 percent ownership will be worth $52.4 million, which translates into an internal rate of return of precisely 60 percent.

The rest is just algebra. If Touchstone is to own 43.7 percent of ZMW and the company presently has 2 million shares outstanding, Touchstone needs to receive 1.552 million new shares [43.7% = 1.552/(2 + 1.552)], which, in turn, implies a per share price of $3.22 ($5 million/1.552 million shares). ZMW's estimated value before Touchstone's investment, or its pre-money value, is thus $6.4 million ($3.22 per share × 2 million shares), and its value after the investment, or its post-money value, is $11.4 million ($3.22 per share × 3.552 million shares).

Cross and Robinson are likely to be of two minds about this valuation: flabbergasted that Touchstone would demand a 60 percent return when all they do is put up money, but pleased to learn that Touchstone apparently puts a $6.4 million price tag on their idea.

The Venture Capital Method— Multiple Financing Rounds

The venture capital method is easy to apply when there is only one financing round prior to the valuation date. Things get more complicated, and more realistic, when there are multiple rounds. To illustrate, let's change the ZMW example by supposing that Cross and Robinson's business plan calls for two financing rounds: the original $5 million at time 0, plus a second investment of $10 million at time 2. Because ZMW will be a functioning company at time 2, it is reasonable to suppose that second-round investors will demand a lower rate of return. Based on Touchstone's experience, let us assume that second-round investors will demand "only" 40 percent. Reworking the earlier figures, as shown in Panel B of Table 9A.1, Touchstone will now demand 2.613 million shares, or 56.6 percent ownership, in return for their $5 million investment.

To arrive at these figures, note that each subsequent financing round will dilute Touchstone's investment. Therefore, owning 43.7 percent of ZMW today, as in our first example, will no longer be adequate. To capture the effect of dilution imposed by subsequent financing rounds, it is necessary to apply the logic described earlier recursively to each financing round, beginning with the most distant. Panel B shows that at a discount rate of 40 percent, the time 2 value of ZMW to a new investor will be $43.7 million, so round 2 investors will demand 22.9 percent of the company for their $10 million investment ($10 million/$43.7 million).

Once we know this number, we are ready to calculate Touchstone's initial ownership. We know that Touchstone wants 43.7 percent of ZMW in year 5 and that round 2 dilution makes it necessary to gross this number up by some amount. To determine how much, we divide 43.7 percent by what is known as a *retention ratio*. Here, the retention ratio turns out to be 0.771, so Touchstone's current ownership must be 56.6 percent (56.6% = 43.7%/0.771). The logic of the retention ratio goes like this. If y represents Touchstone's initial ownership, then $y - 0.229y = 0.437$, so $y = 0.437/(1 - 0.229) = 56.6\%$. The quantity in parentheses is the retention ratio.

Extending this reasoning to an arbitrary number of financing rounds, the retention ratio for the ith financing round is

$$R_i = (1 - d_{i + 1})(1 - d_{i + 2}) \cdots (1 - d_n),$$

where $d_{i + 1}$ is the percentage ownership given to the ith + 1 round investors, and n is the total number of financing rounds. With only one subsequent financing round, Touchstone's retention ratio is $(1 - 0.229) = 0.771$. The need to work recursively from the most distant financing round to the present should now be clear. Because the retention ratio for each round depends on dilution created by all subsequent rounds, it is impossible to calculate the initial percentage ownership of early-round investors without knowing that of all later rounds.

Once we know the percentage ownership at each financing round, it is easy to calculate stock prices as well as pre- and post-money values. As noted in Panel B, ZMW's pre-money value at time 0 is $3.827 million, while the same quantity at time 2 is $33.732 million. The corresponding share prices are $1.91 and $7.31, respectively.

Table 9A.2 confirms the validity of the venture capital method. It shows the resulting cash flows to Touchstone Ventures, the second-round investor, and the founding entrepreneurs—assuming that ZMW can achieve its business plan. Observe that these cash flows yield precisely the target rates of return demanded by the venture capitalists. Note too that although the entrepreneurs lose majority control of their company, the prospect of

TABLE 9.A2 **Prospective Returns to Investors in ZMW**

	Year					
	0	1	2	3	4	5
Touchstone Ventures						
Free cash flows	$(5,000)	0	0	0	0	$52,429
Internal rate of return	60%					
Second-Round Investor						
Free cash flows			$(10,000)	0	0	$27,440
Internal rate of return			40%			
Entrepreneurs' Cash Flows						$40,131

owning shares worth $40.1 million in five years should provide some consolation.

Why Do Venture Capitalists Demand Such High Returns?

There are at least four possible explanations. First, venture investing is a very risky business, and high risk invariably commands high return. When venture investors must screen as many as 100 proposals for each investment made, and when they earn real money on only 1 or 2 investments in 10, target rates must be high to compensate for the many disappointments. Second, high target rates have history on their side. Thus, they have been consistent over the years with adequate-deal flows and with realized returns sufficient to attract new investment capital. Third, venture capitalists argue that they provide much more than money when they invest and that they deserve compensation for these ancillary services. Rather than bill directly for their counsel, connections, and occasional outright direction, venture capitalists bundle their fees into the required target return.

Finally, high target returns may be a natural outgrowth of the dynamic between venture capitalist and entrepreneur. Venture capitalists consistently maintain that the business plans crossing their desks are overly optimistic. It is not so much that the numbers in the plan are unobtainable, but rather that the plan ignores the myriad ways in which a startup business can fail. So instead of representing the expected outcome, the plan is essentially a best-case scenario. When presented with such projections, the venture capitalist has two choices: Try to argue the entrepreneur down to more reasonable numbers, or accept the entrepreneur's numbers at face value and discount them at an inflated target rate.

Two forces favor the "inflated target" strategy. For psychological reasons, the venture capitalist would prefer that the entrepreneur strive to meet his optimistic plan rather than settle for a lower, albeit more realistic, objective. Moreover for practical reasons, the venture capitalist will find it difficult to convince the entrepreneur—who typically knows more about the business than the venture capitalist—that his plan is overly optimistic. Better to concede gracefully on the business plan, and recoup by demanding a high target return. This might suggest a war of escalating projections in which entrepreneurs progressively ratchet up their forecasts to counteract venture capitalists' artificially high rates, while venture investors progressively raise their target rates to offset entrepreneurs' increasingly implausible projections. However, this is unlikely to occur. Venture capitalists are expert at ferreting out overblown forecasts, so unless the entrepreneur truly believes her numbers, she has little chance of convincing venture capitalists of their plausibility.

SUMMARY

1. This chapter examined corporate restructuring, broadly defined as any episodic change in a company's asset mix, capital structure, or ownership composition.

2. The central discipline underlying all corporate restructurings is business valuation, the art of pricing all or part of a business.

3. Before valuing a business, it is necessary to decide whether to value the company's assets or its equity, whether to value it in liquidation or as a going concern, and whether to value a minority or a controlling interest.

4. The discounted cash flow approach to business valuation estimates the present value of the target's free cash flows discounted at the target's weighted-average cost of capital.

5. Major challenges in discounted cash flow valuation are to estimate a forecast horizon and a terminal value for the target firm. The forecast horizon should be at or beyond the date when the target becomes a mature, slow-growth business. Common terminal value estimates include a warranted multiple of the target's earnings or assets and present value calculations presuming slow, perpetual growth.

6. The comparable-trades approach to business valuation infers the value of the target's equity from the prices at which the shares of comparable, publicly traded firms trade. The resulting value estimate frequently must be adjusted to reflect a lack of marketability or the fact that the buyer is acquiring control of the business.

7. The comparable transactions approach to business valuation infers the value of the target's equity from the prices at which recent acquisitions of peer companies took place. The resulting value usually includes a control premium.

8. It is often appropriate for a buyer to pay a premium above the minority value of a business to gain control. The maximum justifiable premium equals the present value of all value-increasing changes contemplated by the buyer.

9. Three controversial, finance-driven, potential benefits from restructuring are increased interest tax shields, enhanced management incentives, and owner control of free cash flow.

10. Empirical evidence suggests that acquisitions typically create value, but the great preponderance of it flows to selling shareholders. Leveraged buyouts appear to create substantial value.

ADDITIONAL RESOURCES

Bruner, Robert F. *Applied Mergers and Acquisitions*. New York: John Wiley & Sons, 2004. 1,029 pages.

A huge book written by a distinguished finance professor at the Darden School to bridge the gap between theory and practice. Topics range from strategy and the origination of merger proposals through valuations and accounting to postmerger integration. About $85.

Copeland, Tom, Tim Koller, and Jack Murrin. *Valuation: Measuring and Managing the Value of Companies*. 3rd ed. New York: John Wiley & Sons, 2000. 592 pages.

Written by three McKinsey & Company consultants, this is a practical, how-to discussion of business valuation. You can spend $60,000 and let McKinsey do a valuation for you or spend $60 for the paperback edition of this book and learn how to do it yourself.

Gaughan, Patrick A. *Mergers, Acquisitions, and Corporate Restructurings*. 3rd ed. New York: John Wiley & Sons, 2002. 632 pages.

A balanced look at corporate acquisitions and restructurings. Less technical and broader in scope than the Copeland book. Includes a historical overview, as well as accounting and legal dimensions of the topic. About $65.

Kaplan, Steven N., and Richard S. Ruback. "The Valuation of Cash Flow Forecasts: An Empirical Analysis." *Journal of Finance*, September 1995, pp. 1059–93.

Empirical support for the discounted cash flow approach to business valuation. The authors compare present values of projected cash flows to subsequent market values of 51 highly levered transactions between 1983 and 1989. Discounted cash flow valuations are within 10 percent, on average, of market values. The DCF valuations prove at least as accurate as those based on comparable trades.

WEBSITES

www.valuepro.net

A free, discounted cash flow valuation model based on 20 input variables. Enter a stock ticker symbol and Valuepro values the business based on current estimates of the 20 variables. Change any of the variables and see how the estimated stock price changes. Created by three faculty at Penn State. Check out how overpriced your stocks really are.

www.mergerstat.com

Corporate merger data, including a running tally of merger activity since 1963, activity by industry, and top advisors.

PROBLEMS

Answers to odd-numbered problems are at the end of the book. For additional problems with answers, see **www.mhhe.com/higgins8e.**

1. Below is a recent income statement for Hegel Publishing.

Net sales	$6,000
Cost of sales (including depreciation of $600)	3,600
Gross profit	2,400
Selling and admin. expenses (including interest expense of $360)	1,200
Income before tax	1,200
Tax	408
Income after tax	$ 792

   Calculate Hegel's free cash flow in this year assuming it spent $480 on new capital equipment and increased current assets net of noninterest-bearing current liabilities $240.

2. A sporting goods manufacturer has decided to expand into a related business. Management estimates that to build and staff a facility of the desired size and to attain capacity operations would cost $275 million in present value terms. Alternatively, the company could acquire an existing firm or division with the desired capacity. One such opportunity is the division of another company. The book value of the division's assets is $140 million and its earnings before interest and tax are presently $30 million. Publicly traded comparable companies are selling in a narrow range around 12 times current earnings. These companies have debt-to-asset ratios averaging 40 percent with an average interest rate of 10 percent.

   a. Using a tax rate of 34 percent, estimate the minimum price the owner of the division should consider for its sale.
   b. What is the maximum price the acquirer should be willing to pay?
   c. Does it appear that an acquisition is feasible? Why or why not?
   d. Would a 25 percent increase in stock prices to an industry average price-to-earnings ratio of 15 change your answer to (c)? Why or why not?
   e. Referring to the $275 million price tag as the replacement value of the division, what would you predict would happen to acquisition activity when market values of companies and divisions rise above their replacement values?

3. Stolid, Inc., is a no-growth company expected to pay a $10-per-share annual dividend into the distant future. Its cost of equity capital is 14 percent. The new president abhors the no-growth image and proposes to

halve next year's dividend to $5 per share and use the savings to acquire another firm. The president maintains that this strategy will boost sales, earnings, and assets. Moreover, he is confident that after acquisition, dividends in year 2 and beyond can be increased to $10.45 per share.

a. Do you agree that the acquisition will likely increase sales, earnings, and assets?

b. Estimate the per share value of Stolid's stock immediately prior to the president's proposal.

c. Estimate the per share value immediately after the proposal.

d. As an owner of Stolid, would you support the president's proposal? Why or why not?

4. a. What does it mean when a company's free cash flow is negative in one or more years?

b. Do negative values of free cash flow in any way alter or invalidate the notion that a company's fair market value equals the present value of its free cash flows discounted at the company's weighted average cost of capital?

c. Suppose a company's free cash flows were expected to be negative in all future periods. Can you conceive of any reasons for buying the company's stock?

5. Procureps, Inc. (P), is considering two possible acquisitions, neither of which promises any enhancements or synergistic benefits. V1 is a poorly performing firm in a declining industry with a price-to-earnings ratio of 10 times. V2 is a high-growth technology company with a price-to-earnings ratio of 40 times. Procureps is interested in making any acquisition that increases its current earnings per share. All of Procureps's acquisitions are exchange of share mergers.

a. Calculate the maximum percentage premium Procureps can afford to pay for V1 and V2 by replacing the question marks in the following table.

b. What do your answers to part (a) suggest about the wisdom of using "avoid dilution in earnings per share" as a criterion in merger analysis.

Company	P	V1	P+V1	V2	P+V2
Earnings after tax ($ millions)	$2	$1	$3	$1	$3
Price to earnings ratio (×)	30	10		40	
Market value of equity ($ millions)	?	?		?	
Number of equity shares (millions)	1	1	?	1	?
Earnings per share ($)	2	1	2	1	2
Price per share	?	?		?	
Maximum new shares issued (millions)		?		?	
Value of new shares issued ($ millions)		?		?	
Maximum acquisition premium (%)		?		?	

6. Ametek, Inc., is a billion dollar manufacturer of electronic instruments and motors headquartered in Paoli, Pennsylvania. Use the following information on Ametek and five other similar companies to value Ametek, Inc., on December 31, 2001.

Ametek, Inc., 2001 ($ millions)	
Net income	$66.1
Number of common shares (millions)	32.82
Earnings before interest and tax	$112.3
Tax rate	22%
Book value of equity	$335.1
Book value interest-bearing debt	$470.8

	Ametek	Emerson Electric	Franklin Electric	AO Smith	Woodward Governor	American Power Conv.
Comparison of Ametek with Comparable Companies: Growth Rates, Financial Risks, Size, Returns						
5-year growth rate in sales (%)	3.3	6.8	1.4	8.1	10.2	15.2
5-year growth rate in eps (%)	5.1	1.3	9.2	(5.4)	19.6	3.4
Interest coverage ratio ($\times$)	4.8	8.0	38.0	3.0	12.3	*
Total liabilities to assets ($\times$)	0.7	0.6	0.4	0.7	0.5	0.1
Total assets ($ millions)	1,029	15,046	196	1,294	585	1,421
Indicators of Value						
Price/earnings ($\times$)		23.2	16.1	32.0	12.4	25.0
MV firm/EBIT(1-Tax rate) ($\times$)		23.3	16.2	34.7	13.2	25.0
MV equity/BV equity ($\times$)		3.9	3.5	1.0	2.1	2.3
MV firm/BV firm ($\times$)		2.7	3.3	1.0	1.8	2.3
Price/sales ($\times$)		1.5	1.4	0.4	1.0	2.0
MV firm/sales ($\times$)		1.9	1.4	0.8	1.1	2.0

*American Power Conversion has no interest-bearing debt outstanding.
MV = Market value; BV = Book value. Market value is estimated as book value of interest-bearing debt + market value of equity. Earnings are fiscal year earnings.

7. Following is a four-year forecast for Torino Marine.

Year	2007	2008	2009	2010
Free cash flow ($ millions)	$-85	$-32	$62	$66

a. Estimate the fair market value of Torino Marine at the end of 2006. Assume that after 2010, earnings before interest and tax will remain constant at $210 million, depreciation will equal capital expenditures in each year, and working capital will not change. Torino Marine's weighted-average cost of capital is 14 percent and its tax rate is 40 percent.

b. Estimate the fair market value per share of Torino Marine's equity at the end of 2006 if the company has 50 million shares outstanding and the market value of its interest-bearing liabilities on the valuation date equals $300 million.

c. Now let's try a different terminal value. Estimate the fair market value of Torino Marine's equity per share at the end of 2006 under the following assumptions:

(1) Free cash flows in years 2007 through 2010 remain as above.

(2) EBIT after year 2010 grows at 4 percent per year forever.

(3) To support the perpetual growth in EBIT, capital expenditures in year 2011 exceed depreciation by $20 million, and this difference grows 4 percent per year forever.

(4) Similarly, working capital investments are $10 million in 2011, and this amount grows 4 percent per year forever.

d. Lastly, let's try a third terminal value. Estimate the fair market value of Torino Marine's equity per share at the end of 2006 under the following assumptions:

(1) Free cash flows in years 2007 through 2010 remain as above.

(2) At year-end 2010, Torino Marine has reached maturity, and its equity sells for a "typical" multiple of year 2010 net income. Use 17 as a typical multiple.

(3) At year-end 2010, Torino Marine has $300 million of interest-bearing liabilities outstanding at an average interest rate of 10 percent.

The following three problems test your knowledge of the chapter appendix.

8. A venture capital company buys 400,000 shares of a start-up's stock for $5 million. If the company has 1.6 million shares outstanding prior to the purchase, what is the company's premoney value? What is its postmoney value?

9. New ventures commonly set aside 10 to 20 percent of company shares at the valuation date for employee bonuses and stock options. Modify the valuation of ZMW Enterprises in Panel B of Table 9A.1 to include an employee set aside equal to 20 percent of the company in year 5. Specifically, calculate Touchstone's required percentage ownership at time 0 under these revised conditions.

10. Using the information below, please answer the following questions below about Surelock Homes, a start-up company. In your analysis, assume the valuation date is the end of year 6, projected earnings in year 6 will be $12 million, and an appropriate price-to-earnings ratio for valuing these earnings is 20 times.

Financing Round	Amount in Millions	Year	Required Return
1	$ 6	0	60%
2	8	2	40
3	12	4	30

In addition, the company wants to reserve 15 percent of the shares outstanding at time 6 for employee bonuses and options.

a. What percentage ownership at time 0 should round 1 investors demand for their $6 million investment?

b. If Surelock presently has 1 million shares outstanding, how many shares should round 1 investors demand at time 0?

c. What is the implied price per share of Surelock stock at time 0?

d. What is Surelock's premoney value at time 0? What is its postmoney value?

11. The Excel file C9_Problem_11.xls available at **www.mhhe.com/ higgins8e** (Select Student Edition > Choose a Chapter > Excel Spreadsheets) contains information concerning the potential acquisition of Fractal Antenna Systems, Inc., by Integrated Communications, Ltd. After reviewing this information, answer the questions given there.

12. The spreadsheet available at **www.mhhe.com/higgins8e** (Select Student Edition > Choose a Chapter > Excel Spreadsheets) presents information concerning The Timberland Company and four of its peers. Use the given information to estimate the value of Timberland.

Present Value of $1 in Year *n*, Discounted at Discount Rate *k*

Period (*n*)	Discount Rate (k)											
	1%	2%	3%	4%	5%	6%	7%	8%	9%	10%	11%	12%
1	0.990	0.980	0.971	0.962	0.952	0.943	0.935	0.926	0.917	0.909	0.901	0.893
2	0.980	0.961	0.943	0.925	0.907	0.890	0.873	0.857	0.842	0.826	0.812	0.797
3	0.971	0.942	0.915	0.889	0.864	0.840	0.816	0.794	0.772	0.751	0.731	0.712
4	0.961	0.924	0.885	0.855	0.823	0.792	0.763	0.735	0.708	0.683	0.659	0.636
5	0.951	0.906	0.863	0.822	0.784	0.747	0.713	0.681	0.650	0.621	0.593	0.567
6	0.942	0.888	0.837	0.790	0.746	0.705	0.666	0.630	0.596	0.564	0.535	0.507
7	0.933	0.871	0.813	0.760	0.711	0.665	0.623	0.583	0.547	0.513	0.482	0.452
8	0.923	0.853	0.789	0.731	0.677	0.627	0.582	0.540	0.502	0.467	0.434	0.404
9	0.914	0.837	0.766	0.703	0.645	0.592	0.544	0.500	0.460	0.424	0.391	0.361
10	0.905	0.820	0.744	0.676	0.614	0.558	0.508	0.463	0.422	0.386	0.352	0.322
11	0.896	0.804	0.722	0.650	0.585	0.527	0.475	0.429	0.388	0.350	0.317	0.287
12	0.887	0.788	0.701	0.625	0.557	0.497	0.444	0.397	0.356	0.319	0.286	0.257
13	0.879	0.773	0.681	0.601	0.530	0.469	0.415	0.368	0.326	0.290	0.258	0.229
14	0.870	0.758	0.661	0.577	0.505	0.442	0.388	0.340	0.299	0.263	0.232	0.205
15	0.861	0.743	0.642	0.555	0.481	0.417	0.362	0.315	0.275	0.239	0.209	0.183
16	0.853	0.728	0.623	0.534	0.458	0.394	0.339	0.292	0.252	0.218	0.188	0.163
17	0.844	0.714	0.605	0.513	0.436	0.371	0.317	0.270	0.231	0.198	0.170	0.146
18	0.836	0.700	0.587	0.494	0.416	0.350	0.296	0.250	0.212	0.180	0.153	0.130
19	0.828	0.686	0.570	0.475	0.396	0.331	0.277	0.232	0.194	0.164	0.138	0.116
20	0.820	0.673	0.554	0.456	0.377	0.312	0.258	0.215	0.178	0.149	0.124	0.104
25	0.780	0.610	0.478	0.375	0.295	0.233	0.184	0.146	0.116	0.092	0.074	0.059
30	0.742	0.552	0.412	0.308	0.231	0.174	0.131	0.099	0.075	0.057	0.044	0.033
40	0.672	0.453	0.307	0.208	0.142	0.097	0.067	0.046	0.032	0.022	0.015	0.011
50	0.608	0.372	0.228	0.141	0.087	0.054	0.034	0.021	0.013	0.009	0.005	0.003

(*continued*)

Present Value of $1 in Year *n*, Discounted at Discount Rate *k* (*Concluded*)

Period (*n*)	Discount Rate (*k*)												
	13%	14%	15%	16%	17%	18%	19%	20%	25%	30%	35%	40%	50%
1	0.885	0.877	0.870	0.862	0.855	0.847	0.840	0.833	0.800	0.769	0.741	0.714	0.667
2	0.783	0.769	0.756	0.743	0.731	0.718	0.706	0.694	0.640	0.592	0.549	0.510	0.444
3	0.693	0.675	0.658	0.641	0.624	0.609	0.593	0.579	0.512	0.455	0.406	0.364	0.296
4	0.613	0.592	0.572	0.552	0.534	0.515	0.499	0.482	0.410	0.350	0.301	0.260	0.198
5	0.543	0.519	0.497	0.476	0.456	0.437	0.419	0.402	0.320	0.269	0.223	0.186	0.132
6	0.480	0.456	0.432	0.410	0.390	0.370	0.352	0.335	0.262	0.207	0.165	0.133	0.088
7	0.425	0.400	0.376	0.354	0.333	0.314	0.296	0.279	0.210	0.159	0.122	0.095	0.059
8	0.376	0.351	0.327	0.305	0.285	0.266	0.249	0.233	0.168	0.123	0.091	0.068	0.039
9	0.333	0.308	0.284	0.263	0.243	0.225	0.209	0.194	0.134	0.094	0.067	0.048	0.026
10	0.295	0.270	0.247	0.227	0.208	0.191	0.176	0.162	0.107	0.073	0.050	0.035	0.017
11	0.261	0.237	0.215	0.195	0.178	0.162	0.148	0.135	0.086	0.056	0.037	0.025	0.012
12	0.231	0.208	0.187	0.168	0.152	0.137	0.124	0.112	0.069	0.043	0.027	0.018	0.008
13	0.204	0.182	0.163	0.145	0.130	0.116	0.104	0.093	0.055	0.033	0.020	0.013	0.005
14	0.181	0.160	0.141	0.125	0.111	0.099	0.088	0.078	0.044	0.025	0.015	0.009	0.003
15	0.160	0.140	0.123	0.108	0.095	0.084	0.074	0.065	0.035	0.020	0.011	0.006	0.002
16	0.141	0.123	0.107	0.093	0.081	0.071	0.062	0.054	0.028	0.015	0.008	0.005	0.002
17	0.125	0.108	0.093	0.080	0.069	0.060	0.052	0.045	0.023	0.012	0.006	0.003	0.001
18	0.111	0.095	0.081	0.069	0.059	0.051	0.044	0.038	0.018	0.009	0.005	0.002	0.001
19	0.098	0.083	0.070	0.060	0.051	0.043	0.037	0.031	0.014	0.007	0.003	0.002	0.000
20	0.087	0.073	0.061	0.051	0.043	0.037	0.031	0.026	0.012	0.005	0.002	0.001	0.000
25	0.047	0.038	0.030	0.024	0.020	0.016	0.013	0.010	0.004	0.001	0.001	0.000	0.000
30	0.026	0.020	0.015	0.012	0.009	0.007	0.005	0.004	0.001	0.000	0.000	0.000	0.000
40	0.008	0.005	0.004	0.003	0.002	0.001	0.001	0.001	0.000	0.000	0.000	0.000	0.000
50	0.002	0.001	0.001	0.001	0.000	0.000	0.000	0.000	0.000	0.000	0.000	0.000	0.000

Present Value of an Annuity of $1 for *n* Years, Discounted at Rate *k*

Period (*n*)	Discount Rate (*k*)											
	1%	2%	3%	4%	5%	6%	7%	8%	9%	10%	11%	12%
1	0.990	0.980	0.971	0.962	0.952	0.943	0.935	0.926	0.917	0.909	0.901	0.893
2	1.970	1.942	1.913	1.886	1.859	1.833	1.808	1.783	1.759	1.736	1.713	1.690
3	2.941	2.884	2.829	2.775	2.723	2.673	2.624	2.577	2.531	2.487	2.444	2.402
4	3.902	3.808	3.717	3.630	3.546	3.465	3.387	3.312	3.240	3.170	3.102	3.037
5	4.853	4.710	4.580	4.452	4.329	4.212	4.100	3.993	3.890	3.791	3.696	3.605
6	5.795	5.601	5.417	5.242	5.076	4.917	4.767	4.623	4.486	4.355	4.231	4.111
7	6.728	6.472	6.230	6.002	5.786	5.582	5.389	5.206	5.033	4.868	4.712	4.564
8	7.652	7.325	7.020	6.733	6.463	6.210	5.971	5.747	5.535	5.335	5.146	4.968
9	8.566	8.162	7.786	7.435	7.108	6.802	6.515	6.247	5.995	5.759	5.537	5.328
10	9.471	8.983	8.530	8.111	7.722	7.360	7.024	6.710	6.418	6.145	5.889	5.650
11	10.368	9.787	9.253	8.760	8.306	7.887	7.499	7.139	6.805	6.495	6.207	5.938
12	11.255	10.575	9.954	9.385	8.863	8.384	7.943	7.536	7.161	6.814	6.492	6.194
13	12.134	11.348	10.635	9.986	9.394	8.853	8.358	7.904	7.487	7.103	6.750	6.424
14	13.004	12.106	11.296	10.563	9.899	9.295	8.745	8.244	7.786	7.367	6.982	6.628
15	13.865	12.849	11.939	11.118	10.380	9.712	9.108	8.559	8.061	7.606	7.191	6.811
16	14.718	13.578	12.561	11.652	10.838	10.106	9.447	8.851	8.313	7.824	7.379	6.974
17	15.562	14.292	13.166	12.166	11.274	10.477	9.763	9.122	8.544	8.022	7.549	7.102
18	16.398	14.992	13.754	12.659	11.690	10.828	10.059	9.372	8.756	8.201	7.702	7.250
19	17.226	15.678	14.324	13.134	12.085	11.158	10.336	9.604	8.950	8.365	7.839	7.366
20	18.046	16.351	14.877	13.590	12.462	11.470	10.594	9.818	9.129	8.514	7.963	7.469
25	22.023	19.523	17.413	15.622	14.094	12.783	11.654	10.675	9.823	9.077	8.422	7.843
30	25.808	22.396	19.600	17.292	15.372	13.765	12.409	11.258	10.274	9.427	8.694	8.055
40	32.835	27.355	23.115	19.793	17.159	15.046	13.332	11.925	10.757	9.779	8.951	8.244
50	39.196	31.424	25.730	21.482	18.256	15.762	13.801	12.233	10.962	9.915	9.042	8.304

(*continued*)

Present Value of an Annuity of $1 for *n* Years, Discounted at Rate *k* (*Concluded*)

Period (*n*)	Discount Rate (*k*)												
	13%	14%	15%	16%	17%	18%	19%	20%	25%	30%	35%	40%	50%
1	0.885	0.877	0.870	0.862	0.855	0.847	0.840	0.833	0.800	0.769	0.741	0.714	0.667
2	1.668	1.647	1.626	1.605	1.585	1.566	1.547	1.528	1.440	1.361	1.289	1.224	1.111
3	2.361	2.322	2.283	2.246	`2.210	2.174	2.140	2.106	1.952	1.816	1.696	1.589	1.407
4	2.974	2.914	2.855	2.798	2.743	2.690	2.639	2.589	2.362	2.166	1.997	1.849	1.605
5	3.517	3.433	3.352	3.274	3.199	3.127	3.058	2.991	2.689	2.436	2.220	2.035	1.737
6	3.998	3.889	3.784	3.685	3.589	3.498	3.410	3.326	2.951	2.643	2.385	2.168	1.824
7	4.423	4.288	4.160	4.039	3.922	3.812	3.706	3.605	3.161	2.802	2.508	2.263	1.883
8	4.799	4.639	4.487	4.344	4.207	4.078	3.954	3.837	3.329	2.925	2.598	2.331	1.922
9	5.132	4.946	4.772	4.607	4.451	4.303	4.163	4.031	3.463	3.019	2.665	2.370	1.948
10	5.426	5.216	5.019	4.833	4.659	4.494	4.339	4.192	3.571	3.092	2.715	2.414	1.965
11	5.687	5.453	5.234	5.029	4.836	4.656	4.486	4.327	3.656	3.147	2.752	2.438	1.977
12	5.918	5.660	5.421	5.197	4.988	4.793	4.611	4.439	3.725	3.190	2.779	2.456	1.985
13	6.122	5.842	5.583	5.342	5.118	4.910	4.715	4.533	3.780	3.223	2.799	2.469	1.990
14	6.302	6.002	5.724	5.468	5.229	5.008	4.802	4.611	3.824	3.249	2.814	2.478	1.993
15	6.462	6.142	5.847	5.575	5.324	5.092	4.876	4.675	3.859	3.268	2.825	2.484	1.995
16	6.604	6.265	5.954	5.668	5.405	5.162	4.938	4.730	3.887	3.283	2.834	2.489	1.997
17	6.729	6.373	6.047	5.749	5.475	5.222	4.988	4.775	3.910	3.295	2.840	2.492	1.998
18	6.840	6.467	6.128	5.818	5.534	5.273	5.033	4.812	3.928	3.304	2.844	2.494	1.999
19	6.938	6.550	6.198	5.877	5.584	5.316	5.070	4.843	3.942	3.311	2.848	2.496	1.999
20	7.025	6.623	6.259	5.929	5.628	5.353	5.101	4.870	3.954	3.316	2.850	2.497	1.999
25	7.330	6.873	6.464	6.097	5.766	5.467	5.195	4.948	3.985	3.329	2.856	2.499	2.000
30	7.496	7.003	6.566	6.177	5.829	5.517	5.235	4.979	3.995	3.332	2.857	2.500	2.000
40	7.634	7.105	6.642	6.233	5.871	5.548	5.258	4.997	3.999	3.333	2.857	2.500	2.000
50	7.675	7.133	6.661	6.246	5.880	5.554	5.262	4.999	4.000	3.333	2.857	2.500	2.000

Glossary

A

accelerated depreciation Any *depreciation*[1] that produces larger deductions for depreciation in the early years of a project's life.

acceptance criterion Any minimum standard of performance in investment analysis (cf. *hurdle rate*).

accounting income An economic agent's *realized income* as shown on financial statements (cf. *economic income*).

accounting rate of return A figure of investment merit, defined as average annual cash inflow divided by total cash outflow (cf. *internal rate of return*).

accounts payable (payables, trade payables) Money owed to suppliers. Obligations due to trade suppliers within one year.

accounts receivable (receivables, trade credit) Money owed by customers.

accrual accounting A method of accounting in which *revenue* is recognized when earned and expenses are recognized when incurred without regard to the timing of cash receipts and expenditures (cf. *cash accounting*).

accrued liabilities *Other liabilities*. A catchall accounting term referring to a collection of unpaid expenses that are individually too small to warrant a separate line on the balance sheet.

acid test (quick ratio) A measure of *liquidity*, defined as *current assets* less inventories divided by *current liabilities*.

adjusted present value (APV) *Net present value* of an asset if financed entirely by equity plus the present value of any side effects, such as interest tax shields.

[1] Words in italics are defined elsewhere in the glossary.

after-tax cash flow Total cash generated by an investment annually, defined as profit after tax plus depreciation or, equivalently, operating income after tax plus the tax rate times depreciation.

allocated costs Costs systematically assigned or distributed among products, departments, or other elements.

amortization The provision for the gradual elimination of an asset or a liability by regular payments or charges. Often synonymous with depreciation.

annuity A level stream of cash flows for a limited number of years (cf. *perpetuity*).

asset Anything with value in exchange.

asset turnover ratio A broad measure of asset efficiency, defined as net sales divided by total assets.

B

bankruptcy A legal condition in which an entity receives court protection from its creditors. Bankruptcy can result in *liquidation* or reorganization.

bearer securities Any securities that are not registered on the books of the issuing corporation. Payments are made to whoever presents the appropriate coupon. Bearer securities facilitate tax avoidance.

benefit-cost ratio *Profitability index.*

β-risk (systematic risk, nondiversifiable risk) Risk that cannot be diversified away.

bond Long-term publicly issued debt.

bond rating An appraisal by a recognized financial organization of the soundness of a *bond* as an investment.

book value   The value at which an item is reported in financial statements (cf. *market value*).

book value of equity   The value of *owners' equity* as shown on the company's balance sheet (cf. *market value of equity*).

break-even analysis   Analysis of the level of sales at which a firm or product will just break even.

breakup value   The value one could realize by dividing a multibusiness company into a number of separate enterprises and disposing of each individually.

business risk   Risk due to uncertainty about investment outlays, operating cash flows, and salvage values without regard to how investments are financed (cf. *financial risk*).

C

call option   Option to buy an asset at a specified exercise price on or before a specified maturity date (cf. *put option*).

call provision   Provision describing terms under which a bond issuer may redeem the bond in whole or in part prior to maturity.

capital   The amount invested in a venture (cf. *capitalization*).

capital budget   List of planned investment projects.

capital consumption adjustment   Adjustment to historical-cost depreciation to correct for understatement during inflation.

capital in excess of par value   (paid in surplus, additional paid in capital)   Cash contributed by shareholders over and above par value of shares issued. The sum of common stock and capital in excess of par value is the total amount paid for common shares.

capitalization   The sum of all long-term sources of financing to the firm or, equivalently, total assets less current liabilities.

capital rationing   Fixed limit on capital that forces the company to choose among worthwhile projects.

capital structure   The composition of the liabilities side of a company's balance sheet. The mix of funding sources a company uses to finance its operations.

cash   Any immediately negotiable medium of exchange.

cash accounting   A method of accounting in which changes in the condition of an organization are recognized only in response to the payment or receipt of cash (cf. *accrual accounting*).

cash budget   A plan or projection of cash receipts and disbursements for a given period of time (cf. *cash flow forecast, cash flow statement, pro forma forecast*).

cash cow   Company or product that generates more cash than can be productively reinvested.

cash flow   The amount of cash generated or consumed by an activity over a certain period of time.

cash flow cycle   The periodic transformation of cash through *working capital* and fixed assets back to cash.

cash flow forecast   A financial forecast in the form of a *sources and uses statement*.

cash flow from operating activities   Cash generated or consumed by the productive activities of a firm over a period of time; defined as profit after tax plus *noncash charges* minus noncash receipts plus or minus changes in *current assets* and *current liabilities*.

cash flow principle   Principle of investment evaluation stating that only actual movements of cash are relevant and should be listed on the date they move.

cash flow statement   A report of the sources of cash to a business and the uses to which the cash was put over an accounting period

certainty-equivalent   A guaranteed amount of money that a decision maker would trade for an uncertain cash flow.

close off the top   Financial jargon meaning to foreclose the possibility of additional debt financing.

collection period   A ratio measure of control of *accounts receivable*, defined as accounts receivable divided by credit sales per day.

common shares   *Common stock.*

common-size financial statements   Device used to compare financial statements, frequently of companies of disparate size, whereby all balance sheet entries are divided by total assets and all income statement entries are divided by net sales.

common stock (common shares)   Securities representing an ownership interest in a firm. Also, on the balance sheet, the total par value of common shares issued.

comparables   A method for estimating the *fair market value* of a closely held business by comparing it to one or more comparable, publicly traded firms.

comparable trades valuation   A valuation technique that relies on prices of shares trading on financial markets and representing small, minority interests.

comparable transactions valuation   A valuation technique that relies on prices of shares determined in acquisitions and representing controlling interest of the companies sold.

compounding   The growth of a sum of money over time through the reinvestment of interest earned to earn more interest (cf. *discounting*).

comprehensive income (loss)   An obscure, technical accounting term equaling net income plus changes in the unrealized value of securities held for resale, foreign currency translation adjustments, minimum required pension liability adjustments, and certain futures contracts qualifying as hedges.

conglomerate diversification   Ownership of operations in a number of functionally unrelated business activities.

constant-dollar accounting   System of inflation accounting in which historical cost items are restated to adjust for changes in the general purchasing power of the currency (cf. *current-dollar accounting*).

constant purchasing power   The amount of a currency required over time to purchase a stable basket of physical assets.

consumer price index (CPI)   An index measure of the price level equal to the sum of prices of a number of commodities purchased by consumers weighted by the proportion each represents in a typical consumer's budget.

contribution to fixed cost and profits   The excess of *revenue* over *variable costs*.

control ratio   Ratio indicating management's control of a particular current asset or liability.

conversion ratio   Number of shares for which a *convertible security* may be exchanged.

conversion value   Market value of shares an investor would own if he or she converted one convertible security.

convertible security   Financial security that can be exchanged at the holder's option for another security or asset.

corporate restructuring   Any major episodic change in a company's capital or ownership structure.

correlation coefficient   Measure of the degree of comovement of two variables.

cost of capital (opportunity cost of capital, hurdle rate, weighted-average cost of capital)   Return on new, average-risk investment that a company must expect to maintain share price. A weighted average of the cost to the firm of individual sources of capital.

cost of debt   *Yield to maturity* on debt; frequently after tax, in which event it is 1 minus the tax rate times the yield to maturity.

cost of equity   Return equity investors expect to earn by holding shares in a company. The expected return forgone by equity investors in the next best equal-risk opportunity.

cost of goods sold (cost of sales)   The sum of all costs required to acquire and prepare goods for sale.

coupon rate   The interest rate specified on interest coupons attached to bonds. Annual interest received equals coupon rate times the *par value* of the bond.

covenant (protective covenant)   Provision in a debt agreement requiring the borrower to do, or not do, something.

coverage ratio   Measure of financial leverage relating annual operating income to annual burden of debt (cf. *times-interest-earned ratio, times-burden-covered ratio*).

cumulative preferred stock   *Preferred stock* containing the requirement that any unpaid preferred dividends accumulate and be paid in full before common dividends may be distributed.

current asset   Any asset that will turn into cash within one year.

current-dollar accounting   System of inflation accounting in which historical-cost items are restated to adjust for changes in the price of a specific item (cf. *constant-dollar accounting*).

current liability   Any liability that is payable within one year.

current portion of long-term debt   That portion of long-term debt that is payable within one year.

current ratio   A measure of *liquidity*, defined as current assets divided by current liabilities.

D

days' sales in cash   A measure of management's control of cash balances, defined as cash divided by sales per day.

debt (liability)   An obligation to pay cash or other goods or to provide services to another.

debt capacity   The total amount of debt a company can prudently support given its earnings expectations and equity base.

debt-to-assets ratio   A measure of *financial leverage*, defined as debt divided by total assets (cf. *debt-to-equity ratio*).

debt-to-equity ratio   A measure of *financial leverage*, defined as debt divided by shareholders' equity.

default   To fail to make a payment when due.

default premium   The increased return on a security required to compensate investors for the risk that the company will default on its obligation.

deferred income taxes   A recognized obligation to pay income taxes in the future.

deferred tax liability   An estimated amount of future income taxes that may become payable from income already earned but not yet recognized for tax reporting purposes.

delayed call   Provision in a security that gives the issuer the right to call the issue, but only after a period of time has elapsed (cf. *call provision*).

depreciation   The reduction in the value of a long-lived asset from use or obsolescence. The decline is recognized in accounting by a periodic allocation of the original cost of the asset to current operations (cf. *accelerated depreciation*).

dilution   The reduction in any per share item (such as earnings per share or book value per share) due to an increase in the number of shares outstanding either through new issue or conversion of outstanding securities.

discounted cash flow   The method of evaluating long-term projects that explicitly takes into account the time value of money.

discounted cash flow rate of return   *Internal rate of return.*

discounting   Process of finding the present value of future cash flows (cf. *compounding*).

discount rate   Interest rate used to calculate the *present value* of future cash flows.

diversifiable risk   That risk that is eliminated when an asset is added to a diversified portfolio (cf. β-*risk*).

diversification   The process of investing in a number of different assets.

dividend payout ratio   A measure of the level of dividends distributed, defined as dividends divided by earnings.

E

earnings (income, net income, net profit, profit)   The excess of revenues over all related expenses for a given period.

earnings per share (EPS)   A measure of each common share's claim on earnings, defined as earnings available for common divided by the number of common shares outstanding.

earnings yield   *Earnings per share* divided by stock price.

EBIT   Abbreviation for earnings before interest and taxes.

economic income   The amount an economic agent could spend during a period of time without affecting his or her wealth (cf. *accounting income*).

economic value added   A business's or a business unit's operating income after tax less a charge for the opportunity cost of capital employed.

efficient market   A market in which asset prices instantaneously reflect new information.

enterprise value   The *present value* of projected cash flows to *equity* and to creditors discounted by the *weighted-average cost of capital*.

equity (owners' equity, net worth, shareholders' equity)   Ownership interests of common and preferred stockholders in a company. On a balance sheet, equity equals total assets less all liabilities.

equity value   The *present value* of projected cash flows to *equity* discounted by the *cost of equity*.

equivalent annual cost or benefit   The *annuity* having the same time-adjusted value as a given stream of cash inflows and outflows.

equivalence   Equality of value of two cash flows occurring at different times if the cash flow occurring sooner can be converted into the later cash flow by investing it at the prevailing interest rate.

Eurodollar   Originally a U.S. dollar in Europe, now any currency outside the control of its issuing monetary authority. The Eurodollar market is any market in which transactions in such currencies are executed.

expected return   Average of possible returns weighted by their probability.

F

fair market value (FMV) (intrinsic value)   An idealized *market value* defined as the price at which

an asset would trade between two rational individuals, each in command of all of the information necessary to value the asset and neither under any pressure to trade.

figure of merit   A number summarizing the investment worth of a project.

Financial Accounting Standards Board (FASB)   Official rulemaking body in the accounting profession.

financial asset   Legal claim to future cash payments.

financial flexibility   The ability to raise sufficient capital to meet company needs under a wide variety of future contingencies.

financial leverage   Use of debt to increase the expected return and the risk to equity (cf. *operating leverage*).

first-in, first-out (FIFO)   A method of inventory accounting in which the oldest item in inventory is assumed to be sold first (cf. *last-in, first-out*).

Fisher effect   Proposition that the nominal rate of interest should approximately equal the real rate of interest plus a premium for expected inflation (cf. *real amount, nominal amount*).

fixed cost   Any cost that does not vary over the observation period with changes in volume.

fixed-income security   Any security that promises an unvarying payment stream to holders over its life.

forcing conversion   Strategy in which a company forces owners of a convertible security to convert by calling the security at a time when its call price is below its conversion value (cf. *call provision, convertible security*).

foreign exchange exposure   The risk that an unexpected change in exchange rates will impose a loss of some kind on the exposed party. With **transaction exposure,** the loss is to reported income; with **accounting exposure,** the loss is to net worth; and with **economic exposure,** the loss is to the market value of the entity.

forward contract   A contract in which the price is set today for a trade occurring at a specified future date.

forward market   A market in which prices are determined for trade at a specified future date.

free cash flow   The *cash flow* available to a company after financing all worthwhile investments; defined as operating income after tax plus depreciation less investment. The presence of large free cash flows is said to be attractive to a corporate raider.

frozen convertible (hung convertible)   *Convertible security* that has been outstanding for several years and whose holders cannot be forced to convert because its *conversion value* is below its call price (cf. *forcing conversion*).

funds   Any means of payment. Along with cash flow, "funds" is one of the most frequently misused words in finance.

G

gains to net debtors   Increase in debtor's wealth due to a decline in the purchasing power of liabilities.

general creditor   Unsecured creditor.

going-concern value   The *present value* of a business's expected future *after-tax cash flows*. The going-concern value of *equity* is the present value of cash flows to equity, while the going-concern value of the firm is the present value of cash flows to all providers of capital.

goodwill   Excess of purchase price over fair market value of net assets acquired in a merger or acquisition.

gross margin percentage   Revenue minus cost of goods sold divided by revenue.

H

hedge   A strategy to offset investment risk. A perfect hedge is one that eliminates all possibility of gain or loss due to future movements of the hedged variable.

historical-cost depreciation   *Depreciation* based on the amount originally paid for the asset.

hurdle rate   Minimum acceptable rate of return on an investment (cf. *acceptance criterion, cost of capital*).

I

income   *Earnings*

income statement (profit and loss statement)   A report of a company's revenues, associated expenses, and resulting *income* for a period of time.

inflation premium   The increased return on a security required to compensate investors for expected inflation.

insolvency   The condition of having debts greater than the realizable value of one's assets.

internal rate of return (IRR)   *Discount rate* at which project's *net present value* equals zero. Rate at which funds left in a project are *compounding* (cf. *rate of return*).

internal sources   Cash available to a company from *cash flow from operations*.

inventories   Raw materials, items available for sale or in the process of being made ready for sale. For financial institutions: securities bought and held for resale.

inventory turnover ratio   A measure of management's control of its investment in inventory, defined as *cost of goods sold* divided by ending inventory, or something similar.

inventory valuation adjustment   Adjustment to historical-cost financial statements to correct for the possible understatement of inventory and *cost of goods sold* during inflation.

investment bank   A financial institution specializing in the original sale and subsequent trading of company securities.

investments   The company's ownership interest in the net assets of unconsolidated subsidiaries and affiliates.

investment value   Value of a *convertible security* based solely on its characteristics as a fixed-income security and ignoring the value of the conversion feature.

J

junk bond   Any *bond* rated below investment grade.

L

last-in, first-out (LIFO)   A method of inventory accounting in which the newest item in inventory is assumed to be sold first (cf. *first-in, first-out*).

leveraged buyout (LBO)   Purchase of a company financed in large part by company borrowings.

liability   An obligation to pay an amount or perform a service.

liquid asset   Any asset that can be quickly converted to cash without significant loss of value.

liquidation   The process of closing down a company, selling its assets, paying off its creditors, and distributing any remaining cash to owners.

liquidation value   The cash generated by terminating a business and selling its assets individually. The liquidation value of equity is the proceeds of the asset sale less all company liabilities.

liquidity   The extent to which a company has assets that are readily available to meet obligations (cf. *acid test, current ratio*).

liquidity ratio   Any ratio used to estimate a company's *liquidity* (cf. *acid test, current ratio*).

long-term debt   Interest-bearing debt obligations due more than one year from the company's balance sheet date.

M

marketable securities   Securities that are easily convertible to cash.

market for control   The active, competitive trading of controlling interests in corporations, effected by the purchase or sale of sizable blocks of common stock.

market line (securities market line)   Line representing the relationship between *expected return* and β-*risk*.

market value   The price at which an item can be sold (cf. *book value*).

market value of equity   The price per share of a company's *common stock* times the number of shares of common stock outstanding (cf. *book value of equity*).

market value of firm   The market value of *equity* plus the market value of the firm's debt.

mark-to-market accounting   The practice of adjusting the carrying value of traded assets and liabilities appearing on a business's balance sheet to their recent market values.

monetary asset   Any asset having a value defined in units of currency. Cash and accounts receivable are monetary assets; inventories and plant and equipment are physical assets.

multiple hurdle rates   Use of different *hurdle rates* for new investments to reflect differing levels of risk.

mutually exclusive alternatives   Two projects that accomplish the same objective so that only one will be undertaken.

N

net income   *Earnings.*

net monetary creditor   Economic agent having *monetary assets* in excess of *liabilities*.

net monetary debtor   Economic agent having *monetary assets* less than *liabilities*.

net present value (NPV)   *Present value* of cash inflows less present value of cash outflows. The increase in wealth accruing to an investor when he or she undertakes an investment.

net profit   *Earnings.*

net sales   Total sales revenue less certain offsetting items such as returns and allowances and sales discounts.

net worth   *Equity*, shareholders' equity.

nominal amount   Any quantity not adjusted for changes in the purchasing power of the currency due to inflation (cf. *real amount*).

noncash charge An expense recorded by an accountant that is not matched by a cash outflow during the accounting period.

nondiversifiable risk β-*risk, systematic risk.*

notes payable The total amount of interest-bearing short-term obligations.

O

operating leverage Fixed operating costs that tend to increase the variation in profits (cf. *financial leverage*).

opportunity cost Income forgone by an investor when he or she chooses one action over another. Expected income on next best alternative.

opportunity cost of capital *Cost of capital.*

option See *call option, put option.*

option premium The amount paid per unit by an option buyer to the option seller for an option contract.

other assets A catchall accounting term referring to a collection of assets that are individually too small to warrant a separate line on the balance sheet.

other expenses A catchall accounting term referring to a collection of expenses that are individually too small to warrant a separate line on the income statement.

over-the-counter (OTC) market Informal market in which securities not listed on organized exchanges trade.

owners' equity *Equity.*

P

paid-in capital That portion of *shareholders' equity* that has been paid in directly, as opposed to earned profits retained in the business.

par value An arbitrary value set as the face amount of a security. Bondholders receive par value for their bonds on maturity.

payables period A measure of a company's use of trade credit financing, defined as accounts payable divided by purchases per day.

payback period A crude figure of investment merit and a better measure of investment risk, defined as the time an investor must wait to recoup his or her initial investment.

perpetual-growth equation An equation representing the *present value* of a *perpetuity* growing at the rate of *g* percent per annum as next year's receipts divided by the difference between the *discount rate* and *g*.

perpetuity An *annuity* that lasts forever.

plug Jargon for the unknown quantity in a pro forma forecast.

portfolio Holdings of a diverse group of assets by an individual or a company.

position diagram A graph relating the value of an investment position on the vertical axis to the price of an underlying asset on the horizontal axis.

post-money value A company's equity value implied by the price per share an investor pays, after investing (cf. *pre-money value*).

preferred stock A class of stock, usually fixed-income, that carries some form of preference to income or assets over *common stock* (cf. *cumulative preferred stock*).

premium for control The premium over and above the existing *market value* of a company's *equity* that an acquirer is willing to pay to gain control of the company.

pre-money value A company's equity value implied by the price per share an investor agrees to pay prior to investing (cf. *post-money value*).

prepaid income taxes A prepayment of taxes treated as an asset until taxes become due.

present value The present worth of a future sum of money.

price-to-earnings ratio (P/E ratio) Amount investors are willing to pay for $1 of a firm's current earnings. Price per share divided by earnings per share over the most recent 12 months.

principal The original, or face, amount of a loan. Interest is earned on the principal.

private placement The raising of capital for a business through the sale of securities to a limited number of well-informed investors rather than through a public offering.

profitability index (benefit-cost ratio) A figure of investment merit, defined as the *present value* of cash inflows divided by the present value of cash outflows.

profit center An organizational unit within a company that produces revenue and for which a profit can be calculated.

profit margin The proportion of each sales dollar that filters down to *income*, defined as income divided by *net sales*.

profits *Earnings*.

pro forma statement A financial statement prepared on the basis of some assumed future events.

property, plant, and equipment The cost of tangible fixed property used in the production of revenue

protective covenant *Covenant*.

provision for income taxes Taxes due for the year based on reported income. Often differs from taxes paid, which are based on separate tax accounting rules.

public issue (public offering) Newly issued securities sold directly to the public (cf. *private placement*).

purchasing power parity A theory stating that foreign exchange rates should adjust so that in equilibrium, commodities in different countries cost the same amount when prices are expressed in the same currency.

put option Option to sell an asset at a specified exercise price on or before a specified maturity date (cf. *call option*).

Q

quick ratio *Acid test*.

R

range of earnings chart Graph relating *earnings per share (EPS)* to earnings before interest and taxes (*EBIT*) under alternative financing options.

rate of return Yield obtainable on an asset.

ratio analysis Analysis of financial statements by means of ratios.

real amount Any quantity that has been adjusted for changes in the purchasing power of the currency due to inflation (cf. *nominal amount*).

realized income The earning of income related to a transaction as distinguished from a paper gain.

residual income security A security that has last claim on company income. Usually the beneficiary of company growth.

residual profits An alternative to *return on investment* as a measure of *profit center* performance, defined as *income* less the annual cost of the capital employed by the profit center.

retained earnings (earned surplus) The amount of earnings retained and reinvested in a business and not distributed to stockholders as dividends.

return on assets (ROA) A measure of the productivity of assets, defined as *income* divided by total assets. A superior but less common definition includes interest expense and preferred dividends in the numerator.

return on equity (ROE) A measure of the productivity or efficiency with which shareholders' equity is employed, defined as *income* divided by *equity*.

return on invested capital (ROIC) A fundamental measure of the earning power of a company that is unaffected by the way the company is financed. It is equal to earnings before interest and tax times 1 minus the tax rate, all divided by *debt* plus *equity*.

return on investment (ROI) The productivity of an investment or a profit center, defined as *income* divided by *book value* of investment or *profit center* (cf. *return on assets*).

revenues *Sales*.

rights of absolute priority Specification in bankruptcy law stating that each class of claimants with a prior claim on assets in liquidation will be paid off in full before any junior claimants receive anything.

risk-adjusted discount rate (cost of capital, hurdle rate) A *discount rate* that includes a premium for risk.

risk aversion An unwillingness to bear risk without compensation of some form.

risk-free interest rate The interest rate prevailing on a default-free bond in the absence of inflation.

risk premium The increased return on a security required to compensate investors for the risk borne.

S

sales (revenue) The inflow of resources to a business for a period from sale of goods or provision of services (cf. *net sales*).

secured creditor A creditor whose obligation is backed by the pledge of some asset. In liquidation, the secured creditor receives the cash from the sale of the pledged asset to the extent of his or her loan.

Securities and Exchange Commission (SEC) Federal government agency that regulates securities markets.

selling, general, and administrative expenses All expenses of operation not directly related to product production incurred in the generation of operating income.

semistrong-form efficient market A market in which prices instantaneously reflect all publicly available information.

senior creditor Any creditor with a claim on income or assets prior to that of *general creditors*.

sensitivity analysis Analysis of effect on a plan or forecast of a change in one of the input variables.

shareholders' equity *Equity, net worth*.

shelf registration SEC program under which a company can file a general-purpose prospectus describing its possible financing plans for up to two years. This eliminates time lags for new public security issues.

simulation (Monte Carlo simulation) Computer-based extension of *sensitivity analysis* that calculates the probability distribution of a forecast outcome.

sinking fund A fund of cash set aside for the payment of a future obligation. A bond sinking fund is a payment of cash to creditors.

solvency The state of being able to pay debts as they come due.

sources and uses statement A document showing where a company got its cash and where it spent the cash over a specific period of time. It is constructed by segregating all changes in balance sheet accounts into those that provided cash and those that consumed cash.

spontaneous sources of cash Those liabilities, such as accounts payable and accrued wages, that arise automatically, without negotiation, in the course of doing business.

spot market A market in which prices are determined for immediate trade.

spread Investment banker jargon for the difference between the issue price of a new security and the net to the company.

standard deviation of return A measure of variability. The square root of the mean squared deviation from the *expected return*.

statement of changes in financial position A financial statement showing the sources and uses of working capital for the period.

stock *Common stock*.

stock option A contractual privilege sometimes provided to company officers giving the holder the right to purchase a specified number of shares at a specified price within a stated period of time.

striking price (exercise price) The fixed price for which a stock can be purchased in a call contract or sold in a put contract (cf. *call option, put option*).

strong-form efficient market A market in which prices instantaneously reflect all information, public or private.

subordinated creditor A creditor who holds a debenture having a lower chance of payment than other liabilities of the firm.

sunk cost A previous outlay that cannot be changed by any current or future action.

sustainable growth rate The rate of increase in sales a company can attain without changing its profit margin, assets-to-sales ratio, debt-to equity ratio, or dividend payout ratio. The rate of growth a company can finance without excessive borrowing or issuing new stock.

T

tax shield The reduction in a company's tax bill caused by an increase in a tax-deductible expense, usually depreciation or interest. The magnitude of the tax shield equals the tax rate times the increase in the expense.

times burden covered A *coverage ratio* measure of *financial leverage*, defined as earnings before interest and taxes divided by interest expense plus principal payments grossed up to their before-tax equivalents.

times interest earned A *coverage ratio* measure of *financial leverage*, defined as earnings before interest and taxes divided by interest expense.

total capital All long-term sources of financing to a business.

total enterprise value (TEV) *Market value of the firm.* The market value of equity plus the market value of debt.

trade payables *Accounts payable.*

transfer price An internal price at which units of the same company trade goods or services among themselves.

treasury stock The value of a company's common stock that has been repurchased. Treasury shares neither receive dividends nor vote.

U

underwriting syndicate A group of *investment banks* that band together for a brief time to guarantee a specified price to a company for newly issued securities.

unrealized income Earned income for which there is no confirming transaction. A paper gain.

V

variable cost Any expense that varies with sales over the observation period.

volatility β-*risk*.

W

warrant A security issued by a company granting the right to purchase shares of another security of the company at a specified price and for a stated time.

weak-form efficient market A market in which prices instantaneously reflect information about past prices.

weighted-average cost of capital *Cost of capital.*

with-without principle Principle defining those cash flows that are relevant to an investment decision. It states that if there are two worlds, one with the investment and one without it, all cash flows that differ in these two worlds are relevant and all cash flows that are the same are irrelevant.

working capital (net working capital) The excess of current assets over current liabilities.

working capital cycle The periodic transformation of cash through current assets and current liabilities and back to cash (cf. *cash flow cycle*).

Y

yield to maturity The *internal rate of return* on a bond when held to maturity.

Suggested Answers to Odd-Numbered Problems

Chapter 1

1. a. The company is better off because it could retire all its debts at a $10 million lower cost, or should it choose not to retire its debts, the annual burden of the debt should be lower than that of new debt with the same face value. Said another way, market value of equity equals the market value of assets less the market value of liabilities. Market value of equity rises $10 million when liabilities fall by this amount.

   b. I would be indifferent between the two events because the market value of equity rises $10 million in both cases. The only difference is that increasing asset value may be due to improved management, whereas falling debt values are usually due to market forces outside the firm. But in terms of the effect on wealth, the two events are identical.

3. Because the accountant's primary goal is to measure earnings, not cash generated. She sees earnings as a fundamental indicator of viability, not cash generation. A more balanced perspective is that over the long run successful companies must be both profitable and solvent, that is, they must be profitable and have cash in the bank to pay their bills when due. This means that you should pay attention to both earnings and cash flows.

5. First, let us account for Golden Gardens' $1 million expenditure. Cash will fall $100,000, liabilities will rise $300,000, and owners' equity will rise $600,000. Next, let us account for the assets acquired. The accountants will write up the value of fixed assets and possibly inventory to their estimated replacement value; they will then add the difference between the acquisition price and the replacement value of assets acquired to a goodwill account appearing in the long-term assets section of Golden Garden's balance sheet; and lastly, they will consolidate the two companies' balance sheets by adding like accounts together.

7. The General Secretary has confused accounting profits with economic profits. Earning $200 million on a $5 billion equity investment is a return of only four percent. This is poor performance and is too low for the company to continue attracting new investment necessary for growth. The company is certainly not covering its cost of equity.

9. Beckey Construction generated economic income equal to $750,000, comprised of $450,000 in operating cash flow plus a $300,000 increase in the market value of its assets. The $500,000 difference between economic income and accounting income consists of the $200,000 non-cash charge of depreciation, and the $300,000 appreciation in the market value of assets, which accounting income does not include.

11. a. In 2006, company sales were $156 million, but accounts receivable rose $10 million, indicating that the company received only $146 million in cash. (This ignores possible changes in bad debt reserves.) Letting bop stand for beginning of period, and eop for end of period, the equation is

$$\text{Accounts receivable}_{eop} = \text{Accounts receivable}_{bop} + \text{Credit sales} - \text{Collections}$$

$$\text{Collections} = \text{Credit sales} - \text{Change in accounts receivable}$$

$$\$146 \text{ million} = \$156 \text{ million} - \$10 \text{ million}$$

   b. During 2006, the company sold $82 million of merchandise at cost, but finished goods inventory fell $2 million, indicating that the company produced only $80 million of merchandise. The equation is

$$\text{Inventory}_{eop} = \text{Inventory}_{bop} + \text{Production} - \text{Cost of sales}$$

$$\text{Production} = \text{Cost of sales} + \text{Change in inventory}$$

$$\$80 \text{ million} = \$82 \text{ million} - \$2 \text{ million}$$

   c. Net fixed assets rose $8 million, depreciation reduced net fixed assets $24 million, so capital expenditures must have been $32 million (ignoring asset sales or write-offs).

$$\text{Net fixed assets}_{eop} = \text{Net fixed assets}_{bop} + \text{Capital expenditures} - \text{Depreciation}$$

$$\text{Capital expenditures} = \text{Change in net fixed assets} + \text{Depreciation}$$

$$\$32 \text{ million} = \$8 \text{ million} + \$24 \text{ million}$$

13. a. Stock price per share = $5 million/500,000 shares = $10 per share. Book value per share = $1,750,000/500,000 = $3.50 per share.

   b. Epic Records will pay $10 per share for the 100,000 shares it repurchases. This reduces the book value by $1,000,000. Assuming all else remains the same, the new book value should be $750,000.

   c. Since nothing else has changed and the market does not perceive any value added to the firm and there are no taxes or transaction costs, the market value should fall by exactly the amount of the cash paid in the transaction. The new market value should be $4,000,000. In practice share repurchases often have a positive price effect at the time of announcement. There are several explanations for this effect, some of which we will cover in later chapters.

15. a. eBay's market to book ratio at year-end 2003 was a robust 8.568 times.
    b. eBay's growth rates in sales in 2002 and 2003 were 62.135 percent and 78.329 percent, respectively.
    c. Market values are forward looking, and any company with growth rates like these can expect to command a healthy premium over the book value of its assets.

Chapter 2

1. Company A has a high asset turnover and a low profit margin consistent with the food industry. Holding a lot of perishable milk in inventory is not a wise idea. This is Dean Foods. Company B has very low asset turnover and a very high profit margin. This is typical of a capital-intensive firm that adds considerable value to the product. Company B is Houston Exploration Co.

3. a. True. The numerators of the two ratios are identical. ROA can exceed ROE only if assets are less than equity, which implies that liabilities would have to be negative.
   b. True. Let L = liabilities, E = equity, and A = assets. Does $A/E = 1 + L/E$? Does $A/E = (E + L)/E$? Yes.
   c. False. A payables period longer than the collection period would be nice because trade credit would finance accounts receivable. However, payables periods and collections periods are typically determined by industry practice and the relative bargaining power of the firms involved; depending on a company's circumstances, it may have to gracefully put up with a collection period longer than its payables period.
   d. True. The two ratios are the same except that inventory, a positive quantity, is subtracted from the numerator to calculate the acid test.
   e. False. Imagine a year in which a company earns no operating profit, and the market value of neither its assets nor its liabilities changes. Economic earnings in this year would be zero. Now suppose the company sells an asset in which it has an unrealized gain for the asset's current market value. Economic earnings would still be zero, but accounting earnings would now be positive. Erratic sales of assets with unrecognized gains and losses could produce a volatile accounting income stream despite stable economic income. In practice,

executives more often manage accounting income to produce the illusion of stability in the face of volatile economic earnings.

f. False. Ignoring taxes and transactions costs, unrealized gains can always be realized by the act of selling, so must be worth as much as a comparable amount of realized gains.

5. a.

	Year 1	Year 2
Current ratio	8.46	2.63
Quick ratio	8.39	2.19

HomeDepot.com's short-run liquidity has deteriorated considerably, but from a high initial base.

b.

	Year 1	Year 2
Inventory turnover	41.2	5.4
Collection period	29.2	29.8
Payables period	43.8	26.6

c. The company lost money in both years, more in the second year than the first. Cash flow from operations is negative in both years but has improved. Liquidity has fallen and the inventory turnover is down sharply. The more than 10-fold increase in inventory suggests that HomeDepot.com was either wildly optimistic about potential sales or completely lost control of its inventory. A third possibility is that the company is building inventory in anticipation of a major sales increase next year. In any case, the inventory investment warrants close scrutiny. In general, these numbers look like those of an unstable, startup operation.

7. a.

	Company X	Company Z
ROE	31%	65%
ROA	25%	13%
ROIC	26%	18%

b. Company Z's higher ROE is a natural reflection of its higher financial leverage. It does not mean that company Z is the better company.

c. This is also due to Z's higher leverage. ROA penalizes levered companies by comparing the net income available to equity to the capital provided by owners and creditors. It does not mean that Z is a worse company than X.

d. ROIC abstracts from differences in leverage to provide a direct comparison of the earning power of the two companies' assets. On this metric, X is the superior performer. Before drawing any firm conclusions, however, it is important to ask how the business risks faced by the companies compare and whether the observed ratios reflect long-run capabilities or transitory events.

9. Collection period = Accounts receivable/Credit sales per day

$$\text{Credit sales} = 0.80 \times \$75 \text{ million} = \$60 \text{ million}$$

$$\begin{aligned} \text{Accounts receivable} &= \text{Collection period} \times \text{Sales per day} \\ &= 60 \times \$60 \text{ million}/365 = \$9.9 \text{ million} \end{aligned}$$

11. Sales/365 = (Cash/Days sales in cash) = 500,000/15 = 33,333

$$\begin{aligned} \text{Accounts receivable} &= \text{Collection period} \times \text{Credit sales per day} \\ &= \text{Collection period} \times (\text{Sales}/365) \\ &= 50 \times 33,333 = 1,666,667 \end{aligned}$$

$$\begin{aligned} \text{Cost of goods sold} &= \text{Inventory turnover} \times \text{Ending inventory} \\ &= 6 \times 1,000,000 = 6,000,000 \end{aligned}$$

$$\begin{aligned} \text{Accounts payable} &= \text{Payables period} \times (\text{Cost of goods sold}/365) \\ &= 28 \times 6,000,000/365 = 460,274 \end{aligned}$$

$$\begin{aligned} \text{Total liabilities} &= \text{Assets} \times \text{Liabilities to assets} \\ &= 5,000,000 \times 0.80 = 4,000,000 \end{aligned}$$

$$\begin{aligned} \text{Shareholders' equity} &= \text{Total assets} - \text{Total liabilities} \\ &= 5,000,000 - 4,000,000 = 1,000,000 \end{aligned}$$

$$\begin{aligned} \text{Current liabilities} &= \text{Current assets}/\text{Current ratio} \\ &= 3,166,667/2.4 = 1,319,444 \end{aligned}$$

Assets	
Current:	
Cash	$ 500,000
Accounts receivable	1,666,667
Inventory	1,000,000
Total current assets	3,166,667
Net fixed assets	1,833,333
Total assets	$5,000,000
Liabilities and shareholders' equity	
Current liabilities:	
Accounts payable	$ 460,274
Short-term debt	859,170
Total current liabilities	1,319,444
Long-term debt	2,680,556
Shareholders' equity	1,000,000
Total liabilities and equity	$5,000,000

13. See Suggested Answers worksheet in C2_Problem_13.xls available at **www.mhhe.com/higgins8e.** (Select Student Edition > Choose Chapter > Excel Spreadsheets.)

Chapter 3

1. A negative value implies that the company has excess cash above its desired minimum. You can demonstrate this on the balance sheet by setting the external funding requirement to zero and adding the absolute value of the external financing required to cash.

3. This would tell me I had erred in constructing one or both of the forecasts. Using the same assumptions and avoiding accounting and arithmetic errors, estimated external financing required should equal estimated cash surplus or deficit for the same date.

5. Pro Forma Forecast for R&E Supplies 2007

Income Statement	
Net sales	$33,496
Cost of goods sold	28,807
Gross profit	4,689
General, selling, and administrative expense	3,685
Interest expense	327
Earnings before tax	678
Tax	305
Earnings after tax	373
Dividends paid	187
Additions to retained earnings	$ 187
Balance Sheet Forecast	
Current assets	$9,714
Net fixed assets	270
Total assets	$9,984
Current liabilities	$4,823
Long-term debt	560
Equity	1,995
Total liabilities & shareholders' equity	$7,378
External Financing Required	**$2,606**

Projected external financing requirements in 2007 are over $1 million higher than in 2006.

7.

Pepperton Income Statement
January 1, 2005–March 31, 2006 ($ thousands)

Net sales	$1,080
Cost of sales	540
Gross profit	540
Selling and administrative expense	540
Interest	90
Depreciation	30
Net profit before tax	(120)
Tax at 33%	(40)
Net profit after tax	($80)
Dividends	300
Additions to retained earnings	$(380)

Balance Sheet—March 31, 2006 ($ thousands)

Assets

Cash	$ 150
Accounts receivable	192
Inventory	1,800
Total current assets	2,142
Gross fixed assets	900
− Accumulated depreciation	180
Net fixed assets	720
Total assets	$2,862

Liabilities

Bank loan	**$1,362**
Accounts payable	240
Miscellaneous accruals	60
Current portion long-term debt	0
Taxes payable	80
Total current liabilities	1,742
Long-term debt	990
Shareholders' equity	130
Total liabilities & equity	$2,862

Comments:

Inventory is estimated as follows:

Beginning inventory Jan. 1	$1,800
+ First quarter purchases	540
− First quarter cost of goods sold	540
Ending inventory March 31	$1,800

Taxes payable are estimated as follows:

Taxes payable Dec. 31, 2005	$300
− payments	180
+ First quarter taxes accrued	−40
Taxes payable March 31	$ 80

a. $1,362,000.

b. Yes, they are the same.

c. Yes, the pro-forma forecasts can be analyzed in the usual manner.

d. They say little or nothing about financing needs at any time other than the forecast date.

9. a. Negative numbers for taxes mean the company is reducing its tax liability. If the company has paid taxes in the recent past, it can file for a rebate of past taxes.

b. Cash balances exceed the minimum required level because the company has excess cash in these quarters. Cash balances are determined in these periods by first noting that external financing required is negative when cash is set at the minimum level. External financing required is then set to zero and cash becomes the balancing item equating assets to liabilities and owners' equity.

c. When greater than zero, external financing required becomes the balancing item equating assets to liabilities and owners' equity.

d. The company should easily be able to borrow the money. The amounts required are less than one-quarter of accounts receivable in each quarter.

11. a. The footnote to the spreadsheet tells us the forecasts are based on linear regression, which is an elaborate form of extrapolation.

b. Mechanically, one could combine the forecasts provided with a few heroic assumptions to estimate future financing needs. Combining projected net worth and long-term debt as given with independent projections of current liabilities, perhaps based on a percent of sales, and other long-term liabilities would yield projected liabilities and owners' equity. Similarly, combining the given projected capital expenditures with independent projections of current assets, perhaps based on a percent of sales, depreciation, and other long-term assets, would yield projected total assets. The implied financing surplus or deficit would then be the difference between assets and liabilities and owners' equity. Such a forecast would only be as good as the heroic assumptions necessary to make it and the presumption that the future will be a simple extension of the past. We should be able to do better.

c. As a portrait of where the company is headed unless changes occur, the projected operating figures might provide a useful benchmark for analyzing a company. I do not think the projected stock prices are valuable. Current prices should already reflect investor expectations about future performance.

13. See Suggested Answers worksheet in C3_Problem_13.xls available at **www.mhhe.com/higgins8e.** (Select Student Edition > Choose Chapter > Excel Spreadsheets.)

Chapter 4

1. a. False. Companies can achieve growth rates above their sustainable levels by increasing their profit margin, asset turnover or financial leverage, or by cutting dividends. The problem is that there are limits to a company's ability to make such changes.

   b. False. Glamorous companies such as eBay with an exciting story to tell can raise equity despite operating losses. More traditional companies usually cannot.

   c. True. Repurchases reduce the number of shares outstanding, which contributes to increasing earnings per share. However, the money used to repurchase the shares has a cost, which reduces earnings and tends to reduce earnings per share. In most instances, the former offsets the latter and earnings per share rise when shares are repurchased.

   d. True. Survey evidence suggests that most managers, most of the time, believe their shares are undervalued. Repurchasing undervalued stock is a productive use of company resources that benefits remaining shareholders.

   e. False. A major theme of this chapter has been that slow-growth companies have subtle and often more serious growth management problems than their rapidly growing neighbors.

   f. False. Good growth that yields returns greater than cost increases stock price. Bad growth at returns below cost destroys value and will eventually reduce stock price.

3. a. PCA's sustainable growth rates are

	1991	1992	1993	1994	1995
Sustainable growth rate (%)	90.6	47.0	9.6	6.9	16.5

   b. PCA's sustainable growth rate in every year exceeded its actual growth rate by a wide margin. The company was generating more cash from operations than it could productively employ. Its challenge was what to do with the excess cash.

   c. PCA coped with actual growth below sustainable levels in two ways. It allowed its asset turnover to fall from 4.3 times in 1991 to 2.4 times in 1995, and it sharply reduced its debt from 5.6 times in 1991 to 1.8 times in 1995.

   d. Stock repurchase made sense for PCA. They appear to have little productive use for the money they earn within the firm, so they should return it to the owners, either as dividends or in the form of a share repurchase.

5. a.

	1999	2000	2001	2002	2003
Sustainable growth rate (%)	10.0	10.6	15.7	17.3	20.9
Actual growth rate (%)	53.2	36.4	46.5	49.3	40.6

   b. UFC does have a sustainable growth problem. Its sustainable growth rate is much lower than its actual growth rate.
   c. The increase in asset turnover and financial leverage is helping increase the sustainable growth rate. But the spread between the two rates is still substantial in 2003.
   d. $g^* = 0.387 \times 1.0 \times 0.4 \times 1.6 = 24.8\%$

7. See Suggested Answer worksheet C4_Problem_7.xls available at **www.mhhe.com/higgins8e.** (Select Student Edition > Choose Chapter > Excel Spreadsheets.)

Chapter 5

1. The percentage of the company owned is most important to the investor. This determines the size of her claims on company cash flows and hence the value of her investment. A company's share price and the number of shares outstanding can be arbitrarily changed by splitting the shares. Share price and number of shares owned are of interest only to the extent that they help the investor calculate more meaningful dollar or percentage ownership numbers.

3 a.

Stock price	$75.00
− 8% underpricing	6.00
Issue price	69.00
− 7% spread	4.83
Net to company	$64.17

   Number of shares = $500 million/$64.17 = 7.79 million

   b. Investment bankers' revenue = $4.83 × 7.79 million = $37.63 million.
   c. Underpricing is not a cash flow. It is, however, an opportunity cost to current owners because it means that more shares must be sold to raise $500 million and each share will represent a smaller ownership interest in the company.

5. a. The holding period return is −4.76 percent [($60 − $110)/$1,050].
   b. The bond's price might have fallen because investor perceptions of its risk rose or because interest rates rose. The price of a bond is the present value of future cash receipts. As interest rates rise, the price of the bond falls. See Chapter 7 for details.

7. a. Suppose Liquid Force stock sells for $40 before the dividend and the dividend is $6. Buy Liquid Force stock immediately prior to the dividend for $40, receive the $6 dividend, and sell the stock for $37. You invest $40 and immediately after the sale have $43 in cash. Easy money.

    b. Liquid Force's stock price would rise prior to the dividend and fall more when the dividend is paid. As more and more investors pursue this strategy, the price drop will approach the full amount of the dividend (in the absence of transaction costs).

    c. Borrow Liquid Force stock and sell it immediately prior to the dividend for $40, pay the $6 dividend to the person from whom you borrowed the stock as his dividend, and buy the stock for $28 and return it to the lender. You invest $34 ($28 + $6) and, immediately after the transaction, you have $40 cash. Again, easy money.

    d. Stock price will fall prior to the dividend and fall less after the dividend.

    e. Such trading will continue until the stock price drops by an amount equal to the dividend payment.

    f. Ignoring taxes and assuming efficient markets, a $1 increase in dividends results in a $1 decline in capital gains. Rational investors are indifferent to whether they receive their return as dividends or capital gains, so increasing the dividend will not benefit investors.

9. The analogy is an appropriate one. The strike price on the owners' option is the value of the debt outstanding. Owners have the option of paying this amount and owning the firm's assets free and clear. Alternatively, if the value of the assets falls below the value of the debt, the owners can walk away, leaving the assets to the creditors. The value of equity relative to the value of the firm looks like the payoff diagram for a call option.

Chapter 6

1. SAP AG, primarily a business software company, would face much higher distress costs than General Motors because a much greater proportion of its assets is intangible. For this reason SAP AG should have the more conservative capital structure.

3. a. There are several reasons. First, companies with promising investment opportunities typically have valuable intangible assets whose value would decline sharply if the company got into financial difficulty; that is, the resale value of their assets is low. Second, it is important for such companies to maintain the financial flexibility that comes with a conservative capital structure to assure funding

for future investment opportunities. They are making money on the asset side of the business. They should not do anything on the liability side to jeopardize future investments.

b. Most would follow this recommendation if they could, but lack of sufficient operating cash flow and the inability to raise additional equity force many small businesses to an extensive reliance on debt financing. For these companies, it is either growth with debt or no growth. Also, many entrepreneurs view debt as a way to stretch their limited equity to gain control over more assets. They like playing with someone else's chips.

5. While bond covenants can help mitigate undesirable conflicts between shareholders and bondholders, they impose costs of their own because they are costly to monitor and they reduce firm flexibility. The covenants might prevent firms from undertaking good projects (if the covenants restrict investment policy), repurchasing stock, or incurring fresh debt for new projects. Also, it's impossible to write covenants that anticipate every possible conflict that might arise.

7. a. An increase in the interest rate would lower the debt financing line in the range-of-earnings chart. This would reduce the EPS advantage of debt or increase the disadvantage if EBIT is below the crossover point. It would also increase the crossover EBIT. Both changes would reduce the attractiveness of debt financing.

b. An increased stock price will reduce the number of shares issued to raise the needed capital, which will increase EPS at all income levels for the equity line. Raising the equity line will improve EPS with equity financing relative to debt and will increase the crossover EBIT. Both changes will make equity more attractive.

c. The range-of-earnings chart will be unchanged, but increased uncertainty will increase the probability that EBIT will fall below the crossover point. This will make equity more attractive.

d. Increased common dividends will not affect the range-of-earnings chart. They will reduce the times-common-covered ratio and will hence make debt marginally more attractive.

e. An increase in the amount of debt already outstanding will increase interest expense and lower EPS for all financing options. This will lower both the debt and the equity financing lines in the range-of-earnings chart by the same amount, but will not affect the attractiveness of debt relative to equity, at least as far as the range-of-earnings chart is concerned. Interest coverage obviously falls as existing debt rises, which makes additional debt financing riskier.

9. a. Each year sources of cash must equal uses. Sources are earnings plus new borrowing. Uses are investment and dividends. So each

year the following equation applies: $E + 1.2(E - D) = I + D$, where E is earnings, 1.2 is the debt-to-equity ratio, D is dividends, and I is investment. Solving for D, $D = E - I/2.2$. The following table presents the resulting annual dividend and payout ratio.

b. Summing dividends and dividing by total earnings, the stable payout ratio is $219/$930 = 24$ percent. Substituting this into our sources and uses equation, $E + 1.2(E - .24E) = I + .24E + CM$, where CM is the change in the marketable securities portfolio. Solving for CM, $CM = 1.67E - I$. The resulting values for CM and the year-end marketable securities portfolio appear in the following table. (Had I carried out the calculations with more accuracy the ending marketable securities would have equaled the beginning value, $200.)

	($ millions)				
Year	**1**	**2**	**3**	**4**	**5**
Dividends ($)	20	−6	34	71	100
Payout ratio (%)	20	−5	20	31	33
Stable payout ratio (%)	24	24	24	24	24
Stable dividend ($)	24	31	41	55	72
Change in marketable securities ($)	−8	−83	−16	34	61
Marketable securities ($)	192	109	93	127	188

c. The company can do any or some combination of the following: reduce marketable securities, increase leverage, cut dividends, sell new equity.

d. The options are ranked according to the pecking order as they appear in the answer to question c. One might distinguish between using excess borrowing capacity and raising the target debt ratio, with the former ranked above the cut dividends option and the latter below.

e. The pecking-order theory follows from the desire to avoid negative signaling effects of new equity issues, supplemented by the desire to maintain access to financial markets. If these goals are important to managers, they will naturally follow the pecking order.

11. a. EBIT $= [40/(1 - 0.36)] + 15 = 77.5

Interest $= $15 + 0.07(40) = 17.8. Times-interest-earned
$= 77.5/17.8 = 4.35$ times

b. Burden of interest and sinking fund before tax $= 17.8 + (14 + 8)/(1 - 0.36) = 52.17

Times burden covered $= 77.5/52.18 = 1.49$ times

    c. EPS = $(77.5 - 17.8)(1 - 0.36)/18 = \$2.12$

    d. Times interest earned = $77.5/15 = 5.17$ times. Times burden covered = $77.5/[15 + 14/(1 - 0.36)] = 2.10$ times. EPS = $(77.5 - 15)(1 - 0.36)/(18 + 2) = \$2.00$.

13. See Suggested Answer in C6_Problem_13.xls available at **www.mhhe.com/higgins8e**. (Select Student Edition > Choose Chapter > Excel Spreadsheets.)

Chapter 7

`1. a.

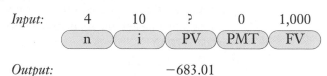

Input: 4   10   ?   0   1,000

          (n) (i) (PV) (PMT) (FV)

Output: −683.01

b. PV = 466.51. Present value is less because the present sum has more time to grow into \$1,000.

Input: 8   10   ?   0   1,000

          (n) (i) (PV) (PMT) (FV)

Output: −466.51

c. PV = $4,545.45 + 3,305.79 + 3,084.35 = \$10,935.59$

Input: 1   10   ?   0   5,000

          (n) (i) (PV) (PMT) (FV)

Output: −4,545.45

Input: 2   10   ?   0   4,000

          (n) (i) (PV) (PMT) (FV)

Output: −3,305.79

Input: 10   10   ?   0   8,000

          (n) (i) (PV) (PMT) (FV)

Output: −3,084.35

d. PV = \$815.66

Input: 10   10   ?   70   1,000

          (n) (i) (PV) (PMT) (FV)

Output: −815.66

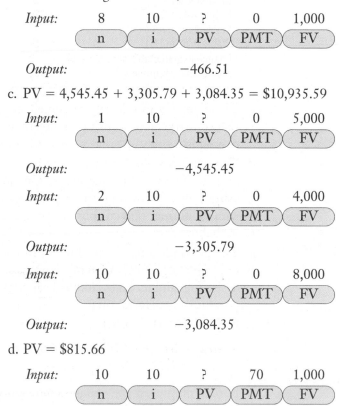

e. PV = 5/.10 = $50.00

f. FV = $23,384.61

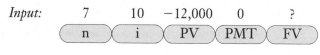

Input:	7	10	−12,000	0	?
	n	i	PV	PMT	FV

Output: 23,384.61

g.

Input:	?	10	−2,000	0	4,000
	n	i	PV	PMT	FV

Output: 7.27

h.

Input:	20	10	0	−500	?
	n	i	PV	PMT	FV

Output: 28,637.50

i.

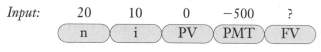

Input:	18	10	0	?	250,000
	n	i	PV	PMT	FV

Output: −5,482.56

j. IRR = 18%. Paying less than $22,470 implies an IRR greater than 18%, and vice versa.

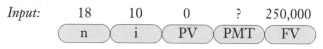

Input:	10	?	−22,470	5,000	0
	n	i	PV	PMT	FV

Output: 18.0

k. If the stream lasted forever, PV = 600/.10 = $6,000.00. Hence, the stream must be a perpetuity. If the stream lasted only five years, the salvage value would have to be $6,000. This is the amount required to be invested at 10 percent to generate $600 per year in perpetuity from year 5 on.

l. The IRR = 8%.

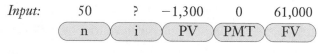

Input:	50	?	−1,300	0	61,000
	n	i	PV	PMT	FV

Output: 8.00

m. The annual payment necessary to amass $150 million in 8 years is $13.12 million.

Input: 8   10   0   ?   150

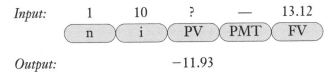

Output: −13.12

If the money is deposited at the beginning of each year, bring the $13.12 million deposit forward one year. The value is $11.93 million.

Input: 1   10   ?   —   13.12

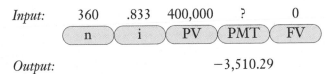

Output: −11.93

3. a. Her monthly payments on the 10 percent loan option are $3,510.29, using a monthly interest rate of 10%/12 = 0.833%, and 360 monthly payments.

Input: 360 .833 400,000 ?   0

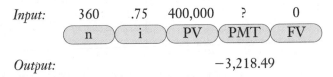

Output: −3,510.29

b. Her monthly payments on the 9 percent loan option are $3,218.49, using a monthly interest rate of 9%/12 = 0.750%, and 360 monthly payments. Her monthly payment is $291.80 lower using this option.

Input: 360 .75 400,000 ?   0

n   i   PV   PMT   FV

Output: −3,218.49

c. Compare the present value of her savings using the 9 percent loan against the loan fee. For 60 months, the present value of the monthly savings at a 0.750 percent monthly rate is $14,056.99. Her loan fee = 3% of $400,000 = $12,000. You should advise her to take the 9 percent loan, as she will save over $2,000 in present value terms.

Input: 60   .75   ?   291.80   —

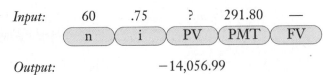

Output: −14,056.99

5. The effective interest rate on the time purchase plan is the discount rate that makes the seller indifferent to a cash sale for $42,700 and a time payment sale for $10,000 now and $10,000 for each of the next four years plus $1,000 fees.

$$42,700 = 1,000 + 10,000 + PVA, \text{ where PVA}$$
$$= \text{present value of 10,000 for 4 years}$$

Implies $31,700 = PVA$. Using $PV = 31,700$, solve for the interest rate:

Input:

4	?	−31,700	10,000	0
n	i	PV	PMT	FV

Output: 10.0

The interest rate = 10%.

7. This is a straightforward replacement problem.

	Old Roasters	New Roasters
Gross profit	$600,000	$1,200,000
− Depreciation	300,000	450,000
Profit before tax	300,000	750,000
Tax at 45%	135,000	338,000
Profit after tax	165,000	412,000
+ Depreciation	300,000	450,000
After tax cash flow	$465,000	$862,000

If they keep the old roasters, NPV = $2.857 million.

Input:

10	10	?	465	—
n	i	PV	PMT	FV

Output: −2,857

The present value of the after tax cash flows from the new roasters is $5,297 million.

Input:

10	10	?	862	—
n	i	PV	PMT	FV

Output: −5,297

If they sell the old roasters and buy the new ones, NPV= −4.500 + 1.500 + 5.297 = $2.297 million. Therefore, keep the old roasters.

Alternatively, one can look at the difference in the cash flows between the two alternatives. This amounts to analyzing the *incremental* cash flows. Subtracting the old roasters' cash flows from the new roasters' cash flows,

Input: 10   10   ?   397   —

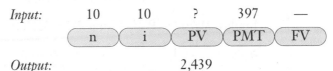

Output: 2,439

and NPV = −3.000 + 2.439 = −0.561 million, indicating that spending an incremental $3 million to buy the new roasters is not attractive. It should not surprise you to learn that this NPV equals the difference in the NPVs of the two options. That is, −0.561 million = $2.297 million − $2.857 million.

The IRR of the incremental cash flows is 5.4 percent, which because it is below 10 percent again indicates the incremental investment is unwarranted.

9. The internal rate of return is 13.7 percent. Once again we see the power of compound interest. This does not suggest that investing in fine art is especially attractive. It ignores the costs of maintaining, insuring, and protecting a valuable painting, and the return on a Van Gogh can be expected to be much higher than the return on a typical fine art investment, even if it is one of his lesser works.

Input: 98   ?   −125   0   36,000,000

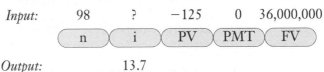

Output: 13.7

11. See Suggested Answers in C7_Problem_11.xls available at **www.mhhe.com/higgins8e.** (Select Student Edition > Choose Chapter > Excel Spreadsheets.)

13. See Suggested Answers in C7_Problem_13.xls available at **www.mhhe.com/higgins8e.** (Select Student Edition > Choose Chapter > Excel Spreadsheets.)

Chapter 8

1. a. False. Future cash flows are discounted more than near cash flows for risk because the discount rate in the denominator is raised to a higher power. A constant discount rate assumes risk increases at a constant geometric rate as the cash flow recedes in time.

b. True. The WACC is the appropriate discount rate to use for projects that have the same risk as existing assets of the firm. If a project is either safer or riskier than average, it should be evaluated with a discount rate other than the WACC.

c. False. This is yet another example of the marginal cost of capital fallacy. A company may have enough other assets such that it can borrow enough for a single project. However, this does not imply that the cost of capital for the investment equals the borrowing rate. Increasing leverage increases the risks borne by shareholders, which increases the cost of equity capital. This means that the discount rate for the investment should reflect the risk of the investment rather than the cost of the particular funding source.

3. When the investment lies below the market line it is possible to make equal-risk investments promising higher expected returns. Conversely, investments above the market line promise expected returns above those available on equal-risk, ready alternatives.

5. Increasing financial leverage increases the risk borne by equity investors and hence increases the cost of equity capital. The company's equity beta will rise as well. Indeed, the rising equity beta causes the cost of equity to rise. Figure 6.1 shows the relationship graphically.

7. a. IRR of perpetuity = Annual receipt/Initial investment. IRR_e = 20% = [$1 million − (1 − .5)8%$X$]/($10 million − X), where X = required loan. X = $6.25 million.

b. 80% = [$1 million − (1 − .5)8%$X$]/($10 million − X). X = $9.21 million

c. An investor would settle for a lower return because it takes less debt financing to achieve it. Leverage increases expected return to equity but also the risk to equity. See Chapter 6.

9. a. It is a call option. It gives General Design the option to "purchase" the expansion.

b. The strike price is the price at which General Design can purchase the expansion, or $500 million.

11. a. Cost of equity capital = K_E = 4.5% + 0.465 × 6.4% = 7.48%

b. WACC = K_w = [(1 − .4)(8%)(916.33) + 7.48%(45.46 × 397.40)]/(916.33 + 18,065.80) = 7.35%

13. See Suggested Answers in C8_Problem_13.xls available at **www.mhhe.com/higgins8e.** (Select Student Edition > Choose Chapter > Excel Spreadsheets.)

Chapter 9

1. Free cash flow = EBIT(1 − Tax rate) + Depreciation − Fixed
investment − Working capital investment

$$EBIT = \text{Income before tax} + \text{Interest} = 1{,}200 + 360$$
$$= \$1{,}560$$

$$\text{Tax rate} = 408/1{,}200 = .34$$

Free cash flow = $1{,}560(1 − .34) + 600 − 480 − 240 = \$909.60$

3. a. Any time one company acquires another, its sales and assets increase. Further, if the acquired company is profitable, earnings will increase as well. This is no surprise.

   b. Value per share before proposal = $\$10/0.14 = \$71.43$

   c. Value per share after proposal = $\$5/(1 + .14) + (\$10.45/.14)/(1 + .14) = \$69.86$

   d. Clearly, owners of Stolid should oppose the president's plan. It may result in a larger company, but it will destroy shareholder value; that is, stock price will fall under the plan. The problem with the president's plan is that it takes money with an opportunity cost of 14 percent to owners and invests it in a venture yielding only 9 percent ($0.45 per year added dividend in perpetuity for a $5 investment yields 9 percent return).

5. a.

	Company				
	P	**V1**	**P + V1**	**V2**	**P + V2**
Earnings after tax ($ millions)	$2	$1	$3	$1	$3
Price to earnings ratio (×)	30	10		40	
Market value of equity ($ millions)	60	10		40	
Number of equity shares (millions)	1	1	1.5	1	1.5
Earnings per share ($)	$2	$1	$2	$1	$2
Price per share	$60	$10		$40	
Maximum new shares issued (millions)		.5		.5	
Value of new shares issued ($ millions)		30		30	
Maximum acquisition premium (%)		**200%**		**−25%**	

   b. This problem illustrates why concern with earnings per share dilution or accretion is short-sided. Here, Procureps is tempted to pay a huge premium to buy V1 but is disinclined to even look at V2. Yet V2 is the exciting firm with future potential.

7. a. FMV = PV(FCF, '07 − '10) + PV(Terminal value)

   PV(FCF, '07 − '10) = −$18.3 million

   Terminal value = EBIT(1 − Tax rate)/0.14 = $126/0.14
      = $900 million

   PV(Terminal value) = $900 million × 0.592 = $532.9 million

   Summing, FMV = $514.6 million

b. FMV of equity = ($514.6 − $300)/50 = $4.29 per share

c.   Terminal value = FCF in 2011/(0.14 − 0.04)

FCF in 2011 = $210(1.04)(1 − 0.4) − 20 − 10

= $101.0

So terminal value = $101.0/.10 = $1,010. Present value of terminal value = $598.2

FMV of company = −$18.3 + $598.2 =

$579.9 million. FMV of equity per share = ($579.9 − $300)/50 = $5.60

d.   Terminal value = Value of equity + Value of interest-bearing liabilities

Value of equity = 17 × Net income in 2007

= 17 × (210 − 0.10 × 300)(1 − 0.40)

= $1,836 million

Terminal value = $1,836 million + $300 million = $2,136

Present value of terminal value = $1,264.7

Therefore, FMV of company on valuation date = −$18.3 + $1,264.7 = $1,246.4 million

Value per share = ($1,246.4 million − $300 million)/50 = $18.93

9.

Employee ownership at time 5	20.0%	
Round 2 ownership at time 5	22.9%	
Touchstone ownership at time 5	43.7%	
Round 2 retention ratio	0.80	=(1 − .20)
Round 2 ownership at time 2	28.6%	=0.229/0.80
Touchstone retention ratio	0.57	=(1 − .20)(1 − .286)
Touchstone ownership at time 0	**76.5%**	=0.437/0.57

Confirmation of answer

Let X equal total shares outstanding at time 5 and recall that the founders own 2 million shares. Then $0.20X + 0.229X + 0.437X + 2$ million $= X$

X (millions)	14.93	
Touchstone ownership at time 5	6.52	= .437 × 14.93
Touchstone % ownership at time 0	**76.5%**	= 6.52/(2 + 6.52)

This confirms that giving Touchstone 76.5 percent ownership at time 0 will result in 43.7 percent ownership at time 5, which, in turn, will yield their target return of 60 percent on investment.

11. See Suggested Answers in C9_Problem_11.xls available at **www.mhhe.com/higgins8e.** (Select Student Edition > Choose a Chapter > Excel Spreadsheets.)

Index